T0161372

A Maiden of Mauritius

CULTURAL LEGACIES

A Maiden of Mauritius

John Gorrie

Edited by

*Judy Allen, Jean Ayler, Marina Carter
and Shawkat M. Toorawa*

Pink Pigeon Press ——◆—— A Solitaire Book

Published by
Pink Pigeon Press
92 Greenfield Road, London, England

in association with
The Hassam Toorawa Trust
P. O. Box 16, Port Louis, Mauritius

Solitaire is an imprint of
The Hassam Toorawa Trust

This edition of A Maiden of Mauritius
© 2016 Pink Pigeon Press

ISBN 978-0-9539916-8-6

Book design by Susanne Wilhelm
Display type Superclarendon 12 pt / Apollo MT 13 pt
Text type Apollo MT 10.5 pt

Printed in the United States of America

Contents

Series Editors' Preface

WE WILL BE UNPICKING THE LEGACIES OF THE BRITISH EMPIRE for generations to come. Studies of colonial officialdom continue to evolve as historians pore over private papers and less reverential scholarship appears.* The present volume represents a small and somewhat unusual contribution to this field. John Gorrie was a respected colonial judge, albeit defiantly and decidedly not on the side of the ruling classes in the territories where he was posted. He believed that everyone, irrespective of race, was equal before the law, and his efforts to practise what he preached led him down many difficult paths. But his legal wranglings are barely touched upon in this book, which introduces the reader to a startlingly different kind of writing from that usually exercised by denizens of the colonial courtroom. Justice Gorrie wrote a remarkable romantic novel. Everything from its fortuitous discovery, to its incisive portrayals of both humble and elevated Mauritians, to its depictions of everyday life in a colonial backwater, form part of its all-intriguing history.

Judy Allen and Jean Ayler have done the hard work of transcribing their shared ancestor's manuscripts and letters; we have had the easier task of steering the project through its final stages. In doing so, it has been a pleasure to work with the talented cover and book designer, Susanne Wilhelm, and bookman extraordinaire, Ian Stevens, both of ISD, LLC. We are grateful also to benefactors and patrons who helped in subventing production, printing and distribution costs.

---

* See for example, Stephanie Williams, *Running the Show: Governors of the British Empire, 1857–1912* (London: Viking, 2011).

Page from John Gorrie's manuscript of 'Maid of Maurice'

Preface

THE MANUSCRIPT OF "A MAID OF MAURICE" was very nearly lost forever. It was in the possession of my great-aunt, one of John Gorrie's two grand-daughters by his second daughter, Isabella. The elder, Helen Marion, was my grandmother. The younger, Alice Noel, nicknamed Noa in the family, was my great aunt. Neither my mother nor I knew of the existence of the manuscript. When Noa died we went through her flat and, when we had removed every-thing of interest (as we thought), my mother paid a house clearance firm to deal with the rest of it.

On the first evening the firm went in, the head of the clearance team, in flat cap and overalls, rang my mother's door bell and handed her a large pile, saying he didn't think she had meant any of this to be thrown away. He had found it all in a cupboard underneath a very narrow window seat, one we had not known was there.

This invaluable "pile" consisted of the huge old family Bible, with births and deaths written on the family record pages by Gorrie; a diary written by his eldest daughter, Marion (Minnie); various family letters and photographs; poems by Gorrie; and the manuscript of a novel, "A Maid of Maurice"!

All the material was fascinating but I transcribed Minnie's diary first. She wrote it in 1876 when she was 19, aboard *The Sea Breeze*, a sugar clipper en route to London from Mauritius, where she and her family had been liv-ing on Gorrie's first colonial appointment. When Gorrie was posted to Fiji, he sent his family back to the United Kingdom until he was able to set up a home in Fiji. (Minnie kept a diary all her life but sadly the rest of them are all lost.)

I then abridged the diary and sent it to Chris Venning, who had directed several of my plays on Radio 4. Chris – who it turned out had once lived for a few years in Fiji, on Gorrie Street! – directed the abridgement of the diary as a one-voice reading featuring Jan Francis, broadcast on 18th February 1985.

Just before the broadcast my distant cousin, Jean Ayler, descended from Gorrie's younger brother, was travelling to visit an aunt. Jean did not usually read the *Radio Times*, but her aunt had asked for a copy so Jean bought one and flicking through it saw the listing for the radio broadcast of Minnie's diary. Jean was already researching on the Gorrie family history and immediately wrote to me, via the BBC. That is how Jean and I, who before this did not know of each other's existence, first met.

Jean urged me to write a book about Gorrie's life but I knew a biography would need an academic author. Even so, I did some research, and Jean did even more. When we came across Bridget Brereton's *A History of Modern Trinidad, 1783–1962* (1981), which has information on Gorrie, I contacted her and as she was looking for a new project, we found the ideal academic. She decided to write a book about Gorrie and in 1997, *Law, Justice and Empire: The Colonial Career of John Gorrie, 1829–1892* appeared. In addition to her impressive research in archives and contemporary sources, Professor Brereton was able to rely on the massive amount of further research undertaken by Jean, and on all the relevant family papers in my possession, including some pamphlets written by Gorrie.

I transcribed the manuscript of Gorrie's novel. One thing that struck me as very powerful was that in the romantic sections his handwriting was a well spaced, elegant copper-plate and therefore easy to read, but when he was describing social injustices and his outrage was aroused, his writing is visibly fast and furious — the spaces are narrower, the words overrun each other, and there are blots and tiny holes where the nib has dug into the paper. The emotion comes through not only through his words, but also physically in the manuscript. I have donated the manuscript to The National Records of Scotland, where it has been conserved and digitised, and can be viewed by appointment.

◆

Some years after Bridget Brereton's biography was published, Dr Marina Carter contacted me. Bridget had put her in touch with me because she had expressed an interest in seeing Gorrie's novel. I happily shared it with Marina who felt that, although it was a romantic novel, it gave a very good picture of Mauritius in the late 1860s and early 1870s, and that it was therefore worth publishing, ideally with annotations explaining or elaborating things that might not be clear to modern readers. Professor Shawkat Toorawa kindly agreed to assist with this task and has overseen the book's publication. None of this would have been possible, however, if all those years ago the material had not been saved by an observant and kindly stranger – whose name, sadly, I never knew – to whom I am truly grateful.

Judy Allen

Introduction

John Gorrie (1829–1892),[1] a Scottish-born judge, sailed to Mauritius together with his family in October 1869, and on 15ᵗʰ December was sworn in as
Substitute Procureur-General, a role similar to that of Solicitor-General in
Britain. The legal system of the island was complicated, a mixture of French
and English law—although a British colony since 1810, the Napoleonic code
continued in force, and senior legal personnel, recruited locally from among
the French settler population, coexisted, at times rather uneasily, with judges
and magistrates imported from England. The fact that Gorrie was considered
"a good French linguist" as well as an able lawyer was an important factor in
his selection. At the time of his arrival, however, the island was struggling to
recover from a devastating malaria epidemic which had literally decimated
the population. Working and living conditions for the large community of
immigrants from India were deteriorating, a direct result of oppressive labour
laws and falling sugar prices. By the time Gorrie left, in 1876, he had played a
vital role in helping to set the colony on a road to reform and amelioration of
the worst abuses to which the labouring classes had been subjected.

It was during his time in Mauritius that Gorrie developed a judicial style
that made him the bane of colonists and settler elites and the champion of local, indigenous, indentured and other oppressed populations, a style Bridget
Brereton has characterized as "combative, interventionist and 'political', always on the lookout for abuses to denounce and correct."[2] He certainly found
a ready field for action in Mauritius where the legal profession was in turmoil. While Gorrie was still en route for the island, the Governor, Sir Henry
Barkly, had received a petition, signed by 11 Barristers and 19 Attorneys,
protesting about the undue influence of the Colin family in the judgements

---

1   See the biography at the back of this volume. See also Bridget Brereton, *Law, Justice
and Empire: The Colonial Career of John Gorrie, 1829–1892* (Barbados, Jamaica, Trinidad
and Tobago: The University Press of the West Indies, 1997).
2   Brereton, *Law, Justice and Empire,* p. xvi.

of the Supreme Court, "owing to the intimate connection subsisting between Mr Justice [Gustave] Colin and certain of his relatives who belong to the legal profession and to the great influence which he was supposed to exercise over his brother Judges."[3] While this complaint was being investigated, the Procureur-General, Jules Colin [Gustave's brother], died. Perhaps rather surprisingly in the circumstances, the Governor decided to offer the newly vacant post of Procureur-General to Gustave Colin, and to appoint Gorrie as 3rd Puisne Judge. Another local lawyer, Eugène Leclézio Jr, was provisionally appointed Substitute Procureur-General in Gorrie's place. The Scotsman believed that he should by rights have acceded to the post of Procureur-General and reacted by penning a letter of protest to the Governor pointing out the dangers of appointing Creoles—he means Mauritius-born French Whites—to key positions where family ties might entail conflicts of interest.[4] Since the Colonial Office very rarely acted against the recommendations of Governors, the appointment to which Gorrie objected was confirmed. This prompted another lengthy missive from Gorrie, written as a "private memorandum for the Secretary of State for the Colonies" on 23rd September 1870, explaining in detail the duties of that post, and his reasons for recommending that the appointment be made from England. "All these matters require careful and firm handling," he wrote, "and I have no hesitation in offering my opinion, that the duties cannot properly be discharged by a Creole of the Island mixed up with the Magistracy and the legal profession."[5] Not surprisingly, among the dozen or so substantive objections to the appointment, Gorrie also raised the question of oppression of and discrimination against Indo-Mauritians:

> The remarks which I have already made as to the supervision of District Magistrates applies equally to the case of Stipendiary Magistrates. The latter administer the labor laws of the colony which are peculiar to the colony and in their incidence too frequently oppressive to the labourer. We have found for example such a case as this. An Indian Immigrant who had completed his period of service cheated out of his money by a pretended shipping agent, and punished by 21 days hard labor on the public roads for using an illegal pass given to him by the pretended shipping agent. The Indian of course being unable to read, and the Stipendiary Magistrate taking the charge of some illiterate policeman as true without enquiry.[6]

3   NA CO 167/525 Barkly to the Earl Granville, 6 April 1870 (Confidential.)
4   NA CO 167/528 John Gorrie to His Honor Administering the Government,
11 September 1870.
5   Ibid., Memorandum as to Office of Substitute of Procureur General of Mauritius, John Gorrie, 23 September 1870.
6   Ibid.

In February 1871, Sir Arthur Hamilton Gordon was appointed Governor of Mauritius. Although Gordon disliked the island and immediately requested a transfer, he remained till 1876. Mark Francis notes about Gordon:[7]

> As a colonial administrator Gordon was one of the most distinguished of the second generation of professional governors who succeeded mid-Victorian figures such as Lord Elgin and Sir George Grey. Unlike those of his more imperialistic contemporaries, Gordon's policies did not favour white settlers and planters over other ethnic groups in his colonies. He was relatively free from the taints of racialism both when this served as a justification for empire and when it masqueraded as a mission to impose the ideals of European justice upon the customs and politics of non-British peoples.

A mutual respect soon developed between Gordon and Gorrie and began to bear fruit. In April Gorrie had drawn the attention of the Governor to the details of a trial he had overseen the previous month of three Indians, Tirmally, Chavrimootoo, and Chunnoo, for arson committed on the estate of Messrs. Desvaux of Cote d'Or, in the district of Moka. Gorrie remarked that the police appeared to be "in the habit of arresting persons on suspicion, and of improperly tampering with them whilst so in custody, to induce them to give evidence of a particular character," which he denounced as "contrary to the maxims and usages of English law."[8] Gordon ordered a formal enquiry into the charge. Then, in June, a petition was submitted to him on behalf of "old immigrants"—time expired Indian labourers—complaining of mistreatment, largely at the hands of the police and of the government department which processed their papers. A Police Enquiry Commission was set up to investigate the claims; Gorrie was one of six commissioners appointed. Between December 1871 and February 1872 the Commission examined 130 witnesses, including several magistrates, police officers, Government clerks, and a number of Indians, some of whom had signed the petition, and others, such as Modeliar, and Sinnatambou, who were "persons of consideration among the Indian population of the colony."[9] The eventual report —largely the work of Gorrie—upheld most of the Indians' complaints. Additionally, the Governor convinced the Colonial Office to send out a Royal Commission to Mauritius to investigate the treatment of Indian immigrants.

---

7 Mark Francis, 'Gordon, Arthur Charles Hamilton, first Baron Stanmore (1829–1912),' *Oxford Dictionary of National Biography*, Oxford University Press, 2004; online edn, Jan 2011 [http://www.oxforddnb.com/view/article/33459, accessed 18 June 2015].
8 *Report of the Royal Commissioners appointed to enquire into the treatment of Indians in Mauritius*, 1875, para 60.
9 Ibid., para 63.

The Royal Commission Report, published as a Parliamentary Paper in April 1875 fully vindicated his and Gorrie's concerns. The Commissioners outlined in great detail the oppressions exercised on immigrant Indians through the labour laws and recommended the abolition of vagrant hunts and thorough reform of the working of the immigration department, police and magistracy. Gorrie was pleased to see that his findings on the Police Enquiry Commission had been upheld, but found some fault with the report, noting in a private letter to Frederick Chesson, a British activist working with the Aborigines Protection Society, among other points:[10]

> the Commissioners suggest that the Pass system should be extended to Creole born Indians. The Secretary of State has disapproved of this, and most wisely, it would be iniquitous to extend a system radically bad. They also suggest badges to be worn by the old immigrants in addition to or in lieu of papers ... a very unhappy suggestion and unfortunately Ld Carnarvon seems not to regard it as pernicious. He seems to have forgot that many of the old immigrants have risen in life and are shop keepers, proprietors, Government servants etc. etc. and these men would look upon it as a degradation to be compelled to wear a badge.

In his private correspondence, Gorrie stressed repeatedly that it was not only laws but the men in place to uphold them, that needed to be changed. He remarked on the "inveterate tendency in the island to stick to their own usages in spite of laws to the contrary," adding, "the Planters will only begin to understand that the Home Government is in earnest when it changes the men." In September 1875 he reiterated, *nothing has been done here* and nothing will be done until the local officials are stirred up from home in a very determined way."[11]

In the event, John Gorrie had to leave the new Governor to fight the reform battle without him. Sir Arthur Hamilton Gordon, appointed Governor of Fiji, needed a new Chief Justice there, and wrote home recommending Gorrie for the post. Gorrie departed Mauritius in March 1876, but not before the residents of the colony had marked the event in characteristically opposing ways. Whereas the planter's mouthpiece referred maliciously to his "relegation to the Fiji judgeship" as an implied punishment, a deputation of municipal councillors, barristers and others called on him at Chambers to pay tribute, "the ability and impartiality with which you have performed the arduous and delicate duties of your post amidst an heterogeneous population, whose manners, customs, and language are so varied that the admin-

10   *Aborigine Protection Society Papers,* Rhodes House, Oxford, John Gorrie to Frederick Chesson, 30 April 1875.
11   Ibid., John Gorrie to Frederick Chesson, 16 September 1875.

istration of sound justice is a task not easy to be accomplished."[12] Perhaps most satisfying for Mr Justice Gorrie, however, was the deputation from the Indian community who attended at his residence, Belvedere, Beau-Bassin, for the purpose of presenting a valedictory address. Read aloud by Mr. V. Rajaruthnum Modeliar, those present announced that "your departure is a calamity felt by all, and a heavy blow and discouragement to us in particular." The address continues:[13]

> Your profound legal knowledge and acumen, vivid perception of the interests brought before you, and also your instinctive love of justice, accompanied by the conscientious and impartial discharge of your onerous and most important duties, have met with the fullest recognition on the part of our community.

> Among the distinguished men who have sat as judges at the Supreme Court in this island, your Honour will occupy a place in the foremost rank, uniting, as your Honour does, great natural capacity to all the advantages derived from a deep and earnest study of the law. In addition to these capabilities, native and acquired, your Honour possesses an unsullied integrity and a fearless determination to act with independence and to put down legal abuses of every kind.

> [Signed] V. Sinnatambou, Ayoob Aboo Taleb, Hajee Jonus Allarakia, S. Ayassamy, Saboo Sidick & Co., V. Rajaruthnum, I. M. Sulliman, C. Kooshalee, Soka Potty Chetty, Abdool Rassul, M. L. Moutou, D. Sinnatambou, D. D'Silva, and 353 others. Port Louis, 21st March 1876.

Despite his struggles there, John Gorrie, for his part, remembered Mauritius with much fondness. This was apparent, some years later, when he described the island as being famous for "canes and hurri-canes" and recollected a memorable stag hunting outing. Gorrie's intimate knowledge of the lives of Indo-Mauritians, derived not only from his travails on the bench, but also from having shared his home for several years with Indian domestic servants, is nowhere more apparent, than in his novel, written in Fiji and set in Mauritius.

The plot of "Maid of Maurice," to use its probably intended title, is straightforward. An English naval officer, Jack Montmorency, falls for Estelle

---

12   *Mauritius Sentinel* 23 March 1876.
13   Ibid.

Beauvallon, a young, naïve woman—a member of the French settler elite, but someone who apparently has a little African blood too. Her neighbor, Isidore Amirantes, also French, is a womanizer who has numerous liaisons with mixed-race women. When Jack is re-assigned to Natal, Isidore's and Estelle's long association and subsequent friendship turn to love, and Jack in the meantime falls for Agnes MacNeill, a strong, independent woman he meets on a returning ship. The several sub-plots include the unfair arrest and imprisonment (and near-execution) of Jean, a mixed-blood worker, and also the fate of the properties and estates of Isidore and Estelle, devastated by a hurricane and consequently vulnerable to unscrupulous speculators. Jack turns out to be the savior of the estates, something he initially conceals by using Jean as a middleman, and in the end, all ends happily.

In her brief characterisation of the novel, Gorrie biographer and scholar Bridget Brereton concedes that it is "competently written," that it "contains many good descriptions of scenery and Creole lifestyles," and that it displays "a real appreciation for Creole society at its best, an empathy for the cultured French families who constituted a local elite of more refinement that could be found, perhaps, in most British colonies."[14] But for Brereton

> the characters are stereotypical (frank, manly English sol-
> dier; corrupt, proud, touchy, passionate French Creole;
> beautiful, shy yet charming Creole girl with a "touch of the
> tar brush") and fail to come to life as rounded individuals.
> Gorrie's crusading zeal for justice, his hatred of oppression,
> his stern moralism and didacticism, are all to be found in
> his novel, and he constantly breaks into the narrative to
> deliver lectures on diverse topics: how dueling could persist
> for so long in a British colony; how the police arrest and
> convict unscrupulously and how the higher officials fail to
> stop this; how oppressive laws made life difficult for poor
> but honest black fishermen.[15]

Is this a fair assessment? In a recent article about the novelist Anthony Trollope, Adam Gopnik observes, "What makes Trollope a novelist rather than a polem-icist is that, although he is on the side of reform, he is capable of empathetic engagement with its victims."[16] This is not unlike Gorrie. Now, this is not to suggest that Gorrie is a novelist of the caliber of Trollope, but to suggest rather that the balance between polemic and novel are not unique to Gorrie. As Elaine Fregood has noted:

> An empire can only be imagined and represented... The
> novel, like the map, the photograph, the survey, the paint-

14   Brereton, *Law, Justice and Empire*, pp. 102, 103.
15   Brereton, *Law, Justice and Empire*, p. 102.
16   Adam Gopnik, 'Trollope Trending', *The New Yorker* (May 4, 2015), p. 28.

ing, the scholarly work, and the newspaper story, contributes to the imagining of empire that is necessary to its conception, production and maintenance. [17]

In fact, in Britain, until late in the nineteenth century, the idea of imperialism was usually negatively associated with Napoleonic France. "The British Empire, as it began to be called in the 1870s," Fregood reminds us, "required considerable fictional sustenance and narrative therapy to win the hearts and minds of its would-be conquerors, colonists and administrators."[18] Gorrie, it would seem, was responding to such needs. He was no radical (neither was Trollope, for that matter), "Yet he was unquestioningly a liberal of an ideologically rigorous kind—exactly what we mean by a 'progressive'."[19] His views on race were similar to those held by the abolitionists of the 1830s and 1840s, "although he went further than them in his unequivocal conviction that persons of all ethnic backgrounds should enjoy civic and legal equality in the British empire."[20] And he was a believer in the project of empire, in its ability to bring progress to all peoples. That Gorrie was a reformer and a progressive, and the treatment he received for his views, is evidence, as John McLaren has put it, "that subservience of the judicial arm of the colonial state to the executive was a sine qua non of law and politics in the Caribbean, and other multiracial colonial possessions during the late nineteenth century. Judges were meant to comply with a governor's vision of what was good for the colony, even if it meant compromising the deployment of the rule of law to protect the disenfranchised and the oppressed."[21]

Importantly, Gorrie's novel is not without literary merit. The following description, contrasting immobility and motion, demonstrates his skill:

> The harbour was thronged with ships, floating motionless.
> The flag on Fort George had turned round the staff to mark
> that its flaunting for the day was done.

---

17   Elaine Freedgood, 'The Novel and Empire', in Kucich and Taylor (eds), *The Nineteenth-Century Novel 1820–1880*, p. 377.

18   Freedgood, 'The Novel and Empire', p. 377.

19   Gopnik, 'Trollope Trending', p. 32.

20   Brereton, *Law, Justice and Empire*, p. xiii.

21   John McLaren, 'The Perils of the Colonial Judiciary: The Indelible Stain of Slavery in the West Indian Colonies', chapter 10 of *Dewigged, Bothered, and Bewildered: British Colonial Judges on Trial, 1800–1900* (Toronto: Published for the Osgoode Society for Canadian Legal History and the Francis Forbes Society for Australian Legal History by University of Toronto Press, 2011), p. 272. McLaren goes on to aver that because the political balance of power in these possessions was set in favour of elite local economic interests to the cost of the majority of the population and because the system could and did preserve the social and economic status quo in these grossly unequal societies, the growth of democratic government was delayed.

So too does the following metaphor:

> If the streets of the city had not been swept of the filth, at
> least disease knew how to sweep the homes of their inmates.

And in organizing the novel into chapters, the transitions are often well-craft-
ed. Consider the end of chapter 3 and the beginning of chapter 4:

> Ernestine did well not to disturb the hallowed moments. They
> were brief enough as it was for the night was at hand, a night
> which threw not its shadow on their spirits then, but which
> came swift and silent from the Unseen, as the unbidden storm
> comes out of the far firmament.
>
> *[Chapter Four, The Wreck on the Reef]*
>
> The weather which for weeks had been beautiful changed
> during the night. A storm of winter rain not often felt at that
> sea level, although common enough on the heights of the is-
> land, blotted out the whole of the fair landscape. The wind
> blew strong from the east, raising the sea, which came rolling in
> throwing up the foam in thunder on the reefs. The day passed
> heavily and drearily. The labourers, easily chilled with the cold
> rain, walked about shivering and hugging their rags. The ani-
> mals even seemed to have lost heart. The carts sank in the soft
> clay, and the long trains of mules refused to pull them out.

But the novel is also a panoply of Gorrie's views about lawyers, judges, the
police, the Creole settler elite, and the rule of law, and race. Of the Procureur-
General, Gorrie writes:

> So long as he kept to the safe ground of representing that
> the French law was this or that, and that by law the priv-
> ileges, duties, and powers of the Procureur General were
> such and such, he could twist the Governor, as the saying
> goes, round his little finger. The very words "French law"
> were sufficient to put any holder of the office, at any time,
> into a cold perspiration, and by judiciously working this
> handle the Creole Procureurs General had the administra-
> tion in their own hands.

Of the Indian cane workers, Gorrie says:

> The labourers had their hours of toil, but also their times
> of recreation and as, gaudily dressed, they went and came
> from the distant town in the carriages of the country, or en-

gaged in their household duties after their return from the fields, amongst their own cows or poultry, they seemed as happy as any peasantry in the world.

He describes the Creole lawyer conducting Jean's defense as follows:

The Counsel for the Crown in opening the case followed the French rather than the English fashion. An able man, fond of display, and not the least moved by any considerations of fairness for the prisoner, he was determined not to lose such a chance of making a brilliant effort so as to astonish, and as he fondly hoped electrify, the community.

Of Amirantes, the French Creole rake who is Jack's rival, Gorrie writes:

he took care never to show by his manner that contempt for the black race which he so profoundly felt.

Of the mixed-blood Creoles, Gorrie writes:

The Creoles were not a provident class and probably could never have been rich, but they would always have been above want had it not been for the harsh laws which caught them into its toils, just as they caught the fish in their nets.

And also:

As they deemed themselves oppressed they fought the law with the weapons of the oppressed, lies or perjury of this description sitting very lightly on the consciences of the men, and the women generally once a year making a clean breast of it to the priest, and getting absolution for that and other escapades of a different and promiscuous description.

Acknowledging the nuances of Kreol Morisien (the Mauritian Creole language), he characterises a conversation as follows:

It would be impossible to give the conversation between the two women except in the Creole patois which they both spoke, when the various ruses and turns of expression showed the remarkable cleverness of both.

The English, Gorries avers, are clueless (the fact that Jack's eventual wife is a Scotswoman is no accident):

The English people have no more conception of curry than
they have of the Koran.

Throughout the novel, Indians and mixed-blood Creoles are shown to be
discriminated against and mistreated, physically and by the institutions of
the State. Gorrie shows the irrational and destructive views about race when
he describes Jack's mother's views about his proposed marriage to Estelle
(which in the end does not come to pass), that is, when the views are held by
an Englishwoman:[22]

> Let us pity the poor lady if she would have preferred a swar-
> thy Portuguese or Indian beauty for her son rather than a
> young lady descended from a good French stock with only
> such a small soupcon of the African as to add a grace and
> relish to her beauty. She had been brought up in a land of
> prejudices and in a prejudiced family. She did not under-
> stand that hereditary ignorance, fanaticism, pride and ri-
> diculous notions of family consequence, might be far worse
> for the mind than any small and faint cross of another breed
> might be for the body.

Jack's father, in a letter to him, writes:

> And now comes one not less delicate and important. The ques-
> tion of health. I have spoken above of the necessity of looking
> forward to the results of marriage in the birth of children. We
> have all, thank God, had excellent constitutions, and inherit-
> ing as you have both your mothers' excellent health and my
> own, the lady's parents need have no fear on that score as re-
> gards you. But frankly, Jack, we don't want the breed spoiled.
> Putting it on the lowest possible footing it is still of the utmost
> consequence that you be able to look forward to the chance of
> having children free from any hereditary taint of disease. Dr
> Podgers who is as often here as ever, but without getting any
> fees, was you may recollect, although I daresay you were too
> young to take notice of all these little details, in the navy at the
> same time as myself; we were messmates in fact when we were
> in Mauritius, but he being much older—and besides it was
> his profession—learned much more about these things than I
> did. He tells me that the danger of an hereditary disease of a

---

22   See Jenny Sharpe, *Allegories of Empire: The Figure of the Woman in the Colonial Text*
(Minneapolis: University of Minnesota Press, 1993), p. 46, who argues that "due to the
long history of racial mixing in Jamaica, the scandal the creole presented to the British
was the possibility of a white person who was not racially pure," this because of the equa-
tion of racial purity with English national culture.

very terrible kind is not only possible but probable, and he has begged me to be perfectly frank with you on the subject, not to frighten you against an alliance which you have determined on, but for your own satisfaction and comfort hereafter to make every enquiry which you can do in a cautious and proper way to make sure that the family into which you propose to marry is free from this evil in the blood. If you could by any means consult some family physician or some man of business—probably your banker could put you on the right track, I say, before God, Jack, you are bound, before everything, to make this enquiry.

Although the novel is a repository of Gorrie's views, one could argue that it is as much about marriage and the rights (and duties) of a wife as anything else. English novelists routinely expressed views about women and marriage. Contrast Laura Fairlie's imprisonment in Wilkie Collins' *The Woman in White* (1859–60), and the prescient Jane's celebrated assertion of equality with Rochester in Emily Brontë's *Jane Eyre* (1847). In fact, in the 1850s and 1860s marriage came under unprecedented scrutiny, both as a legal contract and as a means of transmitting wealth and property,[23] and various developments (such as the Married Women's Property Act of 1870) changed people's views on marriage and on coverture, wherein a wife's legal person was assimilated into her husband's which was deemed inappropriate to a modern society. Gorrie evidently believed a woman ought to enjoy property rights—the resolution of Estelle's and Isidore's property troubles depends on it. And he evidently believed that a married woman ought to be able to assert independence from her husband—Jack's and Agnes's marriage depends on it. The ideal, for Gorrie, would seem to have been an equal, companionate marriage—something he himself enjoyed in his own married life.

◆

Gorrie never did publish his novel—perhaps he was too preoccupied with his work, or perhaps he was daunted by the prospect of publishing a novel in a period when it had become the dominant literary form.[24] Whatever the case

23   John Kucich and Jenny Bourne Taylor (eds), 'Introduction', *The Nineteenth-Century Novel 1820–1880*, The Oxford History of the Novel in English, Volume 3 (Oxford: Oxford University Press), p. 28. See also Mary Lyndon Shanley, *Feminism, Marriage, and Law in Victorian England*, 1850-1895, (Princeton: Princeton University Press, 1989).
24   Kucich and Taylor (eds), *The Nineteenth-Century Novel 1820–1880*, p. 20. A small sample includes: Sir Walter Scott (d. 1832), the most popular author of the early nineteenth century and a Scotsman and lawyer, like Gorrie; Emily Brontë (d. 1848); Anne Brontë (d. 1849); William Makepeace Thackeray (d. 1863); Charlotte Brontë (d. 1865), novelist of contemporary social ills; Mrs Gaskell (d. 1865); Charles Dickens (d. 1870); Charles Kingsley (d. 1875), who railed against social injustice; George Eliot (d. 1880); politician

may be, he seemed acutely aware of the fact that the "genre was largely de-signed with the female reader in mind, offering them information not found elsewhere, and offering a sense of community."[25]

By publishing it now, it is our hope that this early champion of equal human rights find his place, if not in the history of English literature—which will be for critics and literary historians to decide—then certainly in the history of remarkable individuals who helped make Mauritius what it is.

— Marina Carter and Shawkat M. Toorawa

and chronicler of political life, Benjamin Disraeli (d. 1881); Anthony Trollope (d. 1882); Robert Louis Stevenson (d. 1894), lawyer, Scotsman, and traveler to the colonies; Samuel Butler (d. 1902), critic of Victorian morality; Radical politician and realist, George Gissing (d. 1903); George Meredith (d. 1909).

25   Deborah Wynne, 'Readers and Reading Practices', in Kucich and Taylor (eds), *The Nineteenth-Century Novel 1820–1880*, p. 32.

A Note on the Text

In preparing the manuscript of the novel for publication, we made certain editorial decisions and changes, notably:

*Converted underlines to italics.

*Standardised and corrected spellings for consistency, e.g. "Darcy" over "D'Arcy" (the latter appearing thus only in the first 11 pages), and e.g. "coconut" for "cocoa-nut"; adding accents missing from French words; and added or removed hyphens and capital letters as appropriate.

*Added punctuation such as commas and/or dashes for clarity.

*Corrected errors of dating.

*Altered or created paragraphs where appropriate.

*Indented dialogue for clarity.

The manuscript is damaged or defective in places. Whenever possible, we intervened by:

*Adding an obviously missing word, e.g. "and" to "lawlessness and licentiousness" in ch. 9.

*Speculating about missing words or phrases—these are indicated in square brackets. An ellipsis in square brackets means we were not secure in our speculation.

*Deleting material Gorrie himself strikes through. This in-
cludes a stylistic deletion of three words by Gorrie in ch.
9, an entire paragraph in ch. 18, and, most importantly, the
novel's final two lines, which appear out of place, and appear to suggest that Gorrie was experimenting with extend-
ing the novel. Those lines are:

> "Excuse me," said Colonel Montmorency,
> "Come Agnes and let us try to get near Sir Isidore."
> "And near Estelle. Jack don't be a hypocrite.
> My peace of mind is gone!"

Additionally, we footnote foreign or possibly unfamiliar words and expressions, signaled by an asterisk: *; we provide Back Notes to explain anything
that might not be clear to the reader, signaled with an arrow: †; and we iden-
tify most toponyms and proper names (but not the fictional characters) in a
Glossary.

Finally, we saw fit to change the probable title "Maid of Maurice" to "A
Maiden of Mauritius," so that the 21st-century English reader would think of
what Gorrie was evoking, namely a young woman on the island of Mauritius,
rather than a domestic worker in the service of a man named Maurice.

— The Editors

A Maiden of Mauritius

John Gorrie

Chapter 1
A Ball and its Results

AT THE TIME WHEN THIS TALE OPENS THE SOCIETY OF MAURITIUS was still centred in its chief and indeed sole town of Port Louis. The great fever of 1867 has swept away much that was charming in the life of the Colony, as it also swept so many thousands into the gorged graveyards. French and English, Merchant and Planter, Avocat and Avoué* had formerly their homes in those picturesque mansions, shaded by masses of flowering trees and gay shrubs, which adorn the town. They still form pleasant retreats for a class less rich but with all the old taste for music and pleasure.

It was the cool season when the days were somewhat shorter. A delicious freshness of the atmosphere came up with the shades of evening calling forth old and young to the verandah and the pleasant little flower garden, or to mount the carriage which stood ready to join in the promenade around the Champ de Mars or out to the bridge over the Grand River. The scene was one which had not its equal in any Colony of the Crown. The finest carriages from famous makers of England and France, drawn by high mettled steeds, passed and repassed. The Lascar coachman arrayed in spotless white with scarlet girdle and gold embroidered bonnet, sat statue like, scarce needing to touch the glossy coats of the horses with his well-poised whip. Groups of children in the charge of negress nurses whose wooly hair was concealed by bright coloured kerchiefs lit up the streets as if by sun flecks.

The children seemed more numerous, and the grown-up people taking an airing less numerous, than usual. The regimental band was absent from the pleasure ground so that those who had come on foot to enjoy the music ascended instead for a little way the steep hill-side and drank in the beauty and the glory of the sunset hour. The harbour was thronged with ships, floating motionless. The flag on Fort George had turned round the staff to mark that its flaunting for the day was done. There was a low streak of foam upon the reef to right and left, but no sound of break or ripple. The wind had left the trees and sunk to rest among the flowers, gently kissing as it passed the wan cheek of the sick child propped with pillows in its chair. The few faint clouds in the sky blushed to find themselves alone, as the setting sun, unseen by the gazers on the hill, touched with rich evening rays the path it had traversed in the pride of day.

---

* The two principal types of attorney

But amid the peace and rest of the hour there was a feeling of expectancy in the air. The sounds of the hoofs seemed to quicken as they reached the streets, and those persons who passed along the Chaussée could see anxious mothers inside the shops holding up ribbons to the fading light, the last touch to make perfect some charming costume. The shop of the hairdresser was filled with young men waiting the leisure of the assistant, the master himself having been absent for hours in the private mansions, busy with the locks of ladies old and young. For there is to be a ball tonight, given by the officers of one of the regiments in garrison, and the stir in society is great. The regiment is a distinguished one, and its officers have made themselves much liked by their frankness, their air of distinction, and the unusual number of them who could speak tolerable French. They, however, have the worst of the part just at this moment. The juniors, coatless and breathless, are watching the last bayonet or brightly burnished ramrod added to the decorations which cover the walls. The floor polished to perfection with bees-wax in the morning is littered with flowers and coconut leaves, while a tangled mass of banners refuse to hang in the graceful folds so eagerly desired by the Ensigns who lack the necessary skill. A marquee has been put up on the smooth lawn of the barrack-square, where the supper table is being laid; the candles in the numerous silver candelabra have been lit to show the Colonel the grand general effect.

"Would you believe it," said Captain Bloater coming in, flushed and angry, "that old cheat Blancgilet* has not sent up the extra champagne. They will be bringing it when the guests are arriving, just as if we never drank champagne except when we have a dance."

"No one will accuse you of such moderation, my dear fellow," said the Colonel. "Besides, we have sufficient as it is to turn the heads of all the men in the Colony. You, Bloater, and the rest must answer for the heads of the fair."

"Oh," piped the small voice of the last arrival from home, "if the heads of the w-w-women can be turned by w-w-waltzing, I am game till cock-crow."

"Don't crow too soon young cock," said the dashing Darcy Connaught. "Who is for the River for a plunge before we dress? Mike, get a *voiture*."**

"Devil a one is to be had, your honour," said Mike, "they have all gone for the quality. There's nothin' on wheels to be seen but a fire engine driven by a nigger."

"Just the very thing," shouted Darcy, "Now for a ride in an illigant carriage! Mike, stop the nigger." And in spite of the protests of the driver, a band of the young scapegraces mounted the fire engine, Darcy lashing the steeds to their utmost speed, and the whole shouting to clear the street went along like lightning as if rushing to save the capital from destruction.

The capital had indeed been already nearly destroyed by fire shortly after the English capture of the Island. Not only was much property destroyed and many persons ruined, but various public and private offices were consumed

* Lit. white waistcoat
** carriage (lit. vehicle)

which contained the Archives of the island, title deeds of property, registers of births, deaths and marriages, and many similar important documents, so that even up to the present time difficulties are thrown in the way of judicial investigations. Any alarm of fire was therefore sure to create a great sensation from this cause alone, independently of the fact that the town was built of timber and would burn like match-wood if a breeze were blowing to drive the flames through the heart of the city. Extraordinary precautions were accordingly taken to subdue fires, the brigade for the purpose being stationed at various parts of the town, and houses and men in constant readiness.

In addition to the fire brigade an officer was on watch in the Citadel, a commanding position whence the whole streets could be scanned, and by a code of signals he could warn the brigade of the quarter where any conflagration[1] had broken out. So many guns meant this or that district, to which the fire engines accordingly betook themselves. Although all this precaution was wise and beneficial, one cannot help reflecting that after all fire was not the most dangerous enemy the inhabitants had to fear. Amid each mixed population, and especially when the great mass of the people were Indians huddled together in squalor, the great enemy was disease and no care was taken to guard against its approach. Against disease from without, it is true, quarantine laws had for a long time been enforced, but against disease springing up from within, not only were no precautions taken but the whole condition of the town was such as to make disease inevitable and an epidemic deadly. For a long time Port Louis was comparatively safe, but the day came at length when all the neglect, and filth, and evil customs, brought forth the Avenger. If the streets of the city had not been swept of the filth, at least disease knew how to sweep the homes of their inmates.

There was light enough left to enable the Lieutenant in charge of the signal cannon in the Citadel to descry through his glass the fire engine careering along Moka Street, and fearful that he had overlooked a conflagration he hastily fired the signal gun – bang – bang – until he had signalled "Fire at Grand River." Then there was such a mounting in hot haste of horse police, such a hurrying along Moka Street of foot police, accompanied by a mass of people of all nations and colours, through whom the fire engines forced their mad way, racing with each other, the firemen holding on grimly as the vehicles swayed wildly from side to side. It seemed as if the whole town had suddenly become peopled with demoniacs. Arrived at the river the head of the crowd found the captured vehicle, the horses calmly eating the grass by the side of the path, while below in the dim light could be seen the forms of the bathers. Merry laughter rose up from time to time from the ravine.

"We have been hoaxed," said a dashing serjeant of the police troopers. "It has been some of those devils from barracks."

"Just so, Serjeant," said a foot policeman, "I saw them pass me, but not one of you would stop, although I have shouted myself hoarse."

"Well, gentlemen, you have got into a pretty scrape," the Serjeant said, as he saw some of the officers calmly emerge from the ravine with their towels.

"Dear me," said Darcy, "have all these people come to see us bathe? Oh, there's the Superintendent. Look here, Thompson, you cannot take all these fine fellows back to town on horseback. The niggers will laugh at them. We have barely time to get something to eat, and dress for the ball. Let some of them dismount and give us their horses."

And in point of fact, such is the power of good nature and popularity, the officers rode back through the laughing crowd on the horses of the policemen, who ought to have taken them into custody.

About nine o'clock the carriages began to arrive at the barracks, entering by Moka Street gate and retiring by Jemappes Street. The line soon extended along the whole length of the barracks, and up towards the Chaussée, while on the footpaths clustered a mass of Indians, negroes, Chinese and half-castes to see the dresses and the carriages.

There was the usual amount of stiffness at first in the room, notwithstanding the exertions of the hosts to make the affair start well. The ladies, old and young, preferred to crowd together to watch the new arrivals. Presently, after a number of leaders of fashion had been welcomed by the Colonel, the Adjutant introduced to him Monsieur, Madame and Mademoiselle Beauvallon. These, although well-known residents, had not been accustomed to receive invitations to such balls. Their entrance evidently caused a sensation, especially amongst the young men, as Mademoiselle Beauvallon who thus made her first appearance in a ball-room was wonderfully pretty.

"I forgot to say," whispered the Adjutant to the Colonel, after the newcomers had moved on, "that old Soussigné,* the Notary, begged me to invite these people, at the very last moment, and I omitted to mention the circumstance."

"But, bless me," replied the Colonel, "they have a slight touch of the tar-brush. I know all about them. The old gentleman was a very successful planter, but they are not in society. You will find scarcely one of these *jeunes gens*** will have the courage to dance with the girl, pretty as she is.†"

"Oh," said the Adjutant, "I will make Soussigné fils lead off with her, and that will give her a fair start."

This was more easily arranged before the young gentleman was consulted. He had no objection to extract dollars from Monsieur Beauvallon to fill the purse of the Notary, but to make himself publicly responsible for the introduction to society of a young lady whose great-grandmother had been one of his great-great grandfather's slaves, was a strong dose for a white Creole† to swallow. When he found, however, that he had either to do as he was asked, or embroil himself with the Adjutant, he did his part with that charming grace so characteristic of well-bred young Frenchmen. The Adjutant, not to do things by halves, told off two of the juniors who were to keep a special eye to see that the young lady had no lack of partners, and in a spirit of self-sacrifice which he thought did him infinite credit, he resolved to lead Madame Beauvallon in to supper.

* Lit. "Undersigned"
** young bachelors

The Governor had by this time arrived, and the *quadrille d'honneur** was duly formed, while the whole room displayed all the bustle and amusement of the arrangements for the first dance. And the spectacle was in fact a superb one. The ladies of the Colony shine to more advantage in the ball-room than in their own houses, each trying to outvie the other in the richness of their Paris-made dresses and the display of jewels. It is true that more than one ill-natured question was asked by censorious persons as to how many English and French capitalists had been robbed to provide the sparkling diamonds which lent a lustre to the fête but such questions were only answered by light laughs or expressive shrugs, which simply meant that diamonds on women were good things whoever paid for them.

After the first crash of the music all went well. The stiffness thawed like the crisp ice of a morning in spring. During the pauses of the dance the Colonel cast an anxious eye to the set in which the debutante was conspicuous, and found to his relief that everything was going smoothly. Nor did the gaiety flag during the rest of the evening, the Colonel's only fear there being that Jack Montmorency who had been told off to do duty with the beautiful Mademoiselle Beauvallon was paying her so much attention as to be talked about in the room. Indeed when Jack led her into supper and seemed no longer to notice the other guests, the Colonel, when he met his eye, looked grave as a hint that he was going too far, but Jack saw nothing except the soft black eyes with the long lashes and the delicately chiselled features which had made him feel all the witchery of beauty. From time to time Estelle (for so we will now call her) glanced furtively in the direction, not of her father and mother whose presence she completely ignored, but of a young Frenchman, Isidore Amirantes, the son of her neighbour Monsieur Amirantes of Pompadour, who from among a circle of young men, making merry at the end of the table, cast looks black as thunder at the officer who was so openly paying attention to the young lady.

To hasten the conclusion of supper the music struck up a galop, and the young people hurried off to resume the dance. Jack Montmorency was about to start with Estelle as his partner when young Amirantes arrived to claim her. Jack refused to yield, saying that this was an extra dance not on the programme and with that disdainfully nonchalant air which English people are ready to assume, and which wounds more than hard words, put his arm round the graceful figure of the girl to begin. The young Frenchman, blind with jealous fury, for in secret he had long loved Estelle, seized Montmorency by the collar to drag him away, when a subdued scream from the young lady called the attention of the Adjutant to the scene. Although inwardly annoyed at the folly of Jack in putting himself in such a position, nothing could excuse the act of the young Creole in daring to lay hands on one of his hosts, and so in the most polite, but most firm manner, he was requested to leave the ball. This he did in company with a friend, all the hot French blood boiling in his veins, and thinking of nothing but a meeting with Montmorency at

* guard of honor

the earliest opportunity. The affair was fortunately very little observed by the other guests, but for Estelle, the pleasure of the evening was gone. The attentions of the handsome English officer were not disagreeable to her, but knowing the fierce and turbulent character of Amirantes she dreaded the consequences, she knew not what. She scarcely thought of a duel, but of some open act of violence which would bring shame upon them all, and shut for ever to her the doors of the society which had opened so pleasantly and easily. She begged to be taken home, a request which astonished her mother very much, who thought Estelle could not but be enjoying the evening, and she herself would have preferred another visit to the supper room and a little more of the champagne of which she felt she had partaken too sparingly. But the will of Estelle was law to both the parents and they prepared to go.

Jack escorted the Beauvallons to their carriage with the utmost courtesy, as though nothing untoward had happened. Then he stood watching until, the horse trotting briskly in its shafts, the conveyance was soon out of sight.

Chaussée in Port Louis before the fire of 1893

Chapter 2
An Exchange of Shots

NEXT DAY FEW OF THE OFFICERS WERE OUT OF THEIR ROOMS before "tiffin,"[†] but at that meal the various incidents of the ball were discussed and arrangements made to visit the lady guests. The incident with young Amirantes was never once mentioned, and Jack himself would have forgot it had not the unwelcome idea forced itself upon him that the gentleman was in love with Estelle. His rash act of offered violence was put down to account of the champagne, so that when later on in the afternoon, as he was dressing to go out, his servant Mamode announced that a "Français" wished to see him, he ordered him to be admitted, thinking that it was nothing more important than his tailor's bill. He was both surprised and amused to find that the stranger came with a demand for an apology from Amirantes, or in the event of refusal an invitation to meet the challenger on the following morning in a retired valley at the base of the Pouce, the mountain which overhangs the town.

Jack thought the sooner the ridiculous business was over the better, and, begging his visitor to be seated, went in search of Darcy Connaught, in whose hands he placed himself. Darcy, who knew the Continental theories in regard to such matters, saw at once that it was better to accept the challenge, which was, perhaps, he wickedly thought, the last thing the challenger wished. He determined to say nothing about it to his brother officers, in order that if the civil authorities interfered they two alone might be in the scrape. The preliminaries having been arranged, the two young men went out to visit, and after some formal calls, they separated, when Jack found himself, without well knowing how, at the residence of Estelle. He could not pass without enquiring for his fair partner of the preceding evening, and, as the carriage was in waiting to take the mother and daughter for their afternoon drive he went with them. The talk that Jack was smitten with the charms of the fair young Creole became more general.

This was not so fortunate for the Beauvallons as it seemed. Jack was a great favourite, and when it was thought that he preferred the debutante to his old friends the tongues of the fair scandal mongers did not spare either. The fact is that Jack *was* smitten, and more deeply than he himself was aware of. Estelle, conscious of the good impression she had made on the previous evening, had attired herself even more carefully than usual and the lustre of the dark eyes, shaded and softened by the long lashes, as they now met for

an instant Jack's frank and open look and smile, and now more modestly regarded the street, the houses, the passing carriages, completed a conquest she
did not try to make, but the thought of which when she awoke in the morning had made the sunshine appear more bright, and the remembrance of the
scene with Amirantes infinitely less serious than it had appeared over-night.

Jack did not return to the barracks till it was time to dress for dinner.
He had accepted the invitation of Madame Beauvallon to a musical party for
the following evening. Fortunately for the nerves both of himself and Darcy
Connaught in view of the serious work of the morning, the mess dinner was
not kept up so late as usual, and the attempted card parties all breaking
down, there was an early adjournment to bed.

It may appear remarkable that a custom so essentially French as that of
duelling should have survived under the English Government which must at
least have then enforced the law with firmness and impartiality. The very fact
however that the Colony was French often prevented the authorities from
taking any severe views which might have come in conflict with the customs
of the country. We have held the Colony for upwards of seventy years but
all the upper and intelligent classes are still French to the back-bone. The
government has been no sinecure from first to last. Until the wars of the
French Revolution had ended, the vigilance of the English officials had to be
directed to prevent any attempts at recapture of the Island with the aid of
the inhabitants. At this time Bourbon was also in the hands of the English,
and under the same Governor. After the war, and when Bourbon had been
handed back to the French, the great bone of contention was the slave trade.
England had put an end to it so far as an imperial law could do so, and her
cruisers were busy everywhere in enforcing the prohibition. It was very difficult, however, to put the trade down in Mauritius when the Coast of Africa
was so near, and the colony of Bourbon free to run cargoes as it pleased. An
increasing vigilance had to be exercised and stringent penalties enforced.
Afterwards came the struggles about the duty levied on sugar which was settled, against all the principles of geography, by the Island being regarded as
a West Indian and not an East Indian possession. The long contest for emancipation followed, in which which Mauritius did its best to defy the home
government and not without success.

In the midst of these struggles any concession which could reasonably be made to the feelings of the people was made. At a time for example
when Protestantism was both bigotted and aggressive, when statesmen like
Wellington and Peel were still strong in their opposition to the emancipation of the Catholics in Ireland, Roman Catholicism was practically the established religion of Mauritius. The Articles of the Capitulation guaranteed to
the inhabitants the free exercise of their own religion and their own laws and
customs and thus any attempt forcibly to put down duelling before public
opinion in France was the least shaken in regard to its propriety and fairness
would probably have been unsuccessful, and made it even more popular than
it really was. The weapon under which it has gradually succumbed, was ridicule. One of the law officers in recent times proposed to have the heads of

the combatants shaved, while another used the still more cruel threat that he would insist upon the parties fighting if a challenge had been issued and accepted. Men sent challenges who never intended to fight, and who took care, if the challenge was accepted, that the authorities should be warned in time to prevent the meeting. At the earlier date of which we write encounters had occasionally been serious and in one or two cases had led to the death of one of the combatants. Now notwithstanding the hold which the evil practice still has in France, duelling may be said to have died out in the Colony.

Jack tossed about uneasily after Darcy left him, doubtful of the light in which Estelle and her friends would regard his meeting with Amirantes, and still more doubtful whether in general society he would be commended or laughed at. He had, however, quite made up his mind as to the course he would pursue. No thought of danger to himself entered his mind. He wrote no parting letters lest he should fall, but seeing that however the affair might be regarded it was inevitable, he fell into a sound sleep thinking of Estelle and the beautiful gloss of her hair as it waved over the ivory smoothness of her shoulders.

It was the cool season, which meant also that the sun was somewhat longer in rising than in the height of summer. Long before daylight Darcy had aroused Jack and the two were already on their way to the place of encounter. They both thought that the distance was formidable for a meeting which even then they could not be brought to regard as serious. But their adversaries came on the field before them, and for the first time Jack comprehended from the compressed lips and bloodless face of the young "cub" as he called him, that Amirantes meant mischief. A sensation of regret that he had been led so far did cross his mind, not from any feeling of fear, but lest there might be a scandal, and the name of Estelle be mixed up with it, as well as the fair fame of the Regiment be brought into question. But he quietly took his position, and at the signal received the fire of Amirantes which was not intended to be child's play. The bullet passed through Jack's forage cap, a fact of which he was not at the time fully conscious, but feeling that he was unhurt, he raised his own pistol and fired in the air.

Amirantes, knowing how determinedly he had himself sought to take a good aim, expected nothing else than immediate death, and the sudden reaction to perfect safety was too much for him. He threw himself into the arms of his second, and as the two seemed disposed to indulge in antics, the English officers quickly left the field, taking the Doctor, who was in attendance at a little distance, back with them to breakfast.

So far as the two officers were concerned the affair would then have sunk into oblivion but the young Frenchman was too elated with the whole encounter to permit it to remain secret. The announcement flew over the town, the desperate courage of Amirantes, together with the bearing of the English officer, being told in a hundred excited and extravagant ways, sometimes even with tears. Curiously enough the fact of Jack firing in the air was taken to be an acknowledgement that he was in the wrong, while his honour as an officer would not allow him to refuse to meet the other when challenged. Amirantes, without a dissenting voice, was held to have reflected glory on his native island, to have established a courage worthy of a Frenchman, and to have shown that the Creole would neither stand an insult nor show himself inferior to the English in high chivalry. Business was almost suspended. On the *Place* – the street where the merchants congregated – and in the square of the Supreme Court, nothing else was talked of, now one, and now another, incident of the great drama of the morning being brought to light. It couldn't fail therefore speedily to reach the ears of those in authority. But the authorities were discreet.

"Either of the fools hurt?" enquired the Procureur General* from the Superintendent of Police.

"Neither," was the reply.

"Who is the girl?"

"Old Beauvallon's daughter."

"Well, I suppose we had better leave it alone, and not make bad worse by a prosecution."

"I think so, decidedly," said the Superintendent, "to attempt to prosecute would only add fuel to the flame, and it would be impossible to obtain a conviction from any jury."

The Colonel duly consulted the General in Command of the Forces as to whether something should be done from a military point of view, but both agreeing that the conduct of the officers concerned was perfectly proper they too resolved to drop the subject with one proviso – that it was to be kept out of the newspapers. The Superintendent of Police undertook to arrange this delicate part of the negotiation, and hard as it was for the Creole editors to lose the opportunity of printing the ravings which had already been written, even this was arranged, and the incident made a family matter not to be known beyond the bounds of the colony.

When Jack arrived in the evening at the house of Madame Beauvallon that good-hearted and excitable lady was disposed to throw herself into his arms. But the hero of the morning discouraged the attempt. He had no objections however at a later period, when by chance Estelle and he found themselves in the verandah, to receive her warm and almost sobbing thanks for his noble conduct in not firing upon Amirantes.

"He is so violent," said Estelle, "but surely he will now be taught what true courage is."

"I fear the thought of the affair gives you pain," replied Jack. "Think of it no more. I disliked the idea of the encounter on this very ground, and I would rather do something which could bring you pleasure."

"It has brought me pleasure," she said, "in knowing of your generosity," and then fearing she had spoken with too great boldness, she blushed lest she should have been thought unmaidenly. They stood there where the moonlight was bursting through the foliage, where the sound of the song fell softly on their ears, mingling with the cool plash of the fountains which stood in the centre of the little flower garden. Jack took the hand of Estelle and gratefully pressed his lips to the trembling fingers, making the blood

* akin to a Solicitor-General

mount again into her cheeks with a redoubled rush. "Am I too bold," he said, as they resumed the promenade which the action had interrupted. She did not speak, but only glancing her eyes for a moment to meet those of her companion she pressed ever so gently and lightly on his arm, as if to intimate that she would not be unwilling to trust to such a protector. Just then a waltz was started and without another word Jack and his partner glided into the dance. All remarked the perfect beauty of the young girl, her cheeks yet glowing with the rich blush which had mounted so unbidden at the touch of the lips of the young officer.

Madame Beauvallon was too shrewd not to perceive the marks of a growing attachment, and as she thought the match would be in every way desirable, and would enable her to triumph over those ladies who had so long excluded her from society because of her supposed tinge of colour, she resolved to give every reasonable opportunity to the young people. She accordingly sought out her husband, who was enjoying a smoke and a glass of brandy and water with a friend of his own age, and suggested that he should invite Mr Montmorency with one of his brother officers for a few days' visit, to Lorraine, for such was the name of their sugar estate. Monsieur Beauvallon was not as sure as his wife that the invitation would be accepted, and it would be a dreadful humiliation to be refused. Madame argued that they could not be invited to visit them in Port Louis if they had any objection to visit them at home in the country, and the sooner the question was set at rest the better. With very considerable trepidation therefore Beauvallon gave the invitation, and was extremely gratified to find it accepted in the most cordial manner.

"Of course you know, Monsieur" said Jack, "I must obtain leave of absence before I can absolutely say I shall be with you on the day you name, but I have no doubt that I shall obtain it."

When Madame Beauvallon, after the guests had left, informed Estelle in her own room of the expected visit, the tell-tale blood which was so ready to mount, again made its presence seen and felt.

"Oh Maman," she said, "it is too short notice! We require many things for the salon and for the pavilion which the English officers will occupy."

"We are going to entertain them as Creoles of Maurice," said the mother, with a pardonable pride, "and they will see us as we are. But, Estelle, whatever you know is necessary for English bedrooms you can get tomorrow before we leave."

"They must have the double-roomed pavilion, Maman, and each of the rooms must have carpets, and marble-topped basin stands, and dressing tables, and chests of drawers, and handsome lamps. The Misses Britain told me these things were de rigueur in English bed-rooms. And then the bath, Maman, which is always out of order – Oh, dear, what shall we do?"

Madame Beauvallon could not help laughing at her daughter's dilemma. "Oh," she said, "carpets and such things are necessary and suitable to cold countries, but one can make the rooms look very well without them. We can get tomorrow new mosquito nets, and window curtains, new table covers, and lamps, and we shall make the rooms fit for English princes. Meantime, go to sleep my child, and do not dream too much of that handsome Mr Montmorency."

"Oh, Maman," cried Estelle, blushing crimson yet again, as she held her mothers' face close to her burning cheeks and kissed her many times "Bon soir, méchante Maman."

"Bon soir, mon enfant. Que le bon Dieu te bénisse Ma Chérie."*

While this was passing in one part of the town, Jack was finding unexpected difficulties in another. The Colonel whom he found in the Library of the Barracks, after some guests had departed, was very unwilling to give leave for the purpose of such a visit.

"The French people," he said, "do not understand these things in the same light as we do. If you do not take care you will be regarded as a suitor for the hand of the girl. Which of course," added the Colonel, "is ridiculous."

It was now Jack's turn to feel his cheeks somewhat hot, but the veteran proceeded.

"You and Darcy, whom you wish to accompany you, are welcome to the leave, but you will be disappointed. Down on the estates you will find things different from Port Louis, and you will come in contact with a great many objectionable people. Good God, Jack, what would my old friend your father say if you got entangled with a coloured Creole."

"Really, Sir," said Jack, "it is surely possible to enjoy a few days rambling about without all these dreadful consequences."

"I have seen serious consequences flow before now from just such invitations, and such beginnings, as these people are preparing for you. But of course you will not take advice. I never saw a young man yet who did. Enjoy yourselves if you can, but take care, my boy, of these wily old Creoles."

And so in the morning Darcy and Jack after breakfast concocted together a note informing their friends that they had both obtained leave and would be at Lorraine on the evening appointed. This invitation, simple as it had seemed, entailed no inconsiderable amount of trouble on the family of the Beauvallons. Monsieur had to consult with his friend over the weak brandy and water what would be the most suitable mode of entertaining the gentlemen. With fishing, partridge shooting on the estate and visits to a few places of note, it was thought the time would not hang heavily. Dinner and breakfast parties had however to be arranged, and everything required for the household to be thought of and despatched from town. No railways existed in those days and Lorraine was many miles from the capital. Estelle had had various conferences with Mrs Britain, and now believed she had a perfect idea of how bed-rooms should be arranged after the English fashion. She was so resolved not to forget anything that she ordered twice over a large supply of Eau-de-Cologne which led the perfumer wickedly to suggest that the *bonhomme*** intended to give it to his guests to drink.

---

* – "Oh, Mummy… Good night, naughty Mummy." – "Good night my child. May God bless you, my darling."
** Affectionate term for an elderly man, such as the father of the family.

Chapter 3
The Visit

THE AUSPICIOUS DAY AT LENGTH ARRIVED. The Coolie boys at Lorraine had felt the full importance of the visit of the personages who were about to arrive, the "burra Sahibs"* as they were talked about in the Coolie lines. Madame Beauvallon knew how to handle her servants, and what with polishing the floors of the reception rooms, which had always been polished, and the floors of the pavilion which had never been polished, scouring and dusting, cleaning plates, and washing dishes, the distinction of the visit had been thoroughly impressed upon the boys in more ways than one. Even Estelle's voice which was naturally soft had been heard rising in rather harsh accents.

The sick from the Estate Hospital had been pressed into service to weed the courtyard, the mill had received a new coat of whitewash, the *bagasse*** which had lain from the last crop had been swept up, and the mill dam, which was a good place for a plunge, cleaned of its sediment which lay yet unremoved but covered with lime on its margin. The mule stables which generally reeked with filth had been purified. The oxen were stalled among fresh fodder, and in spite of Madame Beauvallons' boast that her guests would see them as they were, everything had the uncomfortable look of being cleaned up for the occasion. Some of the Coolie children were sent out by Estelle as scouts to warn her of the approach of the strangers, as she was still busy in her desperate efforts to adjust the pavilion like an English bedroom, which she had never seen. Her old Mozambique nurse Ernestine was with her, amazed and amused at the little lady who never soiled her fingers, striving as hard as any of them to make the *chambres-à-coucher*** look well. She entertained an Indian girl who was assisting them with stories of her own inventing about the fabulous wealth of the Sahib who was going to marry Mam'selle – and the two had many jokes, not of the most refined description, even in Estelle's hearing, about the best mode of entertaining the strangers.

"Mamzelle," cried Ernestine in her patois, "Moi danse le Sega"**** and she placed the Indian girl before her and began to dance that immodest old African slave dance. The antics of the two made Estelle laugh in spite of her

* Lit. "big sirs," a reference to colonial men of importance.
** Cane by-product.
*** the bed-rooms
**** "Miss" ... "I'm dancing the Sega."

desire to have the work finished. They were interrupted by one of the child scouts rushing in with the cry "Burra Sahibs veni – caless veni."* All was confusion and hurry. Estelle darted off lest she should be caught in the act of doing household work. She had time to compose herself however as the children had seen the mail phaeton a long way off, and it was some time before the vehicle came at a fast trot down the avenue and pulled up before the admiring Coolies in the courtyard of the mill. Ready hands took charge of the horses and poised the portmanteaus and gun cases on their heads, even to the bundles of the officers' coolie servants, who were treated as gentlemen for the occasion.

The house of Lorraine was finely situated on a rising ground which commanded a view of the plain covered with sugar-cane in all stages of growth. At a little distance was the sea, fringed by a belt of filao trees** through which the foam of the tide could be seen kissing the sandy beach of the bay. Beyond, seaward, the break of the wave showed the line of coral reef. The mill and courtyard were partially shut out from view by the fine trees and shrubs which surrounded the house and which afforded also an agreeable shade from the midday sun. The reception of the young officers was cordial in the extreme, and after they had been taken to their pavilion they examined each other's rooms, expressing much satisfaction at the comfortable quality they had obtained.

Dinner passed over more gaily than they had anticipated. Some of the "objectionable" people of whom the Colonel spoke were present, that is to say they were relatives of the host or hostess who were unknown in the society of the chief town, and who were mostly connected in some capacity with the estate. The brother-in-law who acted as the broker in town to sell the sugar and purchase the supplies, the attorney who conducted the legal business, and prosecuted the Coolies before the Stipendiary Magistrate, brothers and sisters who in virtue of their relationship had privileges, or *hypothèques**** on the estate, were all present. The board groaned under a liberal profusion of meats all placed on it at the same time. The profusion was greater than the refinement, and as usually happens in such cases all the dishes which ought to have been eaten hot had become cold. There was one however which remained, and which at all Creole dinners was the true pièce de resistance, the curry for which Mauritius had been famous for more than one hundred years, ever since in fact Indians were first stolen as slaves from the Malabar Coast. English people have no more conception of curry than they have of the Koran. Imagine the messes which are brought in occasionally and called curry! A nondescript yellow mess in a huge dish with a sprinkling of rice round the margin, the rice having been steeped in hot water until it is soft and pulpy and as nauseous as human beings could contrive to make a nourishing article of diet. An English cook is not aware, and few English ladies are aware, that rice is the food of hundreds of millions of the human race, and that it is so cooked as to be not only nourishing and wholesome but

---

* "The Masters have come, the carriage has come"
** casuarinas
*** mortgages

delicious to eat. In England the idea of curry is to make some slop or other the basis, and the rice the ornament, whereas the true principle is that the rice is the dish and the condiment is solely to make the rice palatable. Indians and Chinese live on rice, but it is rice made rich and salty and pleasant to the taste. So the early settlers of Mauritius adopted rice as their national dish, rice for the whites, but manioc* for the slaves.

The manioc was introduced from Brazil by the first Governor Labourdonnais, no doubt from the best of motives, but it may be that the slave race did not bless him as they were fed, from day to day, from year to year, upon manioc and *margoze*, a bitter creeper which grows by the wayside.[†] With the French genius of the colonists, the curry (*carrie*, they wrote it) rose steadily in estimation, until now even the poorest are able to mix up nearly a dozen spices and simples and condiments with the rice which they eat. In the bazaar of Port Louis which is so admirably conducted, the curry mixtures are spread out on banana leaves, and sold for a few pence. When to these are added the leaves of some road-side shrub, such as the tender leaflets of the Pepper plant, the labourers need never be without a savoury meal. The Indians give much more time and care to the making of their favourite dish than the Mozambique Creoles. The latter are not particular about the rice they purchase, the former must have the rice to which they are accustomed. Their women clean the rice by pounding it in a mortar, and then they fan it by tossing it in the air, after which the curry stuff must be rolled out and thoroughly mixed on the curry stone which forms part of the furniture of every household.

The Creole whites pile up a plate with rice which boiled in so careful a manner that the seeds of the rice are not broken or wet, but the whole dry and nice, and then having added the condiment, they proceed to eat it with spoon and fork, even the ladies causing immense quantities to disappear.

The officers were no less struck after dinner with the admirable music played by the ladies, with the spirit and good sense exhibited in their conversation, and the wonderfully varied knowledge which the gentlemen possessed. The most recent literature of England and France, and the best scientific works, were familiar to them, the French authors being naturally preferred. Not a single observation, either on religion or politics was hazarded which could in the most remote decree have seemed to conflict with the opinions of their guests. The ladies who were early risers retired early, but the gentlemen remained till far in the night over cards and cigarettes tempered with a weak brandy.

The officers were occupied at first in visiting the estate, inspecting the mill and the various operations of the manufacture of sugar. In these Jack took less interest than Darcy who had been in other Colonies and seen how the industry was practised elsewhere. He was much struck with the superiority of the machinery and the perfection of the processes in ordinary use compared with what he has as yet seen. In fact the sugar industry in Mauritius had made wonderful progress. Emancipation had not caused there the same breaking up as it had done in the West Indies. Although a certain number of the estates

* cassava

may be said to have been in the hands of London merchants it was not in the
same absolute and complete way as in other slave colonies. The slaves, as is
well known, in the West Indies were not the property of the planters, they
had all been mortgaged with the estate to the London merchants who were
the real owners. It was they and not the proprietors who got the compensation
money, and feeling that they had sucked the orange dry they threw away the
skin. In Mauritius, on the other hand, not only did the compensation money
mostly come to the Island, but two circumstances had wonderfully improved
the position of the estates, just at the time when what is called the blow of
emancipation had fallen on them. The Island sugar obtained the benefit of
protective duties, and Coolies being obtained in abundance enabled the planters to get on with their cultivation with great energy. The best machinery was
introduced, the export went on augmenting year by year, until Mauritius
came to be justly considered one of the most successful of the Colonies of
England. The estates which were originally small, gradually swallowed up all
the little properties in their neighbourhood, so that the estates in this Colony
were probably four times the average size of a West Indian property.

Hence all that Darcy saw was on a much more extensive scale than he
had seen it elsewhere. They stood for a long time watching the carts drawn
by mules or oxen bringing up the canes to the crushing rollers, and the busy
hive of Coolie lads who were heaping the canes on the table from which they
were gradually drawn in between the rollers and crushed into dry fibre. The
grey juice poured into the tank prepared for it and was carried onward to be
boiled and skimmed, purified and concentrated.

Sometimes in the afternoon the officers attempted to pick up a few partridge among the fields, which had been left to recover fertility under temporary abandonment. Ernestine noticed that she was called upon more frequently than before to accompany Estelle to sit under the filao trees planted
on the government reserves, or Les Pas Géométriques as they were called, by
the seashore of the bay. She did not fail also to notice, and to comment on afterwards to her mistress, with shining teeth and merry eyes, that while Darcy
Connaught went inland and obtained a few birds, Jack ordinarily turned towards the shore and by pure accident encountered Estelle and her attendant
under the filaos. Ernestine went to the beach to pick up shells, to show to
Monsieur, while Jack asserting that the sun was still too strong, persuaded
Estelle to remain seated to watch Ernestine wading in the shallows, and to
gaze on the glorious colour of the reef beyond, and the white foam of the
restless wave as it broke on the guardian barrier of the shore.

"How surpassingly beautiful," he exclaimed on one of these occasions,
half unconscious for the moment that Estelle was by his side. She looked
up with an arch glance, intending to banter him upon his absent mind and
enquired, "Who is?" Then fearing he might consider her too bold, as if she
had fished for a compliment, she hung her head and almost sobbed with vexation. It was enough. The remark touched the secret spring in both hearts.

"Thee," he exclaimed with rapture. "Thee, Estelle, my well beloved," and
in a fashion of wooing common to all nations, he caught her in his arms, and

held her close to his heart. She did not attempt to break away, but wept there in silence. She felt that as a modest maid she ought to rise and flee, that on the other hand as she was not unwilling to be his, she must give some token of consent, and this was what the occasion, which she longed for, and yet dreaded, had inspired. Oh, but these English had a warm way of wooing! There was no reserve now, but kisses falling thick as rain, the embrace tightened from time to time, and returned with the faintest pressure of her slender arms, her smiles coming, through her tears, and he kissing the drops from the long eye lashes.

How softly that afternoon sped! Estelle never knew how it was they stayed so long, beneath the filaos, nor why Ernestine did not call her. Ernestine, good faithful soul, had come back from her pretended search for shells, and with noiseless foot approached them from behind. But seeing that the moment which she knew would come had come, that her "enfant" as she lovingly styled her had so soon found a breast to weep upon, she retired to a safe distance, and indulged in a good cry also from pleasure and sympathy.

There was no reason why she should disturb that reverie of joy. It was yet light although the sun was waning, and the rays grew golden. It was yet light although the wearied labourers were returning from the fields, and the mill had stopped, and the Indian women were winding back from the creek with the water jugs poised on their heads. It was yet daylight and there was glorious warmth and sunshine in two young hearts, finding in the mystery of loving and being beloved all the peace and rest and rich content which neither untold wealth nor dreams of fame can give. Ernestine did well not to disturb the hallowed moments. They were brief enough as it was for the night was at hand, a night which threw not its shadow on their spirits then, but which came swift and silent from the Unseen, as the unbidden storm comes out of the far firmament.

The transport of sugar cane

Chapter 4
The Wreck on the Reef

THE WEATHER WHICH FOR WEEKS HAD BEEN BEAUTIFUL changed during the night. A storm of winter rain not often felt at that sea level, although common enough on the heights of the island, blotted out the whole of the fair landscape. The wind blew strong from the East, raising the sea, which came rolling in throwing up the foam in thunder on the reefs. The day passed heavily and drearily. The labourers, easily chilled with the cold rain, walked about shivering and hugging their rags. The animals even seemed to have lost heart. The carts sank in the soft clay, and the long trains of mules refused to pull them out. Redoubled blows and the harsh shouts of the drivers failed to rouse them to activity. High voices were heard from the kitchens and the house, urging on the servants to work, which ordinarily they did without being driven. The two officers sat smoking gloomily in their pavilion, Darcy meditating a retreat on Port Louis, and Jack beginning to realise the difficulty of his position when he thought about his declaration of love. Towards evening the gale increased, but dinner passed over with considerable gaiety, as those within roused themselves from the torpor and dullness of the morning. Song had succeeded song, a card party was busy in one corner and a group conversed with animation in another. Jack hung over Estelle, who had excelled herself in the brilliance of her performances on the piano. Seated at the instrument she seemed to become a new being. All her timidity and shyness vanished, her touch was firm, her time perfect.

All was comfort, gaiety and the luxury of refinement within when a peculiarly dull heavy sound was heard borne along on the wings of the blast. What was it? It seemed as if the wall of a house had fallen, and the gentlemen stepped hastily out to the verandah to listen. They had scarcely done so when the murky atmosphere to windward was lighted up.

"The flash of a gun," exclaimed Darcy, and all listening attentively the same dull report reached their ears.

"A ship on the reef" seemed the only explanation, and scarcely had they thus cried out than one of the servants entered, dripping wet, and exclaimed "Monsieur Beauvallon, there is a ship wrecked on the coast, what shall we do?"

"Where is it?" said the master.

"Opposite the old fort," was the reply.

"Get out all the boats and pirogues,"* said the master, "but take care to keep well inside the reef until some of us arrive."

"You must not go, sir," said Jack, "the night is too tempestuous and wet. The younger men will take this business into their own hands."

"Yes, yes," added Darcy, "we will do all that is needful if you give us the men."

The ladies at once scented danger. The guns were sounding constantly. A blue light was burning from time to time to show the position of the ship, and it was felt some great disaster was in progress.

"Let the *employés*** take the men and go," the ladies cried, "they know the coast, the fishermen will be there, you can do nothing, and may get into danger in the darkness."

"If there is danger," said Darcy gaily, "we cannot allow your employés to reap all the credit of the expedition."

Jack was replying softly to the remonstrances of Estelle, whose face so ardent a few moments before was now blanched with excitement and terror at this unexpected event. But she was called by her mother who with the readiness of one who had long been at the head of a large establishment, recollected that wounds might require to be staunched, that cordials might be necessary to revive the rescued, that food and blankets should be at hand for the ship-wrecked. Never did women so rise to the heights of their mission than that small band of Creole ladies, suddenly interrupted in their music and pleasure by the news of a calamity. And they were admirably seconded by the older Creole servants, who with many exclamations of "bon Dieu!," "pauvres diables!," "quel dommage!"*** packed baskets with the remains of the dinner, with spirits, cordials, lint and medicines, provided blankets, and loaded up a mule cart with stretchers and beds from the hospital. The whole camp was aroused, and responded to a man to the call of the employés, although all had come in weary with the day's work in the rain and after their meal were comfortably smoking "gandia"**** in their huts. Estelle found time amid the cares for the shipwrecked to provide some refreshments for Jack and Darcy who with the manager and a few Creole fishermen who knew the coast were to go in M. Beauvallon's boat. The gentlemen had rapidly equipped themselves for the expedition. The boat laden with ropes and provisions, bounded from the shore to make a long tack into the darkness and the tempest. Estelle watched the light as it danced and faded in the gloom, with a heavy foreboding of danger and coming sorrow.

There was indeed a shipwreck on the reefs and as the boat approached they thought they saw the black hull, lying on one side with only the broken stumps of the masts standing and the sea, as each successive breaker rolled on, making clean breaches over all. A confused wailing was heard, and the

---

* canoe made of a hollowed-out tree trunk
** "the managerial staff"
*** "Good God!", "poor devils!", and "what a shame".
**** marijuana, not illegal at this time

hum of a great multitude. "Great God," cried Jack, "it is a Coolie ship, every soul will be lost."

"She is on the Chouxfleur,"[1] said a fisherman from an adjoining boat. "There is a deep channel between it and the reef." As he spoke something was seen rolling in the shallows, thrown over by the last breaker. It was washed hither and thither lightly for a moment or two, and then drifted towards the boat where Jack and Darcy were eagerly conferring as to the best course to be pursued. A fisherman caught it with a boat-hook, and as he drew it near uttered a cry. He raised it from the water, and lo! The half trunk of a drowned man – a nameless horror!

"The sharks," was gloomily uttered by the men, and the portion of humanity was dropped back into the water. From the position of those who had hastened to the scene there was no possibility of reaching the ship or to make those on board hear their voices, and they soon found that in place of doing good they were causing the shipwreck to imagine from the lights that they were to attempt a passage at that point. A boat was observed through the darkness mounting on the crests of the rollers and gradually but surely approaching destruction. From the deviations of the course, those in her seemed to be searching for the passage which did not exist. Then apparently deeming that the lights must be intended to guide them in, they struck boldly forward, and in another moment were enveloped in the broken water. Still the boat rose on the crests, sinking back into the hollows as the breakers, one after the other, rolled on to burst and lighten up the dark with the spume of their foam. The doom of all was certain. Nearer the reef there was no space between the advancing waves. They trampled on one another, breaking, hissing, foaming, smiting the barrier, and dashing over it in angry leaps and roars. The boat was overwhelmed; half of its occupants were already in the surge, the others felt that their last moments had come.

"Oh God, can we do nothing," cried Jack. "Let us at least get on the reef, where it is not deep, some may be swept over."

"Never!" cried the fishermen, "nothing living will cross the line."

But the young officers more daring, more ignorant of the risks and possibly more humane to Coolies, got with difficulty on the shallows where the water from the making of the tide was already over their knees, and the fishermen reminded them that the tide made fast. Scarcely had they advanced a dozen steps when Darcy disappeared in a hole, soon rising however to the surface, and little the worse for his immersion. Luckily both had stripped themselves of all superfluous clothing before leaving the boat, and they were good swimmers. As they neared the spot where the full force of the sea was breaking, and naught else could be heard but its deafening clamour, the scene was one of awful sublimity. In the darkness the white breaker seemed to mount to meet the sky and curling over to threaten destruction to the solid earth itself. But a greater Power than the sea had said "hither shalt thou come and no farther." The submerged coral, smitten, bathed in the foam and crevassed by the mighty force of the deep was still the stronger. The violence of the tempest lashed against it in vain. The rising tides struggled to surmount the barrier but in vain. And thus it was that at a little distance from the edge of the fathomless ocean there men could stand knowing that each successive wave would be arrested, its violence stayed and beyond its roar and terror and the deluge of its foam, that it could not affect those who dared to approach. Five only of the figures who were in the boat were tossed into still water with fragments of wreck. Seized by the hair, or the clothes, they were dragged from the very jaws of destruction, and carried as rapidly as possible to the shore boats. For the fishermen, encouraged by the example of the officers, had followed them in to the reef, and thus were able at the critical moment to render assistance.

The last who was thus thrown over was a white sailor, and Jack who was nearest where he fell had great difficulty in dragging him a few feet from the wash and boom of the billow. In doing so he felt himself fixed in a position perilously near the breakers. In his exertions to hold up the poor sailor, knowing not whether he was dead or alive, his own foot broke through the softer coral and his leg became fixed as in a trap. He felt he could not withdraw it and as all were busy it was some time before his companions noticed him, his voice as he raised it being swept away and silenced by the thundering sea. Two of the fishermen at length arrived to his rescue, but they could not remove the leg. The waves were coming nearer.

"Quick, Jean, quick," cried the elder, "let us carry this "pauvre diable" to the boats and return with oars to break the rock where the gentleman is fixed."

Jack thus left alone in face of the ever increasing danger, bold as he was, felt his heart sink within him. The boats were at some distance. By the time the fishermen could return the tide may have gained too much to permit of their approach. The men might be brave enough, but he was a stranger, and they could not be expected to risk their own lives for his. Where was Darcy? Eagerly employed, no doubt in applying restoratives to those of the shipwrecked people who showed signs of life, and he might not hear of the predicament of his friend till too late. The last wave came up to the breast of the unfortunate officer. His life was now measured by seconds. The huge breaker as it burst seemed over his head, and as the long deep wash came in retching nearer and nearer to his throat he felt already the first pangs of drowning. No help appeared, and a cry of bitter anguish escaped even that strong heart, as he thought of this horrible death, and of those far away at home, and of her so near who seemed to dread his going, and would be mortally struck were he to die. A strange faintness came over him against which he roused himself as against a baseness for at first he himself thought it was a sinking of the heart morally, but it was in fact loss of blood. The coral, as his leg forced its way through, had cut deep with its sharp points, and he was bleeding profusely. A feeling of desperation was aroused within him. What! To die thus, caught in a trap within reach of the rising tide, unable to do aught to save his own life while his strength and his faculties were untouched. To die by inches a death worse than drowning, when the billow would play with his sufferings, now overwhelming him with its fury, now retiring, to give him space to gasp, and thus to torture him by lengthening out his anguish! In the darkness which seemed to thicken around him, made denser by the ghastly gleam of foam which at short intervals broke and thundered so near, and washed out in long sheets over the submerged reef, amid the horror of the scene when he knew men near him were perishing by scores, but whose death cry he could not hear, although the scene of their agony was only beyond that mound of billows, a vision of home, bright as if an angel's wing had wafted it, passed over his spirit. He saw the drawing room of a winter's evening after the cosy family dinner, his mother rising to search for the book which she had laid aside the previous night, he could see how serene was her look, believing as she did from the letters received that day that all was well with. Jack. He saw his sisters beginning to play some favourite piece of music, and his father tranquilly reposing, with a book unread resting on his knee, while his mind was away to those scenes of his early manhood under the far bright tropic skies, when he too was a light-hearted lieutenant.

"Oh God, to die, and thus," cried Jack as the break of the last wave washed up to his very lips. He struggled violently to release himself, but the remorseless coral cut deeper and refused to relax its grip. "Father," he cried in agony, as the vision died out in the terrible presence of the truth. "Father, help, help." Another wave had succeeded and the salt foam now dashed over his face. "Help," once more cried the despairing youth, "Help, Great God, help!" But the thunder of the breakers drowned his voice as remorselessly, as outside, in the pride of its strength, it was dashing to pieces the strong ship and feeding the maw of the sharks with frequent corpses. At but a few yards distance Darcy Connaught with some of the fishermen were searching for him but could not find him. "Jack, Jack where are you?" he cried, in his turn trembling in the terror of suspense lest his friend should have perished.

"Here, here, Darcy," Jack was still able to utter. "Quick, quick or I perish." One of the Creole fishermen was at his very elbow as he thus cried, searching as the wave went back, in the deeper water. Shouting to his companions he pounded the coral with the butt end of the oar which he carried, causing intense pain to the officer. They were swept over by the foam, and the oar was lost, the Creole having to catch hold of Jack to keep them both from being carried away. Half smothered the man had yet the presence of mind and at the risk of being himself entangled, like the poor captive, to press heavily with his naked foot on the coral, which still held fast. The spines gave way, the ends remaining in the leg, at the very moment when another wave, more huge, more loud, more like to death itself, broke over them.

———◆———

A breathless Coolie messenger arrived at the mansion house. More blankets were to be sent to the huts of the fishermen as some of the shipwrecked had been saved but were barely able to struggle against the cold. More blankets; and as he finished the message he had been sent to deliver, he gave news on his own account to the Indian girl and Ernestine. One of the sahibs was dead. One of the burra sahibs. One of the officer sahibs.

"How, how, where," cried Madame Beauvallon, who just entered. "Tell me, tell me Molbaccus, who is it, how did it happen?"

"Drowned," said Molbaccus sententiously. "Drowned and killed." For he had seen poor Jack carried from the boat, drenched, pallid, covered with blood which could not be staunched.

"Which of them, O, which of them," eagerly again enquired Madame Beauvallon, but as she spoke Estelle in her turn entered, and Molbaccus, with a look at the Indian girl was silent. He had that tenderness which the lowliest have to spare pain to the young and gentle.

"Which of them Molbaccus," almost screamed his mistress, but the Indian turned round and left the apartment. The girl followed him.

"Is it the Fiancé?" she asked, herself breathless with surprise and horror, for by that title Jack had come to be regarded by the people of the household. "Yes," replied the Coolie, and stepped from the verandah out into the darkness. Estelle had heard something but she did not comprehend. "Are any of the people saved?" she cried, looking in her mother's face of pain, "are many drowned? Oh what is it!"

"Mon Dieu, Mon Dieu, Monsieur Montmorency."

"What, what?" the poor girl ejaculated.

It would have been mercy to have spared her, but the excitement of the mother had got beyond bounds. In her own pity and horror she shrieked out to her sister who was in another apartment, "Clémence, Clémence, come here. Monsieur Montmorency is dead."

The sudden announcement was too much for poor Estelle, but Ernestine, whose thoughts were ever of her "enfant,"* was beside her and caught her as she fell. There was no need for concealment now, and the piteous cries of the women were heard over all the courtyard.‡

* "child"

‡ It would appear that Gorrie intended there to be an intervening chapter between this one and the next.

Chapter 5
Beneath the Surface

IN A FEW DAYS THE INVALID WAS ABLE TO BE CARRIED OUT under the filaos when the strength of the sun had declined, and there sometimes alone with Estelle (for Ernestine had a remarkable faculty of making herself invisible on such occasions, although theoretically supposed to be present), and sometimes in company of the ladies of the household who took tea in the shade, they sat enjoying the calm of the evening. The sea which so lately raged in its fury was now for days together calm as the sky itself, dimpled it might be during the sunshine with a gentle breeze just sufficient to carry the busy coasters, the boats of the fishermen or some stately ships from India with rice and Coolies, sailing in safety where the less fortunate [had perished and the ship had] found her doom. The murmur of the reefs was of peace. The wavelets lapped the sand all around the perfect curve of the bay with a gentle motion. They would linger until the star of evening came forth from the haze amid which still floated the rose tinted clouds of the West.

This kind of existence had great charm for the young English officer. How natural, even patriarchal, was the life of the estate!

M. Beauvallon seemed to be at the head of a large and united family. In those pleasant hours when the ladies were at tea, the overseers, who all seemed to be on terms of friendship and even affection with the planter came to report the proceedings of the day, and to get instructions for the morrow. The sirdar, leader of the gangs of labourers, came to Madame Beauvallon to obtain medicines for the sick, or perhaps some little comfort for their wives about to give birth to children, or suffering from the effects of the climate. Each day had some fresh incident of interest. Now it was the arrival of a new gang of Coolies, who had to obtain huts and rations, now it was a lot of mules from Montevideo which had been purchased at an auction in town and which had to be trained to the collar.

The labourers had their hours of toil, but also their times of recreation and as, gaudily dressed, they went and came from the distant town in the carriages of the country, or engaged in their household duties after their re-turn from the fields, amongst their own cows or poultry, they seemed as happy as any peasantry in the world. The negro fishermen also, who lived in the village near, appeared to take life easily and to have always enough to eat, if nothing to spare. The sound of the men beating on their boats as they drove the fish into the nets at early morning became familiar to Jack. He was anxious to go to the village to thank and reward the young man who had so gallantly rescued him from the breakers, and he asked Estelle if she would go with him to show him the house. She laughed and said she had never been in the village in her life, except when passing through it on two occasions to go to the old Fort which lay beyond. But she added she would send for the brave youth Jean LeBlanc who was a relative of Ernestine. The latter had told her proudly that it was he who had been so nearly drowned in trying to save the young officer. A message was accordingly dispatched to Bail to request Jean to come to Lorraine to see Monsieur Montmorency in the evening, but the boy returned and stated Jean was not at home. Where was he?

Ernestine soon found that he was in prison, but as that was by no means an unusual incident in the lives of the fishermen it was with an air almost of indifference she announced the fact to Estelle. The latter also seemed to think that it was the most natural thing in the world, and turned to the piano without further comment. The cool manner in which one who loved him heard the news that the youth who had saved his life was in trouble pained Jack not a little, and sending for Ernestine to his room he begged her to ascertain what had happened, and to inform him whether he could do anything to assist. "Is your nephew a wild young fellow, Ernestine, that he gets into trouble?" "He is often in trouble," she replied naievely, "but he is not wild. He is a good son to his parents and well beloved by all."

"Why, then, has he been arrested?"

"Oh," she replied, "it is the police who cannot leave them alone to get bread for their children. Some contravention, I suppose," she added bitterly. The term did not convey any definite idea to Jack's mind, but he resolved to go himself to the village to enquire.

For two whole days after the wreck there was a truce between the fishermen and police. Serjeant Stocks who had charge of the station was a man zealous for duty, but having the contempt which the low Briton entertains for the rights of the coloured race, and especially for a coloured race which was additionally contemptible by speaking French. He had been in town on the day when people began to be excited about the events of the wreck and the shipwrecked having been cared for without having obtained *pratique*,[†] was quick to discern the signs of the times, and he had also been stung by the reproach of the Adjutant of the Police Force that there were fewer convictions in his quarter than any other of the Island. That this was a good sign of a law abiding population never occurred to the Adjutant, but he put it down without hesitation to the inefficiency of the police of the district. The pride of the office was to have entered year to year in their Returns a greater and greater number of convictions and the unscrupulous means by which this was attained was well known to every inhabitant of the Island. It was known also to the officials who ought to have stopped it, but no one had the courage to do his duty. Anyone who did so would be a marked man and among the charges which would be raised against him, and the plots which would be instituted to catch him tripping, he might be dismissed from his function. One official at a later period, who of all others was responsible for the remedying of abuses, made no attempt to stop the iniquities which were going on while he was in the island, but after he had got safe home, and obtained his pension, he made report to the Colonial Office in order that someone else might have the trouble of dealing with what was a grievous situation. The vicious system thus proceeded from bad to worse. While the poor were oppressed several of the smaller officials who profited by a share of the penalties went home with snug little fortunes, and their names were cherished by their own circle of friends in the island as those of good men whose services had been lost to the country.

The Serjeant resolved that in future there would be no need to reproach him with want of zeal or success in procuring convictions. As he found the fishermen united with the English officers in the universal condemnation, he rightly judged that the time of their stay at Lorraine was favourable for a renewal of severity. As soon as he returned, therefore, to his district he took steps to get up a case. His Indian constables, at least a few of the older ones, were admirably adapted for the purpose, themselves more or less mixed up with all the bad characters of the district, they used their knowledge for the purpose of betraying their friends and comrades. They held their consciences at the service of the department to which they were attached. If there was no evidence against any accused person they made evidence. In cases where that was impossible, they compelled the accused by bodily tortures, such as compressing his finger nails with twisting ropes, or by hanging him up by the hands and punching his spleen to make an acknowledgement of guilt, and this they were always ready to swear before the Courts to be a free and voluntary confession. The Serjeant knew that he had only to give a hint to these hounds and they would soon run the quarry to earth. But he was aided also in another way and from another quarter.

Isidore Amirantes had seen the visit of the English officers to Lorraine with feelings of the most bitter kind. The subsequent events which occasioned the sojourn of Montmorency to be prolonged filled the cup of envy to the brim. We have already seen how in town he had eagerly fanned the flame of the popular outburst against the landing of the shipwrecked, and at home he plotted the wildest schemes in order to get Estelle into his power. His father shared his dislike to the visit of the English officers to Lorraine. He had for several years thought of a marriage between Isidore and Estelle as a means of uniting the two estates and increasing the wealth and prestige of both families. He was a bigoted Frenchman and Catholic and looked upon the anticipated union with an Englishman and a Protestant as a disgrace to the Colony. He eagerly caught up the popular notion as to the danger to the public health by the landing of the people from the wreck and had passed his spare hours since the event in writing letters to the journals to keep up the excitement. Isidore had accordingly a sympathising friend in his parent for all the strong feelings of dislike to which he gave expression. But the former had views and schemes for the accomplishment of his object which he deemed it prudent to conceal from his parent, schemes which while they furthered his main object were in keeping with his licentious character and irregular life.

Madame Beauvallon had a female servant, Lucille, the daughter of a negress mother, by a coloured employee on one of the neighbouring estates, who had since become a planter in Natal. She therefore considered herself very superior to her mother's kindred, and as her wages and the kindness of Madame Beauvallon enabled her to dress well when she went to her village she was looked upon as quite a great lady. She had when a girl been the playmate of Jean LeBlanc and when she grew up to be a tall handsome woman Jean's childish admiration warmed into love, and he formed for his old playmate an attachment of the most passionate kind. Lucille could not but be friendly with Jean, but she did not reciprocate his love, although not unwilling to accept his admiration, and to employ him as her cavalier until someone more eligible came forward. In fact Lucille, like all women of a shade of colour somewhat lighter, looked forward to a husband who was still further advanced in the whitening process and would not, except under special circumstances, think of marrying one who was darker. She had not of course the same repugnance to Jean as a woman of the white race would have had. She saw herself truly a [milat*]', and all her relatives were almost pure negroes except where illegitimately mixed. And Jean was in many ways a very desirable lover. He was handsome in person, had been educated at the public schools, and wrote letters expressing in very good French the fervour of his attachment. Beyond the natural gaieties of his age he took no part in the drinking bouts of the fishermen. But for repeated convictions for imaginary breaches of the fishery laws, and the frequent confiscation of his nets and boats, he would have been rich for his station in life. It was just such a young Creole, however, whose presence was offensive to the District Serjeants and white policemen. He aped the white gentlemen of the neighbourhood in his dress. He was better educated than the policemen, and had sometimes a malicious pleasure in pointing out their mistakes publicly in Court. Worse than all, he was known to be the lover of Lucille and one who watched over and guarded her with a jealousy which prevented the unscrupulous from getting the opportunity to attempt her ruin which they eagerly sought.

The competitors of the police in this respect were the young planters and employees among whom Amirantes was one. But Isidore had so many affairs of the like nature on hand in town, and on the estate, that his pursuit of Lucille had of late been much less ardent. She in her turn was piqued at his coldness, for she well knew the reason, and the fire of jealousy often burns more fiercely in the humblest than in the higher echelons. Moreover she greatly admired Monsieur Isidore. He was always so gay, he took care never to show by his manner that contempt for the black race which he so profoundly felt, and he did not spare his gifts when he was in pursuit of some affair of this description. On the other hand Jean was pressing Lucille very hard to name a time for their marriage and this pressure Amirantes learned

* "mulatto"

with the other gossip of the estate just at the time when these events happened which have already been narrated. He thought that it was most desirable to keep Lucille from accepting Jean, in order that she might continue in the service of Madame Beauvallon. Through her he hoped still to work on the hopes and fears of the mother of Estelle to prevent the dreaded marriage with the Englishman. And he had in view also a still wilder and bolder project which would require the assistance of some confederate inside the house either of Lorraine or in town in order for its successful accomplishment.

He therefore resolved to renew relations with the girl and attempt to get her completely within his power. As a preliminary he wrote her a note stating that for some time he had been endeavouring to wean his affection from her, as he feared that it would annoy his father, but that he found it altogether impossible and begged her for an interview, but praying her to keep secret his letters and attachment for fear his father should hear of it. He had also, he said, left with her mother at [Lorraine] for her use a piece of silk for a dress which he had bought for her last time he was in town. It had in fact been purchased for another, but was now employed in what seemed the more pressing service! He sent off the note by a safe hand, and it was received and effected its purpose just in time to prevent Lucille committing herself to Jean, for, proud of his courage on the night of the shipwreck, and touched with his real devotion to her, she was on the point of promising to accept him. Poor Jean felt that someone had crossed his path. He had been lately received so kindly, that he had been encouraged to offer an [assurance that was] not refused. He felt confident his long devotion was now to meet its reward. But he soon had occasion to meditate bitterly on the instability of such hopes. There was a triumph in Lucille's manner on the occasion of their next meeting, which puzzled while it irritated him, and in his jealousy his attention was directed to the wrong object. Could it be that the English officer, the man whose life he had saved, was to reward him thus? When he angrily gave expression to these feelings the girl was more amused than before. She would have thought it a success indeed if the lover of Estelle had thrown favourable regards on herself, but finding the suspicions of Jean aided her in the concealment of the real lover, she did not dispel the extraordinary fancy which had taken possession of the brain of the young fisherman. He parted from her in anger, but the girl did not the less greet him on leaving with one of the most pleasant of her smiles, and the softest of her musical "good nights."

Amirantes was not the man to do things by halves. After dispatching his note to Lucille he took the usual vehicle in which he was accustomed to make his tour of the estate, and directed the heads of the mules to the village which contained the District Court and police station. The Serjeant and he were old friends. Many a turkey and duck, many a sucking pig and bag of sugar had gone from the Estate of Pompadour to the Serjeant in charge of the station. There was nothing in this, it was said, but neighbourly kindness. The Serjeant was frequently laid up from the effects of the climate, as he called it, but everybody knew, nevertheless, it was from the effects of drink, and these little presents not only assisted in the Serjeant's recovery, but smoothed over many difficulties in the way of getting the police to prosecute cases from the estate. Amirantes considered that the latter was a good and lawful object for he had no doubt in his own mind that if he forwarded a Coolie to the station it was the duty of the police to prosecute and of the Magistrate to punish. Therefore when the young planter threw the reins of the smoking mules to his servant, with the patois phrase "chombo li"* and swaggered into the station house – he was pretty well assured beforehand of the co-operation of the functionary of the law. The Serjeant was all deference to Monsieur Isidore. When he got the confirmation, just as it were part of the news of the day, that the fishermen were constantly contravening the law by landing on the beach at Pompidou within the prohibited areas he was so pleased with the opportunity of putting up a case, that he sent secretly to the shop of the Chinaman† and increased his debt to him by the purchase of a bottle of the best brandy. He did this in order that he might both show respect to his visitor, and regale himself on the head of the good chance thrown his way. Monsieur Isidore pretended to be hurt by the eagerness shown by the Serjeant to make use of the information he had given, and he required, and very readily obtained, a promise of absolute secrecy from the Serjeant as to the source of his information. The Serjeant equally had no doubt that Amirantes was doing this to further some scheme of his own so he took the opportunity of borrowing ten pounds from the young planter to enable him to tide over a deficiency which had accrued that very evening.

An Indian carter who supplied hay for the two or three government horses at the police station had not been paid for a long time. Pressed by some of his own creditors he had employed his lawyer to enquire at the Treasury when the money to pay the hay for the horses in the District would be remitted. He having received for answer, as he expected, that it had been regularly remitted every month, armed with this information he had asked payment of his bill from the Serjeant who had received the money and kept it, in a tone which the latter saw was getting serious. He indeed had no intention of paying to the Indian the whole of the ten pounds. He would give him half to gain some weeks' further indulgence and the other half he would pay to the Chinaman whose account for necessaries and luxuries was getting portentous. With the Chinaman he resolved to square accounts by proceeding against him for selling rum on the Sunday, but the time was not exactly favourable for such a stroke, as the mean spirited Governor, it was said, had been poking his nose into a similar transaction at [Mahebourg].

The Serjeant, deeming it exceedingly probable that before the bottle of brandy was finished he would be intoxicated, sent for his most trusty Indian Constable and informed him that at daybreak tomorrow they must lie in wait at Pompidou to establish a contravention against the fishermen. Amirantes having seen that everything was in train in this quarter and resisting the entreaties of the Serjeant to make a night of it, mounted his vehicle and drove round the village. He talked and joked with the fishermen whom he had

* "hold him," or "restrain him."

known from boyhood, and then as he was about to drive off he asked if they would be good enough to leave at Pompidou a good dish of young fish as he wished to make a present of them to Madame Beauvallon who had promised to the young officer that he should have whitebait as in England. "Take care not to break the law, Albert" he said to Jean's father, but let me have them as small as you possibly can. Isidore in this was laying a cruel and dastardly snare for the fishermen, but he rather thought it a good joke. He had no idea of the long train of events which were to spring from the invitation he had given to the Police Serjeant. All that he hoped for was Jean would be placed hors de combat for a few weeks while he worked out his own designs by means of Lucille. But whatever he thought, the mode he adopted was not the less treacherous. Having laid the mine he drove home in high spirits to await the explosion.

Chapter 6
The Fisherman's Pride[1]

THE DAWN FOUND THE FISHERMEN BUSY AT THEIR TOIL. First a thin bar of brightness heralded the day, then almost suddenly there was light, as it were the light of the moon, a softened mellowness which transfused itself throughout the atmosphere. After a brief interval the clouds above the far rim of the sea were touched with radiance and floated in crimson glory over the dark band of the horizon. It was at that moment, when as yet the high peaks were not smitten with the rays, when all earth, and air and sea were still, and the East clad in robes of rose promised peace, that the fishermen, long toiling in laying out their nets, advanced in a widely drawn circle of boats to the shore. While some beat in time on the sides of their boats others plied the oars slowly inwards over the sea which was changing from the black of the night to the blue and beautiful of the morning. As they crossed bits of submerged reef they could begin to see the gorgeous colours which the full day reveals. They were a merry set of men and as they felt the warmth of the coming day they made light of their toil, singing, or with laughter exchanging banter from boat to boat. The business in these tropical seas was very different from the hard fare and hard toil and dangerous nights of fishermen at home. The Creoles were not a provident class and probably could never have been rich, but they would always have been above want had it not been for the harsh laws which caught them into its toils, just as they caught the fish in their nets.

At a very early period the fishermen had been brought under severe regulations professedly intended by the law givers to increase the supply of fish in the basket, but which in reality only tended to destroy competition and to throw the trade into the hands of favourites of the men in power. The slave owners in fact kept a tight rein over those who could supply fugitive slaves with chances for escape.

The first regulations on the subject were made by the French authorities at least one hundred years before the time of which we speak. The reason given for their enactment was that fish having become an article of food most essential to life, on account of the scarcity and high price of all other articles, and especially on account of the difficulty of procuring butcher's meat, the lawgivers wished to protect the source of supply and to prevent the abuses which might lead to the total destruction of the breed of fish. They proceeded to hamper the fishermen and the mode of fishing in every conceivable way. Anyone wishing

to engage in fishing had to make a declaration to the police office of this intention, and to mention the number of pirogues or boats, and the names of the
men he proposed to employ, and whether freemen or slaves. He had to take out
a permit from the police before he could begin his industry. Nets with meshes
of one inch square were alone to be used, and they were to be knotted according to sample. A permit had again to be obtained for permission to use each
individual net. One of the regulations was very remarkable as showing the
precautions which a state of slavery, and the fears of slave holders, necessitated.
The owners were bound to have in each boat pistols in good order, with half
a pound of powder, and half a pound of bullets, in order to be able to prevent
the boats from being carried away by fugitive blacks. For the same reason, and
because of the generally unsettled state of the colony, the fishermen were forbidden to leave their boats along the coast at night. Whenever they could not
reach a harbour they were to repair to creeks under the batteries of the military
posts. To land at any port on the coast where there was no military post was to
subject them to heavy penalties with confiscation of the boats. Even when they
were under the batteries the owner and masters were to keep careful watch
by day and night and to sink the boats and pirogues by opening a hole in the
bottom, which all boats were bound to have, lest they should be used by the
fugitive slaves to aid in their escape. And although fish were adjudged to be a
first necessity of life in the island, the fishermen were expressly forbidden to
employ nets at the mouths of rivers as being the places apparently where it was
supposed they would meet with most success.

If anyone, whether fisherman or not, threw line, or any of their stupefy-
ing drug, into a river or stream they were to be flogged at the discretion of the
Judge. It was forbidden to fish in rivers or creeks along the coast in spawn-
ing time, that is three weeks before and after equinoxes. Masters were held
responsible that their slaves obeyed these regulations, but the slave had the
honor of a special regulation for himself, in so far that if he was found fishing
without a note signed by his master "or a well-known mark if his master does
not know how to sign" he was to be flogged for the first offence, and to have
a more severe flogging for the second, although the severity of the first was
not stipulated. Fishing turtle was expressly and absolutely forbidden.

During the revolutionary period in France the regulations were much
softened but a whole code for the fishermen was enacted in 1841 under
British authority, with the result that the fishermen were the favourite game
of the police and became perhaps the most persecuted class in the island. The
most amazing regulation was one in regard to the size of the fish to be taken.
The sea swarmed with sharks which could swallow at a mouthful more than
the fishermen, even by intentional [...] could dispose of in a month but it
was an offence for the fisherman to take the young fry. The cry was got up
that it was necessary to preserve the breeds of fish. It was imposed upon the
Government in the island and at home, and it kept the fishermen in a debased
and poverty stricken condition. By no human ingenuity could they escape
snares laid for them. If the lawgivers had only paid half as much attention to
improving and preserving the breed of fishermen as of conserving the fish,

which the Almighty intended to be devoured, they would – or ought to have been – ashamed of their laws. But they left these toilers to be hunted to earth, as they had no friends powerful enough to protect them, and it was always easy to screw up the fishery laws a bit tighter.

The boats neared the shore, and the men had not forgotten the request of Monsieur Isidore Amirantes to have some small fish for the breakfast of the young English officer. The first rays of the sun had touched the sea and land. The waters sparkled in the joy of the morning, and far away round the bay the blue smoke was rising from the fishermen's dwellings where the wives were astir to prepare the morning meal. The leading boat containing Jean LeBlanc and his father had drawn into the beach and the others were close behind, when the Indian Constables headed by Serjeant Stocks dashed out of the bushes and gorse which lined the bay.

Quick as they were they were not so quick as the lithe and active Creoles. With one vigorous shove the boat was again afloat and those who had been dragging it to shore were in and pushing off from land. The Serjeant feared his prey would escape. He wished to seize the fish and prove that some of them were only three and a half inches long whereas the law required them to be at least four inches! He had a convenient tape measure, so old and worn that it permitted his conscience to swear to any length which might suit the purpose. He dashed through the water, followed by two of his Indian Constables, the latter of whom were soon disposed of by the Creoles, but they feared to touch the Serjeant who had hold of the gunwhale of the boat. Jean stood erect on the seat, oar in hand, as he had been pushing off.

"Ah," exclaimed the Serjeant, noticing him for the first time, "it is you, you black puppy, we will soon teach you to fancy yourself a gentleman, and court girls better than yourself." His was a most unfortunate allusion, for Jean, feeling at once all the danger to Lucille, and smarting under the sting of the vulgar insolence, raised his oar and with a blow on the head tumbled the Serjeant into the water. The boats were soon all out of reach.

The Creoles cheered as they saw the Serjeant fall, but they could not underrate the importance of the event, and that the act of Jean, much as they sympathised with it, would bring them all into more trouble than even the quarter of an inch on the tail of a "Cordonnier."* They had seen two of the Indian Constables on shore taking a note of the boats and the names of the men, and pulling together for a brief colloquy. They afterwards rowed vigorously back to the village to make arrangements for their defence, before the Constables could arrive with a warrant for their arrest. The arrangements were soon made. The men changed clothes with each other and with some of their number who had not been out so as to confuse the Constables when they attempted to recognise them by details of dress. Whoever might be arrested, the rest agreed to swear had not been at the fishing that morning. As they deemed themselves oppressed they fought the law with the weapons of the oppressed, lies or perjury of this description sitting very lightly on the consciences of the

---

* Literally "cobbler-fish," this is the African pompano (*Alectis ciliaris*).

men, and the women generally once a year making a clean breast of it to the priest, and getting absolution for that and other escapades of a different and promiscuous description. They felt the strength of the fight would be around Jean and various efforts were made to alter his appearance from what it was in the morning and to dress up in his clothes some of the other men of nearly the same size. They were not kept long in suspense. Serjeant Stocks at the head of the whole considerable police force of the district appeared with a warrant to arrest five of the fishermen for assaulting the police in the execution of their duty, of whom Jean was the first. The Serjeant made Jean the peculiar object of his attention. For a police Serjeant to be struck by any man was an enormous crime in the eyes of that functionary but for a white Serjeant to be struck by a nigger! He had no words to express his rage and astonishment. His smallest pair of handcuffs was produced and forced upon the muscular wrists of Jean causing intense pain, and when he complained the officer, beside himself, struck him on the mouth shouting "Silence, canal," which was the best approach the Serjeant could make to "canaille"* which he had once heard used in a play and tried to use on all occasions afterwards. Jean's face was covered with blood. The women, seizing the opportunity, made the neighbourhood resound with their cries. Several persons unconnected with the fishermen came upon the scene and saw the effects of the Serjeant's violence. Their testimony had a very favourable effect afterwards on the fate of the accused. The men were all marched off handcuffed to prison, while Albert, the father of Jean, who was not arrested, took boat for town to see a Counsel to attend the proceedings before the Magistrate.

Montmorency, on learning the chief facts which we have related, determined to proceed at once to interest the Governor on behalf of the young fisherman. He had dined once or twice at Government House, and finding the Governor socially very agreeable, took it for granted that he would feel the same indignation against oppression and chicanery which he himself felt burning within him. But his project received little encouragement from M. Beauvallon who at last to convince his guest that the moment was not favourable for such action, showed him a copy of one of the newspapers which had hitherto been kept from him, in which he and his brother officer were attacked in the most savage fashion as enemies of the Colony for permitting Coolies who had not been passed by the medical authorities to mix with the Coolies on the island. The facts of the shipwreck were shockingly distorted, and every effort made to excite the minds of the population to fury as if a premeditated defiance of the law of the island had been carried out by the English officers. The facts of the duel were also recalled and as freely distorted. A prosecution for the breach of the quarantine laws was loudly demanded. Jack felt indeed that there was more to be thought of for the moment than the care of the young fisherman, but with the confidence of inexperience and conscious innocence, he imagined that a conversation of a few moments with the Governor would place the facts in their true light.

* Lit. "rabble."

Wearied with his unwonted exertions, Jack felt little inclined to renew them, and gave himself up for the remaining day of his stay to the more agreeable pursuit of courting the fair Estelle. Estelle was so ignorant of the world and of Society that one of his chief duties of an evening was to tell her of the manners and customs of that other world of which she had as yet only dreamed. That first ball was to her the grandest of all conceivable things. Formed by nature to dance she did not know how she had acquired it, but she looked upon dancing as the chief pleasure in existence. Gifted with an exquisite ear for music she could easily without effort time the motions of her feet to the tune, and thus, whether it were waltz, or Mazurka, which was her favourite dance, she felt as if she were moving in her natural element. Her face lit up with an expression of brightness and pleasure which was irresistible, and her innocent enjoyment communicated a like feeling to her partner. There were many little dances at Lorraine in the evening. It was not difficult to push back the obtrusive tables and chairs in the salon. One of the more elderly ladies would play. The bees-waxed floor was always ready for such impromptus. During the visit of the officers the neighbours were frequently invited to dinner and often came uninvited after dinner when they knew that the piano would not be idle. The chief pleasure in a dance, however, as many imagine, is the little tête-à-tête with the partner afterwards, in some cool corner of the verandah where the ordinary members of the company do not presume to come. Jack was not so selfish, or so destitute of good manners, as to monopolise Estelle, who had always been a favourite in her own district, but it would not be saying too much that he had every third dance and a long talk in a very nice corner after them. Strange as it may seem, considering the work he had been doing, and the hostility he had showed to Jack, Isidore Amirantes was invited more than once to dinner. Old M. Beauvallon and Amirantes père had been friends from their boyhood, and Isidore had walked about Lorraine as freely as about his own estate. They did not feel justified in cutting him off because of the new acquaintance.

On one particular evening he had not only been at dinner but had made himself most agreeable. Estelle was surprised, and almost charmed with him. It was with a feeling of vexation that she could not understand, and which haunted her for a long time, that after she and Jack had danced their last dance for the evening, and had enjoyed their last talk in secret, she had observed Isidore come out of the dark in such a position that he must have seen the leave-taking. Fortunately Jack did not see Isidore and Estelle held her peace. During the few moments they still lingered she was, however, very careful and circumspect, almost cold to Jack. He felt a little mortified, but not suspecting what had crossed his path, put the stiffness down to an access of maidenly modesty, and retired to his room. Estelle when she in turn retired did not feel satisfied with herself. Why should she care whether Isidore had seen her or not, he was nothing now to her, as she had preferred another. But Isidore was certainly a bright and amusing companion, an exquisite dancer, a handsome fellow. Estelle wondered why she had at one time disliked him so much. That dislike was much modified, probably because she was no longer afraid of his proposing for her. But on that occasion, when she thought of his proposing for anyone else, a very curious feeling took possession of her, a sense of personal loss, and almost of anger that Isidore should presume to do anything of the kind.

Chapter 7
A Scene in Town

THE EDITOR OF THE NEWSPAPER WHO WROTE REGARDING the quarantine laws and the danger to the health of the Colony arising from the events of the ship wreck was an associate of Isidore Amirantes. He was the sharer in town of all his adventures and dinners, and a ready hand at billiards or cards when the humour of the young planter demanded such recreations. He was perfectly sincere in his abuse of the English officers as he detested them with all the bitterness of a low adventurer for those who quietly take up the position of leaders of society, and who by their mere presence at table or race-meetings, threw into the shade all those who like himself had nothing to recommend them but their imitation of the Parisian beau monde in dress and gait, the gloss of their patent shoes and the badness of their characters. He had more-over a malicious pleasure in making a sensation.

The population had been cruelly scourged by epidemics. These, chiefly up to that period of cholera, had been terribly destructive to the old slave class, and their descendants, and to all the olive coloured people of all walks of society. One epidemic in particular had come like a plague.[†] It had swept off its victims by hundreds, breaking up family after family, leaving only in many cases one grief-stricken survivor to tell the number who had been carried to the tomb. The events of that year had been burnt in on the memory of the people, just as those of a year which had still to come, but which is now also away in the dim past, have become part of the history of the Island. In this last plague, fever took the place of cholera,[†] sparing no class, but laying especial-ly its gaunt and bony fingers on the Indian labourers. The population of the capital was lessened by nearly 20,000 souls, and all over the Colony whenever you see a churchyard more than ordinarily covered with the wooden crosses, which mark the graves of the poor, you may be sure that fever in the year of the epidemic was busy in that quarter. Many deeds of heroism were done. The sisters from the convents made themselves familiar with the scourge, and met and not infrequently vanquished it on its own chosen ground. The po-lice, awed for the time into humanity and moderation by the greatness of the suffering around them, themselves fell victims at the call of duty, and were buried side by side with the poor Indian pedlars and carters whom before the day of the terrible visitation they had deemed to be fair game.

The doctors laboured without ceasing, chief amongst them one who survived the ordeal and has now gone to his rest, but who notwithstanding the greatness of his perils, the immensity of his labours, the abundance of his humanity, especially to the poor from whom he could hope to secure no reward, had to wait for many weary years before he got the much coveted recognition from the home authorities of his devotion to duty. Alas, if instead of striving to save human life he had been one of those favoured beings who belong to the professions whose duty it is to kill, and if when called to active service he had been so fortunate as to do an ordinary act of pluck or courage, if he had captured a hutfull of savages, or followed a Caffre* to strike him with a lance, or even gallantly fled from the enemy with a dismounted solider behind him – how swift his reward would have followed his deed! A civilian may spend his life in doing acts of courage, especially in those Colonies where from many causes a man is sorely tempted to forget his manhood, but no special correspondents being present to waft him into fame, his very name and existence, unless by a fortuitous concourse of circumstances, may be utterly unknown even to the department which he serves.

Should the remembrance of that last greatest and deadliest of epidemics raise in the mind of some dweller in the Island, on some day of surpassing beauty even for that clime, thoughts higher and better than the quotations of sugar, the following lines may not be unwelcome as a reminiscence of the time of mourning, lamentation and woe:

> *Beauty and Terror – children of one birth,*[1]
> *Repose and Revolution – Calmness, Storm;*
> *How oft walks Sadness hand in hand with Mirth,*
> *Or Danger, Safety's grim companion form;*
> *No sea more fair than yonder gracious girth*
> *Of this fair Isle, in Southern Sea forlorn,*
> *Where I these measures pen; but in its treach'rous deep*
> *Huge monsters swim, and hurricanes their terrors keep.*
> *How beautiful on this all beauteous day*
> *The blue belt stretcheth out to meet the sky*
> *How lazily the white foam of the bay*
> *Laps gently o'er the reefs which round it lie,*
> *How peacefully the fort reflects the ray,*
> *How loftily and slow the sea-birds oer us fly;*
> *Hath peace with wide sphere more fitting home,*
> *Or beauty fairer shrine than that last azure dome?*
> *Lo! as I muse a gentle breeze hath rippled*
> *Oer the sea's cobalt, and the floating cloud*
> *Casts deeper shadows, blue with white is dappled*
> *While sea-birds dip and sweep of swifter motion proud;*
> *The ships which vainly with the calmness grappled*

---

* Derogatory term used to refer to a person of African origin.

All sail with eager expectation crowned
And, sparkling like a jewelled coronet, the waves
Dash the glad shore and laugh into its caves.

A few years ago Death did its worst,
The graves were gorged with victims ere the pest
Had well begun; the city seemed accurst;
Whole fields were taken for the place of rest
And they were filled; the poor, the very poor, at first,
But Death grew nicer, and then chose the best;
The field of graves is sown; row after row.
How well in such a soil the thriving saplings grow!

While men's hearts failed for fear, Nature was gay,
The sea, over which the smell of corpses passed,
Was blue and radiant, weltering in the ray,
Each day of death more beauteous than the last,
Ah! is she then as keen as Death for prey?
Can Nature smile where Pity stands aghast?
Nay, nay; in gentle league with all consoling Time
She heals the broken hearts with sympathy sublime.

Having such material as the terror of a scourge-smitten population to work upon it is not wonderful that the editor achieved success in his vicious plan. The people feared the effects of the contact of the shipwrecked Coolies with the healthy population, and were angry and excited in regard to events, a true narrative of which had been purposely withheld from them. A deputation to the Governor was determined upon to insist upon the due carrying out of the laws of the Colony, and to have those prosecuted who had infringed them, and above all it was resolved to demand that the Estate of Lorraine with all the people on it should be provisionally put in quarantine. The glee of the editor in announcing his success roused into action those who are not easily stirred by similar ravings. Darcy Connaught had returned to town, and communicated to his brother officers the events of the night, and in particular the courage of Jack in his eager endeavours to save life and his narrow escape. The news soon spread throughout the English society with whom Montmorency was a great favourite, and a large proportion of the Creole element were equally well informed through the exertions of the friends of the Beauvallons. Both of these sections saw that it was necessary to take action.

Next morning two letters, to which the editors were forced to give peculiar prominence, appeared in the two leading journals. One in the English organ was signed by Darcy who had obtained the permission of his commanding officer for the purpose, and the other in the organ of French society was signed by an Avocat, a friend of the Beauvallon family, an eloquent and popular man whose name was a guarantee at least of honesty. The facts set forth were so different from what the public had hitherto been led to believe that a great reaction set in in favour of the officers. The Colonel had ordered Jack to rejoin his regiment and his appearance in town on the morning after the letters had been printed created as much interest as on the day of the duel. The affair had every chance of blowing over, although the friend of Amirantes returned to the charge and tried his very best to keep alive the feeling of insecurity and terror.

He would have failed had it not been for the incident which must now be related. Some two or three days had lapsed when the police boat was seen approaching the harbour after a visit to Quarantine Island† where the Coolies of the wreck had been taken. A fresh trade breeze was blowing which enabled the boat to come rapidly along the reef but after rounding the point it had to tack up the harbour through the crowd of shipping. The breeze coming down from the mountain in gusts requires care in the management of sailing boats in the harbour. On this occasion the police boat pushed on with so much energy and haste that more than once she was on the point of capsizing. The sailors of a French man-of-war so fully expected it to come to grief that they had run to their places to lower a boat to be ready for a rescue. The mates of the English vessels at anchor came to the perhaps natural conclusion that the men in charge were drunk. When the boat reached the landing place, a police Serjeant hurriedly left for the chief police station. The police crew were not slow to tell friends on shore the sad news. Cholera had broken out among the Creoles in quarantine, both those landed from the *Mofussel,*† and those from another ship which were formerly on the island. They were dying by scores every day.

The boat had not been permitted to approach but an urgent message had been sent by her for medical assistance as the Irish doctor who had come from India had lost his head and taken to drink in the middle of the crisis. Before the Serjeant and the Inspector-General of Police reached Government House to make their unwelcome report the news was fast stealing through the town, causing dread and consternation everywhere. But worse was to follow. The Executive Council which had been hastily called together† was in deliberation when a letter marked "urgent" was put into the hands of the Governor. It was from the Chief Medical Officer stating that a mounted messenger had arrived from Pompadour with information that one of the Coolies on Lorraine had been seized with a complaint which it was feared was cholera. The members looked at each other in silence. They knew the excitable population among which they lived, they knew how terror would make all classes predisposed to disease, and they knew too well what its effects would be if unfortunately it should make its appearance in town. The first thing was to have a conference with the Chief Medical Officer to ascertain if possible the grounds for supposing that the Lorraine case was one of cholera. That functionary had already been at the work of investigation and fortunately had learned that Doctor Malade,* the medical officer of the district was in attendance as a witness at the Supreme Court. Monsieur Malade scorned the idea that cholera could exist in his district without his having known it.

* Doctor "Sick"

"Who has brought the news?" was his first question. On being informed that it was an employé of Pompadour he proceeded to find him; and the following colloquy took place:

"It is thee – Jules," said the Doctor. "Who is ill at Lorraine?"

"I do not know."

"Then how do you know the person is ill with cholera?"

"I do not know that."

"Who told you to come here to say so?"

"Monsieur Isidore."

"Had he been to Lorraine?"

"No."

"Who had come from Lorraine to Pompadour?"

"Some witnesses who were coming in to the Supreme Court."

"Oh, of course!" exclaimed the Doctor. "How could I have forgotten it. They are sitting under the banyan tree now. Go for Leelookee" he continued to a peon who stood near, "and bring him hither."

Leelookee having come the conference was resumed.

"Leelookee – you saw Isidore Sahib this morning?"

Leelookee gave the nasal grunt which represents the Hindu-stanee "Yes."

"Did you tell him anyone was ill at Lorraine?"

"No, sahib," said Leelookee who was as yet unaware of the news, "I did not tell Isidore Sahib any one was ill at Lorraine. Isidore Sahib asked how many witnesses were going to the Court, and I said three were going and a fourth was sick."

"Did he ask about the sickness?"

"Yes, sahib, he asked about the sickness and I told him it was here" (the man put his hand on his stomach, bent double, and made a grimace.)

"Who is it that is sick?"

"Old Ramdoss, Sahib."

"Whew," whistled the Doctor, "why he is in hospital and has been for several days."

"Yes, Sahib, and the *huissier** got a paper from your house to show to the Judge."

"Yes, you are right, Leelookee, quite right. Now if you hear anyone say today that there is cholera at Lorraine you can contradict it and say it is only Ramdoss ill with his old complaint. "

As Leelookee retired the doctors took their way to Government House, and thus when he entered the Council room the Chief Medical Officer could give a very satisfactory explanation of the origin of the rumour as regarded Lorraine.

"But what," asked the Governor, "could be young Amirantes' reason for sending in an express to you if that was all."

"One part funk, and three parts spite," bluntly replied the Medical Officer. This part of the business was soon disposed of by asking Doctor Pillule to return at once to the District to visit Lorraine and if any worse

* "Usher"

disease than that of Ramdoss existed to send an express in at once that precautions might be taken.

   They turned now to the undoubtedly serious affair of the Quarantine
Island, and the afternoon was far spent before all the necessary arrangements
could be made. One of the staff of surgeons, a small determined man, volunteered to go to supersede the Irishman who had lost his head. He did go, and
it may be added that by separating the well from the sick, by placing the latter on a small islet divided from Quarantine Island by a fordable channel, and
infusing courage in to those who were faltering he was able after a week of
horror to get the mastery of the disease and to report to headquarters that all
was going on well. Needless to say that the gallant volunteer who thus faced
a danger to which that of leading a troop into battle is as child's play, got no
special thanks for his endeavour. The last action of the council was to draw
up a proclamation informing the inhabitants of what had occurred, warning
them against the effects of panic and explaining that the case reported from
Lorraine was one of an ordinary nature and not a case of cholera.

"La Flore Mauricienne" in Port Louis

Chapter 8
An Inexcusable Flight

THE GOVERNOR, AS HIS HORSES TOILED UP THE STEEP TURNPIKE on the way to his country residence, had little heart to admire the beauty of the scene as he rose higher and higher above the sea level. So many things were constantly occurring to prevent his seat being a bed of roses. Sir Foulis Foolscap was not a strong man mentally. He had become a Colonial Governor no one very well knew why,[†] and having no brains or strength of character to prevent him rising in the service, he was on the fair way to get all that was best in the peculiar line in which he found himself. Moodily he entered his dwelling, and when reminded that it was a guest night, his first impulse was to stop the dinner party. But a moment's reflection convinced him that such a course would be impolitic, and little disposed as he was for gaiety, he was obliged to put on his receiving face. Fortunately not much was expected of this particular Governor in the way of conversation, and even he reflected after the first few glasses of wine that it was only after all Coolies in the Quarantine Island who were sick!

In town there was a perfect scare. Long before the newspapers had received copies of the Governor's proclamation, the most alarming rumours were flying about everywhere. Busybodies ran from house to house and with their tales froze the blood of young and old. The shops of the Druggists began to be crowded with people who already felt ill from fright. The doctors were kept running hither and thither, but amid the terror incidents were not wanting which supplied food for laughter when sense and reflection obtained the mastery. A company of actors from Paris were at the time performing in the theatre. About the middle of the performance one of the actors became too ill to appear. He had in fact drunk too much rum in the excess of his fright. When, however, the Manager appeared before the curtain to explain, with doleful face, that a somewhat lengthened interval would take place in consequence of the sudden illness of M. Buveur,[*] the boxes emptied with a rapidity which was soon imitated by other parts of the house.

The performance came to an end and this contributed not a little to heighten the prevailing excitement. Several families had already gone to the

---

* Mr. Drinker

country. Those who had no carriages of their own were squabbling with ter-
rific energy at the stables of the hirers of public vehicles. Among the ladies
who were panic-stricken we regret to say number Madame Beauvallon and
her sister. But they perhaps ought to be excused as they remembered but too
well the horrors of the last visitation, and in addition, they had heard many
rude and cruel remarks from excited neighbours. The carriage had accordingly been ordered early in the evening and the two elder ladies with Estelle
and Ernestine were driven off, but not to Lorraine. They had determined to
go to a house on the table-land of Plaines Wilhems belonging to M. Rempart,
to be away if possible from all risk of contagion, notwithstanding the dis-
comforts and gloom of this camping, as they thought, in the wilderness. Both
of the old gentlemen refused to go. They were rather pleased than otherwise
with the excitement in town, and over their brandy and water and cigars
discoursed of all the methods by which frequent communication could be
kept up with the ladies.

Amirantes came to town to watch the effect of his message, and had the
pleasure awaiting him of hearing of the undoubted outbreak at Quarantine
Island. He invited the editor and a few more kindred spirits to dine with him
at the Flore Mauritienne[†] in order that they might rejoice over the success
they had thus far achieved. Coming out after ordering dinner he noticed the
carriage of Madame Beauvallon pass and saw who were within. Guessing at
once the reason of their journey, he went towards their house for the purpose
of ascertaining from the servants whether Lucille was to remain in town, but
as the evening was fine he went by the Jardin de la Compagnie, a reserve of
banyan trees in the middle of the town, with a statue of a local celebrity in
the centre, where it was often cool and shady while the streets were ablaze.
The name was a remnant of the time when the French East India Company
owned Mauritius, but they failed to secure success, and the Island was retro-
ceded to the French Monarchy.

A goodly number of children attended by their nurses played around,
the word of terror which they had heard so often during the day beginning
by its repetition to cease to have any effect on the very young. The nurses
were huddled together, conversing in under-tones, careless for once of the
young men who were passing home from the Government and other offices. Amongst them was Lucille herself, who finding that for the moment she
was her own mistress, had come for a gossip with her friends. Always well
dressed when she went abroad, with her gay parasol and her neat boots, she
was never unnoticed, and she liked town accordingly, for her vanity which
was great was gratified by attentions which more modest girls might have
resented. She did not observe Amirantes as he approached, but he was well
known to all the chattering damsels present and a "Voilà! Isidore!" from one
of them made her turn round as he, having already espied her, was coming
forward. Under pretence of enquiring after the health of the family he drew
the not unwilling damsel away from her friends behind a large banyan tree,
which had girth enough, with its numerous aerial roots, joined into one mass
with the trunk, to hide them during their colloquy. The women looked at

each other with meaning smiles, well knowing what attentions like these from Isidore were to lead up to, and having all, indeed, passed through that particular stage several times with someone and being quite ready to begin again with any well dressed young white who had sufficient money to give them presents. Their intuition was not at fault, for Amirantes was pressing the girl for an appointment now that the coast was clear by the departure of her mistress. The only thing which troubled Lucille was the dread of cholera. She thought a little of Jean, but it was la Mort* hovering over the city with his huge outstretched wings which made her hesitate most. Her new lover hastened to calm her fears by assuring her no one was ill at Lorraine as had been thought, and that the Coolies at Quarantine Island had often had cholera and no bad effects had resulted in town. The appointment was made; Lucille agreeing to meet him after the late dinner in the little garden behind the house which sloped down to the Ruisseau des Blanchisseuses.** A foot-bridge crossed the stream giving access to a door in the garden wall which she would open at the hour of appointment.

Thus it was that while the two gentlemen were seated where we left them, in the verandah, smoking, telling their tales of old epidemics, and watching what was passing in the street, Lucille had slipped away unperceived to the back garden to open the gate for Isidore. It was a night of the most perfect loveliness. Situated on the lee side of the Island, and on the sea level, there is little rain in town except during those hurricane bursts of the hot season by which the whole Island is saturated.

A full rich moon shone overhead in a cloudless sky. Scarcely a breath of air stirred the vegetation. A million tiny cigales*** piped their unceasing song. The countless fowls which make the din of the day were all perched for the night, to be silent till morning. The leaves of the Flamboyant tree, so common in the gardens, and so beautiful when its flame-coloured flowers come forth in the months of summer, were folded up, each pair of tiny leaflets on the spray shutting together as if they were hands clasped in rest. The Oleanders and the Jasmines were only in sufficient number to slightly scent the air; but Lucille herself, handsome young fool as she was, had not forgotten to make free use of the perfumes of her mistress.

There was an occasional champ from stables near, a sound also of far off music, and as she put her hand to the gate a bugle from the barracks sounded the retreat for the night. Leading her lover into a bower which her master had constructed for a smoking retreat for just such nights as these, the thoughtless creature bent a ready ear to all the praises which Isidore lavished on her beauty, her grace and her superiority to all of her sex. Flushed as he was with wine, he was careful not to hurt the girls' self-respect by any gross words or phrases of offensive familiarity, for her vanity made her believe she was a lady, and she desired to be wooed like one. It was indeed a night which

* "Death"
** Launderesses' Stream
*** cicadas

would have sanctified an engagement made between kindred hearts, where a pure love burned brightly in each breast, and a holy and lawful purpose was the aim of the lovers. The bower, it was true, in which these two sat, and where the first kisses which she had conceded were fast inflaming the youth to a pitch of madness, was not from the absence of these sanctions less beautiful. The flakes of moonlight stole as softly through the trellis, the witchery of interlaced twig and leaf and bough were the same as if there were no flashing eyes or breasts heaving with too ardent hopes within.

The dangerous dalliance of the lovers was arrested in a very remarkable manner. A strange and mysterious Form was seen crawling among the bushes, or rather advancing by leaps like those of an immense toad. "One of the boys!" was the ejaculation of Amirantes, for he felt the girl suddenly cling to him as if in mortal fear. He had firm nerves; he had firm nerves for exactly this kind of incident, either in town or country, where he sometimes had been most fiercely interrupted, and had occasionally come off only second best. He was a man of remarkably firm nerves, but when he saw this strange and terrible sight come leaping towards them, half hidden by the bushes, and felt the girls' clasp of fear, and the beating of her heart, his own heart began to beat faster and faster, the perspiration came unbidden to his brow, and it was with a quaver in his voice he could not control that he called out, "Est-ce toi, garçon?"* When no answer was returned to this appeal, but the strange object came nearer and nearer and nearer – leap – leap – nor dog, nor goat, nor man, nor beast, Lucille could no longer master her emotions. Thoughts of cholera – of death – of sin – of the grave – in bodily form passed across her mind.

Superstitious like all her race, she seemed to see at last the Evil One in bodily shape come to take her down to the remorseless regions. With a scream of terror which was heard in that still and lovely night far and near, she broke from the convulsive embrace of Amirantes and ran towards the house ejaculating in the extremity of her terror "Le Diable! Le Diable!"** She rushed alone onto the verandah where the two gentlemen were seated, Amirantes in his terror having now fled by the postern, and crouching down behind her master's chair, she covered her face with her hands and sank helpless. Leap – leap – the Object followed her to the verandah. Both the old men quaked for a few seconds until as it came nearer they could see that what was before them was a human being, so long accustomed to move about like a beast that to go on all fours had become natural to it. Its long hair was matted into mops hanging over lack-lustre eyes, the rags which covered the person were dirty and torn, the open breast was covered with hair and stains of food, its smell was that of a pig, and the whole aspect horrifying and humiliating. He, for it was a male, dragged, in one of his fore paws, a tin vessel, and as he held it up to the gentlemen in the verandah it was evident that he had been drawn out of his lair by the pangs of thirst.

* "Is it you, boy?"
** "The Devil! The Devil!"

It was an idiot youth – the son of one of the neighbours – who having lost his wits in the manner to be hereafter narrated, was treated thus. He lived in an out-house like a dog, he leapt about the back court-yard all day like a tame animal, and when thirsty, as he constantly was, he dipped his tin into the water of an old fountain in which the ducks waddled and swam, and the fowls' droppings were deposited, and over which a green scum grew as it stagnated and evaporated in the stifling heat. The fountain had got out of repair, and in the excitement of the day, no water had been provided for the Object in the back yard and in search of this he had managed to leap into the garden of Monsieur Beauvallon, and now held up his tin with beseeching eyes for the water to cool his burning tongue.

It was liberally supplied to him, with a touching kindness, and food also, which the poor wretch sought to run off with as soon as it was placed in his hands. After he had eaten and been refreshed a servant led him gently back to the court yard from which he had escaped.

"I thought," said M. Rempart, "that poor *misérable* had been in his grave long ago. I have never heard it mentioned for years."

"No," replied his friend. "We do not ordinarily speak of our skeletons in the closet. There are some terrible ones in this Island of ours, but this is I think the worst form of human suffering."

"Nay, I fear, my friend, there is one worse – where reason remains but the bodily frame drops like diseased fruit and life becomes one long terrible punishment such as the imagination even of Dante could not compass. But let us not talk of it, we have supped full of horrors today."

"Do you know that I never heard the correct story of that poor wretch. I remember him well when a boy at the Royal College, a trifle soft but showing no signs then of this bad end. As we have made this a day of horrors would you mind telling me how it happened, while I fill another pipe, and mix up a little more brandy *pannee** to steady my nerves after this visit from the Old One."

"Let me first send this poor girl to bed,[†] and make arrangements for someone to sleep in her room. Here, Lucille, take a little weak brandy and water, you see it was not the devil but something worse, a man who having lost his reason has become like the beasts that creep and crawl.

---

* "water" (from Hindi/Bhojpuri *pani*)

Chapter 9
Inner Life of a Coolie Camp

BY MERE CHANCE JACK MONTMORENCY FOUND HIMSELF SEATED at the Mess dinner on a stranger's right beside one of the law officers of the Island. Of course he knew nothing about the mode in which the legal business of the Colony was worked or what were the relations of the legal hierarchy to one another. But having mentioned that the Creole fisherman who saved him was in gaol, and that he thought some very improper work was going on in that remote district, the official he addressed encouraged him to tell what he knew and appeared very much interested in the state of affairs. The papers concerning the assault by the fisherman on the police had been laid on the table of the appeal that very day, and he had himself been struck by the extreme proposals which had been made, the least of which was that Jean LeBlanc should be tried for an attempt to murder the Serjeant.

The Magistrate, belonging to the old white aristocracy of the Island, looked upon an assault by a black on a white, as a much worse offence than an assault simply upon the Serjeant of Police as such. He therefore not only sympathised with the views of the Serjeant but went far beyond them, and it would have fared ill with Jean if these two functionaries only had had to be consulted. But the Magistrate, desiring to have the support of the higher authorities from the first, had referred the case for directions and the official consulted having both seen though the extreme views which were submitted to him, and having had the benefit of the explanations of the officer, sent back the papers with instructions to proceed for a simple assault, and took occasion to caution the Magistrate and policeman as to the necessity of administering the fishing laws with care and discretion.

The Magistrate was by no means a fanatical person at heart in regard to colour and disliked the ways of the Serjeant very much. When the case came on he did not permit the police to have the whole say to themselves. The advocate whom Jean's father had brought down overdid his role, as is not infrequent with young counsel pleading before a [district] tribunal. He started on the theory that the Magistrate would be against him and wished to impress him with the idea that unless he took the same view as himself, the case would be taken to the Supreme Court for a ruling. He all but turned the Magistrate against his clients from the way in which he disputed every point and lengthened out the proceedings until the afternoon was far spent. But fortunately the witnesses whom he called spoke out most clearly and decisively as to the brutality of the Serjeant in striking Jean when manacled, which although not necessarily part of the case showed at least the spirit in which the proceedings had been taken and conducted throughout. The advocate was astonished at his success (as he imagined it to be) in having the offence received by the Magistrate as a simple assault, and in Jean getting off easily with three months imprisonment and the others with even shorter terms.

The Serjeant was thoroughly disgusted, and having business at Pompadour at all events he drove over after Court to see Isidore Amirantes. The business of the police at Pompadour was never-ending. The estate employed upwards of six hundred Coolies, which meant with the women and children the population was that of a large village, and it was unfortunately one of those estates which never seemed to be in good order. The simple reason was that Isidore living an ill regulated life his example was followed by the Managers and employés, who all had their favourites among men and women, and their objects of dislike whom they persecuted by constant complaints before the Magistrate for neglect of work, illegal absence, or desertion as the case might be. The same causes which led the employés to adopt this course to the men, led the sirdars also to adopt it towards some of their gangs, and the men to adopt it towards each other. In no place in the world did women cause more mischief than on a sugar estate in Mauritius at the time of which we speak. The disproportion of the sexes was so excessive that the competition for the women was like the battles of the fowls of the air for their mates.

As the Serjeant rode slowly along through the straggling camp of hovels, he knew nearly every man and woman who passed, either intimately or at least by sight, from their frequent appearances as accused, complainants, or witnesses before the Court. That rather fine looking woman, for example, who has just descended from a *carriole** on which she has travelled from the town, he knows well. She looks the perfection of modesty, as having paid the carriole driver she arranges her red calico over her head and breast, showing only one fat finely moulded arm covered with gold bracelets, and walks towards the door of her hut straight and erect as a palm, with only her style of walking a little spoiled by the numerous bangles on her ankles. Modest, yes, as modest as the wife of six husbands can well be. She had only five previously but by a family arrangement recently concluded, she is to take a sixth, and has been to town to purchase some delicacies for the wedding supper. The advantage of the arrangement is obvious. As the female companion of one man, unless he were a Sirdar, or a usurer, she would be kept in squalor and poverty, but by an arrangement such as she has been able to effect she gets all the spare wages of several, and an amount of attention which pleases her vain heart. Ostensibly of course the men are lodgers, or boarders, but all the men in camp, and all the women in camp, and all the children in camp, and the employers, the police, the doctors, the whole world of the estate knows that they are quasi-husbands. The Magistrate knows, the law officers of the

* A small, open horse-drawn carriage

Crown know, the officers know, the Governor knows of many such cases, but what of that? These people are wanted for their work, not for their virtue, and if it pleases them to live in the state of polyandry it does not cost anyone else a thought. Evil comes of it, as we shall presently see from this particular case. The law wakens up to punish deeds of violence but it does not trouble itself about the prolific source of the evil. There is happily much less of this kind of life now, time having partially cured the very great disproportion of the sexes which once existed.

She of the many husbands was called Jothee, and the new husband whom she was about to espouse was Bhootan, a Sirdar who a couple of years before had sold his daughter for twenty pounds to Isidore Amirantes. When the Serjeant saw Jothee descend from the carriole his first thought was that something has been stolen and that she had been away to dispose of the stolen goods, but on second thoughts he recollected that she, a successful and busy woman, did not belong to the class of thieves. Another woman passes, a Madrassee,[†] different in tongue, shape, style and complexion from the other. The cloth which covers her is not her holiday costume, it is a common white calico, not over clean. How mean she appears without the gay dress, and yet one can see that her arms and legs are also plentifully covered with ornaments. She is the wife of two brothers. One is a gardener, the other is a night watchman. They thus do not come into collision. That slim delicate-featured creature driving half a dozen goats round to the back of the hovel has also her history.

A man is now serving ten years in Port Louis gaol for her. He is one of the gang in chains who may be met at four in the afternoon as they pass, heavily clanking, along the street to their prison home for the night. She was his wife and he loved her, loved her devotedly, but with a jealousy sharpened by the atmosphere of lawlessness and licentiousness around him. A young man who had recently arrived from India begged that he might have his meals cooked by the woman as he occupied the adjacent hut. Tempted by the trifling profit, the man consented, and lost his peace of mind from that moment. Not possessed of more virtue than her class the woman was still true to him from fear. For the Indian husband, sanctioned by his religion, and by custom, takes prompt and awful measures with his wife should he deem her to be unfaithful. On one occasion the woman, out of innate politeness, had accepted some trifling service from the neighbour, which her husband had also proffered. The latter was stung to the quick believing it to be a proof of an attachment between them. He seized the stick which is used for pounding the rice, and laid her, as everyone thought, dead at his feet. Carefully attended to by the estate Doctor, and nursed after she was able to be removed to her hut by the man for whom she had suffered, she recovered, but the husband was tried and condemned to ten years labour on the roads. She lives now with the man of whom her husband was jealous without cause, and they are saving up every farthing of money they can earn in order that they may be able to flee from Mauritius before her husband's time is up, as his first act on regaining his liberty would be to kill her.

"She must have the lives of a cat," murmured the Serjeant to himself, who remembered the case, and how he had given her up for dead, and would never even have taken her to the hospital, had the Doctor, who had more experience, not been luckily on the spot.

Two bright looking boys come in from the fields, shouldering their *pioches** and having all the airs of grown men. They have grown old before their time for they are practically orphans, and have become the heads of the house as the result of a domestic tragedy. Their father, a white bearded Punjaubee, old Sheik Mahmoud, was at a merry-making one Saturday night with his elder children when a man whispered in his ear that the young and strapping Memdee had been taken by his wife stealthily into the house. The villain who told had himself besieged the wife in vain. Old Mahmoud went down rather with the view of getting evidence to confound the slanderer of his wife's fair name – but, ah me!, entering suddenly, for who could have expected him home from the merry-making so early, they were caught in their guilt. The lover flees from the house, but a knife is at hand and despite a cry from the victim, the weapon is plunged into her heart and a sheet cast over her corpse. Never flinching for a moment, but with set teeth, Mahmoud sends for the assistance of those of his gang upon whom he can rely to aid him in the capture of the lover and to punish him as he deserved.

They caught him, and while the sounds of music from the booth of the dancers pervades the camp, and the moon shines bright overhead, and while many men and women are quietly smoking the hubble-bubbles at their doors, the wretch is set upon, and notwithstanding a desperate defence, is slain in the very midst of the camp. The same field-knife which pierced the heart of the woman has been driven through the body of her lover, and Mahmoud giving some direction about the burial of the bodies, stalks off, all bloody from the sacrifice as he was, to the police station and gives himself up as a murderer. His appearance so frightened the Inspector who happened to be at the station, that he had not presence of mind to order his arrest, and the criminal had actually to thrust himself upon justice. He too, not for the death of his wife which the French as well as the colonial law looks on leniently when the circumstances are such as to deprive the man of his reason, but for the cruel vengeance on the lover afterwards in cold blood, was condemned for a long period of penal servitude. He expected to die, he wanted to die, he sought to plead guilty to the worst charge, and the law's mercy was no mercy in his eyes.

The boys with whom the Serjeant had been brought frequently into contact during the awful time of the tragedy and the enquiry, knew him well and greeted him cordially, one of them running after to hold his horse when the great man should alight. Then there were the ordinary ruck of deserters from work, confirmed malingerers, men who had been tried for gang robberies but had escaped, all in addition to the many honest, hard-working Coolies, who strove to keep straight with the Sirdars and employés, until their five years

* A tool rather like a pick-axe, used by cane workers.

engagement should be at an end, when as old immigrants they would choose their own field of labour,[†] and most probably become market gardeners, and grow rich by cultivating three acres of vegetables for the bazaar of Port Louis.

Isidore and the Manager of the Estate were away having a plunge when the Serjeant arrived. They had been hard at work all day repairing some portion of the machinery which had given way, and both looked upon the visit as a great bore. The Manager especially, for it generally fell to his lot to entertain the police functionary. Isidore was not sorry to hear the result of the trial as it gave him all the chance he wished and he was a little ashamed of the way in which the affair had originated. Having given the Manager a hint to ask the Serjeant to dinner with him, Amirantes was about moving off when two more important functionaries appeared unexpectedly in the field. These were the Magistrate and the Inspector of Police, who merely said as they drove up that they were passing on duty and as night was approaching they would, if Monsieur Amirantes père had no objection, remain for the night. Neither of the three persons, Isidore, the Manager nor the Serjeant felt comfortable. They had all done many things which would not stand investigation and they feared the two functionaries had arrived on an enquiry. Deciding with wonderful readiness the next course to be pursued, Isidore took them to the "great house," and after starting his father's domestic on the preparation of an invigorating swizzle for the two gentlemen, he went off in search of his father.

That gentleman was returning from an inspection of the work of the day, and as he approached one field where two of the Coolies had been kept as a punishment to finish their uncompleted task, he saw the two sitting among the young canes idling, so deeply engaged in conversation that they did not hear or perceive the master driving along the cane-road. He stopped the vehicle and passing noiselessly across the ground, came suddenly upon the culprits. The first notice they had of his presence was the full weight of his cane on their bare backs, not merely a smart reminder, but as hard as he could give it till the wretches winced again – "Ah, it is you, Carpen," he exclaimed, "good-for-nothing villain that you are. Never your task finished, lazy, disgusting dog, I will have you up before the Magistrate once more." Carpen grasped his pioche so menacingly that the planter hesitated. "Dog" he at length exclaimed, striking the Coolie over the head with his stick, "would you dare to menace me?" The blow cut the head open, and blood streamed over the face of the helot, who was awed however by the vigour of the attack.

Carpen was one of those bad bargains whom the planters are obliged to take among the new gangs from India. A criminal probably in his own country, it was not to be expected that a voyage with plenty of food and without work will make him all of a sudden begin a new life. Properly handled by employers with a stock of patience greater than that of Job, such men sometimes turn out fairly good labourers, but the chances are that long before the natural hardness of their hearts has melted, the patience of the employers has been exhausted and a desperate strife has begun for the purpose of breaking in the bad bargain by punishment and the weight of the law. The latter course is sure to fail. More obstinate than the employer, having no fear of gaol and not valuing life, he has the employer at a disadvantage. The strife moreover is apt to bring discredit on the plantation. When the wages of the Coolie are constantly cut for bad work or desertion, he does not obtain sufficient food to keep him strong. Disease more readily attacks him, and he is taken to the hospital a half starved miserable wretch where only half rations were then given, and his wife and children, if he had any, starve also. The list of deserters, and the sick list, swell up by the constant entry of the same names, and the officials whose duty it is to keep a kind of eye to the welfare of the labourers shake their heads and begin to point to such and such an estate as badly managed, and a disgrace to the Colony. Moreover the Coolies know very well that they can appeal to the law and where the employer or any of his assistants resorts to blows they are not infrequently summoned before the Magistrate by the servant, but woe unto that servant through whose instrumentality a Master is fined!

It was the possibility of this appeal to the Magistrate which quickened the step of young Amirantes, as he hurried to meet his father. He had seen the uplifted stick and feared a scene while the Magistrate himself was on the premises. But he was always ready with some device. Having told his father of the visitors who had arrived and what he feared, he requested him to go at once to the house to keep them in talk and employment for the evening, while he went into the field to speak with Carpen and Gungadoo. With all his faults, Isidore was much more popular with the men than his father. The latter was a keen money making hard man, the former was a lover of pleasure, and usually allowed the men to take their own way with the work. He very seldom lifted his hand to a Coolie, although it was a frequent practice both with his father and the employés. Carpen had a wife or concubine but he was not jealous of Isidore in regard to her. One of the chief causes of his trouble was that the woman was employed by the Manager as a domestic, and was frequently in his pavilion when Carpen returned from his work prolonged, as was not infrequently the case, by the direct interference of the Manager himself.

"What did you say to my father, Carpen, that irritated him," said Isidore as he approached.

"I said nothing, sahib, but being struck from behind I did not know who it was, and I took hold of my pioche."

"Threatened to strike him," said Isidore, "how could you think of striking the burra sahib?"

"I did not know it was he," replied the Coolie, shrinking now in cold blood from what he only thought of doing. "I thought it was Missié* Eugène—"

"But why should you think of striking Eugène, Carpen?"

"Sahib, he gives me tasks I cannot finish, he comes and makes me finish, and speaks bad words to me, he keeps me here till the stars are out, and when I come home, I find Chinacontee in Missié Eugène's house. I cannot make

---

* Monsieur

enough money to live upon, and my rice is not cooked by the woman when I am hungry."

"All right, Carpen," Isidore replied, "if you think Eugène is hard upon you I will put you in another gang, and give you another hut. Now, look here, I wish this note taken into Port Louis tonight so that the stores may come out first thing in the morning. I came to ask you as I know you would go quickly. Wash yourselves, you and Gungadoo, in the canal, and set off at once. I will tell your wives where you have gone, and will look after Chinacontee, Carpen. Here is a dollar to buy your food for tonight and tomorrow."

The sight of the two rupees dispelled all doubt and hesitation from the minds of the men, and after washing themselves in the canal, they set off for town by a road which did not bring them through the camp.

Cutting sugar cane

Chapter 10
The Chasse*

THE HUNTING PARTIES IN THE ISLAND ARE GREAT GATHERINGS of from fifty to sixty guns, and the mode adopted is to post the chasseurs at definite stations in a long line on which the deer are driven down by a multitude of *piqueurs*** with dogs. The meet was usually a three-day holiday for the more distant chasseurs, one day for going, another for the sport, and the third for the return with the spoil. The *chasse* on this occasion was given by a leading planter whose place was distant from the City rather by its inaccessibility than by the mere measurement in miles. Several of the officers were invited, and as the day approached there was a general cleaning of guns, and a general borrowing by those who had not the proper description of arm, and were going, from those who had but were not going. Jack and Darcy with two of their comrades started in a hired vehicle, a little crazy on its wheels, but which was thought sufficient to take them up to the point where the public road crossed, whence they would have to walk through the forest.

The drive up was long and toilsome, for the horses were old, half starved, and one fell lame. The weight of four young men with their guns was rather too much for the steep climb to an elevation of sixteen hundred feet. The day was accordingly past the meridian before they reached the end of civilization as represented by roads passable for vehicles, and found their servants who had gone on before waiting for them in all the varied attitudes of repose. The domestics having to shoulder the *malles**** it was necessary for the gentlemen to carry their own guns, but at the beginning of the tramp this seemed a very light thing indeed. They saw a party far ahead mounted on the small Estate ponies which are admirably adapted for the woods, and they rather envied the planters the possession of all those luxuries.

The afternoon air on those breezy heights was most exhilarating. They were above all vegetation strictly tropical, and were now in the region of lycopod and fern, of the tree-fern in place of the palm, and of the old moss grown trees of the ancient forest. Although cultivation had not yet got up so far, the wood-cutter had been busy. Great trees were rare, and the ground

* "The Hunt"
** A whipper-in, or huntsman's assistant
*** baggage

was cumbered with the debris of others, small and great, while many of those which still stood erect were smitten with mortal disease and stretched their gaunt leafless limbs into the silent air. The aspect might have had a melancholy influence on a solitary traveller, but it was barely noticed by these young men in the full flow of animal spirits, rejoicing in the sense of freedom from the restrictions of the town and in anticipation of the sport of tomorrow.

As they neared a river which had to be crossed they saw deer feeding in the ravines and took care not to startle them, for the animals are wonderfully acute in their knowledge of the preparations for a great drive. The river had to be forded, a feat which, gaitered and booted as they were, was about as easy for the gentlemen as for the bare footed and bare-legged attendants. But they did not calculate on the depth or the coldness of the water, and it was with many ejaculations and drawings in of breath that, holding high their guns, they gained the further bank. They soon reached a stretch of the ancient forest which had not been invaded by the devouring axes of the wood-cutters. Before penetrating the gloom they stopped under a magnificent dome of tree-ferns to adjust the burdens of the servants, to tighten the buckles of their own belts, and to stimulate their energies by an application to their flasks. It was a march long to be remembered. The path wound amid the stems of giant trees whose mingling tops obscured the sun-light, and made a sombre shaded stillness as if one had entered the confines of the silent world. The deer deterred by the density of the undergrowth seldom ventured within, the few birds which still remained of the feathered tribes of the forest after the remorseless slaughters encouraged and commanded by the law in the infancy of the Colony preferred the outskirts where it was not always afternoon. A waft of perfume occasionally passed over from the male flower of the pandanus of the woods, and a gleam of colour from a cluster of white orchids.

Silence, twilight and the depth of colourless gloom generally prevailed. The young men felt the awe of the place and the hour. The laughter and the repartee ceased, the gabble of the domestics was no longer heard, only the tramp of feet, the crackling of the dry twig, the deep drawn breathing of the men toiling under their burdens. It was doubtless thus with all the Island, Jack thought, as he moved noiselessly onward, when the Dutchman first ventured to choose it for a home, it was thus when the Frenchman, sick of the gaudy splendour and abject misery of the monarchy of Louis succeeded the Dutch when they retired to join their brethren elsewhere.

To these glades the Solitaire, driven from the coast may have fled for shelter from the unwelcome presence of man,[†] and later, as the years rolled on, and misery came in the train of the pioneer, here the hunted maroon may have laid him down to draw his panting breath, hearing in the far distance the baying of the baffled hounds. But what is man in presence of the infinite yearnings which possess the soul when one treads the aisles of the ancient forest, breathing the breath of the woods, and feeling the awful silence? Thought rises to higher moods. We begin to speculate upon the condition of things in the remote centuries before even the hills were raised above the waters. What existences told of the greatness of the Creator before these wondrous girths were brought forth which now overshadowed the land? Their massive limbs make night while it is yet day, but what of the time before they had burst through the conscious soil, and still dwelt in night and the unknown? In those glades he that hath ears to hear may hear much of the greatness of the Creator. The sap coursing through its countless channels may utter the full volume of praise and tell us of the wisdom of Him who made all things very good. Can we interrogate the Past, as we seem, or think we can, to be able to question the heart of Nature? Can we search the record of the works of the Parent of Good to learn of the dawn of things; to enter reverently the vestibule, to see the deep foundations whence the structure springs? In such a flight the mind soon droops her weary wing.

The Past had still a Past, even as these great types had progenitors, or as the animals whose bones are preserved for us in the tombs of the rocks had descended from a long line which lived and moved and had their being before this so solid seeming isle had been heaved above the surface of the great deep. We cannot see the end from the beginning, or know whether man as now developed is a mere passing existence on the world's surface, or is toiling pilgrim-like to a heaven of purity and peace which he will reach and enter without sensible change. But what is man, that he should survive when so much that is wrought with infinite cunning is hourly hurled to annihilation? The race may live although the units constantly die, and after knowledge has become complete, and science has laid her last golden crown at his feet, man may be changed as Moses and Elias were on the mount of transfiguration and become fitted in perfection of body and mind to fill a sphere where change hath ceased to operate, and where a new Eden hath been formed without a Serpent. Then, indeed, the last war drum will cease to roll, the last slave's cry be heard, the last embrace of agonized hearts be given, the death bell's last knell be tolled.

But lo! the sunshine on the clearing beyond the wood; the gloom is behind and the travellers come forth into freedom and light. The afternoon is fast waning but the spectacle before them keeps them transfixed with admiration. The slope of the Island here is towards the South and West. The heaven is already yellowing into sunset. The forest crowns the tops of the hills, which multiply around. Cleared fields planted with sugar cane occupy the plain and divide the mountains from the sea. The "Hangar" to which the travellers are bound, shining out white amid the surrounding green lies below, and beyond is the ocean with its white fringe where the tide dashes itself on the reefs. With renewed energy at the prospect of rest all push forward. The dusk overtakes them, and they enter the Hangar and receive the hearty welcome of their host, as the first star of evening comes forth from the waning splendour of the day.

All is bustle and life. Carriages of all descriptions had already arrived, and were picqueted about in picturesque confusion. Coolies squatted around or searched in their dirty *kupras** for cold rice with which to refresh themselves while awaiting better fare. The host and his assistants were busy allotting sleeping quarters to the new comers, which in some instances consisted

---

* clothes

of simply a place on a sloping plank in roughly constructed huts, but for the officers from town was a separate comfortable pavilion, with camp beds. A stream which babbled near invited a plunge.

Before the bath was finished, and some suitable garb for the evening found, the verandah of the dining room was filled with guests, who continued to arrive till late in the night. The hand-shaking was incessant for besides old friends there were planters from distant parts of the Island who had not yet met the English officers and had to be introduced. No formality or stiffness hampered the hilarity of this meeting. All had come for enjoyment, quite resolved to make the best of everything. The only drawback was the extremely late hour for dinner which did not appear until everyone was nigh famished. It is not easy to get ready to feed so large a number in the wilderness, but to make up for the lateness of the hour there was generally more than enough of the best of everything. Nine o'clock had struck before the doors were opened and the happy moment came for hungry men. Fully sixty guests sat down and did full justice to the rude plenty of the feast. Amid the profusion of turkeys, roast pig, venison, beef and other solid dishes, cakes and comforts from the chief restaurant of the capital were there in profusion and the flowers of the forest decorated the centre of the table.

The drinking was very moderate, consisting almost exclusively of claret but after dinner, when cigars were produced, and the verandah became the favourite lounge for story or song, there was much popping of soda water corks for what is properly called b. & s.* and frequent adjournments by old comrades of the Chasse, who had found each other after dinner for the first time, to cement friendship by a mutual drink.

The morning was wet, dismal, and dreary. In place of turning out in the pouring rain most would have preferred to remain in bed, but the programme was fixed and could not be deflected from. Moreover enthusiasts were present who would have gone out in search of the game if a hurricane had been blowing or an earthquake shaking under their feet. The dogs were ready and in the charge of the piqueurs, so after a cup of scalding coffee had been swallowed, the gun-lock well bound up to protect it from the wet, and the ammunition safe under the water-proof, a start was made.

The place to be first tried was in the plain, a portion of waste land rather than of forest for the trees had nearly all disappeared, and in their place thickets of wild strawberry plants or clumps of matted young shoots, had come up helping to conceal the decaying trunks which nature was covering up with a mantle of green. The gentlemen were placed each at his own particular post, and told in which direction they might fire with safety to their neighbours and where not, and then they were left to their own solitary musings until it might please a stag to come straying in their direction. The rain continued to pour. A musket shot was the signal that the last chasseur was posted and for the dogs to be loosened to drive the deer down upon the guns, but the deer lay close and the dogs all wet and miserable would not face the

* brandy and soda

wild strawberry brakes. The majority of the chasseurs stood for four weary hours, wet and hungry, and did not so much as see one head of game of any sort. This was dull work and the company were recalled for a late breakfast which developed into rather a substantial lunch.

On the way back to the Hangar, the rain stopped, the thinned clouds were blown over the hills, and the sun came out to cheer and enliven the whole prospect. Old hands were unanimous in predicting that the deer were out in the plain so that it was with quite renewed hope of some genuine sport that the guests followed their guides for the afternoon attempt. This time the flank of the party was high up on the hillside where the officers emerged from the woods. The other flank was thrown back and continued in the direction of the Hangar. The sun had done wonders for both men and beasts. The piqueurs went away with a will predicting good sport, the dogs were eager to be unleashed.

After a long walk to their respective posts as before, scarcely had the musket sounded as the signal to begin, when the continuous yelping of the dogs was heard as they drove the deer before them from thicket to thicket. Guns were loaded and the posters** waited with eager expectation.[†] The rule of the field is that none but stags are to be shot at, and as the stags are most frequently in the centre of a crowd of does it is not easy to single them out for a shot. At times however either the dogs cut out a stag and drive him down on the guns, or the herd becoming separated by fear when the reports of the guns are heard and confusion begins the stags leave the females behind and attempt to break through the circle of fire to escape to the hills.

In about an hour after the piqueurs had begun to beat, a fine herd was seen coming over the rising ground opposite that portion of the line where the officers were posted. Cautiously, as if they knew the real danger was in front, and not from the yelping curs behind, the herd reconnoitred the shallow valley and opposite hillside. Two fine stags were in the middle. They seemed to hold converse with the does as to the probable position of the hunters, and where it would be possible to get through. With frequent stoppages they stepped forward, taking little runs in the open, and then suddenly changing their course. Arriving opposite where Darcy was stationed, although they were still too far for effective work with the musket, he could not restrain his impatience and fired at one of the stags which was uncovered for a moment by the females. The stag swerved and nearly fell, having received the bullet in the hind quarters, but was not disabled. The herd scattered and fled down the line of posters. The wounded stag could still keep up pretty closely although evidently hurt. The course down the line was like a charge of cavalry in front of hidden batteries. Bang!, bang! went the guns as the animals flew past. Both stags fell while the scared and flying females got back to their retreats by the lower side of the rising ground. Another herd had tried to break through at the other end of the line and had been dispersed in the same manner. All the stags had fallen but one, which, knowing beyond its years, kept out of range until it gained the height, when believing it must have passed

---

* chasseur

all the guns, it was making for the retreats around the Grand Bassin when it
stopped behind a rock to reconnoitre the part of the hill where Jack was posted. Hidden behind the root of an overturned tree which had sprouted again
he was not easily seen by the animal, while kneeling he had an admirable
rest for his elbows to take a steady aim. All that was visible of the stag was
its horns and a small piece of its head over the rock. Taking a cool and steady
sight Jack fired. The horns disappeared, but whether he had hit or not he
could not say, and the chase was too hot to permit him to go out, as his next
neighbour might have shot him in mistake for a stag.

A little chagrined that he saw nothing, and that no one came to congrat-
ulate him, Jack loaded again, and scarcely had done so before a young animal *à trois cornes** came bounding along. It is lawful to kill these as they are
no longer fawns although not yet stags. He took it on the bound, a difficult
shot, but it was a capital one, right behind the fore shoulder, and the animal
dropped and never stirred. After this there was a long lull, and Jack was
thinking of creeping down to his friends to establish to his own satisfaction
whether or not he had got the first stag when another herd was driven out
nearly in the same direction as before. They scattered in fright when they
came to the rock where the first stag had disappeared thereby raising hopes
that they had seen something to cause terror, and making right across they
were in between the lines of posters before any one could draw trigger. It
was impossible to shoot to right or left although Jack had a stag on each side
of him, for had he fired he might have missed the stag and brought down a
friend. Following them therefore with his gun at his shoulder until they had
got to the rear he fired and hit but not mortally. A second shot from an old
chasseur posted higher up brought down the very noble old stag which Jack
thought to have been his. But the law of the field is that he who kills, not he
who wounds, is to have the stag. He sent a hurried shot after the second but it
was already away sniffing safety in the hills. Scarcely had Jack emptied both
barrels than turning around towards the rising ground where the dogs were
still keeping up their yelping din he saw not twenty yards off a very fine old
stag whose coat hair was almost black. Its horns were magnificent as it stood
eyeing the officer with as much astonishment as he beheld it.

The spectacle was one of the most superb and thrilling kind. Jack could
not move to get a cartridge, for if he had, he knew the stag would instantly
have disappeared. For several seconds they thus gazed at each other until
the yelp of a hound close at hand caused the noble animal to start afresh and
with one bound he was hid behind the brushwood. A noise and rustle were
all that could be detected, until he was seen again turning round to breathe
on a mound far out of reach of bullet. The passing of the dogs beyond the
line of posters shewed that the chasse was over, and the men from right and
left came up to talk of their luck. Darcy had got a stag besides the one he
had wounded at the beginning, and the others had at least had shots if not
successful. They all went towards the rock where Jack thought he had hit at

* three-pointed

first, and there sure enough was a fine stag stark and dead, struck right on the top of the forehead which he had seen above the rock. Its body was already swelling as he had not used the knife. The experienced chasseur always goes out after a successful shot to cut the throat of his victim which prevents the carcass thus swelling with foul gas.

The piqueurs were loud in praise of the promptness of the officers who were new to the work, but one of them, with a knowing look (for he guessed at once the cause, having heard both barrels fired immediately before) asked Jack what the old stag had said to him that he did not fire when it was so close. Jack thought it judicious to give the man a tip of five shillings and ask that he should say nothing about it, as the chaff against anyone who gets chances and misses them is not always pleasant. Numbers of estate labourers were already coming on the field to carry back the trophies to the Hangar. It was a rare and stirring sight, after some refreshment had been hurriedly partaken of, to see the beasts brought in swung by the feet to poles carried by a couple of men. The chasseurs mark their own stags so as to distinguish them, because the head with its panoply of horns belongs to him who brought it down, while the body is cut up and divided among all who have been present.

The night had already set in while the piqueurs continued their work by torchlight. As the officers watched them at their labours, the Host came and said "What has become of old Beauvallon? I have not seen him since lunch." The officers had not seen him either, and others who were interrogated knew nothing of him. The head piqueur was applied to and he mentioned where he had posted him, and who were his neighbours but neither of the neighbours had seen him coming home, although one said he had observed him packing up a little basket as if getting ready to start. Four of the most experienced of the men were sent back to the post with instructions to keep along the path by which he would naturally come to the Hangar. A kind of uneasy feeling began to spread itself throughout the company. "Oh, the bonhomme has perhaps lamed himself leaping a ruisseau,"* said an old comrade of his, "he will be here immediately with the help of the two Mozambiques." But a small band of old chasseurs who had become very anxious about their friend started also, resolved to solve the mystery of his absence before dressing for dinner.

They had been gone about half-an-hour when one of the piqueurs who had set out first reached the hangar and without speaking to anyone else went direct to the host. He had terrible news to communicate. The bearers were approaching with the dead body of Monsieur Beauvallon. It was impossible to keep the news from the guests, and when it passed from mouth to mouth a deep awe fell upon the whole company. As if moved by one impulse they ranged themselves in two lines from the door of the hut which the unfortunate gentleman had occupied, watching for the party to approach with the remains. Nor had they long to wait. A faint light in the trees first told them where the torches were passing, and then the lights, leaving the wood, came out to the road.

* stream

Slowly they approached as if their burden was heavy, and when step by step they at last neared the buildings, the sad company saw the body stretched on a rude bier covered by the cloak of one of the friends who had gone in search, and with bated breath they watched it carried into the hut and laid on the bed from which the victim had risen so well and cheerful in the morning. The cause of the accident was easily explained. The gun which Monsieur Beauvallon carried was a percussion muzzle-loader, and he had not withdrawn the charge before starting. At a short distance from his post the musket was found in a clump of bushes with a *liane** caught round the trigger, and the body lying on its face a few paces in front of the clump. The charge must have been almost instantly fatal. At the moment of the breaking up, when friends are proceeding to rejoin each other, when the muskets are being emptied, and when the talk over exploits which is continued all evening has begun, a stray shot, like that which finished the career of Monsieur Beauvallon, excited no attention. Nor was the spot where he fell in the direction of any one else returning, so that it was not until the general muster in the evening that his absence was noticed.

The pleasure of the occasion was gone for everyone. The host busied himself in making arrangements for transporting the body homewards on the morrow. To be in advance of rumour, which travels so rapidly and mysteriously, an express had been sent off through the dark and silent night with a note to the Priest to go at once to break the terrible news to Madame Beauvallon.

* creeper.

Chapter 11
The Trials of Widowhood[1]

THE BODY OF POOR MONSIEUR BEAUVALLON was duly laid in the old churchyard of Pamplemousses. That spot was consecrated by frequent use even at the time when Bernardin St Pierre was in the Island, and on its many monuments can be read the names of all the chief families of the Colony. An immense concourse attended the funeral, for no man was more respected and loved, and the manner in which he met his death caused an universal feeling of pity and of sympathy with his family. The service of the church was held in the Cathedral before the cortège started from Port Louis.

It was crowded in every part. Ernestine was there in order to narrate most faithfully to her sorrowing mistress and her beloved "enfant" all that took place, and the giddy Lucille, clad in mourning and weeping bitterly, also looked down from the gallery on the dismal ceremony. Cut to the heart as she was however that did not prevent her, in coming out, when she saw one of the young men of her acquaintance, from raising the skirt of her mourning dress, to show the elaborate white petticoat beneath. In the depth of her grief the nature of the coquette was still strong within her. Her eyes had wandered everywhere in the church until she discovered Isidore, and when she had she remarked with secret pleasure how much better dressed he was than those who were near him. For many days sadness reigned in the house in town, and had it not been for the necessity of attending to business the unhappy widow would have preferred to have spent months in weeping.

But the French laws are very peremptory and very precise on the occasion of death. As soon as the news of the accident reached town, and after the first shock of surprise was over, old Monsieur Soussigné had taken a clerk with the requisite material, and gone to the house of mourning to compile an inventory of everything it contained, especially every scrap of written paper, and afterwards to seal up all the repositories with infinitely greater care and solemnity than if a peer of the realm had died and his estates had passed to a line different from the family in possession.

Harsh as this proceeding may seem, it really has a beneficial effect upon the bereaved. Every French man and woman has a natural turn for business. It is saying the simplest truth that if few of them could turn to any passage in the Bible which was peculiarly adapted to give comfort to mourners, they could all turn with readiness to the Chapters of the Civil Code which regulated their rights. Madame Beauvallon in consequence of the easy nature of her husband, had long been the real head of the house and knew the condition of affairs only too well. The estate was heavily mortgaged as is usual with most if not all the sugar estates in Mauritius. The French law gives much more facility for borrowing on mortgage than the English from the ease with which the land which forms the pledge can be sold if the amount borrowed be not repaid, or the interest be not regularly remitted. In fact land can be as easily mortgaged as an article of *vertu* can be pawned. The consequence is that the chief desire of French capitalists is to get hold of landed securities which in England are rather shunned, or left to great capitalists who cannot easily place their money anywhere, or to Life Insurance companies whose accumulations of Capital have become immense. The ease of borrowing has both a good and a bad side for the planter. It is good when he wishes new or improved machinery which may largely improve his annual returns that he should have facility to raise money on the security of his estate, but when such facility exists loans are frequently arranged for novelties which do not turn out improvements, or for real improvements the benefits of which are lost by some change of climate, or some disaster the effects of which are not recovered for years.

Lorraine was suffering from drought. When Monsieur Beauvallon first became proprietor the climate was all that could be desired for the growth of sugar. For many years he made excellent crops and became rich, but since that period the great extension of sugar growing which had taken place, owing to the facility with which Coolie labourers could be obtained, had caused the destruction of the forests on the high lands, and the consequence was a most material reduction of the supply of moisture to the properties below. It was necessary to employ irrigation on a great scale, but notwithstanding the immense sums spent on canals the mass of water which was suddenly poured upon any given field by this means did not equal the benefit of a few fine showers of rain – the plants in fact, as every well informed agriculturalist knows, take in much of their nourishment by means of the leaves. While they were deprived of that resource by the cessation of the showers, the water poured on the volcanic soil too rapidly disappeared into fissures and subterranian hollows. Madame Beauvallon knew well that a very large proportion of the income of the estate had to go to pay the interest of the mortgages and she knew well what effect the death of M. Beauvallon might have upon the mortgages.

Many people have no faith in enterprises of which women are the nominal as well as the real heads, although they might have no objection where the husband was only nominal and the wife the real manager. Besides, she knew the customs of the country too well not to be aware of the openings which any change of circumstances, such as the death of a proprietor, offered to those who were ambitious to become owners of an estate. In a small Colony where the opportunities for men to establish themselves are limited, where wits are very keen and the openings given by the law to manoevring and chicanery very numerous, many dangers arose from ambition and from the competition of interests. A mortgagee might think that the safest way for himself would be to obtain possession of the estate and have it worked by his own managers and in his own style, having little doubt that all the other mortgagees would continue their loans to him, while the sum he had lent would go as far as part of the price to be paid. The family in possession would thus be got rid of. A neighbour might think the moment opportune to extend his estate by getting hold of the adjoining one, the two being much more cheaply and easily worked under a single management. Such a neighbour, as we have seen, was Amirantes père and the mode in which he hoped to realise this ambition was to purchase up a mortgage, force a sale and buy the property for himself. Or a mercantile house in town which trafficked in sugars, or a place of business which dealt in lending money, might think the opportunity a good one to extend their operations, and the way they would proceed would probably be to back up some man of straw to purchase a claim over the estate, and to press it until the estate had to be sold, when they would assist him with the proportion of the price requiring to be deposited at the sale, and then either instal him as nominal proprietor, or throw him aside and put up another in his room more suited to their purposes. In fact scarcely was the body of Monsieur Beauvallon laid in the tomb than all these descriptions of speculators began to buzz around the property like carrion flies after a dead ox.

There was therefore abundant cause for Madame's anxiety but the French law while laying her open to attack on one side had placed her in an advantageous position on another. Her own rights were extensive and they were defended by what is known in French law as a *privilège* ranking before all the mortgages, and the moment her husband died both the rights of her daughter and herself came into full play. In addition several members of the family had money invested in the estate, and the whole, whatever little differences they might have with each other, would pull together if any outsider attempted to get possession of the property.

There was both approbation and a menace to the estate in the knowledge of its affairs, and of everyone else's affairs, possessed by M. Soussigné the Notary. If he remained true he could certainly find means to baffle anyone attempting to gain possession, but a Notary in France, and equally in Mauritius, may have the interests of many people in his keeping, all having different views as to the same property. The powers of the Notaries for good or evil are immense. Probably in the old and simpler days, that is, the days of less extensive operations, when his clients were all colonists living on their own properties, or concerned with their own *habitations** in town, the influence of the Notary was solely for good. But great companies had begun operations, and commercial houses carried on business on a scale of unprecedented magnitude, luxury had come in with its influence on the style of living, which required Notaries and all others to increase their incomes as much as possible, and thus he was obliged to cultivate not only the proprietor who might be a victim, but the Bank, the Credit Company, the financial house,

---

* country residences or estates.

which might wish to be the victimiser. It did so happen in this instance that M. Soussigné was the Notary both of the Beauvallons and of the Amirantes, and a very few days after the funeral he was closeted for hours with old Amirantes. Madame Beauvallon knew this, because she herself had called at the office, and one of the Clerks who was deeply touched at seeing Madame for the first time in her widows' garb, told her who was with the Notary.

Ernestine going down town to make some purchases later on saw Amirantes leaving the door of M. Soussigné and duly informed her mistress of the fact. Madame Beauvallon instinctively guessed what the object of her neighbour would be. She had herself occasionally thought of the possibility of a marriage of Estelle with Isidore, before they had become acquainted with Montmorency, and in her present state of sorrow and dejection, feeling for the first time what a deprivation it was to have no one with whom to consult or on whose advice she could implicitly depend, she sometimes asked herself whether she had done wisely in looking out for an alliance for Estelle beyond her own old acquaintances and friends. This was a dangerous feeling to entertain so far as the interests of Jack were concerned. Unfortunately, it so happened, that like so many young Englishmen who have no sense of tact, or of the fitness of things, he had somehow managed to create a less favourable impression upon both Madame Beauvallon and her daughter than his wont. Overwhelmed with grief at the death of the father, he had, with what he believed to be the truest kindness, hung back from tending his sympathy in person. His daily notes to Estelle, with frequent little gifts were all that could be desired, but she wished to see him, she expected to see him, she longed to throw herself on his shoulder and to weep there, but he came not. The mother expected to see him as one whom in the ordinary course of affairs she would have the right to consult more freely hereafter; she felt the want of a male friend on whom she could rely; in the first bitterness of her widowhood she wished an arm to lean upon when walking in the valley of the Shadow of Death; but with a false delicacy, prompted by the most generous of feelings, he came not. Of his notes to Estelle, some which came afterwards to light ran as follows:

On the morning after the accident he wrote: "Estelle, my heart bleeds for thee. Oh that I could comfort you. I weep with you and your poor mother."

On the following day: "I have been weeping with you all the night. God bless and comfort you. What can man do in such an hour. In your bitter grief, Estelle, I share but cannot help. May God help you."

And again on the same day – "The suddeness of internment in these climes is even more terrible than death. No time to weep even over the lost one. May the earth in whom your father now dwells send comfort and dry away thy tears."

His next was still written under the influence of his own strong emotions. "My heart was with thee, Estelle, as all that was mortal of him you all loved was hid from our eyes. Every one sobbed and many wept bitterly. Behold how they loved him! When such was the grief of more distant relatives, of friends, and of neighbours, what must yours be, my beloved. What the grief of your mother and aunt. I can pray for you all, but cannot speak words of comfort because I know of none fitting at such a time. I mingle my tears with yours and pray that the heavenly father may have pity on an afflicted child."

Estelle having pencilled a few words in reply – "I cannot write, but thank you, dearest, thank you. EB." Jack wrote next morning once more.

"How pleased I was, my own one, to get your note. I knew you could not write and did not expect any answer, so your thoughtfulness made it all the more welcome. I fear that even the expressions of love may jar on your feelings while your sorrow is still so fresh, but I kissed your note, Estelle, many many times, and did not cease to think of you all day in your solitude and tears. I know what it must be now and cannot but be for many days, but time the all consoler will at last enable you to look upon your bereavement with more calmness, and I hope you will then be able to see me as before. We drove out to Pamplemousses yesterday and I noticed the wreath of flowers upon the tomb. This showed me if any proof were needed how all your thoughts are still of him and him only. How I sympathize with you, my own one, and look forward to the time when the bitterness of your grief will be assuaged."

But while Jack was thus simply penning his consolation, Isidore taking advantage of his old friendship and the fact of his being the nearest neighbour had called to proffer his sympathy to Madame Beauvallon in person. Overwhelmed with grief as she was, when she heard who had called she put on her new dress with even more than the usual care. Nay after she had left the glass and had picked up her handkerchief she went back to the glass again and saw not only that the cap was in perfect order but also that the sweep of the skirt was as it should be. Isidore was known to be a critic and Madame even in her grief retained her desire to be *comme il faut*. The sympathy which Isidore tendered was perfectly genuine. He was warm-hearted, and he had always looked up to old Monsieur Beauvallon with real affection. Accordingly as he warmly pressed the hand of the widow and put it to his lips the tears which came to his eyes were perfectly genuine. He too was struck at seeing Madame for the first time in her widow's dress, and it brought home to him her isolated and forlorn condition. It was therefore with a tremor in his voice, which Madame Beauvallon could not doubt was of real sorrow for the friend of his childhood, that he proffered his aid in every way, to look after any private matters until things were arranged. He would willingly he said have attended to the running of the estate, but that he knew was already managed for her by her own relatives. But in any difficulty she might depend upon him. Isidore had a handsome face, and it was almost with a qualm of conscience Madame remembered how she had encouraged the suit of the English officer in preference. But here was the old friend at her side and the new… nowhere. Would it not be so always? Were the differences between Estelle and Jack not too great ever to be smoothed over, the gulfs too deep ever to be bridged. Thinking in spite of herself of such things she gradually became more frank and confident in her interview with Isidore. When he asked for Estelle she told him with much of her accustomed volubility how much the dear "enfant" had done for her, and how it was only for her sake she did not allow herself to be overwhelmed by the calamity. She even ventured upon more dangerous ground and spoke of the devotion and kindness of the servants, and amongst others of Lucille, who, she said, giddy girl as she was, proved herself to be all heart and had fully won her confidence and esteem. Isidore winced a little while mentally taking a note of the greater hold this gave him over the fortunes of the household.

Madame Beauvallon did not know of any intrigue of Isidore with Lucille, but she had no illusions about the kind of life he led, and it did not affect her in the same way as it would have done an English matron who knew nothing about these things. Madame had known of all these customs from her youth up. She had known how slavery in the old days had sapped the virtue of the men so that wives had sometimes to tolerate concubines living in their own courtyard, and she knew well how the hereditary immorality, so to speak, had been maintained and continued by the presence of the Coolies. As to what the conduct of her servants might be in their private relations she cared no more than she did of the horses in the stable, or the cattle in the stall. That it reacted upon the young men was known full well, but it was necessary to take the country in which they lived as they found it. The advantages of the Coolies were too great to permit them to quarrel with the source of their prosperity. She proceeded to ask Isidore news of his family and amongst others of that species of half-sister who had been sent to France for her education and whose fate we have already learned. Madame knew the reason of her being sent away, a reason which was hinted at in the letters of the poor girl herself.

Abandoned as she had been to her own devices, getting her food and lodging and some showy accomplishments, acknowledged by the father but [having] been inveigled away by an employé of the establishment, and after discovered by Isidore, who brought her back to her mother. The consequences soon showed themselves, and to hide the scandal if possible from the father and the neighbourhood Isidore had, under pretence of getting her educated, taken her first to Paris (where the child was born and placed with the creche of the Foundling Hospital) and after to the establishment of Madame Biggerade. Isidore told Madame that the marriage, which had been duly announced in the Island, had not turned out as well as had been expected, and that he feared Rosette was far from happy.

Chapter 12

Doubts, Fears and Dissipation

AFTER THE DEPARTURE OF THE VISITOR, Madame Beauvallon went to her daughter's room. "That was Isidore, Estelle'," she said.

"Yes, Maman."

"He asked so kindly for you, and indeed he behaved altogether in a very friendly and affectionate manner."

"He always seemed to like Papa."

"Yes, and I think the accident seems to have had a good effect in sobering him and making him think more seriously of the realities of life."

"Indeed, Maman, I am glad to hear it. He always seemed to me to be so reckless and perverse."

"All young men are, I fear, Estelle, at certain periods of their lives. It is good when they do not carry it too far, and become serious before great harm is done."

"But what could have induced him, Maman, to take such a course as he did about the shipwrecked people at Lorraine, if he were becoming serious and respectable. And oh, Mama, have you forgot the duel with Jack and how he actually tried to kill him," and Estelle shuddered at the thought.

"What he did was quite indefensible, he must have been off his head I believe at the time," said the mother. "And I can scarcely believe," she added slyly, "what was said by all the neighbours that it was any real love for you, Estelle, which was at the root of his conduct, for he must have known that he could not have taken a better way to disgust you."

"He could not, and I never liked him from his boyhood. He was always self-willed, violent, and evil in his thoughts words and deeds."

"You speak of him very strongly, are you sure not too strongly, Estelle, it is such a pity to entertain any animosity of that kind against one who may not deserve to be so thought of, and who as a neighbour may be very useful to us. His affection for your father quite touched me, and he spoke so kindly and affectionately of all like a true neighbour and friend."

"I would forgive many things if he loved Papa as much as that," said Estelle, with the ready tears beginning again to flow.

"I wonder," replied the mother, thinking it wise to change the subject, "what has become of Monsieur Montmorency. Have you heard from him today, Estelle?"

"Not to-day. But I did yesterday. He will call when he thinks we can bear the presence of strangers."

"But he is not a stranger. I wonder at his absence. Has he no feeling for you, Estelle? It is quite like those English, really they have no savoir faire. "

"Oh Maman, that is too hard upon our English friends. His notes are so beautiful," she added weeping afresh as she did indeed feel that her accepted lover might have been at her side during these dreadful days.

"Humph!" replied Madame. "Has Clémence come back from Madame Garderobe?"

"Not yet. She has scarcely had time. What is there to be done for you, Maman, that I can do, or shall we wait till Aunt returns?"

It was the first of not a few conversations the mother and daughter had on the subject of the two young men. Scarce a day passed that Isidore did not either call or send, always, however, to Madame Beauvallon, to enquire after the health of the family and he sent many little trifles which he thought the ladies would like. Jack by some unaccountable fatality kept away, longing most earnestly to be with Estelle, but withheld by a false notion of what was proper and becoming. While in this frame of mind, kept back from doing a most obvious duty by an over-strained sensitiveness, it so happened that the very morning he had at length made up his mind to call he got an order to proceed at once to Mahebourg to make arrangements for an exchange between the companies stationed in the barracks there and those in Port Louis, in order that the latter might go through their course of musketry instruction at Pointe D'Esny.

Before starting Jack who quite expected to be in town again in a day or two, wrote Estelle of his absence on duty and that on his return he would, if she permitted, hasten to visit her. He received no answer for the note written in haste appeared to Estelle at first to be a mere excuse, and her feelings were deeply hurt that he should have left town without visiting her Mama and herself, and still more at the unfortunate phrase that he would come to visit her if she permitted, as if they were still strangers. The note was unkind, the leaving in this way cruel, and Estelle felt it all the more that she could not confide the secret of her distress to her mother. Bit by bit she had come to comprehend that her mothers' views were changing as to what would be best for her future, and she looked forward to any difference of opinion between them on the subject as a trial too hard to bear. Now that her father was gone she felt she owed all the more respect and affection to her only surviving parent, she knew well how little parents in France cared for the sentimentalities of love when they interfered with the material prospects of the young, and she could not but guess, from the tenor of her mother's conversations, that she thought it might not be disadvantageous to unite the two Estates of Pompadour and Lorraine. She had even hinted that there might be a question between that and losing Lorraine altogether, and the thought crossed her mind of their being obliged to live in penury, and that then even Jack would perhaps despise them – "Oh that he had come," she half ejaculated, "how cruel to leave me thus." She dreaded that her mother would enter and ask the question so often asked – "When is Mr Montmorency coming to call for us?" Happily Madame was busy with her household cares and did not return until Estelle had time to reflect, and had come to the conclusion that it was very silly for her to doubt his love because he had been ordered off on duty.

While on his way to Mahebourg the young officer overtook one of the Magistrates of the Island returning to his home at Beau Bassin which was then a favourite place of residence. As they were going in the same direction, the official invited Jack to take a seat in his carriage that they might converse on their way up hill. It so happened that the conversation turned upon the Creole families of the Island. "I have just taken part," said the official, "in a very sad piece of business. You know that we have still here an old fashion of divorce that where the married persons come before the proper authority and declare that they wish the marriage tie to be severed, and after twelve months come back with their Notary and say they are still of the same mind, divorce is then and there pronounced without any reason asked or given. Now two young married persons have been before me today for the second time on this mission. They are young, that is to say, for married people. But they seemed to be perfectly good friends, the husband was most kind and attentive to the wife, the wife looking on the husband with tenderness more like a bride than one come up to claim a divorce. And, by --- " he added, "they are divorced now and no mistake."

"What could have been the reason?" enquired Jack.

"Well, I do not know. Anyhow, these two people, husband and wife, young and handsome both of them, but especially the wife, have divided partnership by mutual consent, and so far as I could see they treated each other in the most loving manner."

The conversation flagged a little, as Jack did not wish to press the narrator further than he himself chose to communicate.

"Do you see that house?" the Magistrate at length said. "When I came here first it was inhabited by two single ladies, sisters, people of colour. How they lived no one knew. They had a little garden and some friends in town used to be kind to them I heard. In a year or two, only one used to be seen, but the other was known not to be dead. One morning going down to town very early when we expected the mail in, I saw a figure in the garden moving about in such a strange way as to make my very flesh creep. It was the sister. Whenever she detected the sound of wheels she disappeared at once. Poor creature! God only knows what some of them suffer, and what their friends suffer before death brings them release. I think if there is a hero in this world it is that Scotch soldier who volunteered to take charge of the island, where these patients are sent, and where he must be daily and hourly in the presence of the most horrible scourge ever sent to afflict the human family."[†]

Jack knew from this reference what was meant. He had known of it in a general way, but had never thought of the disease as being in existence at the present day, and of patients suffering from it actually living in some of the private houses near.

"Are many families so affected?" he asked at length.

"Too many," was the answer. "And now you had better come in and have a glass of sherry before you drive on."

The conversation was not forgotten. Jack pondered it over and over, but the ills of life sit lightly upon young hearts. As he mounted the road to the top of the Island he felt the invigorating influence of the cooler climate. It was crop time, and on all the estates great bands of Coolies were levelling the sugar canes and exposing the deformity of the stony soil beneath which had been concealed by the waving leaves of the crop. He had to keep a sharp look out to pass the trains of oxen or mules taking the canes to the mills, or coming helter-skelter back for more with the reckless Coolies whipping up their cattle, and trying to extract as much enjoyment for themselves as they could out of the hard labour of crop time.

The town of Curepipe was not then begun. It has only sprung up since the great fever of 1867, and since the making of the railway made it possible for men in business to live out of town in the cool mountain air. This change of quarters has been the salvation of many Creole families. It is indeed impossible to over-estimate the benefit which the youth of both sexes may obtain by living in what is practically a temperate in place of a tropical zone. At that time, apart from some small clearings which had been made for sugar, there was an unbroken forest at the top of the Island and for several miles down the other side towards Mahebourg. As the road was excellent Jack, driving down in his dog cart, felt all the charm and beauty of the scene. The chasse season was now over, the meeting in fact at which poor Monsieur Beauvallon had been shot having been the last which had been given. The deer seemed to know this as well as the officer, and that out of season they were protected by the game law of the Island. As the vehicle approached they did not move from the pasture close to the high road where they were feeding. It was only when his dog, which had been asleep under the grooms' feet, woke up, having smelt them in his dreams, and made desperate efforts to get out, barking and howling as he struggled, that the deer thought it better to move off, the stags as usual being well surrounded and protected by the females.

His brother officers at Mahebourg welcomed the new arrival with a noisy cordiality. They were delighted when they learned that some of the Companies were to exchange the dreariness of Mahebourg for the comparative cheerfulness of the town. "It is so deuced slow in this beastly hole," said the Ensign with the squeaky voice whom we first heard of at the ball. "By Jove, Jack," he added, "you are not in mourning [dress], how is this?"

"Come, Pig," said Darcy, the appellation being one of affection, as showing both that the Ensign was a young shaver and had a squeaky voice, "there are some subjects which are not to be food for jokings."

"All right, D-D-Darcy, I was not speaking of your p-p-possible father in law."

This sally was received with roars of laughter as Darcy, to pass the time, had been seen talking on several evenings with a coloured young woman, whose father, or rather the husband of whose mother, was a well-known negro tradesman in town.

"I vote we make a night of it," said Pig again, "now that Jack has come. It's good for him to exchange the house of m-m-mourning for the house of m-m-mirth."

"I agree with Pig," said Captain Bloater, "out of the mouth of babes, and especially of sucklings, wisdom has been ordained–"

"I wonder," replied Pig,"what would be in the m-m-mouth of young B-b-bloaters."

"Hold your tongue, sir, or I will order you to be served up for dinner."

"Then I would know," replied the incorrigible, "what would be in the m-m-mouth of an old B-b-Bloater."

Pig having thus come off triumphant so far, thought it prudent to subside.

"Jerry," shouted Bloater to the Adjutant, "who are coming to dinner tonight?"

"The Judge for one," was the reply, "Father Doherty from Black River way, the Magistrate, the little Doctor and two planters."

"By Jove, a capital set for a real night of it."

And a real night of it there was. The table was quite full. The Adjutant had impressed into the service more than the ordinary mess servants, and had so thoroughly drilled them into their duties that he had rather overdone it.

It was thus that when the Judge asked for a spoon the soldier-servant behind him paid no attention. Having repeated the request, the man stepped forward and in a confidential tone whispered into the ear of the guest, "beg your pardon, sur, but I am the man told off for the pertaters." In these times, and indeed the observation is good of all times, the military on foreign service did not starve. They paid no duty on their wines and could always get them forwarded at reasonable freight by the many sailing ships which touched at the Island. The wines were always thus of the very best quality, and guests were not slow to shew their appreciation of their excellence. In the absence of the Colonel the Major took the head of the table. He was a most loveable character, whose peculiarities were constantly mimicked by the youngsters, but he bore it all with the greatest good humour, and when any of them wanted money he was always ready to assist, first giving them a lecture on extravagance, and then adding, "but if it's a fiver you want, me boy, by Jove you shall not want it so long as the ould Major has one to lend you."

After dinner the cards were the order of the night. The youngsters who had kept their heads cooler rather got the best of it, Pig coming off with gains of between five and six pounds. They got the hint to retire as some of the seniors were showing signs of over conviviality. That those who were left had gone to great lengths may be judged from the fact that when the Magistrate awoke he found himself stretched on the table with grave clothes on, and candles burning all round him, while those who had been at his wake were reclining or lying in various attitudes on the field where they fell. Comprehending the position of affairs at once, the undaunted Magistrate shouted out "Garçon, garçon, bring the corpse a brandy and soda!" His excla-mation awoke most of the sleepers, who, after a moment taken to recall their wandering thoughts, rushed off to their rooms as the servants came to open the shutters and admit the daylight on the scene of the orgie. Scarcely had this been done when two miserable looking half drowned objects appeared.

They were two of the Lieutenants who thought that it was their duty to go off in the middle of the night to Pointe d'Esny to look after the practice ground. They had taken a "pirogue," one of the very narrow native canoes or boats from the beach – so narrow that even the most sober man has a difficulty in keeping his balance in them.[1] Somehow the two zealous Subs had got a certain distance from town, and fortunately were in shallow water inside the reef when one dropped his oar overboard. In attempting to regain it he fell out. The pirogue having first dipped suddenly the one way, and then relieved of the weight capsized to the other, away went the second oarsman. All their efforts to get in again proved unavailing. When they tried to clamber up the one side of the pirogue invariably turned over. They came to the conclusion therefore that it would be better to wade themselves and push the pirogue along with them, and thus they continued all night, sometimes in water up to their knees, sometimes up to their necks, and sometimes plopping into deep holes out of which they managed to help each other. When morning dawned they found they had been going round in a circle and had come back to the part of the beach from which they had started. They entered wet, hungry, exhausted, perfectly sober, and very much ashamed of themselves.

An order was shortly after received from the General Commanding the troops appointing Jack to be instructor of musketry for all the companies going through their course at Pointe d'Esny.

"Give him time to reflect, the young fool," said the General when he signed the appointment. "The number of young fellows who wreck their prospects with these Creole marriages is astonishing. I have known," he said, with a little stretch of the imagination "both in Nova Scotia and the West Indies half a regiment engaged at one time, and nothing lying about but love letters."

Chapter 13
Paternal and Maternal Admonitions

By ONE OF THOSE CHANGES WHICH FREQUENTLY TAKE PLACE in Colonies, Isidore got an ally in his designs upon Estelle and Lorraine whence he least expected it. The religious adviser of the Beauvallon family had been a good-natured Irishman who took very sensible views of affairs apart altogether from their religious aspect. He would have been very pleased to see Estelle marry a Catholic and a Creole if that was consistent with her own wish, but he was too much a man of the world to pretend any regret when he saw the chance of her obtaining for a husband a protestant English gentleman of good family. He very well knew her own family might soon require all the wealth they could command to keep them afloat as the district was going back. Like a true friend he gave Madame good advice for the future of Estelle whom he had known from childhood, and looked upon with as much affection as if she had been a near relative of his own. But his turn came to go elsewhere, and a new priest arrived on the scene, of a very different temper and inclination.

He was as lean as his predecessor was fat. His face was as austere as that of the other was jolly. His whole appearance showed him to be a bigot and a zealot, of a sour domineering spirit, but earnest withal for the good of the Church, and the saving of souls, according to his own lights. The two priests were together for some time before the good Father left so that the new Abbé had become acquainted with the history of all the principal people in the district, and did not fail to come, as soon as he possibly could, to call for Madame Beauvallon in town. He took possession of their spiritual interests at once as being in charge of the Parish where their home was situated, although they were very well satisfied with the ministrations of the clergy in town.

The Rev. Père Vendredi as he was called did not allude in the slightest degree to what he had heard as to the possible marriage of Estelle, but he was assiduous with his attentions and consolations to Madame Beauvallon because of her recent loss. His plan was first to get the confidence of the mother before making any attempt to rescue the daughter from what he regarded as little better than perdition. And it was astonishing in what a short time he had obtained the full confidence of Madame and was able to advise her as regard to her worldly matters as well as her spiritual. The burden of his teaching was that severe afflictions were always sent as a means of drawing back to God and his church those of his people who by vanity or wicked complaisance had placed themselves in a position of danger. Many a time by his exhortations he made Madame feel how vain she had been of that dinner at the Governor's, of the picnic, and of the chance of her daughter being allied to a prominent English family. "Is it possible," she would bitterly say to herself, "that my husband had to be taken from me in such an awful manner to bring me back to my duty? God forgive me!"

Estelle had never been confirmed and her religious instructor without even asking her whether she desired to be so, took it for granted, and began a course of instruction to prepare her for the rite. At the time of her engagement to Jack, Estelle had looked forward without the least compunction to becoming a Protestant, for in truth religion sat pretty lightly on the class to which she belonged, that is, the dogmas of religion, for they had all been brought up in the tenets and practice of the Catholic faith, and the women at least paid a fair amount of attention to the outward forms of religion. The men were almost wholly imbued, like the majority of French men in the towns, with sceptical views, yielding only such respect to the Church, and attending such services, as to prevent any open rupture. The priests knew the spiritual condition of the men perfectly, and did not attempt to worry them, but on the contrary joined their breakfasts, and card parties, and were thus all things to all men, as well as paying constant and zealous attention to the spiritual wants of the women.

When Père Vendredi began to map out for Estelle a course of instruction which would take her several months of study and preparation she began seriously to question herself whether this was right in view of her engagement. She had never spoken to Jack on the subject of religion, and he had never spoken to her, but she had almost taken it for granted that she would require to be nominally at least a Protestant. She feared to speak to her mother, as she saw that day by day she was becoming more and more under the influence of the Abbé, and indeed she had no doubt whatever that her mother would decide as the Abbé wished. She shrank from opening her mind to Jack. Indeed a something, she knew not what, not a coldness, for it was far from that yet, but an absence of that entire trust in the devotion of each other, seemed to be growing up between them. She felt from not having seen him since her father's death that she could not write to him exactly as before, for she feared he was becoming lukewarm and she could not be so unmaidenly as to appear to woo him back if he wished to go. The form of words in which they addressed each other was the same, but the undefinable spiritual essence was gone. So was the flower, perfect in its every part, but without the perfume. Her letters were now so difficult to write as she had to ponder whether each phrase was the right one to use, and did not appear unmaidenly in its warmth, and they were still more difficult because she had now little time for disposal.

The Father was so exacting with her religious instruction that it occupied her hours in place of minutes, and her prescribed devotions were also of an inordinate length. Nor did she feel she could turn with any amount of satisfaction to Aunt Clémence. She was not a devotee as her mother bade fair to become, on the contrary she was rather too worldly and sceptical in nature. She did not hesitate to make fun of Père Vendredi himself, to question the purity of his motives, and the quality of his charity for others. Aunt Clémence was a diligent reader, but not in works of devotion. She read the *Feuilletons** of all the French newspapers which arrived by the mail, and it must be added, all the French novels which she could lay hold of, but these she tried as far as possible to keep from Estelle. The latter had once, out of curiosity, taken up one in which her Aunt seemed to be more than usually interested – it was a novel of Georges Sand's, the burden of which was that if a woman loved a man she would follow him and continue to love him whatever in his baseness he might do, even to selling her to another, and assisting the purchaser to gain possession. The girl had laid it down horrified at the results of the broad brush with which the artist worked, and her idea. She feared therefore that Aunt Clémence would not be able to enter into her doubts and distractions, probably looking at confirmation as mere form, and that it signified little in what Church one was confirmed, so that it enabled you to pay a decent amount of attention to religious observances for the sake of a good example.

Thrown back on her own resources poor Estelle thought her lot a very hard one. She was not conscious that these very self-doubts and attempts at solving difficulties, were in themselves a work of education fitting her infinitely better for the life before her. She could not make up her mind to rebel against the Abbé, she could not and would not at present touch upon the subject in writing to Jack, she decided not to speak to her mother, and she abstained from consulting her aunt. She did not the less, however, ponder much within herself, and in reading the religious books the priest had given her, in place of striving to understand the text, her mind was very often trying to solve the puzzle which had thus been presented.

As for Jack Montmorency, he also on his part had had much to think of. Scarcely had he assumed his duties at Mahebourg when he received a letter from his father with reference to his engagement, not as he expected severely blaming him, but in the kindest manner pointing out the difficulties of his position, and requesting him to think over them carefully. Indeed the letter was so much to the purpose that we see no reason why it should not be given entire:–

Three Poplars. —shire. June 27th 18–.

My dear Jack
Your mother and I were certainly unprepared for your letter announcing your engagement, which you see we have left unanswered for a mail or two. But as we notice from your other letters since received that you make reference to your position as if all were quite fixed, we cannot do otherwise than wish you joy, and to send our united love to your fiancee, with our best and warmest wishes for your mutual health and happiness. I presume you do not intend to get married either immediately

---

* serialised novels.

or soon, as you are so young yourself, and the lady appears from your description to be scarcely ready for this serious step. It is possible therefore that we may see you home before the event takes place, and we need not say that if the young lady's parents think of taking a trip to the old country to allow their daughter to see a little of the world that we invite them to make their home here.

Should we be wrong in this, and indeed whether you intend an immediate marriage, or after a year or two of waiting, which we would much prefer and strongly recommend, there are one or two subjects, which I as your father, Jack, am bound to bring to your notice, however lightly young men may regard these things, as upon them may depend very much if not the whole of your future happiness.

In the first place I presume the young lady, from what I recollect of Mauritius, although it is very many years since I was there as a middy and my ideas were rather hazy on these subjects, is a Roman Catholic in her religion. Now living as we do in a tolerant country, especially at a time when many of the best Christians in our own church are seriously questioning whether the schism of 300 years' ago has not gone too far, and whether we ought not in our observances to hark back to some of those celebrated in the old days, I need not tell you that neither your mother nor I are the least likely to raise any objections on that score. But it is always to be guarded against if possible that the husband and wife should belong to different churches. A domestic schism of this kind is very apt to produce dispeace, especially after the children, to whom you must look forward, come the length of being educated. We take it for granted you do not yourself propose to leave the Church of your fathers and of your Lord and country, and therefore it would be advisable in every way if you were to sound the young lady herself, and if she has no great objections to the course to get her to promise to allow whatever church you may select. Our communion is wide enough to embrace many shades of Christian belief, but I need not remind you, although our estate is very small compared with others, that it would be productive of great inconvenience if the heir should be brought up in any other way. Indeed your old friends Parchment & Parchment have written me very strongly on this subject, but that is all I need say on this point.

And now comes one not less delicate and important. The question of health. I have spoken above of the necessity of looking forward to the results of marriage in the birth of children. We have all, thank God, had excellent constitutions, and inheriting as you have both your mothers' excellent health and my own, the lady's parents need have no fear on that score as regards you. But frankly, Jack, we don't want the breed spoiled. Putting it on the lowest possible footing it is still of the utmost consequence that you be able to look forward to the chance of having children free from any hereditary taint of disease. Dr Podgers who is as often here as ever, but without getting any fees, was you may recollect, although I daresay you were too young to take notice of all these little details, in the navy at the same time as myself; we were messmates in fact when we were in Mauritius, but he being much older – and besides it was his profession – learned much more about these things than I did. He tells me that the danger of an hereditary disease of a very terrible kind is not only possible but probable, and he has begged me to be perfectly frank with you on the subject, not to frighten you against an alliance which you have determined on, but for your own satisfaction and comfort hereafter to make every enquiry which you can do in a cautious and proper way to make sure that the family into which you propose to marry is free from this evil in the blood. If you could by any means consult some family physician or some man of business – probably your banker could put you on the right track, I say, before God, Jack, you are bound, before everything, to make this enquiry.

As to money matters, you will be pleased to hear that we can make you pretty comfortable in this way without finishing ourselves, or in fact altering our income in any way. An Aunt of your mother's who died when you were quite young, left a few thousands to be invested for the heir when he came of age or got married. Young Parchment tells me the fund is now close on ten thou', and this on your marriage, can be invested by the Settlement in any way you desire. It is for such matters as these that we would like you to come home first, as Parchment & Parchment would greatly prefer it to sending out great deeds to such a distance, but do as you please yourself. The money is at your absolute disposal and whenever you choose to draw for it you can have it, and with it I need not say you have your mothers' blessing and mine, for yourself and her whom you desire to make your wife.

Ever your loving father
P.P.M. Montmorency.

Jack knew that his father had little humbug in his composition, but the friendly and affectionate tone of the letter, when he expected expostulations, and remonstrances, touched him to the quick. He went out immediately and took a long walk under the filao-trees at Pointe D'Esny to think over all the serious questions which the letter raised. His feelings were about evenly balanced. He delighted to have the consent of his parents, and was not aware of the ten thousand which was in store for him – but on the other hand the two other points upon which his father had touched troubled him greatly.

The facts which he had accidentally learned on his way down came back to his mind with an unpleasant force. He was the more troubled when he recollected that his fiancee was descended from a family which had a touch of African blood, and he remembered with regret that he had not hinted this to his father who had been so frank and kind to him. His first impression was to take no farther step until he had communicated this fact, and then he thought that it would be much more satisfactory if he could at the same time give undoubted assurances in regard both to the religion and the health. But how could he broach such a subject as the former to Estelle, without running the risk of seeming to raise difficulties with the view of breaking off the match now that her father was dead, and at the very time too when in consequence of that death she had been thrown back more than ever on the consolations of the Church in which she had been brought up. While she in her lonely room with the forbidding treatises before her which the Abbé had presented was wondering how she ought to approach the subject with Jack, he, pacing under the no less lonely filao trees beside the murmuring sea was considering the same question, and as the evil luck which seems sometimes to preside over the destinies of men would have it, neither had the courage to write frankly to the other. As to the question of health Jack felt an utter repugnance at the idea of speaking to any one even most confidentially on the subject. What if she were to hear of it, she so sensitive and spirituelle! It would kill her, no, whatever the risk there can be no enquiry. Tossed about upon this sea of doubt, Jack became silent and absorbed and as soon as the duties of the day were over tried to get away to have solitary walks. This was not unnoticed by his brother officers who came to the conclusion that the "old folks" had forbidden the marriage. Darcy, who had been very reticent of late, as he in fact, had a little affair of his own in hand which made him rather sensitive to banter and ridicule, at last spoke to Jack on the subject, and was really pleased to hear that not only did the parents not refuse their consent but that some money to which he was entitled was set apart for him as soon as he wished it.

"Will it come off immediately?" continued Darcy.

"No. Well I don't know. I cannot say for certain as the unfortunate accident has prevented me speaking to Estelle about it. And besides there are other things — there are some things — there are a few arrangements — there are — are — hang it, Darcy," he added as a sudden thought struck him, "you are my dearest friend out here, and are to be my best man, read the letter for yourself and we can talk about it again." So saying Jack put his father's letter into Darcy's hands, seized his hat and gun, and went out for one of his usual solitary saunters.

Nothing would satisfy the juniors until they had a picnic to the Islands on the reefs at the entrance to Mahebourg harbour as it was called, but really simply the usual opening in the reef which is found opposite the mouth of a river. At one time a faction of the troops had always been posted on the Islands, to guard the entrance, and the barracks and houses still remained intact with the tombstones of many gallant fellows who had there died. An officer's wife had just joined who was a woman of remarkable beauty. She had been for some little time in Port Louis and when there had been present at one or two entertainments, and her beauty was such that when she entered a room there was a pause while every eye was turned to her, the men with admiration, the women with envy and with sincerely critical intentions, as the way she turned the heads of all gentlemen whether married or single was notorious. As in every similar case it is difficult to say in what her beauty consisted. Her complexion was perfect, pure white and pink, and her shoulders and neck of the most delicate white. Her hair was a kind of light auburn and it was said to be of wonderful length. The feature of her face however was the eyes. She did not appear to wish to use them with any destructive effect, but they had the power nevertheless of bewitching most men, and many of the more staid ones who were proof, as they thought, against such follies had made fools of themselves. The war which she unconsciously excited raged with great violence.

The women all declared that such a complexion was not natural and that she painted. Her pearly teeth were fake, her hair purchased, and if they could they would also have insisted that her shoulders had been made white by cosmetics and that no woman who was what she ought to be would wear her dress so décolleté, merely to show off her skin. The lady in fact having seen a good deal of the world in continental towns, and having been much in the society of men on long expeditions on horseback, and in the life of a barracks, had a freedom of manner which contrasted with the prudes of her own sex. She was too transparently courageous to be other than everything she ought to be, but that did not prevent her character being made the subject of conversation among the French as well as the English. On her arrival at Mahebourg the youngsters wished to show her something of the place, and to have the pleasure of asking some people to meet her. Pig had also the deep design of getting Jack to pay some attention to her when he hoped that on the principle of a counter irritant he would be cured of moping.

The affair came off one afternoon and was in every sense a success. The Isle de la Passe was visited in boats from the shore. The visitors duly peered down into the blue depths of the sea at the entrance to endeavour to distinguish the wreck of an English ship which was sunk there by the French in 1810.[†] The lighthouse was inspected,[†] standing up grimly facing the great Southern ocean which breaks in foam on the rocks. The epitaphs on the tombstones were deciphered. An excellent dinner was eaten composed in part of fish caught by some of the party and cooked in the ashes of a fire which had been kindled. After the repast there was song, and joke and laughter, the Irish gift of repartee being not confined to the men present, and after the songs, when the party were waiting for the moon to rise for the row home, there was a brew of punch. Stimulated by this compound, as by their own love of mischief and frolic, the youngsters, led of course by Pig the youngest of all, began to carry down the floors of the buildings, the rafters, the flooring which they tore up and every piece of wood upon which they could lay their hands, and piled them on the fire until the blaze lighted up all the Isle, and the Lighthouse and the sea, and made the people assemble in crowds on the beach as they believed it was a ship on fire. After the moon rose there was a pleasant row home with more songs and choruses.

Pig's counter irritant to cure Jack of his melancholy was only too successful. He had joined the party without any thought that it could be wrong for him to go with his brother-officers, and once in for an afternoon of fun his natural flow of spirits returned to him, and he not only made himself agreeable generally, but particularly agreeable to the new-comer, the fair Syren. He kept close to her side the whole day. When they sat down he feasted himself upon her eyes, he applauded more than anyone else when she sang, and himself sang songs of love at her invitation. He had fallen like so many others for the moment under the spell. Had there been no one but the party from the Barracks no harm would have been done. But the daughter of a neighbouring planter and her aunt were present and they having correspondents in town gave an animated description of the picnic and all that had occurred to their friends so that before Jack had done with his squad next afternoon all had been told to Madame Beauvallon.

The morning had indeed been a trying one for Madame. She had found Estelle in tears not on account of her dear father, but because the time for the post from Mahebourg had passed, and there was nothing from Jack. He had become more and more remiss in his correspondence, at first because of the pressure of his duties, and now from the difficulty in which he was placed by the letter from his father, and his wish not to write until he could tell Estelle all the good news about that consent, and his being in an independent position as regards money to marry at once. But on Madame Beauvallon going to her banker, who was the agent of an English banking company, he congratulated her on her daughter's prospects. Before she could ask what he meant, he, never dreaming that Jack had not himself told all, as the news was now several days old, incautiously let out that they were authorised by the head office in London to cash Jack's draughts for £10,000 so soon as he should require it for the purpose of his marriage. Deeply mortified that she should have received that information, which implied that his parents had consented to the match, from other lips than his own, she came too rapidly to the conclusion that Jack wished to conceal from them the consent of his parents in order to found a plea upon their refusal to break off the engagement. "He must have learned that we were poor," she murmured to herself, "and will prefer to seek another ten thousand to add to his own."

And then her jealousy about the tinge of black blood rose up and blinded her reason by the excess of anger which the thought aroused. "Yes, yes a momentary passion; he would have ruined my daughter if he could have got the chance, and now he throws her up because he sees some colour about myself and my relatives. Contemptible English puppy!" It was too much for her, and hoping, strangely enough, that it would help to dry Estelle's tears, and that she would view it in the same light, she foolishly went and told all to her daughter and sister. When she heard her mother raving in this manner against her lover, her accepted suitor, the heart of poor little Estelle was like to break. She sobbed herself into a fever, and Madame Beauvallon had only left her for a moment in the care of Aunt Clémence, to attend to some household duty, when Isidore Amirantes called.

Tempted to deny herself, she deemed it better policy to receive him, and to learn the news about Pompadour and Lorraine. The special object of Isidore was to press to be allowed to see Estelle, as Lucille had faithfully communicated to him the turn of affairs as regarded Madame Beauvallon, and that Estelle did not receive from the English officer nearly so many letters as before. When the mother told him Estelle was sick, Isidore jumped to the right conclusion although he said nothing, but he begged he might be allowed to leave a bouquet for her sick chamber. There was much chit-chat to tell about all the different occurrences on the estate. Isidore mentioned there was a very bad spirit among some of the men, and that his father had been obliged to punish a good number. The people on Lorraine were now getting so much of their own way that the example was catching for the Coolies of the other estates. Respectful and kind as ever, and with a flow of talk and animal spirits which never flagged, he kept Madame occupied and amused for quite an hour, and she could not refuse him the permission for which he again asked to send in a bouquet for Estelle's room.

He had not been long gone when a note arrived from the Notary stating that he had learned, and he thought it right to let her know, that M. Amirantes père had purchased up the first mortgage on Lorraine having given it was believed a rather handsome douceur to induce the holder to relinquish it. The old gentleman had himself carried through the whole transaction. "Ah, the beginning of the end," said the widow, wearily and bitterly. "At the first favourable moment now, that is, the first moment he hears we are embarrassed, he will serve his commandement, and the Estate will be sold. Oh that I had a son like Isidore to protect me now that my husband is gone." And then the tempter whispered, "Why not Isidore as a son-in-law, and there need be no fear of the Estate going." In Estelle's condition she did not think of communicating the news to her but she and Aunt Clémence had a long conference on the subject, the latter dwelling with much more satisfaction upon the prospect of Jack with ten thousand pounds for Estelle, than Isidore with his eventual right to the mortgage his father had purchased, and with both estates stricken by the drought.

The series of remarkable events for this day was continued by the receipt of one of the handsomest bouquets which Isidore could procure and for which he had sent to the Botanical Gardens at Pamplemousses, and a note from him to say that he had arranged for flowers to be sent to them from the Gardens late on the evening before the Fête des Morts* which was approaching, in order that they might have wreaths ready for the tomb, and placing his carriage at their disposal for the occasion. "How very very thoughtful, Clémence, Isidore has become. If he has sown his wild oats and becomes steady, he will prove a very successful man."

The day closed by Clémence herself receiving from her correspondent at Mahebourg a full and complete account of the picnic, and of the appearance, dress and manner of the Syren, and of the most particular (thrice underscored) attentions which Mr Montmorency had paid to her.

"A picnic," blubbered Madame Beauvallon, "and the father of Estelle so recently buried. Oh, the unfeeling wretch. Clémence, how can you any longer think of such a man as the husband of our own child. If he had had a spark of love for her or respect for us or feeling for him who has been taken from us, he would even for decency's sake have kept some semblance of

* All Souls Day.

mourning. But there he is already singing and making bonfires, and paying attention to that odious woman." Clémence had really nothing to say. She was herself shocked, and though unwilling to give up the idea of Jack for Estelle, thought his conduct had been perfectly indefensible.

Chapter 14
Partings and Remembrances

ONE OF JACK'S FAVOURITE RETREATS WAS TO GO OUT to Blue Bay ostensibly for the purpose of fishing but really because he could there enjoy perfect quiet and repose, and could dream of his lady love, and muse over all the difficulties which had started up in his path. On the one side of the bay were the tall filaos of the plantation which stretched all along the coast, and on the other young coconuts with their graceful sweeping fronds, which had been planted on an abandoned sugar estate. The water of the bay was the still, clear, deep blue-green of sea within the reef, and in rowing slowly up to the head of the bay you looked back upon the mound of white foam caused by the waves of the great ocean mounting on the outer barrier. A distant moan could be heard, but it was too far off to observe the motion of the waves. The colours were everywhere so brilliant and perfect! There was one green of the filao (an *Auracaria*) and another green of the coconut palm, there was one blue of the sky flecked with white clouds, and another blue of the sea within the reefs shut in by the mound of foam. The corals below were like the shrubs and flowers of a parterre, the fish which swam above them or sheltered in their branches were tinted with all the exquisite spots and freckles which nature can produce, the very shell-fish for bait which lay in the skiff were of cream shading into yellow, spotted with red, and the inside of the shell of a ripe glossy beauty such as no human artist could hope to imitate.

Dreaming in such a scene Jack alternately felt his course to be clear or overshadowed just as the bay sparkled with sunlight or became shaded for a brief space by the passing cloud. On one of these occasions the time had passed quite unheeded and the day was far spent when he thought he heard a faint shout from the shore at the edge of the filaos. He thought he could discern a figure waving to him, but having little doubt it was only some trifling business connected with the troops, he felt the reverse of thankful for the interruption. As he neared the spot, resting on his oars and looking around he could make out that it was Darcy Connaught, and so quickening and putting more strength into his stroke he made the little skiff skim along and sent her bow up among the broken shells and sand of the shore.

"News with a vengeance, Jack," said Darcy, "We are ordered off to Natal."

"The devil!" was the reply, in a half amazed, half dubious voice. "Now what a confounded bore!"

"Well you are the only man among us who thinks so, but we can feel for you all the same, Jack."

"What is the matter, any row amongst the Caffres?"

"We don't know rightly, and of course no one has seen any of the officers of the ship."

"Good heavens, you don't mean to say that the Transport to take us has arrived?"

"She has; you will have to moderate your own transports, my boy, and go!"

"The devil!" ejaculated Jack once more, "did ever anything happen so untimely. One would have been so glad to go if things had been properly arranged."

"Important private affairs – it won't do Jack; it would not look well if there is any chance of active service in the field, and besides we know old General Gommeril would not listen to it."

"But he must listen if I prefer my request, or I will resign my commission."

"It would not be accepted, and you would not only get into a row with the General, but into disgrace at the Horse Guards, and with your father. Besides I don't know if it is not the best thing that could have happened."

"What do you mean?" asked Jack almost fiercely.

"Oh nothing of that kind, Jack, you may be sure. If I thought you could leave the girl, or do anything in the least disgraceful I would be the first to let you know of it. But don't you see your father wishes you not to be in any hurry, perhaps you will be able to get a run home from Natal before you return here, to arrange business matters as the Governor would like, and then we may hear, I or you, without making any special enquiries at all, something which we hope may be satisfactory on the other subject. She will write freely as you may suppose – page after page by every mail, Jack."

A cloud passed over Jack's brow as he recollected that his own correspondence had already begun to flag, and now he remembered he had had no letters from her either for some days.

"What transport is it?" he at length said.

"The old Himalaya – she is always on the move bringing joy or sorrow as the case may be to the service. Come along, we are to march in to-morrow. You will have a busy night of it before you get your passes all filled in, your reports prepared and your baggage packed."

"So soon as that?"

"Yes, to-morrow – that's sudden," replied Darcy – "I like Natal I must say."

"Shall I row you back?"

"No, let us walk through the filaos once more. Mahmode can come for the skiff. Besides we will walk faster, and you can take farewell of this blissful retreat. There is someone here who will be weeping for me tonight, but, by Jove, I am glad to get out of it."

"Virtuous man, and you were all but threatening me a moment ago!"

"Oh yours is… autre chose, mon cher. Won't I give them lots of French in Natal where the beggars don't know when you make mistakes!"

Yes, they were ordered off to Natal. The transport was waiting for them in harbour, and on the day after they would steam away westwards with snorting engines regardless of the [tearful eyes] and the heavy hearts which would be left behind. Jack laboured all night squaring up his reports for his superiors, and when he awoke in the morning after an hour or two feverish sleep, the troops had already marched. The Major was waiting at breakfast for him, to take a place beside him in his dog-cart for the drive to town.

Scarcely had he arrived at the Barracks, and was looking forward with mingled pleasure and pain to his meeting with Estelle, when a packet was put into his hands, which when he received, although he knew nothing whence it came, made his heart beat violently as he felt that it was something fateful and crushing. It was from Madame Beauvallon, and when it was opened the trinkets and jewels he had given to Estelle, and the letters he had written her fell out on his table – while with eyes scarcely able to read from the mist of shame, grief and stupefaction which blinded them he made out the following words. "Madame Beauvallon begs to return to Monsieur le Lieutenant Montmorency his letters and gifts to her daughter, as she is satisfied that M. Montmorency by his recent unfeeling conduct intended to insult the family with which he ungenerously pretended at one time to court an alliance."

"What in the name of all that is holy have I done," exclaimed Jack as he stood aghast at the announcement he had read. "It surely cannot be that they have heard anything of the picnic and been offended at my going there. Such a trifle, too. If this is to be the way of it could we ever get on together?"

And then he thought of Estelle, to whom he was on the point of flying to communicate to her the news of their departure. Could she be a party to this sudden breaking off of the engagement for so trifling a cause. He thought how their acquaintance and love commenced, and of all her gentleness and beauty, her apparent trust in him and her love, all to be shattered in a moment because he went with his comrades for an afternoon's outing! There must be something else than this, Estelle cannot be so fickle and heartless, and there must be someone destroying my character in the interests of a rival. "The cub!" he almost screamed to himself. "Could it be he?"" And yet although they had known him all their lives Madame Beauvallon equally with Estelle favoured his suit in preference to that of Isidore.

Urged by desperation, Jack determined to get to the bottom of the affair and like a true Englishman taking the wrong way about it, rushed off to call for Madame Beauvallon. "Not at home," replied the boy who had already received his general instructions. "Mademoiselle?" "Sick," was the anvswer. Once more, while his colour went and came, he assayed with the name of Miss Clémence, "Not at home." He heard a door open and someone pass from a neighbouring room. Hoping it would be Madame Beauvallon he pushed past the boy, and found it was Ernestine. He could not in his agitation recall French enough to ask what it all meant, but Ernestine knew all about it, and his agitation was question enough of itself. "Madame is not at home," said she aloud – and then dropping her voice to a whisper she said as she led Jack gently towards the door – "Assez pour le présent – Elle vous aime toujours."

"But I leave tomorrow Ernestine – am ordered off on duty – perhaps never to return?"

Ernestine stood motionless, she had not heard of this, and considered the resolution of the Mistress to be one of which she would soon repent. But the boy, proud to carry out his orders, had shut the door, just as Ernestine screamed rather than ejaculated – "Mon Dieu! Mon pauvre enfant!"

The Transport was to sail next afternoon, and in spite of her weakness, in spite of the remonstrances of her mother and aunt, Estelle insisted on going out to see it from the heights as it sailed. The poor girl was sick and ill, her frail frame was little able to endure the rude shocks to which it had recently been subjected, and her mother who doted on her of whom she was the perfect idol, and next to her God the only existence of whom she ever thought, feared that in her zeal for the honour of her family she had gone too far and imperilled the health of her precious child. Beyond therefore objecting and remonstrating on the score of her own health, she could no longer oppose a decision which she saw was not to be moved, and ordering the carriage, she, Estelle and aunt Clémence drove out.

They took a road where at a moderate height they could see the harbour, and the sea beyond. It led up to a house situated at the head of the valley of the Pouce, not a road used for a pleasure drive and in many points it was so high and so unprotected at the sides that at any other time the ladies would have been terrified to have attempted it. It was however the only way to gratify Estelle, and after they had attained a good position they could see the Transport lying well out, still surrounded by swarms of boats and with the Blue Peter flying. "There is the Governor's barge," said the coachman as a large impressive boat with an awning swept out from the shore. Estelle had no doubt Jack was in it. He was so important a person in her mind that she thought he must be equally so in the minds of others. Poor Jack had been on board more than an hour, and was mechanically making his cabin comfortable although his heart was sore and he scarcely knew what he did. The barge contained the General in Command and the Major who was to command the detachment, and as the General simply went to see the troops off and to bear the report that all was right – the moment of departure was very near. Scarcely had he touched the deck when the bell rang to clear the ship, and servants, boatmen, washerwomen, and the friends and associates of the officers who were leaving began to come over the side.

It was a stirring and busy scene. Estelle knelt on the seat of the carriage looking over the folded hood, watching everything with a keen interest, her eyes every now and again filling with tears, and the lump rising in her throat as she thought that he was going perhaps forever – and thus! Oh that she could have seen him for one brief moment, to have given him one embrace, and to have said that she should ever be faithful. But he thought her fickle, he was striving to drive her image from his heart, and he would meet some other who might make him happy! That woman might be going too, and all the sea voyage she would try to steal his heart! Oh how often the ship and harbour, the town and all the view, was blotted out as she could see nothing for her tears. And the two older women wept silently with her.

At length a white churn of foam appeared astern. "She is going now," said the coachman, and gently, almost imperceptibly, the noble looking ship went slowly astern until she could find sea-room to turn her prow to the ocean. That effected, in the stillness of the air and in the dead stillness of these watchers, they thought they heard the tinkle of the bell which sounded "full steam ahead!"

Great gusts of black smoke came from the funnel, contrasting so strangely with the white ship, the blue sea and the golden western sky; the gusts of smoke came faster and faster and now appeared as one long stream of black cloud, shadowed in the sea. The coast burst into one glorious glow of richness and colour as the sun descended, and in a moment became cold and grey, the steamer disappeared round a projecting headland, and Estelle slipped back into her seat, cold and pale as the sky, with the thought in her heart that her day of enchantment and love and pride had also passed, and that there was nothing for her now but night, night, night. Night and the Grave.

When the carriage returned Mahmode, Jack's Indian servant was in waiting. Estelle did not see him, saw nothing in fact as Ernestine assisted her to her room. But he came forward when the two ladies descended, and asked if they wanted a servant. They knew him to be a good one, and servants who had been trained to wait at English tables were generally preferred. Madame Beauvallon looked at Aunt Clémence, who nodded in acquiescence.

"How much?" said Madame to the youth. "Huit piastres!"

"Bon," was the reply, "demain"* – and the engagement was completed. Estelle was agreeably surprised to see the boy at work next morning. "Bonjour, Mamzelle," he said, and looking furtively around to see that no one was near, took from his *kupra* a letter which he handed to her saying simply, "Mishié,"** and going on with his work as if nothing had occurred. Estelle seized it with a burning hand, and having secreted it soon returned to her room where having locked herself in she tore open the letter and read as follows:

My dearest Estelle,
For you must permit me to address thee thus yet once more. I have little time left to write, and my heart is too sad to permit me to say much, but I cannot leave the Island without one word of adieu. I know not in what I have offended, but if I have it was without thought or intention of hurting the feelings of thee, my fiancee, or of those who are dear to thee. I cannot believe that thou, Estelle, wish to renounce me forever, after our hours of love and constancy, after our engagement, after thou hast won my heart and I thought, alas, that I had won thine. Not even the cruel blow which I have received will alter my affection towards thee, but if it be thy desire – though God forbid it – to throw me off forever I can only bow my head and resign thee – I presume to another – I have had no word from thyself to say so, and cannot take as final on such a

---

* – "Eight piasters." – "Very well… tomorrow"
** Mishié = Monsieur

subject any word but thine own. Oh may it never be spoken! If it be, I feel that life to me will be a heavy burden, that my profession will have no charm for me, friendship no colour, and the summer no sun. For thee and in thee and with thee, Estelle, I have learned to live and move, thou hast taken my heart and all, and whatever thou mayest decide, it must ever remain with thee although you may prize it not. Thy dead father believed I was to be thine, and thou wast to be mine, we had his consent, and a few days ago I got the consent of my father to our union. I had waited in the hope of being able to see you personally, I was eager to fly to meet thee and to claim the fulfilment of thy promise when that cruel message came. Someone must have been whispering falsehood into thy mother's ear – she whom I loved so much, who was ever so kind to me! What can I have done, what can she believe I have done, that in one moment her friendship should be turned into hatred. Let me hope that she will soon be undeceived. If we never meet again, for time flies and I must be abroad, farewell, my beloved. – Oh may the Good God bless thee and keep thee! Oh may he shower down his best blessings on thy head! May he shelter thee from all evil and endow thee with all happiness. Do not forget me, Estelle, think sometimes of me, when I am far away. I will never cease to think of thee, never cease to love thee, and never, God helping me, ever love another. – Farewell, farewell.

　　Thine to the death

　　J.R. Montmorency

We turn from the restless torture of the poor sufferer, thus driven to seem cold towards one who was so true, to what was taking place in another part of the town. Isidore gave a dinner that evening at the Flore Mauritienne to a few of his intimate friends, and indeed they might almost be termed accomplices. He was their leader, and they, for favours frequently received, were devoted to his interest. Not a word was said about the departure of the English officer but all understood perfectly well why their friend was in such pre-eminently good humour, and why the "Flore" had not wines good enough for their entertainment. The dinner had been given also for another reason. Isidore had need once more of the services of the press. His father had been getting on worse than ever with his Coolies, and having taken the law into his own hand, not only in striking, kicking and beating them perpetually, but imprisoning them in houses, cutting their wages, and falsely accusing them of being deserters to get the Magistrate to punish them, a band of them had gone to the Governor's country house to complain, and he had, in answer to their petition, promised to look into their grievances.

　　This unprecedented step on the part of the Coolies, this still more unprecedented step on the part of any Governor, had filled the minds of many of the planters with fear and indignation. Isidore wished the editors to take up the subject, and by making an attack upon the government to force them to assume the defensive, and thus prevent any of those formal enquiries which might not end satisfactorily for Pompadour at present. The Coolies in fact had not been paid for several months, for the estate, as we have seen from the stoppage of the interest of the poor girl in France was not paying its way. The present crop did not promise to be a particularly good one. Nothing was done by positive promise or arrangement, but the topic of the hour came to be the dangerous state of disorder into which the Island would be thrown if the Coolies were encouraged to go with their unfounded complaints to the head of the Colony and if they should be listened to. The discussions of the night were thus duly reflected with fiery and frothy leading articles which began to appear.

While these boon companions were making merry in town, a number of Coolies had met at a lonely spot on the estate of Pompadour. It was in the dead of night, they sat crouching behind a cane road which at that point was considerably raised from having to crop a gully. They were plotting a crime, and therefore anxious to escape all observation. One of the employés, preceded by a boy carrying a lantern, had passed along shortly before from some merrymaking and never imagined that more than a dozen men were crouching below who might have risen up to murder him if he had been the game they sought after. They saw him, as the light shone on his face, but he passed their retreat utterly unconscious of their presence. If he had discovered them it is possible what afterwards occurred might have been prevented, and the whole course of this history been changed, but he passed homewards and the plotters continued their talk, arranged their several parts, and as is not uncommon with Indians went dramatically through the details of the act they had in contemplation.

The days glided on, and All Saints and All Souls days were near at hand. The latter – la Fête des Morts – is one of the most touching festivals in Mauritius. Keeping up the old French customs, the habit of the whites to repair to the Cemeteries to place wreaths and bouquets on the tombs has spread through all the coloured and black population, and even very many of the Indians, especially those who are Creole-born, thus pay honor to their dead. At early morn when the first service of the Catholic chapels begin, the graveyards become crowded, and the tomb stones become gay, if such an expression were allowable, with garlands. Here an old woman whose locks of snow tell of her great age, and of her having in all probability been a slave in the old time, may be seen kneeling beside a grave marked by a humble wooden cross, and depositing upon it bouquets corresponding to the number of those who are beneath – kneeling there and weeping, and as it were whispering to the dead that she will not be long now of also coming to the narrow bed. There a father with hat in hand, surrounded by a group of children has decorated afresh the mother's grave, and the little ones who have already had a holiday gathering the flowers, wonder why he weeps, as they but dimly remember their lost and loving "Maman." There is a young man of colour standing respectfully aside and half hiding himself behind the tomb stones, waiting till the white sons and daughters have gone from the grave of his father, that he may furtively add his wreath to theirs. His mother lies apart; he has duly honoured her grave which is covered by the choice flowers he has culled for her; even in death his father and she are divided; but it will make no difference hereafter, in that land where there is no marrying or giving in marriage. How they crowd in, the young and old, the tottering grandparents and the wee toddling children, all bearing flowers.

It is thus that they who lie below have come and gone. All ages have come to the silent house, one by one, ceaselessly, until they have peopled this city of the dead with a countless population. The old generations have passed away. No one now remembers them. Their dust has long mingled with the kindred dust, and the very memory of their labours has dropped into oblivion. Their sons and daughters have followed them. They, remembered for a day, will in their turn be forgotten, and new generations of children will scatter flowers on the graves of those who have come with their childish prattle this morning to gaze at the flowers and to lay their own little offerings down. The mansions of the Father's house must needs be many, for the human race steps swiftly from the cradle to the grave. It is so strange to see many races of mankind mingling together in this celebration of the common doom. And yet it is as it ought to be, and is a spectacle which teaches yet once more the profound truth that God hath made of one blood all the nations of the earth.

Estelle, and her mother, and Aunt Clémence were early astir. At a late hour the previous night a great heap of the most beautiful flowers had arrived from the Gardens, all wet with the dews of the night, provided by the thoughtful care of Isidore, and they were now being worked up into crosses, wreaths and bouquets for that grave at Pamplemousses which was not there on the last Fête des Morts. The carriage was ready waiting and they soon drove off. How sweet the morning air, how tempered the heat as the sun had not yet mounted above the hills which cast their grateful shade on the plain. The trees by the wayside were putting on their summer garb. The mangoes were covered with their straw-coloured flower, exhaling a delicate perfume, the red tinted young leaves of the banyan looked like flowers in the glints of light which fell on them, the flamboyants were in their richest, densest robes of green with only here and there a crimson flower beginning to open. Crowds were passing and repassing, some clad in mourning, others gay in holiday dress. Frequent carrioles with parties from the country bringing to town those whose relatives were buried there, or groups of Indian women, with their lithe forms clad in gay calicoes carried their bundles easily and lightly, as it seemed from the graceful poise of their heads. Children naked as they were born ran with their little faces gleaming alongside of the carriages, and then rolled in the grass and dust of the side paths.

Past the village of Terre Rouge they went, and then the square tower of the church of Pamplemousses could be seen, the coachman as he neared the entrance to the graveyard gradually checking his career until he drew up quietly and noiselessly at the gate. The cemetery was already filled. The groups the ladies met on the paths stepped respectfully aside to let these new mourners pass. All knew them, and could feel for them in their own grief, the blow had been so sudden and terrible. With slow and sorrowful steps they approached the grave. With their own hands the ladies laid their offerings and hung the wreaths as if it were truly an altar they had raised and were beautifying. Long they stood in silent converse with the dead, until the morning sun became fierce in its heat, and Ernestine, who had come from the graves of her own people, drew them away to return to town.

The time of year when the festival occurs is a beautiful one. It is the beginning of the summer months in the climes South of the Equator, the cooler days have added vigour to the population, the new sugar crop has commenced, and the hurricane season, which indeed sits lightly on a population accustomed to such episodes, has not yet begun. The following description of the day and season was penned in the island on All Saints Day in one of those pleasant years which have gone to the grave of all the years, and in memory of it I now hang up the wreath on its tomb–

> The sky already darkens with the clouds
> Which bear la pluie de Tous-Saints; Nature
> True to her laws, brings forth the season's gifts,
> And now our scanty streams from bank to bank
> Will pour a fuller flood – the drooping herbs
> Will burst in brighter beauty, earth with flowers
> Her bosom deck, life everywhere and growth.
> The first rich drops now stain my page, as here,
> Within an ancient wood, I pen these thoughts –
> To-night, when Mothers dream of culling flowers
> To place tomorrow on the loved one's grave,
> The grateful shower will fall to bless the Rose,
> Begonia, Lily, all the herbs which bloom,
> To make them fit and meet to deck the tomb.
> And if some deem that 'tis the Souls who feel
> The throbbing heart, and with responsive love
> Send cloud and rain to bless and beautify,
> And make their feast-day rich with hues of heaven,
> It is a thought as beauteous as the flowers.
> The air is very still, those sounds I hear
> The women by the stream, the horses champ,
> Chime with the hour –
> The bower which I have sought is near a brook
> Whose sloping banks with velvet moss are clad,
> The tree-fern fronds their graceful shade bestow.
> The ground and trees with snow-white orchids rare;
> Hark how the songsters prattle with their notes!
> From branch to branch, from tree to tree, they flit,
> And chirp and talk, and gargle forth sweet notes,
> They know that summer with its wealth and warmth
> Has come, the time for love, and nests, and song:
> The little "bengali" hops over-head –
> I love to see the gentle creatures near,

They bring us sweeter thoughts and artless songs.
And lo! appears the brilliant "Cardinal" —
He putteth on today his summer robe,
Scarlet as rare flamingoe's wing, or like
That it of all our trees whose crimson flower
Shall soon flush oer the green and brighten all the plain,
Behind him gulfs of blue in heaven, he adds
a wondrous beauty to the scene.
If we but knew the language of the birds
How vain our boasted love! That brilliant thing
Could tell me how he knows the season's change,
How he can imitate the flowers which blow,
And paint with native power his scarlet hue,
Whether to charm his mate, or lure his prey,
Or please created things with radiant hues!
These clouds that come like argosies with freight
Of fruitfulness, whence are they, who hath sent?
The seas no seasons know, and these rich rains
Come with the certainty of sun or star —
What know we of the rain or of its power
Which can impart a life where growth hath ceased,
Or quicken that which if not dead hath slept.
When in the night I hear the welcome shower
Beating with myriad drops on drooping leaves,
Each drop I know its grateful mission hath,
Its influence, its life-restoring balm,
Some little stem to fill with sap, some bud
To swell with bloom, some seed invisible
To which to whisper "Rise, thy time is come,
Earth waits for thee, and all that in thee is!"
Some hue to make the finest flower more fair,
Some pollen to secrete in secret cell,
Or with its elements the cell to weave
As spider weaveth wondrous web at will,
I know that while we sleep all earth will wake,
And weave and work, and work and weave bright things,
The how and why, the why and how all dark,
All dark as night without her beaming stars.

Chapter 15
Temptations and Crimes

LUCILLE WAS NOT PLEASED OR GRATIFIED by the sudden turn of Madame Beauvallon's feeling against Jack. On the contrary, she admired the young Englishman very much. She was so tickled when Jean Le Blanc became jealous of the young officer that she took no pains to disabuse his mind, and even let fall hints, and expressed preferences, which were intended to keep up the delusion. But Jack never having even glanced at her in any way which she could construe into admiration, her enthusiasm for him decreased, and her preference for Isidore led her to desire to do him a service. She was therefore most anxious to convey the tidings of the rupture. The evening before Jack arrived from Mahebourg, having overheard most if not all of the discussions between the sisters, she adroitly managed to get herself sent off to Lorraine, to look after the linen and plate. She was too full of her story and mission to stand upon much ceremony, so believing she could cover her purpose of a visit to Isidore by a pretended visit to the housekeeper at Pompadour she boldly sent for a carriole to La Baie and dressed herself for the occasion in her very best attire. And she certainly looked handsome! But even the coolness of Lucille was put to the proof when Jean himself arrived as the driver of the carriole!

He had just come out of prison, the owner of the vehicle was ill, and had requested Jean to take his place. She knew Isidore disliked Jean, and if the latter was not yet jealous of Isidore he was suspicious of him as of every young white and coloured man in the neighbourhood. It would take very little indeed to light the fire of his jealousy and to make it burn with a fierce ardour. On the other hand with her quick wit she saw how the very boldness of taking Jean with her on such an expedition might be in her favour. It would cover her intention from the inquisitive eye, and it might, and she hoped would, deceive Jean. At all events she could not now turn back. She had hired the carriole for the special purpose of going to Pompadour and to alter her intention would in itself be suspicious. All these things crossed Lucille's mind by intuition in the few moments between her first discerning who was driving the carriole and its arrival in the Cour.* She accordingly resolved not only to make Jean accompany her (and the expectation that Isidore would not like it tickled her vanity amazingly) but in the meantime, and before they started, to

---

* Courtyard.

please him so much by her gracious reception as to deceive him and make his head *virer*,* as she herself inwardly phrased it. Poor Jean's warm greeting was thus more than warmly returned. She tenderly squeezed his hand, and after he had paid his respects to the housekeeper, Lucille took him into her own hut. She soon, as she promised herself, turned the poor fellow's head. "Jean," she said as she shut the door "tell me, hast thou not had a kiss during all these months? Hold." And she took his cheeks between her palms, and gave him such a kiss as would have made any man white or black imagine himself in the Paradise of the Houris. But no more than one.

She kept him in his place, nor did indeed the poor fellow attempt to ask for more. Lucille was to him a goddess, to whom he looked up with boundless admiration, and whose shrine was sacred. She wore a mourning dress on account of Monsieur Beauvallon's death. It suited Lucille somehow, although anything black contrasts so badly as a rule with a coloured complexion. But Lucille had studied the art of dressing. Born in Mauritius she was almost a Frenchwoman in her ways, and above all in her taste and style. She bemoaned to Jean the necessity for wearing mournings, and took out of her chests her dresses to show him, for they had recently been replenished. Madame Beauvallon had declared that she would wear black for the rest of her life, and had divided her silks between Ernestine and Lucille. The latter counted up the months before she could appear in them, and chatted away to Jean of the colours she would wear with this or that, and the ribbons which would match. She shewed him her trinkets, with the pictures of saints on the wall, and as she did so leant on his shoulder, and playfully pulled his hair congratulating him that it had grown so well after having been cut in gaol.

Although she was in fact completely dressed before Jean arrived, she pretended that she was not, and commenced to decorate herself anew. Jean rose up to go, but with an imperative "restez tranquille"** she made him sit down, for the process was wholly for his benefit. She wished to shew Jean some little details to intoxicate him all the more with the sight. She wished him to see that she washed with scented soap like a lady. She took his handkerchief and put Eau-de-Cologne on it first that she might have an excuse for coming near him with her shoulders uncovered. Having loosened and flung out her long hair she brushed it anew and re-adjusted it. She put her leg up on a chair and undid and then tied afresh her garter. "Tenez, Jean,"*** she said to the poor fellow who was speechless with admiration, and felt as if he had suddenly been taken up to the seventh heaven. "I have something here for my friends," and she took out a bottle of maraschino (whence obtained there could be little doubt) and poured him out about half a cup full.

Jean knew there was a pony in the carriole, and that they were going over very rough cane roads, but with Lucille beside him, so gracious and kind, he felt as if he were living a new life. It was his first day of liberty,

* "spin."
** "stay put."
*** "Here you go, Jean."

and such a day! While he was still thrilling under the influence of the lips of the one he had loved so long and devotedly, she was already cogitating how to dispose of him in order that she might visit Isidore in his pavilion.[†] It was partly her reason for delaying a little longer when Jean arrived that she wished the afternoon to be a little more advanced to make quite sure that Isidore would have returned from the fields. She knew the habits of the place well, and was aware that he came in generally about three o'clock to have a bath and get dressed before four. She did not wish to leave Jean and the cariole in the road for she might have to wait some time, and now that she had made up her mind to it she was by no means sorry that Isidore should see Jean and know how she was escorted.

The hut of the housekeeper was in amongst the other huts of the camp, and she feared that if she once went there, it would be difficult for her to get an excuse to go to the mansion house at the back of which stood the pavilion of Isidore. Her bold policy however turned out to be the best. She drove up to the hut of the housekeeper and being told that she was at the great house, she alighted, and requesting Jean to await her return, went in search of old Alice, her friend. That important personage was quite pleased with the visit. Lucille with an address which made every one assist in her purposes, led her, while she left the old woman in the belief that she was leading Lucille, to the back steps of the mansion-in full view of the pavilion. Here they sat talking until Isidore himself made his appearance, in undress, with a towel around his neck as he had come from the bath.

"Is that you, Lucille? What news from town?"

"Oh great news Missié Isidore," she replied, "news you would like to hear."

"You don't say so – shall I come over to you or will you come here," he said, as he put a chair for her in the verandah. Lucille arose to go over to him, and the old housekeeper knowing she was de trop and with a simple but earnest "Prenez-garde, ma fille"[*] went about her own business.

Lucille did not sit down in the verandah. She was let into Isidore's room, and there sitting on his couch, she told him what was really great news for him. It is unnecessary to describe all that took place, the game of Lucille being exactly the same with Isidore as with Jean, only she had to stimulate the one, and repel the other, leaving them both however under the sweet spell of her influence. Isidore on this occasion needed a great deal of repelling, but that did not prevent Lucille from agreeing to come to him again of an evening under the same pretence of paying a visit to the housekeeper.

Jean did not see where Lucille went, nor did he know of the engagement she had formed. The interview was not however unnoticed, nor their arrangement wholly kept secret, for Bhootan's daughter the young Creole Indian whom Isidore had purchased from Bhootan was, unknown to him, in the house, and seeing the "Lady" there, whom she knew well, and of whom by instinct she felt jealous, she had slipt into another apartment where she had heard what made her little heart bitter, and also the arrangement made

---

* "Take care, my girl."

for another visit. Lucille brought away with her on this occasion a diamond pin as a gift, the only thing Isidore could find at the moment. The news was so good he was anxious to make some return. He asked Lucille to get it made up in another form and he would pay for the work. "Take care of it, Lucille, for it is worth ten pounds," and thus so much the richer for her confidences she crossed over in search of the housekeeper. Having found her she walked beside her to her own hut, as if they had never ceased to be in conversation since Lucille arrived. Jean was sitting on the doorstep watching the pony feed, his mind still dwelling on the beauties of Lucille, and proud of her acquaintance with such persons as the housekeeper at Pompadour and other influential people. Bhootan's daughter was also watching at a distance. She asked who the carriole driver was, and on ascertaining asked further whether he was to be married to Lucille. Her informant, one of the negro sugar Coolies, laughed and said, "he would like it, certainly – all La Baie knows Jean has been the lover of Lucille for a very long time." Armed with this information the little woman was not long in making up her mind to the course she would pursue.

After tea with the housekeeper, and a promise cleverly made, in answer to her request for another visit before Lucille returned to town, of a visit some evening after dinner as she was busy at Lorraine with the clearing up and airing of the rooms, Jean and she departed. She had managed so well on this occasion in deceiving Jean though Isidore's kisses were on her lips, which felt so pleasant to her, the foolish coquette that she was, as hers did to Jean, that she boldly asked him to come to drive her when she came again. She would she said acquaint him with the evening fixed.

It was getting dark by the time they returned. The Coolie women were preparing the evening meal, so that a rich smell of curry pervaded the camp. Jean was invited to stay for dinner and Lucille and the housekeeper at Lorraine prepared to entertain him. The former tucking up her dress, both to save it, and to show off her petticoat of which she was vain, began to boil the rice and prepare the curry on a *resso** in the open air. The evening was of that perfect beauty so common in the tropics. A large lustrous star shone in the western heavens which still glowed with sunset, the other stars stole out one by one, the cigales made the trees vocal with their tiny sounds, the smoke from the camp fires rose slowly into the calm air, picturesque figures passing and repassing, the hum of many voices was heard, and the dark was lit up by the lights of many household fires.

Such was the scene where Lucille in the foreground was preparing food for her entranced lover. She kept the housekeeper near her, as she had done enough to turn Jean's head for one day, and after dinner followed by a little rum which she purchased at the Chinaman's shop, she allowed him to depart. She soon herself retired to rest, to gloat over her diamond pin, to recall the caresses of Isidore, to think of the coming interview, and how she ought to deport herself, not forgetting however to say her prayers notwithstanding her

---

* A makeshift oven (Fr. *réchaud*, stove).

avocations for the day, and to smile and whisper as she dropped asleep, when she remembered how foolishly fond he had looked – "Ce pauvre Jean!"*

In a day or two Isidore was free to think of another interview with Lucille. He wrote on a scrap of paper, "Vendredi à huit heures, venez,"** and calling to one of the Indian labourers, the favoured suitor of Lothee, he ordered him to take it to Lorraine and to wait an answer, as he wished for some medicine. It was addressed to "Mlle Lucille à Lorraine." Bhootan's daughter had watched Isidore's every movement since the day Lucille had been in his pavilion, and no sooner had the Coolie left his master's presence than she was beside him: "Where are you going Jebal?"

"To Lorraine," he said. Taking the note from his hand she said "first bring me water for Missié Isidore's room." Undoing the gum of the envelope she took out the little scrap of paper, and hastened to the cottage of one of the mechanics on the Estate, who like so many of the superior workmen was a Creole negro. His little son had attended the Catholic schools, and was often in requisition to read or write letters. For Bhootan's daughter he would do anything as they had often played together, and even now when she had been promoted, they often met, and Augustin received many little gifts, and especially the illustrated newspapers after the mail from his former friend.

"Augustin," she said, "read this for me."

"Friday at 8 o'clock, come," he read and then added "Ah, you have a lover."

"No, no, no," she cried, not foreseeing this application of the document, "not me. Chup chup," she added, "you wicked thing, I won't ask you again if you say that," and ran off to reseal the envelope before Jebal had finished with the water. The letter was delivered to him and he went and brought back from Lucille not medicine, but a verbal message, "Mamzelle veni." It was enough and Isidore was happy, but the little handmaiden had heard too, and she was very unhappy.

There was a second visit to Augustin that day: "Augustin, you know Mamzelle Lucille?"

"Ah yes, I know her well, the maid of Madame Beauvallon."

"You know Monsieur Jean, at La Baie?"

"Oh yes, the man who struck Sergeant… and has been in prison."

"Is it?" said the handmaiden, "I did not know that."

"Yes, Jean Le Blanc, the fisherman. I know him."

"He is the lover of Lucille."

This was a view of it which had not hitherto presented itself to Augustin, but he responded a little doubtfully –

"Peut être!, they were both here a few days ago in a carriole like lovers."

"But you know Monsieur Jean loves Mamzelle Lucille."

"Oh all the world knows that – he is a fool about it – that was why he struck the Serjeant."

"Then, Augustin, will you write for me on a piece of paper, Monsieur

* "Poor Jean!"
** "Friday at 8, come"

Jean, A friend tells you Mamzelle Lucille is to visit Missié Isidore on Friday evening at 8 o'clock."

Augustin hesitated – he thought he had better not mix himself up with the affairs of Monsieur Isidore or he might get himself and his father into trouble. The handmaiden observed his reluctance and taking his hand, looked into his eyes and said, "Ah, Augustin, you will not do that for me."

"I will do all you ask me, Camille," he replied, "but Monsieur Isidore will be angry."

"How can he know," she said disdainfully, but Augustin would not consent, when as they spoke he cried – "Look, there is Monsieur Jean himself, bringing fish for the household!"

And so it was. Jean, all eager to press his suit with Lucille having returned to his old occupation with a determination to make himself independent and rich for her sake.

Camille, quick as thought, but with no motion which savoured of haste, placed herself in his way as he went towards the kitchen, and saying that the housekeeper was in the verandah led him towards the pavilion of Isidore.

While stooping and professing to admire the fish, she took from the basket two beautifully spotted with red and pretended to put them in a plate – but when they wouldn't lie, she brought their heads together as it were accidentally, then laughed a little laugh, and said, "They kiss, like Missié Isidore and Mamzelle Lucille."

Poor Jean leaped as if a serpent had stung him, but she paid no attention, pretending still to make her fish lie as she wished, saying with a mocking air, "do not go, do not go, my dearest, one kiss more," and then breaking into a Creole song she sang:

> *pourquoi na ouli content moi*
> *Jeune fille – Jeune fille!* *

Jean stood gasping for breath like the fish which were still alive but Camille did not once look on him.

At last he was able to articulate with a ghastly attempt at a smile –"You know Mamzelle Lucille, Madame?"

"Ah oui," she answered, "she sometimes comes here – she was here on Monday last."

"Yes, yes," said Jean, somewhat relieved, "I drove her over to visit the housekeeper."

"To visit the housekeeper," she replied, with a laugh, "oh yes, to visit the housekeeper," and again another laugh.

Jean was not relieved – he hastily added, "Missié Isidore sometimes see Mamzelle Lucille?"

"Oh oui, but no great things, only a little plaisanterie – Missié Isidore he sit on the sofa (pointing to it in the room) and he say (imitating the action of

* "Why don't you love me, young girl, young girl"

one trying to steal a kiss) 'donnez-moi, donnez-moi, Lucille, mon amie, ma Chérie;'* and Mamzelle if she not give she let him take plenty, plenty."

"But, Madame, you do not mean, you do not say – but it cannot be, Mamzelle Lucille from Lorraine."

"You think I do not know her. Do you know her, Monsieur Jean? If you like to see a little bit of fun, you come Friday evening and I let you see. But you must not tell anyone, as Missié Isidore would kill me. It is very amusing, Monsieur Jean."

"I will try," said Jean, husky with emotion, "what hour did you say, Madame?"

"Eight o'clock. You remain outside, where you are not seen, and I bring you here when the play begins."

When Lucille sent for the carriole on Friday evening, Jean did not arrive with it. "He has gone to fish," was the message of the owner, who was again able to come out. Although equal to any emergency, Lucille certainly felt relieved by the absence of Jean. She preferred to have her lovers with her on separate occasions if it could be managed. Her present driver was an old Indian, and it mattered nothing to her whether he saw her go into the pavilion of Isidore or not. Her thoughts on the way were accordingly much more unrestrained than on the previous occasion, and few of them, indeed, very few, were of Jean.

The housekeeper was in her hut, but under pretence of talking more freely she was easily drawn as before to the steps at the back of the mansion house, where Isidore passed on leaving the dinner table to go to his own pavilion. He stopped of course and asked Lucille to step across to his verandah to give him the news and the housekeeper, with her, but the latter, saying she would come presently, went to lock away the liquors, and otherwise arrange the house for the evening. Lucille had heard still more of the position of affairs with the English officer and that being communicated she listened in her turn to the adulations of Isidore, his munificent promises, and his earnest protestations of love. He had not spared his embraces, and each time she objected less, when a foot-fall was heard in the verandah.

"It is old Alice," said Isidore.

"No," replied Lucille, listening, "it was the foot of a man slipping away – who can it be?"

"It may be Camille, perhaps."

"No, no," she replied, "it was not the foot of an Indian girl."

Isidore got up and called out but there was no response. He certainly also did hear a foot pass down the back steps. When he went to look he saw no one but little Madame Camille coming with a pitcher of water on her head as if attending to her household duties. Lucille startled into propriety, seeing old Alice in the other house, returned to her position on the steps. Isidore tried by every means in his power to induce her to return, but she would not, and having gone to the hut of the housekeeper for a few minutes, she soon returned in the carriole to Lorraine.

---

* "Give me, give me, dear friend, my sweet."

It was the foot of Jean which had been heard. He had been horrorstruck at seeing Lucille in such a position, and would have interrupted the tête-à-tête had it not been for the whispered entreaties of Camille, who saw she had gone too far. In revenging herself on the girl she had brought Isidore into danger. As Jean was pushed from the back entrance he stooped down to put on his shoes and lift up his bill-hook, which he had hid in the grass, and on raising himself he ejaculated with an oath – "I will have his blood." The father of Augustin was passing at the moment, and knowing Jean familiarly said – "Whose blood, Jean?"

"That scoundrel Amirantes," he replied – and disappeared in the darkness.

Not knowing very well what he did he took the first path he could find. It was one densely shaded by orange trees which M. Amirantes père frequently followed when he went after dinner to visit a friend who lived on the confines of the Estate. In his haste Jean stumbled and fell over something in the path, and on getting up saw with horror that it was a dead body in a pool of blood. In his fright he dropped his bill-hook in the pool, but taking it up again he fled from the spot, not knowing whither he went. The perfidy of Lucille, and the terrible shock which he had just received had for the time deprived him of reason. He had only sense enough left to reflect that his bill-hook might have blood on it, and he accordingly whirled it into the canes as he hurried along. The body over which he stumbled was that of M. Amirantes père. In the morning it was discovered. The marks leaving no doubt he had been murdered, a thrill of indignation and horror passed over the whole community.

Chapter 16
A Pursuit and Capture

THE INSPECTOR OF POLICE AND SERJEANT STOCKS with his Indian detectives were soon on the spot. Isidore – overwhelmed with grief and shame and contrition – for his father had left the dinner table at the same time as himself the previous night and must have been murdered immediately after when Isidore was with Lucille – had not allowed the body to be moved until the police arrived. The Inspector took full notes of the position of the body, the footsteps so far as they could be traced, and the spot immediately around was searched for any evidence of a struggle, or of a weapon which had been used. There were faint foot-prints of several bare-footed men, but there were apparently the marks of one man with shoes in addition to Monsieur Amirantes père himself, whose foot-prints could be traced from the steps leading from his own room to where the body lay.

The alley was particularly dark and densely shaded at the spot, and the conclusion of the Inspector was that while there had been repeated blows there had been no struggle. With one blow the unfortunate gentleman had been felled, and with others dispatched, but he had apparently been able to offer no resistance. With cautious steps the detectives began to search everywhere for the weapon, while the crowd of Coolies and negroes was kept back by orders of the police. The sensation in the camp had been terrible. A murder at any time in a crowded camp would produce intense excitement but the murder of any white gentleman was an extremely rare occurrence in the Island, and this was the case of a white gentleman murdered on his own property and within a short distance of his own door. The Doctor had been sent for, not because they had any doubt that they were dealing with a dead man, but that he also might be able to give his skilled evidence as to the position of the body and the nature and direction of the wounds. When he arrived and had made his observations the body was carried into the house and the women had begun to prepare it for burial. But the more formal *Post Mortem* examination had still to be made, and they were stopped in their preparations until the Magistrate had been consulted and another Doctor provided.

Monsieur Amirantes had recently been setting up a claim to the exclusive right of fishing in a corner of the bay, which he said belonged to him under his grant of the foreshore, or rather the lease of the Pas Géométriques, held by the government around the Island, and which were usually leased out on easy terms to the adjoining proprietor. The claims had been opposed by the fishermen, and so strongly opposed that Monsieur Amirantes had allowed it to remain in abeyance for some time, until lately when he had become soured by the falling off in the yield of the estate, and his quarrels with his Coolies, and then he had re-asserted his right in a very determined manner. Serjeant Stocks had had complaint quite recently from the murdured gentleman about the encroachments of the fishermen, and an [instruction] from him that he would insist on his rights while claiming the protection of the Police in doing so – the Serjeant accordingly no sooner heard of the murder that he jumped to the conclusion that it was the fishermen who had done the deed. He believed that men who could assert rights in the public against any private proprietor, and above all who had in their midst a man who had struck a police serjeant in the execution of his duty, were fit for anything. It was accordingly with something like triumph in his voice that the Serjeant said to the Inspector –

"It has been some of those d— fishermen."

"Don't be a fool, Stocks," was the rejoinder, "this is not the work of a Creole.

"You will see," said the Serjeant in the assured faith that his own inspiration would be found to be the correct one.

And sure enough an Indian constable came up at the moment with the information that Jean LeBlanc had been seen lurking about the premises the previous night.

"I told you so!" triumphantly exclaimed the Serjeant," you will find that desperate scoundrel has been the murderer."

The mind of the Inspector was by no means disposed to take this view. He knew very well the bad feeling which had existed between the proprietor and his Coolies and he thought from the boldness and atrocity of the deed, that it was by practised hands, and not by any Creole who had not a deeper grievance than the quarrel about the fishing ground.

"Go on with your search, Stocks, "he said, "let us get something sure to go by."

"If the man was lurking about this place, he was here for no good," argued the Serjeant, "let me at least send to the village to ascertain if the man is there and to keep an eye on him lest he should escape."

"Well there is no harm in that," replied the Inspector, and a discreet man was dispatched accordingly to make enquiries about Jean, and to find out where he had passed the night, but to be very careful not to permit it to be known that any suspicion existed.

The search continued. The Inspector began to see those persons about the camp who had seen LeBlanc the previous evening, for in spite of himself, as he had been told the man had been lurking about, he was bound to make enquiries. Several of the people confounded together his coming on the previous Monday driving the carriole, and his being there the previous night – making the statements so contradictory that the Inspector, whose knowledge of Creole as spoken by the Indians was not perfect, was vastly puzzled. A fisherman driving a carriole appeared to him a most suspicious circumstance, and he wondered whether he had come in disguise for the purpose of recon-noitring, and espying the habits of Amirantes père, and especially to note the road he took in his usual walk after dinner.

It was while he was pondering over these singular facts that Isidore came to him in tears, bringing the father of Augustin, pale and trembling. He had come to Isidore to tell what he had seen of Jean the previous night and of his threat. He protested that he had known Jean from his childhood, that he of all men was quite incapable of doing a deed of this kind, but that having heard the threat, which he would have taken as a joke, had it not been for the terrible earnestness and anger of his manner and what had since happened, he felt bound to come to communicate it. "You have done well," said the Inspector, "it might have been a very serious matter for you if you had con-cealed that important fact." The witness had not seen Jean put on his shoes, he had only seen him lift a bill-hook and utter the threat with an oath, and then take a road which could have brought him to the place where the dead body was found just about the time the deed must have been committed.

"Do you think it possible that Jean would do such a deed as that," ex-claimed Isidore after the examination was over. "It is impossible!"

"There is no saying what a nigger will do when he is rejected," replied the Inspector taking refuge in the general theory that the hearts of all black men were generally depraved and desperately wicked.

The thought did pass through Isidore's mind that it might have been Jean's foot which he had heard the previous night in the verandah, and that his having seen him with Lucille might have been the cause of his anger, but he kept this to himself in the meantime, and as he reflected he thought it would only show Jean's guilt more conclusively, although he might have mistaken the victim and slain the father for the son.

The Doctors were by this time busy with the post mortem examination, and they concluded that more weapons than one had been used and that one of the weapons had been a bill-hook. No sooner did the Inspector begin to make his enquiries about Jean LeBlanc than the circumstance became known, and several people came forward to say that they had seen him enter the camp, and go towards the main house, while others had seen him endeavour-ing to conceal himself near Monsieur Isidore's pavilion.

The Indian constable returned from the village to say that Jean had gone out after dinner the previous evening – that he was observed to be in a state of great agitation and refused to say where he was going, and that he had not since returned. "There can be no doubt about it," remarked Stocks who having come to his conclusion already found every action to fit quite pat with his theory. "The man has committed the murder and fled." The Inspector cer-tainly began to waver. Here was a man in the camp who had no business there at that hour, attempting to conceal himself, and then shortly before the crime overheard to utter a threat against the victim with an oath, and this man being at the same time the leader and most reckless of the band who had a quarrel with Amirantes père about the fishing ground. His character moreover was not good. He had been often in gaol for contraventions of the fishing laws, and only just out after assaulting the Serjeant of Police himself. Evidently a desperate character, who was not at all unlikely to have committed the murder.

The Inspector mounted his horse and galloped into town. It was still too early for business although in the country the camps had been astir for hours and all the labours of the fields were in active progress. The Inspector General had not arrived at his office, but the town Superintendent was there and the Adjutant soon arrived. They, like every one else, were horrified at the news, and an Orderly was at once despatched for the Inspector General. He was a kind of muddle-headed well-meaning man, whose notion of a police force was to work it entirely like a regiment, and with regard to everything like the detection of crime he was entirely in the hands of his subordinates and let them do as they thought proper. On hearing the proposition of the Inspector that a warrant should be applied for in order to arrest Jean LeBlanc he at once acquiesced and taking it for granted that his officers were on the right scent, he did not hesitate to tell everybody in the course of the day, from the Governor to the reporters for the Press who soon came for news, that the murderer was a Creole fisherman and that a warrant was already out against him. Notice was sent to all the out-stations to be on the look-out for him, with a general description of his appearance and dress so far as known.

The Inspector, borrowing a fresh horse, galloped back again to the seat of the Magistrates Court and had no difficulty in obtaining the necessary warrant, he himself swearing to the information and that Jean was believed to be the criminal. Even before the journals were out next morning the news had flown over the Island, and produced everywhere the greatest consternation and rage against the murderer. Who would be safe if this kind of thing was allowed to go on? A gentleman murdered almost at his own door, and by a blood-thirsty black! It was time to put an end to it, and to teach these scoundrels a lesson they would never forget. That the murderer was at large filled many families with mortal dread. In the course of the afternoon it was whispered that he had been seen making for Black River by the Plaines Wilhems road, and immediately the nurses who were out walking with the children, snatched up the young ones and dragged home the elder behind them, as if they had seen the fiery eyes of a wild beast in every bush by the way-side. The children half-dead with terror, reached home to add to the excitement by the stories which they had imagined, and thus fear grew by what it fed on. It is impossible to understand how an event of this kind excites a community of divided races. The whites lose all command of themselves. They make sweeping deductions reflecting on black races generally. They talk wildly at dinner and are over-heard by the servants, who in their turn, with all their added comments, send it on through their own circle.

On the newspaper appearing next day the passion of the community was increased. The editors had not been idle, and had constructed a harrowing tale of innocence made the victim of a brutal revenge. Not only was it stated that a warrant was out against Jean, but he was without the least compunction or saving clause stigmatised as the murderer. No other theory was even discussed. All that had to be done was get hold of him, to get over the examinations before the Magistrate as rapidly as possible, and to have him before the "Cour d'Assises"* not for trial, but as the formal mode of condemning a man to death. "Let there be no maudlin talk of humanity this time," wrote a furious editor, "the community demands that the perpetrator of such an atrocious act shall die," and all this with the supposed criminal still uncaught, and the evidence against him known in only the dimmest possible way!

This wild burst reacted on the police. They never doubted now about Jean being the murderer. They ceased to pursue a patient investigation into all the circumstances; the Inspector above all, so busy in attempting to secure the imaginary culprit, forgot his own shrewder theories of the morning, and dropt the threads which might have assisted him in arriving at the truth. All Jean's friends and all those persons who could have given testimony to show that there was another cause for his being on the premises, were thoroughly cowed down. The public indignation was so great they were afraid to speak, and even if they had volunteered they would no doubt have been heartily snubbed by Serjeant Stocks. Little Madame Camille who could have given the most important evidence of all was horror-stricken by the death of the proprietor, and terribly afraid lest Isidore should discover that it was she who had introduced the murderer to the premises. The frightened creature hearing every one say that Jean was the murderer believed that he had murdered the father in his rage against the son which was so great on the previous night. The time corresponded so well that appearances were all but conclusive against Jean. Neither Isidore nor Lucille had seen him in the verandah, but the latter as well as the former concluded that it had been his foot which they had heard, and if it were that he must have murdered the father in mistake for the son. Thus Lucille thought anything she could say, would only make his guilt appear more clear. Good-hearted and compassionate as she was the incident well-nigh killed her. The horrible end of Isidore's father, her own lover branded everywhere as the murderer, and the secret feeling that her own thoughtless conduct had contributed to it, threw her in a fever from which she did not recover until a much later period of the marvellous incidents which were to follow.

The search for weapons had now extended outwards in a great circle from the Mansion House, the importance of the event having made the police much more attentive than usual to perform their duty well. Some of the more trustworthy men of the estate were also employed as additional help. The pond in which Isidore and the Manager used to swim had been cleaned out, and thoroughly searched but as yet nothing had been discovered. At length however the newspapers which were continuing to inflame the community in every way were able to announce in a sensational manner – "Discovery of the weapon" – "Finding of the bill-hook of the murderer." "The bill-hook proved to be that of Jean LeBlanc." And it was so! They had got their confirmation from the police who had discovered the bill-hook in the cane field where it had been thrown. It was peculiarly ornamented on the handle with plaited

* Court of Assizes, i.e. criminal court.

twine such as the fishermen use for their nets, and there was not the slightest difficulty in proving that it belonged to Jean. It had moreover upon the blade certain marks, and in order to discover what these were it was submitted to the Government chemist, and he had no hesitation in declaring it to be animal blood, and as he believed human blood.

There was only one thing now to be done, to discover the haunt of the murderer. The traces were very meagre, so not being able to get on the trail by any discovery of their own, the police determined to try to force evidence from his friends and neighbours at La Baie. A detective in plain clothes called upon Lucille, but the fever had taken to her head, and she could not be disturbed, the doctor in attendance stating that it was as much as her life was worth to attempt it. All the members of Jean's family were bullied and threatened, but they could give no information. The person suspected most of knowing his retreat was a young man of his own age named Emile who had also been punished for the assault upon Serjeant Stocks. It was the great desire of the Serieant to get authority to examine him himself out in the country where he would no doubt have exacted satisfaction of some sort for the indignity done to himself, but the heads of the office ordered the examination to take place in town. Emile was handed over to one of the old detectives, an officer whose experience went back to the days of slavery and to the unscrupulous methods employed in those days. He got no instructions from his superiors, but he knew very well if he extracted information no enquiry would be made as to the mode which had been adopted.

So entering into the cell with an Indian constable well experienced in such matters in India, as well as on the Island, the detective told Emile he had come to examine him and that it would be better for him to tell at once all he knew. It was quite in vain for the terrified young man to declare that he did not know where Jean was. The cords were produced and his finger-nails squeezed as in a thumbscrew. Yelling out with pain he continued to declare that he knew nothing when the second degree of pressure was employed. He was seized and cords tied to his thumbs and in that position he was drawn up to a hook in the ceiling. The torture of the weight of the whole body hanging in such a manner was intense – but he did nothing but cry out and protest he knew nothing. "Squeeze him, Akbar," said the Detective, "the obstinate brute, he knows well enough." He was squeezed in a manner which cannot here be described, and in the intensity of the pain Emile screamed out that he knew nothing but that Jean might possibly be at Petite Rivière. Lowered after having said so much, the poor wretch, pale, bathed in a cold sweat from fear and exhaustion, gasped out in answer to questions that Jean had a "petit-cousin"* at Petite Rivière and that he might be there, or they might know if he had come that way. "Now, Emile," said the detective, "you have caused yourself and us a great deal of trouble, don't be a fool but help us to discover whether Jean is there or not, and you will be handsomely rewarded. We don't wish you to take him, but we merely wish you to find out for us, and if you

* cousin's son

come in here in two days with trustworthy information you shall have five pounds." Emile, glad to escape from their clutches for a little, professed to acquiesce, and that afternoon, after dark proceeded with a detective constable in the direction of Petite Rivière.

The police were now on the right scent. Jean, on the night in question, not knowing very well what he did, found himself at Petite Rivière, and going to the house of this distant relative told him what had occurred and asked for shelter. He had not been there for more than one day before the story of the murder was heard and that Jean was denounced. Fearful that if apprehended he would have no way of clearing himself he begged his friends to keep his secret, and went to live in a cave in the vicinity, to the mouth of which his cousin's wife brought him food after dark and told him from time to time of the news which they had heard. Jean carried his food far into the recesses, and beside a fire which he kept burning but which was entirely hid from observation by the windings of the cavern, he ate it while brooding over his danger, and the fickleness of Lucille.

The cave had at one time been an underground river, not a few of which are to be found in Mauritius. The water had cut a path for itself through the porous lava strata, the course having been widened and deepened from time to time by the floods of the hurricane season. By dint of watching the cottage, the detective, who had got an assistant in the person of one of the local constables who knew the district well, saw the woman leave and go to the cave with food for Jean. They waited concealed, and when she had returned cautiously entered the cave, and by dint of closely listening, followed the slight sounds, creeping noiselessly into the darkness. At length coming to the projection where the cave turned they saw still far inwards the fire and Jean sitting beside it gloomily eating the food which had been brought. They watched him take a smoke after he had concluded his meal and, after he had replenished the fire, throw himself down on the couch of grass which he had gathered for his bed. They allowed him to sleep; and when he awoke he was a fettered prisoner.

Chapter 17
Blood for Blood

THE WHOLE COMMUNITY SEEMED TO REJOICE over the capture of Jean. The stories which circulated about his desperate resistance and the bravery of the police in securing him were numberless as the narrators. The secrets of the cave were described, the vividness of the imagination making up for the necessary want of accuracy. It had formerly been a very ordinary cavern, seldom visited and little known, but a legend being now attached to it, it became the resort of numbers of all classes, and was thenceforth known as "the murderer's cave." How such legends idealise and elevate as it were very commonplace objects! In countries which have been once inhabited by a native race, every portion of the sea coast has its pinnacle of rock from the top of which a Chief or a Chief's daughter, as the last warrior of a brave host, are supposed to have thrown themselves. Incidents of the kind have happened, and have no doubt frequently happened, and when one locality possesses such an object of interest others seem never to rest content until they too have their romantic legends associated with rock or mountain or cavern. But the tales of the desperate resistance of Jean did not elevate him as they might have done in some countries into the dangerous position of a hero.

The feeling of the whites was so intense that it impressed itself upon the whole community, and thus Jean, poor wretch, had few friends, and a dismal prospect before him when he was brought to trial. Unfortunately for him also the Assizes came close at hand, and the Magistrate stimulated to unwonted despatch by the public interest which the case incited began immediately to take the depositions. The police were certainly able to bring forth a formidable array of evidence, from the eye witnesses who saw him stealing around the camp, trying to evade observation, to those who saw him near the spot where the body was found uttering threats and grasping his bill-hook, and still more to the silent testimony of the weapon itself found where it had been hidden away in the cane fields prior to the accused's flight to hide himself from justice. The prisoner was duly committed for trial.

The mode of trial in Mauritius is the English method by jury, although the law administered is that of the French penal code. The jury consists of nine and a verdict may be returned by a certain majority. The Attorney General of the Island, still called by his old title of Procureur General, is the public prosecutor. In his name all the criminal informations are laid, and he himself, or his deputies, appear to prosecute for the Crown. The juries may be composed of French or English, Creole colonists of colour or Indians, the only qualification necessary, in addition to the small property or money valuation which entitles them to be placed on the list, being a competent knowledge of the English language. The proceedings of the Court are now conducted in English, a strong minded Judge having about the year 1853 insisted upon the change, to the great disgust, and in spite of the bitter opposition of every interest in the Island. The French law, however, being the law, and the great majority of the witnesses speaking French, or at least the French patois of the Island, the French language still rules if it does not govern.

When Jean's trial came on the jurors answered promptly to their names, there being no excuses on the grounds of ill health, or of not understanding English, such as are made on ordinary occasions. The Court was crowded by the white element; the Creole coloured people and the Indians, who usually take as so much interest in the proceedings, being pushed for this occasion to the back benches. Isidore and some of the neighbours of the late Monsieur Amirantes were seated at the Registrar's table. The passages were blocked, and other seats being occupied the Judge's Clerks, the Magistrates and other officials were seated on the steps of the bench or anywhere they could find room. Jean was already in the dock, a long railed-in enclosure at one side of the Court, which had had to be enlarged because of the frequency of the trial of gangs of Indians for robberies by house-breaking at night. Just as plants and weeds are carried in the train of man in his migrations from one country to another, so his good customs and his bad accompany him and take root in his new home. The gang-robbery was a crime especially prevalent in India, and the Tamil Coolies brought it with them to Mauritius until it was put down by the strong arm of the law.

In the long dock, frequently filled by such criminals as these, Jean was seated in a dejected manner at the upper end. He could feel that everyone was against him, he was of sufficient intelligence to know the strength of the evidence as it was unfolded at the Magistrates Court, and he had almost ceased to struggle against fate. If Lucille had been to him what she was during that brief day of more than mortal happiness then would he have regarded his present position with horror, and would have fought for his life inch by inch for her sake as well as his own, but now he was almost tempted to regard the prospect of his doom as a boon rather than a calamity. Once only was he roused into anything like a feeling of desire for life, and a resolution to fight for it, when Isidore entered the Court, but it was a passing feeling which soon died away in presence of the scowling looks and universal hatred with which he was regarded. Jean pleaded not guilty. His Counsel was unfortunately over-awed by the intensity of the public feeling. He was the same young man who had defended the fishermen before the Magistrate. However pert and even insolent on that occasion, he was nervous and without resource on this, being apprehensive (a very base feeling for a Counsel to entertain) that simply by defending Jean he might share the universal odium in which his client was held. He did not use the power of challenge at the calling of the jurors as he ought to have done, the consequence being that a worse panel for Jean's interests could scarcely have entered the box. Among them was the editor of the newspaper which had been most bitter in assailing him and calling for his trial as a mere form and his execution as a grim certainty.

The Counsel for the Crown in opening the case followed the French rather than the English fashion. An able man, fond of display, and not the least moved by any considerations of fairness for the prisoner, he was determined not to lose such a chance of making a brilliant effort so as to astonish, and as he fondly hoped electrify, the community. He accordingly sketched the supposed character of Jean in the blackest colours, and described the crime with every rhetorical artifice of exaggeration which could work up men's minds to frenzy. And then he began triumphantly to marshal his evidence. He had even a surprise in reserve for the counsel for the defence. He dimly hinted at it in his opening speech, but it was only when he had given orders to call an Indian Constable, who was known to be always ready to prove confessions, that the counsel saw what was in store, and at last made something of an effort to save his client. He objected that the witness had not been called before the Magistrate, but after an hour spent in wrangling the Judge decided that the witness could be heard.

The public prosecutor soon brought the witness to the particular evidence he could give, which was that Jean had confessed in prison that he had been in the alley at the time when the body of Amirantes père was lying in the pool of blood, the point of the prosecutor evidently being that if this were so, and Jean had given no alarm, so that an attempt might have been made to save life, and had fled from justice, it must necessarily have been he who killed the victim. Although the Indian constable coolly swore to this as a confession, he had only over-heard it when placed in a secret chamber to listen to what prisoners said to their friends or to fellow-criminals or detectives in disguise who were locked up with them for the night in purpose to induce them to speak. The person to whom Jean had spoken was his own father, who had implored the son to tell him how he had come to be suspected. Jean also told him why he had been at the house on that night, but that not suiting the purposes of the prosecution was suppressed by the Indian constable in giving an account of the "confession." The evidence was considered as most damning against the prisoner, but fortunately it did not pass unnoticed by the Judge, whom it struck differently, as he was better aware of the methods by which the confessions of criminals were extorted and manipulated.

The last witness called was the Doctor who swore to having detected marks of blood on the bill-hook and more significant still on the trousers. To the surprise of the jury, and it must be added the rage and mortification of the friends of the deceased in Court, the summing up of the Judge shewed that he by no means regarded the evidence as conclusive or satisfying. He was a venerable old Creole gentleman who had been already on the bench at the time of emancipation, and whose whole boyhood had been passed in familiar contact with the slave race, and who had known them intimately and well also in the days of their freedom. He instinctively felt that this was not the work of a Creole.

The motive on which the public prosecutor had founded, of the quarrel of the fishermen with the deceased about the fishing ground, he knew could not have led to such a murder. He was well acquainted moreover with the habits of Amirantes père, and feared that his conduct might have excited much more serious enmities than those of the fishermen. His quarrels with his Indians were notorious, and his harshness, and mania for punishing them, both legally and illegally. The judge suspected that the police, as was not infrequently the case, had started on a wrong theory, and shut their eyes to other circumstances which might have led more surely to the truth. The counsel put forward the defence that Jean being at Pompadour for perhaps no good purpose, morally speaking, had in leaving stumbled over the body, and fearing to be accused had fled. However weak that argument might appear to those whose minds were already made up against the accused, the Judge felt that it was a very likely thing to have occurred, and in the absence of sufficient motive, and more direct evidence, he cautioned the jury against being influenced by the public clamour against the prisoner.

The jury retired simply to express to each other their wonder that the Judge, a Creole like themselves, should have made such a fool of himself in so clear a case. As it was one of murder they thought it would be better to appear to deliberate, and so smoked a cigar before coming back into Court, when they returned a unanimous verdict of guilty. The Judge had no option but to pronounce the penalty of the law, although resolved that he would leave no stone unturned to prevent the execution, the verdict being to him so unsatisfactory. He felt convinced the murder had not been properly investigated and that other evidence of a different complexion would afterwards come out.

It was late before the trial ended; the public slowly dispersed having hung about the Court yard to talk over the incidents of the day, and especially the firm manner in which the Judge had refused to follow the lead of the Counsel for the Crown, and had even been more favourable to the accused than his own Counsel. The coloured races, and especially the Indian, seem to have a rooted suspicion of the integrity of judges. It comes to them from the venal character of their own judges in the days before the English supremacy had at last brought purity to the bench, if it had also brought humiliation to the kings and chiefs, and a new element of political oppression to the people. They suspect a bias in the judge from a hundred circumstances which a white would not dream of. What affects them most of all however is that the Judge necessarily moves in the circle of the leading whites of the Island, and they cannot imagine him raising himself above these influences in order to do justice to a man of another race who has no friends, at the expense probably of furious attack in the local journals, of controversies with the heads of the police, with the Magistrates, and the Governors, it may be with the authorities at home to whom any independence and impartiality of action will probably be represented as factiousness, and a desire to embarrass the local government.

In this very Colony, on one occasion, the Judges having decided some ordinary question against the public prosecutor, he requested the Governor to write home that they had done it factiously and asked that a despatch should be written out reminding them that they held their offices not for life but during good behaviour. No such despatch, it need scarcely be said, was ever written. Probably when the request was received at the Colonial Office the graceless young clerks made great fun of it, as showing the kind of folly of which Colonial rulers could be guilty. Not that the aforesaid young gentlemen have any high standard by which to judge of men and things, but because their familiarity with all sorts of questions and all kinds of controversies must sharpen their sense of the ridiculous, which is so good an ally to common-sense.

The Judge sent in the notes of his evidence to the Governor in the usual way, in order that the sentence of Death which had been pronounced might either be sustained by the Executive Council or the sentence be commuted to something less than death. Notes had been circulated amongst the members of the Council, a meeting was held at which the Judge was present. He stated his own impressions as to the evidence, and gave some very substantial reasons why the verdict of the jury in this particular case should not be regarded with the same favour as in an ordinary trial where the public was not excited, and class prejudices were not roused. Indeed the light and heartless conduct of the jury had shocked the minor officials who had reported their demeanour and jokes to the Judge. The Executive Council, of which the Procureur General, who had prosecuted, was a member, and not the least, indeed we may say at once, the most, influential member, did not share the Judge's views. They were men of like passions with the rest of the community, and had been too completely led away by the popular indignation against the crime itself to be sufficiently careful to discriminate as to the criminal when a victim was presented.

The Governor, upon whom the responsibility necessarily more directly lay in sanctioning the punishment of death, was unfortunately among the panic-stricken. The circumstances of the crime were certainly calculated to strike terror, and if it could have been proved, or even reasonably inferred, to be part of a system, or conspiracy, or an incident likely to be repeated, then he would even less have been justified in consequence of mere scruples, or refinements in connection with the evidence, to have interfered with the course of justice where there could be no doubt they had got hold of the right man. But the Judge who tried the case was not clear they had got the right man. He was very clear the other way, and although he had not the faculty of putting his views very well, there could be no mistake as to what those views were. It is well in such cases for the executive not to be over hasty in carrying out their own notions and opinions. They have ample justification for caution, and calmness, in the attitude of the Judge who would not take up such a position without reason, or without having fully weighed his responsibility. After the Judge left, the Executive Council continued its deliberations, and came to the conclusion, unanimously like the jury, that the penalty of death should be enforced.

The newspapers were triumphant. The decision of the Executive was communicated to them, and they began at once to clamour for a speedy execution, and to assail the Judge in every possible manner. Even his personal appearance was caricatured, and insulting reference made to certain peculiarities of his shape, and the expression of his face when on the bench. But they had reckoned without their host. The gentleman in question was not of that strong mould of men who having once made up their minds that they are right, can push on through the crowd of opposers with a cool and determined air, without any fear of consequences, and perhaps with only a little, and even it may be a very proper, contempt, for other men's opinions on matters to which they have not given the same undivided attention. He had, however, on this the only occasion in his life when he had put his foot down, the determination to keep it down, and his unexpected spirit and obstinacy as it was termed, greatly annoyed the authorities, or to put the saddle on the right horse, the Governor, for many of the men who held this position imagine that any one who differs from them in opinion, even in matters affecting their own special duties, must necessarily be doing it to dispute the Governor's authority. Happily for Jean LeBlanc, the Judge had not only the spirit and determination to do right, but the law in that Colony had given him the power to put an effectual barrier in the way of the execution. In England, when a person is condemned, the judicial authority loses all direct power of control over his fate. Of course in the elevated regions of the political atmosphere at home no such storms rage as in a little Colony. The Home Secretary and the Circuit Judge are not by any means likely to come into collision. The one will give his opinion calmly, judicially, and judiciously, about any question which may be referred to him, the other will from the most elevated stand-point of justice and humanity carefully consider the case of any criminal, and his duty most frequently is to insist upon the sentence of the law being carried out in spite of popular passion to obtain a commutation, rather than to stand between a prisoner and a populace clamouring for his blood. When the condemned man at home, therefore, is left in the hands of the Sheriff, we do not fear that his fate will be decided by a gust of passion.

In this particular Colony, the ancient system was that the Judge should sign a Warrant addressed to the head of the Police authorizing him to take the body of the prisoner from the gaol and to have him executed in conformity with is his sentence, and this Warrant the Governor counter-signed. The Judge refused to sign the Warrant. The Governor sent for him and by entreaties, commands, and even threats endeavoured to shake his resolve. He was told that when the Executive Council had decided upon carrying out the sentence the duty of the Judge to prepare and sign the Warrant was merely ministerial, and not judicial, and therefore that his privileges as a Judge could not shelter him from the consequences. "I am prepared for any and all consequences," said the old man quietly.

"Very well," said the Governor in a fit of spleen, "I see how it is, I will require to issue the Warrant on my own authority."

"You may commit murder if you please," replied the Judge, looking the indignant and fuming functionary full in the eyes, "but I will not."

"Then I understand from you that you finally refuse to grant this Warrant," said the Governor as his last attempt, with a significant air as if the annihilation of the Judge was to be the immediate consequence.

"You may so understand," was the answer, "and now I may wish your Excellency good morning." The Procureur General was in the ante room waiting for the termination of the interview. He immediately began to work upon every weak point which he knew the Governor to possess with the view of inducing him to grant a Warrant for the execution upon a simple minute by the Procureur General detailing what had occurred. The controversy had now assumed the phase of a conflict of authority between the Executive and judicial departments, or even a little closer than that, between the Procureur General and the Judge. It was bad enough for the latter to be obliged to differ from the opinion of the Governor. That might cause temporary unpleasantness, but no permanent estrangement, but to presume to differ from a Procureur General, and to assert an authority against his, was to begin an embittered personal war to end only with life.

In his eager haste, the ardent functionary went too far. So long as he kept to the safe ground of representing that the French law was this or that, and that by law the privileges, duties, and powers of the Procureur General were such and such, he could twist the Governor, as the saying goes, round his little finger. The very words "French law" were sufficient to put any holder of the office, at any time, into a cold perspiration, and by judiciously working this handle the Creole Procureurs General had the administration in their own hands. But when the Governor was told what the rage of the populace would be if he commuted the sentence and the probable rioting that would occur, he touched the chords of the exact rebound of which he was ignorant. "What!" exclaimed the Governor, "Do the mob of Port Louis imagine I will be deterred by their threats from doing whatever I believe to be my duty?" The Procureur General felt he had made a mistake and in his eager desire to wipe out the bad impression, contrived to awaken the conscience of the Governor as to the danger of yielding to their cry for blood. Might there not be some mistake. But what told most was the remark made by the Judge – "You may commit murder if you please." Would it indeed be murder to execute a prisoner otherwise than in the manner authorised by law? He would take an opinion from one more likely to be less swayed by the passion of the hour than his official adviser appeared to be.

Sending for one of the other Judges, an Englishman, with perhaps somewhat too great devotion to the technicalities of the English law, he put to him the question and speedily received an answer that the law having laid down the forms and modes of carrying out a capital sentence it would be murder to do it in any other way. That settled Jean's fate in the meantime. Immensely relieved when he had at last come to a determination which did not involve the irrevocable step of putting a fellow creature to death, the Governor called the members of the Executive Council together and briefly intimated to them that the judge had refused to sign the Warrant for the Execution, and that he having been advised by an authority to whom he was bound to pay deference, that he could not depart from the letter of the law in a case of this kind, had determined to commute the sentence. No remonstrance was made, the decision had been so quickly taken and so curtly announced that none were ready with objections, and within half an hour the Judge had received an official letter informing him that the Governor had commuted the sentence to imprisonment with hard labour for life, such being the equivalent of penal servitude for life in the old country.

The Judge glad to be relieved of the disagreeable business, at once ordered a special sitting of the Criminal Court, at which only the officials, and one of two of the public were present. The prisoner was brought over from the gaol which was in the same Court yard, and the letter of commutation was read to him. To Jean, although the announcement was literally a change from death to life, so fully had he made up his mind to his fate, the reading of the English letter was looked upon as one of these mere forms of the law which had to be gone through before his execution, and he paid no attention to it. The decision to commute had been so suddenly taken that the officials of the gaol had not yet heard of it, as they usually do in time to prepare the prisoner for the momentous change in his destiny. The Judge, more interested than the prisoner, and with his heart full of a conviction of his innocence, which would one day be established, noticing from the careless demeanour of Jean that he had not understood, explained to him in the Creole patois, what the meaning of the ceremony was. Jean grasped the railing in front of the dock, and fearful that he had not heard aright ejaculated, "Your Honour, do I rightly hear, that the sentence of death is not to be carried out?"

"Yes," was the reply, "you have understood quite rightly."

"Yes, yes," said the huissier who had known Jean at school, while opening the dock, and pushing him along the passage towards the door. "You are not to be hanged this time, Jean." The hurried manner of the officials, and the rush to see him of Indian coolies and others who usually hang about the Court-yard, and sit for hours under the large banyan tree, kept Jean from giving way to the excess of his emotion until he was once more within the prison gate, when his limbs simply refused to obey him, and he sank on the ground unconscious and to all appearances a dead man. The Doctor of the prison was fortunately within the walls, and being informed of the circumstances, rightly judged that it was the mental emotion which had been too much for the prisoner. He had him removed to his cell, and copiously bled, when consciousness gradually returned. The sale of an Estate had been proceeding in the "Master's Court" in another portion of the square, and as the bidders and lookers-on came out they were informed of the astonishing news which flew through the town even more rapidly than if the rumours had been false.

Chapter 18
Isidore's Prospects Improve

THE EFFECT UPON MADAME BEAUVALLON OF THE MURDER of Isidore's father was only second to that occasioned by the accidental death of her own husband. Another victim, she bitterly thought, was necessary to punish her for her back-sliding, and this time it was the father of the youth whose suit she had discouraged. Pity for Isidore in his bereavement had taken a strong hold on her mind, so strong that when he came to call for her, and consult with her, in the first days after the murder, when Jean was not yet captured – she took him in her arms, embracing him, and calling him "mon pauvre Isidore,"* as if he had been her own son. The compassion of woman is infinite. She must have something upon which to lavish her devotion; in youth some real or imaginary lover, in more mature age her children, or where she has none, other objects more or less worthy of regard. We see it frequently take the form of philanthropy, a desire to do good to classes or races of human beings, a desire to alleviate the sorrows and woes of others afar off.

And God knows! There is abundant scope in the world for the labours of all who are fired with the noble ambition of doing good. So many centuries after the general acceptance of Christianity, and still so much misery! How can such things be, cry the tender hearted, and the great hearted. How can such things be, cry the pious with agonizing views of duty and self abnegation. How can these things be, cry the sects who own no fealty to religious creeds, but who have what they believe to be the larger religion of humanity. How can these things be, cry the champions of the poor from the midst of their poverty and suffering, and the cry would have remained unheard and unanswered un-til the day of doom had not the transfer of political power to the masses taken place. How can these things be, cry now the public writer, the public orator, and the political leader, not very much concerned to have the answer, but pleased with the cry for it has been uttered of late so widely, so loudly, so im-periously, that it is something to conjure with. Ah how different is their desire from that of the hearts who are full of compassion and love for mankind. They do not feel that intense sense of suffering with them who suffer which has been the spring of action in devoted men and women for so many generations. The question put by the new converts will be sufficiently answered by a Blue

* "my poor Isidore."

Book which not one man in one million will have the courage to read, or if he reads have the capacity to understand, and while money will be poured out without stint to get information which every one knows, and statistics which no one wants, the poor will continue to suffer, and thousands will go down to the grave unsuccoured, uncared for, unblessed, who might at least have been decently buried with the money to be wasted on an enquiry.

Poor Madame Beauvallon was not in a good position for indulging in a wide sympathy with the human race. She knew little beyond the scope of her own role. Her sister Clémence knew more, but her knowledge was of that strange, and naughty – nay, do not let us use terms which may appear to trifle with such things, let us call it that abominably wicked world in which French romance writers seem to revel and which for the public of Paris seems to have such a fascination. Even she had scarcely never heard of the suffering thousands of the great cities, and of the down-trodden, poverty-stricken wretches in the country. In their own Island there was no beggary, poverty was of that kind which can be measured and relieved, the poverty of families which have sunk from middle class opulence to the penury of old age, and the change of circumstances which may equally affect all.

What actual misery did exist was among those other races, between whom and Madame Beauvallon there was the unseen but iron barrier. For it is astonishing how soon those who may themselves have been descended from another race, assume the manners, forms of thought, prejudices and antipathies of that to which they have been converging, or into which they have been received. What love and compassion therefore she had to spare after she had lavished much upon her daughter, sister and household, was concentrated into a much more narrow channel than the general philanthropy of those who lived in wider scenes. The overflow of her heart was like the streams of her own island, which rush mainly in narrow beds, cutting deep into the strata until the channels become ravines, and the stream a torrent, tumbling over cataracts, and brawling under rocks on its way to the sea. Isidore she had wept over before she saw him, and when he appeared she could not disguise her emotion. Her tears flowed freely, her sobs were unrestrained, her expressions of tenderness and compassion such as to assure him that there was now no obstacle in that direction to the realisation of his hopes.

The death of his father had greatly improved even Isidore for the moment. Not that it had changed his heart, or made him resolved to live a more worthy life for the future. But he had loved his father, he was deeply shocked by the manner of his death, his conscience did not cease to upbraid him in regard to Lucille and Jean, the latter of whom he suspected to have murdered his father in mistake for himself. The whole circumstances of the time, the public agitation, the trial, and the fierce discussions as to the execution had made him walk circumspectly while the public eye was, as it were, upon him. Then his personal appearance was so improved by his being in mourning. Talk as we may about what constitutes the real man, we are nevertheless impressed in spite of ourselves by the outward appearance.

Isidore, it need scarcely be said, was always well-dressed when he went to visit, and his clothes were not now better than they had ever been, but the demure black made him more interesting, toned him down as it were, and made it impossible for the moment to believe that he was altogether wicked.

Estelle could not on this occasion refuse to see him. Although she could not bear the thought of marrying him, and indeed disliked him generally, yet that did not prevent her feeling genuine compassion for him in his bereavement. "If he loved his father," she thought, "as I loved mine, how great must be his grief!" She could show she felt for him without giving any encouragement for other advances. Indeed, it must be owned that of the latter she thought nothing, or scarcely anything, at the time. Her mother wished her to see him, and she was glad to have the opportunity to offer her sympathy. When she entered the room it was a touching sight to see these two young people, both so handsome, dressed in deep mourning for their fathers who had both been lost in circumstances so sudden, and striking and sad. It could not escape the notice of Madame Beauvallon, but both the young people seemed also to feel it, and the meeting was an affectionate one on both sides. Isidore was all kindness and attention and respectful sympathy. One would have thought that it was he who had come to condole with Estelle, not she who had willingly come down to offer her sympathy with him.

He talked in a saddened tone of voice, which was perhaps put on for the occasion, for his grief was not such as to affect him so deeply, but it made him more interesting. Estelle was too artless to imagine that he could possibly be acting. But if he was acting in this he was perfectly genuine in the desire from which it sprung, the intense overpowering desire to secure the regard and love of Estelle. Isidore in fact had a double nature as most men have. He was not wholly bad, although his training and manner of life had placed temptations in his way which he could not and never tried to resist. He had scarcely even in his boyhood known what goodness was. Everything evil was known to him from his youth up, having been communicated both by the loose manners and loose talk of the Mozambique [nurses], and by the language and manners of the Indian boys and girls among whom he had been reared. When a boy he spoke three languages with equal fluency and knew the bad words and the bad actions which were represented by the words in each. The language of the nursery was of course the Creole patois, but the languages of the mill and the mill yard, the camp, the side of the stream in the ravine where the clothes were washed, the pasture and the cane fields were Hindustani and Tamil. He had no training in a virtuous home, no examples of goodness set him from early life, and no backing which went to the pith of the matter. How could he in such unpromising circumstances blossom out to be one of those noble, good and pious young men of whom we read in romances.

How different had been the training of nearly all the officers in Jack's regiment, for example. The poorest village child in England or Scotland would have been as ashamed to speak a bad word in the presence of a well brought up child from the mansion house, as they would have been to speak it before the schoolmaster, or the curate, or their mothers. And indeed the chances for any such contamination from the vulgar is as small in a home county, as on a sugar estate abroad it is certain. But these officers brought up so carefully and well, with every good example before them, and every wise precept inculcated from their childhood, they do not all become saints. They have a proneness to the ordinary sins of the world, the old Adam now and again asserts itself so that drinking bouts and unlawful love are things not unknown. How can we then expect to find a youth like Isidore overflowing with virtues, and blossoming like a rare flower on a dung pile? The only advantage the officers had over him, and it was certainly a great one, was that they all knew when they were doing wrong, and only did it occasionally, and as a rule were sorry for it, but to Isidore these evil things came quite as a matter of course, and he only knew that the world had a kind of prejudice against them being openly paraded. Virtue in fact in his creed meant the practice of vices in such a way as not to be found out. But he could readily see that something more would be demanded of him if he aspired to the hand of Estelle.

The bringing up of girls in such scenes as we have mentioned is generally as strict as the care of boys is loose. When they are Catholics they are sent to a Convent school at an early age, and carefully watched and tended until married, but the atmosphere is not a good one in any circumstances. Estelle had been fortunately placed, her nurse had not been worse than the nurse of Juliet, at least not worse than Juliet's nurse would have been if she had been a negress and brought up in Mauritius, and then her religious and home training had been in every sense good. Isidore knew this; he knew that if his conduct were known his chances would be at an end, or rather he felt he had had no chance from Estelle being perhaps conscious from instinct as well as knowledge of the lives of such young men as he, what he was. As yet he had never made vows that he thenceforth led a virtuous life. If he made any mental reflection on the subject, it did not rise higher than a determination to be more careful. The air he assumed with his mourning garb was one of greater staidness and respectability, but such as it was it easily passed muster with Madame Beauvallon as the evidence of a real change in life and character. It unquestionably impressed Estelle also.

She was anxious to be on terms of friendship with their nearest neighbour. She could not but feel for him in his solitary condition, and what to all appearance was his deep sorrow. She could not be cold and reserved to his respectful demeanour, and bright conversation. Unconsciously she allowed herself to be drawn into a frank and confidential talk with him upon old times, mutual friends, and his future arrangements now that he had no longer to study his father's wishes and habits. He thought of building a wing to the house and of abandoning his pavilion life. He did not go much further, but Estelle began to fear that he would. On looking around she found her mother had quietly left the room, Estelle having been too much interested in the conversation to notice her absence. The position caused her a little embarrassment. Isidore noticed it, and with a quick courtesy which did him credit and affected Estelle not a little, he instantly got up and proposed to go. "Stay, Isidore, till my mother returns," she said in her pleasantest way with a smile which might have turned heads less susceptible than that of Isidore. "With too much pleasure," he replied, "if my presence does not bore thee, Estelle."

He was deeply grateful for this first pleasant and gracious word to him since the Englishman crossed his path. She, thankful to him for his courtesy, and grateful that he had not abused the opportunity which she feared her mother had given him, sat down again, and for a moment their eyes met; from his a look of deep and respectful devotion, no it was more, there could be no mistaking it, a look of ardent love; and on her part a glance of friendship and of something more; could it, could it possibly be of coquetry? Oh heart of woman, what an inconstant thing art thou? This artless maiden, deeply in love, devoted to another, whose absence she daily and hourly lamented, for whom she would cheerfully have given her life (she thought) and from whom to be eternally separated would be as death, could not help, just at that moment, and animated with the feeling of gratitude, compassion and old friendship which swayed her, flashing from her eyes a look close, very close, to that of more than friendship, and thus fanning into a flame of devotion, such as only strong men feel, all the sentiments of regard, devotion, and love, which Isidore already entertained for her.

Fortunately for Estelle, unhappily for Isidore, Madame Beauvallon at that moment returned. One word, if he had ventured to utter it, had the mother continued absent would have undeceived him. Estelle was scarce conscious of the havoc she had wrought, of the hopes she had excited, of the fierce and overpowering passion she had fanned into a flame. She knew of course that she had returned the look with favour, with recognition, with friendship, with a little dash more and above which she intended to mean of forgiveness for the past, and of friendship for the future, but it is very hard for the owner of such eyes as hers when she wishes to say all this not to say something more than she intended. As bad luck would have it too, everything was on the side of Isidore in the prosecution of this lawful pursuit of Estelle just as everything was against him in his unlawful pursuit of Lucille. Madame Beauvallon had slipped out to see what there was for tiffin, and to give orders to add some dainties to the meal, and on her return asked Isidore to share it with them. He looked at Estelle, who with a sweet smile, the memory of which haunted him, pressed the invitation of her mother. Consent, yes one would think so, and if the same feeling which came over poor Jean, when Lucille showed her trinkets and combed out her back-hair, now came over Isidore, so that he walked as if on air, and saw the earth transfigured before him, one can easily understand how deep, how overwhelming was his love.

Aunt Clémence at once felt the difference in the presence of Isidore from that of Monsieur Montmorency – the latter could not speak French with that fluency and particular turn of phrase which expresses so much; they in their turn could not speak English well for the same reason. The talk when Jack was present was the talk of children, or of commonplace, amusing sometimes from the slips of the tongue on both sides, but neither instructive nor entertaining. Isidore talked on this occasion like one possessed. He was a well-educated man because all the youth in Mauritius had had the invaluable advantage of the Royal College and amidst all his wildness he had managed to keep up a fair acquaintance with French news and with French literature not merely on its shady side, but its classical and elevated productions. He was a subscriber to the *Revue des Deux Mondes,* not merely for the sake of laying it on the table, but in order to read it, and he kept well posted up in the questions of the day. He was especially devoted to science. The nature of his daily avocations, engaged in the growth and manufacture of sugar, led him to watch the progress of the world in the matter of machinery, and he and a friend had made up their minds that the success of sugar in the future would be bound up with a chemical discovery. They had made certain experiments together in this direction, and already visions of patents and boundless wealth from such a source formed part of Isidore's waking dreams. He was moreover a politician, and one of a school not very popular then in France, although we have seen changes of a great and sweeping nature since that time.

The Empire was then throwing its spell of power over France and Europe and Isidore could talk quite feelingly of the base men who were coming to the top, and of the great and good men who were in exile. Aunt Clémence went in for the Empire, as she thought the literature which she was fond of had shown peculiar piquancy and power since the period of the revolution had come to an end. It certainly had not occurred to her that the flowering of this species of literature betokened a bad and not a good state of the body politic which would go on getting worse and worse until the disease culminated in the most awful calamity which had ever overwhelmed a nation since the time of Julius Caesar. Isidore was almost prophetic in his forecast of the future of the Empire, divining with a wonderful intuition how the necessities of his position would oblige the Emperor to rely upon men who could be bought, and who therefore would not hesitate to sell themselves and their country when the necessity arose. The Court of the Empress came under review with its ephemeral splendour, and its style of woman's dress fitted to draw men who could not be allured by the attractions of virtue.

To hear Isidore discourse, and as it referred to the conduct of others he was for the moment sincere, of the benefit of a good example being set to the people by Crowned Heads, and of the political disasters which had always followed a reign of profligacy, one would have thought him a Republican of more than the severe virtue of a Roland, and a nobleness of ambition worthy of the mother of the Graces!* How his sentences seemed to accommodate themselves to his theme, now full rolling and eloquent, now light, piquant, and recherché, as the thoughts which they embodied. Madame Beauvallon sat entranced, Aunt Clémence was delighted beyond measure to find an antagonist worthy of her steel, and even Estelle had tried in vain to appear unconcerned. She was obliged to listen, and in listening to admire.

Could this indeed be the wild, gloomy, dangerous and profligate man she had thought Isidore to be and as she represented him to Jack at the time of the duel? Had she been mistaken, or had he changed in consequence of

* Hera, the wife of Zeus.

the calamity which had overtaken him? But how could such a change as this have been wrought in an hour? He was pouring forth the full treasure of his knowledge which could only be acquired by reading and thought and study, and she had always imagined that he spent his nights at the card table when not in more questionable company. Strange that either he had not hitherto shown himself in his true character, or she, from her misconceptions, had not noticed the real superiority of his talents. And then another thought obtruded itself. Had this change not been wrought because of his love for her, the shock he had received by her engagement to the English officer and his determination yet to win her. "Could I ever love Isidore?" she thought, and as she thought her eyes were instinctively raised to his face. He was looking at her, his black eyes flashing with the light of what to her seemed genius, and his handsome swarthy face all radiant with the excitement of the conversation.

Their eyes met again, but she lowered hers instantly. She could not bear the light of his, it was so intense, but of that intensity which pleases and captivates not repels. There was nothing of the earth in that light. As rays from a gem it seemed to be away from the eye itself, an emanation rather than an innate brilliancy, but it could not be encountered without a tell-tale look of admiration, and she resolved not to permit him to read her thoughts. But she forgot that the sudden lowering of the eyes can tell a tale as well as a more steady look. [And] she was unwillingly forced to look at him by sympathy with his conversation, and admiration for his eloquence, but she would not for the world that he should catch her stealing back a glance. Isidore felt it so, and as Estelle also felt that his eyes were still on her, that same tell-tale blood, which rose so often and so unbidden to her cheeks when the English officer was her companion, again came stealing up and added a brightness and bloom to the countenance worth more to Isidore than even her look in the drawing room. The afternoon quickly sped until the time when the visitor was forced to depart.

"I think we will come down soon to Lorraine," said Madame, "it is getting hot in town, and I think Estelle will be better of the change."

"In that case," said Isidore, "I hope to be allowed to call to tender my best services as soon as you arrive.'

"We will at all times be glad to see you, Isidore, as a neighbour, and to be useful to you in any way."

Ah, Jack Montmorency, away in Natal, kicking thy heels in tiresome barracks, or spending precious time in breaking in young horses, what are thy prospects worth at the moment? Not much, for in the conversation which followed the departure of Isidore, Estelle heard Aunt Clémence, who had always stood his friend and defended him when the Priest and her mother assailed him, speak in almost eloquent terms of the superiority of Isidore "as a companion."

There can be no doubt about it, that Jack was wondrously ignorant. Like other English boys of good birth he had been sent to one of the public schools, and there he had a certain amount of Latin grammar hammered and flogged into him, and a modicum of Greek which had been forgot as soon as he entered the army. He knew a little of the history of his own country from the orthodox view, that is he had quietly swallowed as a dose the views of the school historians in regard to the men of whom they spoke, just as he had implicitly believed Livy and Tacitus in the few selections he had ever read, but he had never thought out for himself the meanings of any of the great movements of history, or their connection with his own age. Science was a sealed book to him notwithstanding that he was in a profession which ought to deal with all science. Not only was science [scorned] but all the higher literature also. The talk of the mess room was chiefly of dogs and horses, of men and women whom they knew, of actresses whom they had wished to know, of the annoyances of the Park, and of the curiosities in character of Mauritius and Natal. A considerable number of the officers had been at Gibraltar, and one had picked up a considerable amount of Spanish just as Jack had somehow managed to get a top dressing of good French upon his school exercises during six months spent at Boulogne. But he was infinitely behind Isidore in the range of his acquirements and in natural aptitude. Isidore knew not the points of any cattle more elevated in the scale than a mule or an ox. He seldom rode, and when he did he found it a bore in a warm climate. Jack knew the parts of a horse better than he did his Bible. Not even the most knowing of Natal dealers could deceive him, and he was a famous horseman. He could not have spoken of the philosophy or politics of his own country as Isidore did of that of France. He had not indeed any very clear conception of the parties of the State, and of the politics of France he knew no more than that the Emperor was Louis Napoleon and the Empress, Eugénie. If you had asked him who Victor Hugo was he would probably have answered that he was some madman or other. Of his writings he knew nothing, any more than he could have told you wherein lay the peculiar strength of Carlyle or Tennyson. He thought that the author of The Stones of Venice was a man down in Edinburgh who had been a stonemason and that Ruskin was a portrait painter. This one day had found out Jack's weaknesses just as other revelations had formerly laid bare the great weaknesses of Isidore. But if there is anything that a French woman, or a woman of French descent, loves more than another it is literary greatness, the fame of an orator, of a scholar, of a politician. Aunt Clémence could not be silent on the subject of the wonderful culture and knowledge Isidore had manifested. "Oh but his French is beautiful," she exclaimed more than once. To her he was vivid as Dumas, as cutting and strong as Voltaire, as witty as Molière, and in science as great as Arago. He must rise to distinction she contended, if he had only a wider field than Mauritius, and perhaps some day they might be as proud of him as of others of their Isle who had gone to France and become famous. Estelle went to bed with the phrases and the praises of Isidore ringing in her ears, and she dreamed of him rather than of Jack, of brilliant scenes in the French capital, with Isidore as the centre of attraction, and Estelle Beauvallon – oh faithless one – dressed in splendour, bearing the name Madame Isidore Amirantes.

Chapter 19
A Crime to Punish a Crime

THE RAGE OF THE WHITE COMMUNITY WHEN IT WAS FOUND that Jean was not to be hanged was something terrible. All the vials of their wrath were now poured out on the unhappy Governor who had been so very willing to agree to the execution if the resolution of the Judge had not prevented him. Every sinister motive which could possibly be surmised or invented was laid to his charge, he was accused of cowardice, and of a base sacrifice of the best interests of the country to the whims and follies of the English philanthropists who disliked the punishment of death. Wherever men met their talk was of the weakness of the act in allowing the murderer to escape. The excitement was such that the superior officers feared that some attempt would be made to force the gaol and to lynch the prisoner. The Guards were doubled at the Governor's official residence, and a strong force of picked police kept within the gaol square ready to resist any attempt to master the building. Nearly every official thought the decision of the Governor was criminally weak. He on his part had not the approbation of his own conscience in the matter, for he thought the Judge wrong, and had only hastily determined on the respite to get rid of a difficulty. He looked upon the Judge as the person who had got him into all this unpopularity and odium and detested him accordingly.

The law officer again saw his chance of getting his own views carried out by playing upon the fears of the Governor, and his desire to escape from the false position in which he found himself. He was determined that the man should be hung at all hazards in spite of the Judge, and the only difficulty was to know how to manage it. A zealous clerk put an idea into his head which at first he recoiled from, but which he nevertheless came seriously to entertain as every day seemed to cause the public anger to wax greater. The editors found an admirable opportunity for mischief and vied with each other in the violence and virulence of their articles which lashed an excitable and unthinking populace into fury. The weakness of the government in dealing with the great scourge of these small Colonies, an unscrupulous and violent set of public writers, was great at any time, but on this occasion when the writers knew that all the officials were with them and that the Governor and the Judge had scarcely a friend in the community, they took a disgraceful licence.

In the midst of the turmoil and fury the law officer surprised the community by a brilliant coup. The Assizes in the confusion had not been adjourned, and Jean was now indicted afresh for an attempt to murder, the attempt be-ing nothing more than the old charge of his assault upon Serjeant Stocks on the morning when the police tried to seize the fishermen. By the French code an attempt at murder is punishable by death whenever the attempt has failed by a cause not attributable to any act or change of intention of the assailant. Severely logical, the French make the same general rule with regard to all at-tempts to commit crime. And no doubt if the world were to be ruled by logic there would be much to say in favour of the theory. Intention is the essence of guilt, we take the intention into account, and must do so in nearly every criminal enquiry, and if the criminal is to get the benefit if his intention be good, or at all events not so evil as the nature of the crime presupposes, why should he not be held to a strict accounting if the whole evil intention be there and his design has only been thwarted by something over which he had no control. The consequence of this rule is that in the Colony men have been frequently condemned to death for an attempt to murder an individual who may be present and sitting all unharmed in the Court. Of course the practical carrying out of the law is more humane than in theory, and while criminals may be so condemned to death, the rule is to commute the punishment to such term of penal servitude as may be supposed to be a just punishment for the offence. The boldness of the stroke electrified the community. It neces-sarily meant that the Governor had given way, that he regretted the reprieve, and was willing to do the community the pleasure of having the man hanged at all hazards. He was not like Pilate going to wash his hands in testimony of his innocence of the blood for which they clamoured, but he was willing to consent to such a method as this in order that the former reprieve might be practically recalled and the man hung to please the people.

Never was a trial so rapidly prepared for since the Colony had been con-stituted. All the legal forms were carefully observed. It was a lynching, but a lynching by the law-officers, with the aid of magistrates, juries, and all the paraphernalia of the court. On ordinary occasions there is in Mauritius a large amount of pity for any criminal condemned to death even where justly condemned. Where race hatreds are not aroused the people are perhaps on the whole more tender hearted than other communities. Some years ago a very bad murder was committed by an Indian upon another Indian who was his employer, and upon a fellow servant who went to the rescue of the master. The case was clearly proved, but a delay arose in determining the fate of the criminal as the Governor was absent in a dependency of the Colony.

The delay was not very long, not longer than the time usually given in England and Scotland to a criminal to prepare for death, but that was sufficient to raise all the compassion of the community in favour of the con-demned. When the Governor returned the sentence was confirmed, but a petition was so numerously signed in favour of commutation and the wish of the people was in general on the side of mercy, that the Governor afterwards commuted. There have been many theories about the hair turning grey in a remarkably short time under the influence of strong emotion. In this case the criminal had when condemned hair which was completely black. He was altogether a dark, swarthy scowling savage, but when brought out of gaol into Court to have the respite read to him his hair had become not white but certainly grey during the three weeks or so which had elapsed, and thus so far justifying the contention of the people that the time of uncertainty was of itself a terrible punishment. But with regard to Jean if there were any who were shocked at the course adopted they were so completely in the minority or so wholly taken by surprise as to be able to make no sign. The town rang with the praises of the Governor General for his courage and ingenuity.

Jean was again placed in the dock. The chief witness on this occasion was Serjeant Stocks who described the attack upon him in the worst colours, and a jury composed of wild and fiery partisans like the first were easily induced to bring in a verdict of guilty. In ordinary circumstances they would have estimated the evidence which was given in its true light, but it was patent to every one, and accepted by the jury, that the present trial was only a mode by which the error of the Executive on the first occasion was to be got over, and a notorious criminal receive his deserts. Again Jean entered the portals of the prison doomed to death. In front of the gates of the Courtyard his old father, supported by some of his neighbours, was tottering along to a carriole, bowed down to the earth, as if with a burden which was too heavy for him to bear. There was now no hope of a respite, and the execution it was known would not be referred beyond two days.

While all this was in progress, Lucille continued ill, but she was convalescent when Jean was condemned for the second time, and she aroused herself with the desire of doing something to save him. In La Baie where all the events which had led to the second conviction were known the feeling was dangerously strong against the authorities. It would probably have fared ill with Serjeant Stocks had he ventured to return to his station that night, but he did not, or rather he could not, because he was drunk in town. From La Baie the indignation of the negro race was manifested as it were simultaneously throughout the country. It was felt that whether Jean were guilty or not of the first murder that this condemnation a second time would not have been attempted on any white, and probably not on any Indian, as they had the government of India to look after and protect them.

One little sheet in town was edited by a Coloured man who had kept himself more or less independent of the cliques and factions, and who while he had a hatred of injustice was not without the courage necessary to express it. He had been shocked by the second trial, but had not ventured upon expressing an opinion until it was absolutely necessary to save the man's life. Many intelligent persons of the negro race had been with him the morning after the trial, and he found that he would not be destitute of support if he went boldly in to prevent the execution. When he had once made up his mind his language was not a bit more measured than that of his white brethren. Indeed violence of language seems to be the only idea such men have of telling articles. And on this occasion that he did not spare it may be gathered from the heading of his column of indignation. It was entitled "Murder by chicanery worse than murder by the knife." And not to do things by halves he got a number of those who had called upon him in reference to the trial to send his article to the Governor and the Procureur General from various parts of the country, drawing their attention to it, and stating that they approved of its contents, and if Jean were executed they would certainly bring the affair to the notice of the Queen in Council. This was quite a new aspect of affairs.

The Governor had been told by one and all of his officials that the whole community without exception called for an example in the case of Jean as the murder had been so atrocious. It was thus and thus only he had been induced to lend any countenance to the scheme which had been proposed for getting rid of the commutation, but he had never liked it and he felt that such a choice would not be approved of in England. It was bad enough to be told by a Judge that if he wished to murder the man he could do so, but after yielding at that time to be now told publicly that his alternative action was also regarded as little better than murder, and would be brought officially to the notice of the ruling authorities from whom he derived his Commission, was the reverse of comfortable. His first resolve was to have it out with the Procureur General who had induced him to sanction the second trial.

"Well, Monsieur Parquet," he said to him as he entered his room. "Do you see what the little *En Avant* says of both of us this morning?"

"Oh the miserable sheet! Is it possible Your Excellency reads such a rascally production as that."

"Yes I have sometimes seen wholesome truths in it, but what I would like to know is how much these views expressed in it are shared by the coloured population."

"Scarcely one man in the community besides the Editor I should imagine," said the official. "He has no influence and no following."

At this moment a peon entered and placed a letter before the Governor who carelessly opened it. A copy of the *En Avant* fell out on the floor, and the Governor turning to the letter found it to be a solemn protest from one of the community against the trial, and an approval of the doctrines of the little paper. It was in fact from Mr Blancgilet whom we first heard of on the evening of the ball as delaying the champagne to the small consternation of Captain Bloater. The Governor handed the letter to the law officer with the remark, "The Editor has at least a following of one, Monsieur Parquet, and I should imagine Blancgilet to be a man of considerable importance in that section of the community."

"Oh no," replied M. Parquet, "he had some influence at one time but he has entirely lost it. He is of the most immoral character!" The Governor smiled. This charge was always made against political opponents, and generally by those whose own conduct could scarcely bear investigation.

"But don't you think if the proceedings shock even an immoral man that there must be something wrong about them?"

"It is because he is a noir that he sympathises with the murderer," argued the official.

"In that case probably others, perhaps many, perhaps the whole of the black population, will also sympathise with him."

"What if they did, they have no influence. Your Excellency is supported by the whole body of the respectable press and by all the influential inhabitants of the Colony."

"I know what the support of the respectable press means. It means that if by their false and exaggerated views they get me into a difficulty, they will instantly turn round and assail me, and you whose advice I have followed will never be mentioned except in terms of adulation. I know your people, M. Parquet, a little better now."

The Peon again entered and another letter was laid before the Governor which on being opened was found to contain another copy of the *En Avant*, and the sender of the letter this time was a venerable missionary of the London Missionary Society who had laboured in the island for fifty years, and who was the trusted friend and leader of all the old slave class and of the coloured population generally which had sprung from them. His letter was conceived in terms of the utmost respect, but it contained a grave warning in regard to the course which had been followed, and such an intimation of the dissatisfaction of the black and coloured people that in reading it the Governor changed colour and said hastily:

"D— it, Parquet, you have led me into a pretty mess."

It was now Parquet's turn to change colour, and he said, "Surely your Excellency does not doubt that the advice I gave you was good although it may not meet with the approval of a Protestant missionary bigot who was always stirring up the blacks to resist the government."

"Now, Parquet, you know that you are talking at random, for more loyal men than these do not exist in any of the Colonies, and that makes their interference on such occasions the more significant. I at least do not intend to ignore their views."

Another letter was now handed in. It contained a Petition drawn up by Jean's Counsel, who had at length felt a force of opinion around him sufficiently strong to induce him to act with decision, as he saw some hope of obtaining credit by a big, if delayed, effort to save his client. He put the facts of the second trial in a sufficiently strong light, and intimated that His Excellency could obtain the real facts if he were to send for the record of the first trial for assault in the District Court. He reminded the Governor moreover that although condemnations for attempts at murder were not uncommon, executions had not for a very long time followed upon any such convictions.

"But you don't mean to tell me, Parquet, that the prisoner had already been tried for the same offence before the Magistrate."

"For the same offence, no! How could that be, your Excellency, the Magistrate has no jurisdiction to try attempts at murder."

"But on the same facts, Monsieur Parquet, he appears to have been tried for assault, if this Counsel's statement be true, and it can scarcely be false as he said he defended in the Magistrates Court. Surely all this ought to have been explained to me before you got my sanction to the course you have followed."

"Your Excellency has probably forgotten all that was said at the time in explanation. I certainly mentioned the facts fully, and with regard to the attempt at murder I even said that a *nolle prosequi** had been entered in the full assurance that we could obtain a conviction in the other case."

"But you did not mention, I can vouch for it, that when you proposed to proceed for an attempt to murder the same offence had been already treated as an assault and the man been punished for it. We must have an immediate meeting of the Executive Council."

All morning before the Executive Council met, letters and remonstrances, petitions and anonymous threats continued to pour in upon the unhappy Governor who had been assured by every one of his official counsellors that the whole community without exception would approve of his vigour and determination to have Jean hanged. "This comes," he said to himself, "of having one's councillors solely from one class of the population – and not very honest at that," he added with his lips compressed and a scowl on his brow which boded no good to any of them if they had not kept out of his sight. For the whisper had gone round the offices that the Governor had been talking in a very loud key to Monsieur Parquet, and that he was in "a devil of a wax" about the trial.

Lucille first went to Jean's family at La Baie and from the father bowed down with grief she got the first authentic intelligence that it was indeed Jean's foot which had been in the verandah on the evening when she had visited Isidore. In rushing away he had stumbled over the body of old M. Amirantes already murdered and hence the marks on his bill hook and clothes which had staggered even those friends of Jean who were most disposed to believe in his innocence. Understanding now how her lover had come to be suspected, Lucille resolved that she would try whether she could not discover the actual murderers.

It might seem a bold thing for a young woman to attempt when the police had failed, but she knew more about the ways of all classes of the people than all the police in the country. She was a girl of clear intellect if of a vain and somewhat licentious disposition and now that one who loved her so devotedly, and whom she found that she also loved when he had got into so grave a position that his life was only worth a day or two's purchase, she rose almost to a height of female heroism in endeavouring to atone for her former lightness of conduct which had been productive of so much evil. In her long conversations with the housekeeper at Pompadour she had learned of the proceedings of the murdered man with his coolies, and knowing how absolutely impossible it was for any of the La Baie people to have been concerned in it, she came to the conclusion that it was the work of the Coolies and of the Coolies alone. Jean had not failed to mention to his father that it was little Madame Camille who had let him into the house and for what purpose, and with this clue in her hand Lucille betook herself to Pompadour. The same carriole, and the old road, but how different her feelings now from then! Lucille was reformed by the danger of her lover. She had vowed that if

* "unwilling to pursue/prosecute."

she could save Jean she would marry him at once if he would have her, and if not that thenceforth she would think and do only what was right, as the Priest might direct her. There was no necessity now to manoevre about the position to which she wished to be taken in the Camp or the Mansion house. She went at once to Madame Camille, and in a few words told her errand. She told her how sorry she was for her conduct in meeting Monsieur Isidore but that she loved Jean and if the girl would only assist her she would not only never interfere with her position, but would liberally reward her.

The Indian maid was glad to be informed that Jean had not murdered Isidore's father, but if not he, who could it be? She had never thought of the matter so terrified had she been lest Isidore should find out that it was she who had introduced Jean to the house. She was as much concerned as ever that this should be concealed and now she found that Lucille knew it and would probably inform Isidore if she could not find out the murderers. Her little brain became busy, and she told Lucille that there was one person who knew more about the doings in the camp than any one else, and that was Jothee. But that she and Jothee were not friends, and the only way to get any information out of Jothee was to pay her well.

Madame Camille explained about Jothee's marriage to Bhootan, who was her father, and that Bhootan had been killed because of this marriage by Jothee's other lovers but they had never been discovered or punished. Jehal was now her husband, and he and Jothee, to assure their own safety, had to make themselves acquainted with all the movements in the Camp. Lucille heard the name of Bhootan with a shudder for she remembered too well the ghastly evidence she and Isidore had had of his murder by discovering the head in the canal. They had agreed to say nothing about it in order to save themselves the exposure of being called to give evidence before the Magistrate, but the knowledge now gave her something by means of which she could approach Jothee. Lucille felt it would be a matter of the greatest difficulty to get the Indian woman to state what she knew unless she could arouse either her cupidity or her desire for revenge. She accordingly proceeded to the hut of Jothee with mingled hopes and fears.

It would be impossible to give the conversation between the two women except in the Creole patois which they both spoke, when the various ruses and turns of expression showed the remarkable cleverness of both. Jothee soon discovered, as Lucille had no desire to hide it, that it was her love for Jean which prompted her interference, and having this legitimate interest Jothee had less suspicion of her, and more certainty that so far as she could afford it, she would pay liberally for any information. She expressed the utmost indifference about the discovery of the murderer of Amirantes, keeping her sari well over her face in order that Lucille might not observe her eagerness to discover something about the other murder which was so much more important for her. When Lucille cautiously approached the subject and intimated in a vague way that she knew something of the latter, it was impossible for Jothee, try as she might not to display her eagerness and attention.

At last it was arranged that for a payment of ten pounds and the disclosure by Lucille of what she knew as to Bhootan's murder that Jothee would give important information as to the real murderers of Monsieur Amirantes. But without the money in hand, Jothee would not speak, or proceed further. The discovery of Bhootan's murder might be much, but the possession of ten pounds, to be added to the stock which she kept buried in her hut, and of the amount of which neither Jehal nor any one else knew, was greater far. The woman's avarice was so great that there was nothing she would not do to acquire money.

We have seen how she lived, but she was also one of the chief usurers of the camp, lending out money at a cent per shilling per month, so that on pay night she received in interest a larger sum than the wages of three or four able bodied men. She was always engaged also in transactions about marriage, advising the mothers of the young girls in the camp to whom to contract their daughters at the earliest possible age, even while they were yet infants, and assisting the men who made offers for them with the money necessary to purchase the consent of the father and mother, and for this money also the borrowers paid extortionate interest.

The authority which she thus gained throughout the camp was immense, and the debtors in order to get an extension of time for the payment of interest or instalments were always willing to communicate any facts about the lives of others which Jothee wished to know. Her eyes had already begun to burn with greater brilliancy at the prospect of the ten pounds but it must be paid before she would utter another word. Lucille was too weak to go back to Lorraine and return to Pompadour in the heat of the day, although she knew that Madame Beauvallon would at once give her the money for the purpose, and her next thought was to apply directly to Isidore. But she shrank from this, both because she feared she might again excite the jealousy of Madame Camille, and because she dreaded he might prematurely interfere with her plans, and thus spoil her prospects of saving Jean. Nor was she quite sure of obtaining the ten pounds from Isidore, who was not of a disposition much given to retain ready cash about him. The happy thought struck her of applying to Augustin's father who since he had been forced by his conscience to give evidence against Jean had been the most miserable of men as he was thoroughly convinced Jean could not be the murderer, and it was therefore with delight he welcomed Lucille, and from his own resources and those of one or two of the skilled workmen on the estate provided what was necessary. The interview which Lucille had with Jothee thereafter was of the most important description, and so certain did she feel of being able to do Jean essential service that she prevailed upon Jothee to come with her to town, when they resolved to go straight to the Governor.

Chapter 20
A Run Home

THE SOLDIERS WERE NOT WANTED IN NATAL. It was only one of those innumerable scares which are got up wherever there are native races, of disaffection and mysterious messages passing from village to village. The alarmists are bad enough at home when they get hold of such an idea as a French army of a hundred thousand men coming over in a night, without their assembling being known to us, or the vast fleet to bring them being detected, or their landing seen by any but a Coastguardsman who is promptly to be silenced. The gullible in such a nation as Great Britain are naturally numerous, and those who have the chance of profiting by their terrors do not spare them. But in a Colony where the whites are in the small minority the conditions for getting up a scare are still more favourable. The pettiest incident is magnified into a proof of the most determined intention of the blacks to rise and exterminate the ruling race. It was so in the old slavery days when the planters had uneasy consciences, and where wars between the European powers were frequent, affording opportunities which might be taken advantage of by the intending rebels.

At the close of the last century the rising in Haiti was naturally looked upon in the West Indies as the beginning of the end. Every slave who shewed the least independence of character was supposed to be brooding over the part of Liberator and had to be dealt with accordingly. The whites by their terrors told their slaves more of what had taken place than they could ever have learned by themselves. So it is everywhere throughout the world where the numbers of the races are unequal. Natal was no exception to the rule. Wars of a sort were numerous enough but rumours of wars scarcely ever ceased. It was during one of these temporary panics that the Lieutenant Governor had demanded more military assistance, and the wing of Jack's regiment had been sent from Mauritius. Long before it arrived the panic was over, and forgotten, only the expense of the scare had to be met. The officers who were new to the country obtained leave of absence and went off to the interior to hunt large game. This was every bit as dangerous as war and infinitely more beneficial. Some people wonder why our Government does not try to make its army of use to civilization in some way. The Romans built roads and our own brave fellows might help to do some useful public work.

In war the more people who are killed, the greater number of helpless beings are left behind without bread-winners, the more acres go out of tillage, the less food is there for the world at large. We seem somehow to be afraid that the manhood of our race will be questioned if we are not always killing off thousands of savages. We can see very well the absurdity of the Americans imagining that their prowess will be disputed unless they sweep away every remaining tribe of Indians with whom they may come in contact. We can detect the weak points and vanity of the French policy when they go swaggering to Tonquin and elsewhere.[†] How much better is the manhood of a race proved by saving life!

When in a tempestuous sea a boat is lowered from a passing ship, where all the crew are safe, to rescue a handful of shipwrecked mariners clinging to a vessel in the last stage of jeopardy, mankind acknowledges without a dissonant voice that here is true heroism. When men descend into the bowels of the earth where an explosion has rendered the atmosphere of a mine more dangerous than if it were filled by ten thousand arrows or with shells thicker than gnats in midsummer, to rescue, or attempt to rescue, others already standing face to face with death, then we feel all the thrill which the noblest of actions sends vibrating through the soul. The race degenerating because there has been no butchers' bill of savages armed with inferior weapons, and who can be comfortably slain at a distance with all but assured safety to ourselves! Pshaw! Let us revise our dictionary definition of manhood if it has come to this!

Jack was among those who went up country. Being a splendid horseman and good shot he enjoyed himself thoroughly. The excitement, the novel scenery, the strange wild beasts with which they became familiar, served to keep him from brooding, and gave him abundant materials for letters back to Estelle and home. Not being quite sure whether Madame Beauvallon would permit her daughter to correspond in the altered views she had adopted, he had not written many letters to Estelle but had sent some to a friend to be forwarded according to his discretion. It was not difficult for his friend to arrange this as Mahmoud, Jack's old servant, still continued in his new service and was generally to be found about when wanted. At home the letters said so much of the new country, and so little of the old Island, that his parents began to entertain hopes that the change of scenery had been good for Jack's love weakness, and that time only was needed to wean him entirely from the thought of an alliance which would be so embarrassing for all. They imagined that if he could only be brought home for a few months that change of scene and the old home ideas would entirely cure him. The family mentors, Parchment & Parchment, were all in favour of this course. Their notions of propriety had been sorely shaken by the proposed alliance which threatened to introduce new and alien elements into the family history. And they were aided in a way and from a quarter they least suspected.

A letter arrived one morning from the Revd. Père Vendredi, written in French, a very long letter indeed, setting forth what he represented to be the objections of Madame Beauvallon to the match, which we need not say, coming through such a channel, were mainly on religious grounds, and begging that the respectable and honoured Father and Mother of M. Jean Montmorency would use their influence with him to abandon his pretensions to the hand of Mademoiselle Estelle Beauvallon. This was quite a new view of it which certainly had never occurred either to Jack's father or mother or to Parchment & Parchment. They had taken from the beginning the same view as the Colonel of the regiment that it had been an attempt only too success-ful of the wily Creoles to entrap the young officer into an unsuitable match. That a Mauritian family would presume to entertain the idea that a marriage with the Montmorencys of —shire would not be suitable for their daughter seemed too preposterous. The pride of Jack's mother was severely wounded. She had not been indisposed to let her boy have his own way, believing that he would not have chosen one unworthy to be his wife. She had dreamed of the home-coming and of taking the bride entirely under her own protection, of adopting her in short fully and completely as one of the family there being in England no other family to which she owed divided allegiance.

The good lady had also views and hopes that when the son's wife came home and saw their beautiful church and heard the service, as high as it could possibly be without calling for the interference of the Bishop, that she would be gradually led to see the errors of Popery and become recon-ciled to a Church which was Catholic without any admixture of the errors of Romanism. But the mother of the young lady had been beforehand with her, and actually, by the hand of her priest, or Confessor, or Chaplain, or whatev-er post he might hold, objected to any association with an English protestant family. The letter would not have been required if the young lady herself had seen reason to change her mind. The information which the Priest gave on this matter was very meagre, he apparently taking it for granted that her wishes had little to do with it. But they had a great deal to do with it in the eyes of the English mother. She began at once to paint to herself a delicate young girl, desperately in love with Jack, and for his sake willing to flee from all her evil surroundings, and to become accepted as a humble member of the true Church, pining away in secret, while a cunning Jesuit in order to pre-serve his influence over the family, was doing his best to thwart her wishes, to ruin her health, and it may be cause her death, to the life long sorrow of her beloved son. This must not be, and from that moment the excellent lady adopted a more energetic policy and became a partisan of the Mauritius mar-riage. She wanted Jack more than ever to come home as she wished to console him in the difficulties which he was meeting with, and to assure him if he succeeded of his mother's unalterable love both to him and his. The father had not exactly come to the same conclusion although his pride had not been the less painfully wounded by the new development. Apart from this phase of it he was not so sure that an effort should not be made with Jack so as to meet Madame Beauvallon half way. Separated as the young people now were, it would not be difficult to keep them so long apart that time would have so softened the impressions in their hearts as to make a formal break-off easy enough.

He remembered full well that in the ship in which he was, a young officer got engaged to a Ceylon girl who after several years had elapsed was brought home to marry him, and at the Station, to which he went to meet her, he did not know her again, and had to be freshly introduced! Absence makes the heart grow fonder, yes, let us not contest the ancient and well-worn propositions. But absence certainly makes the memory grow weaker, and with growing forgetfulness comes all absorbing indifference. Men go away on foreign service leaving their wives and children behind. They return after years of separation, during which the most affectionate letters have been interchanged, and find themselves strangers in their own house. New friends come in to offer their congratulations whom the head of the house has never seen, and probably of whom he has never even heard. The wife of his bosom looks on him curiously as if she were inwardly comparing him with his former self, and his children have outgrown his knowledge of them and their knowledge of him. It is only after weeks or months when new ties knit them together once more that the sense of being a stranger is completely overcome.

Jack's father had gone through all these experiences, and he was inclined to value absence greatly as a good friend in the circumstances in which his son was placed. How often had he himself formed attachments in foreign ports! How often had his heart been torn by partings, ay, just such partings as Byron describes so well as taking the very life out of young hearts. And yet how soon had the torn heart mended! The friendships, the flirtations, the attachments, were looked back upon in after life as pleasant reminiscences, and the retrospect rather added to than took from his happiness. When he remembered some of them as he sat by the winter fire a smile would steal over his face, and he would be teased to explain to his wife of what he had been thinking. Sometimes he did tell the story, sometimes he found it more convenient to abstain, and to pass off the smile with a laugh. Jack the son was now passing through the same waters. He had certainly got deeper in than his father ever went, but it is only a question of a few inches nearer the chin after all, indeed what of it if he only gets out by swimming, so that he does get out in the end. It would be so much more seemly and like the old Jack to marry one of the neighbour's girls, and settle down among his own people without having attractions and interests at the other side of the globe. But in spite of this, notwithstanding all that had been thought of and said to Parchment junior and the Doctor, and the Clergyman, and others, if he found his son's affections were too deeply engaged to permit him to draw back, or the young lady desirous that the engagement formally made should be adhered to, he was not going to be deterred from giving his consent, or induced to withdraw the consent already given, by the plotting of any d— Priest, Jesuit or otherwise.

In employing such an intermediary Madame Beauvallon, from her ignorance of England and English ways, had made a great mistake, a much greater one than Jack had made in abstaining from calling after the accident to M. Beauvallon, or going to the picnic at Mahebourg. She had touched English sensitiveness to the quick, mortified the family pride and obtruded the religious difficulty in its most offensive form. "How am I to reply to this rascally Jesuit?" was Mr Montmorency's question every morning between the reception of the letter and the going out of the next mail. "Must I write him in French? I suppose it would be the proper thing to do. But I cannot; I could have done it very well at one time, but not now." Indeed the worthy gentleman was flattering himself in this. He never, at any period of his life, could have written a French letter which would not have excited shouts of laughter if read aloud to a French audience. One has met young English officers occasionally who would converse in another tongue than their own, but very seldom indeed. Civilians who speak foreign languages well are much more common. But we compare badly with Foreign services in this respect. Most German naval officers for example speak English if not perfectly at least with ease, and they are generally good enough to say that it is necessary for them to do so as English is the maritime language of the world. They are exceedingly modest withal, not many being like that Commander who imagined himself to be a young Bismarck, and who boasted "that ven the American Captain did not go ven he had said he vould go, I told him you are a liar! And he vept!" On every French ship officers are found who know English. There is a decided change for the better in the English service, and it is to be hoped the improvement may continue.

If the learning of modern languages were only placed first in the list at public schools instead of last, if Latin and Greek were recognised to be admirable in their own place, but very much out of place when they alone are badly taught, and nothing absolutely needed in everyday life taught at all, then we shall find our young men more truly instructed and less frequently made to feel to their humiliation that their education has been grossly neglected. So Mr Montmorency was not quite correct in imagining that he could at any time have written a decent French letter, but in the end he came to the conclusion that it was his duty to write in his own language, as it was of course perfectly well known to the educated Creoles of the Island, although not perhaps to this French Priest. The letter was more guarded and diplomatic than might have been expected, but it expressed surprise that there should be any objection to a union now which had lately been so much approved and appreciated (the writer thought that a good word as implying a great deal) but that in the absence of his son, and in his ignorance of the true sentiments of the young lady, he could give no promise of any kind. He added that at any future time he should be very happy to hear the views of Madame Beauvallon from herself, but that he did not think it desirable that family affairs should be discussed through the medium of others, however pious, learned and respectable. This was the portion of the letter which gave most satisfaction to the Mother, who could scarcely be prevailed upon to abstain from writing to Estelle herself to offer her a home in England whenever she chose to avail herself of it.

It was not difficult for Mr Montmorency next time he went to town to learn at the Horse Guards that there would be no objection to his son getting leave of absence if applied for in the usual way. He accordingly wrote Jack by the following mail that they would be all glad to see him home for a short spell, and sending him what pleases a young officer so much — a Draft without its having been asked for. Being thus flush of cash Jack thought it better to come across country to Cape Town in order to see the Colony and the life of the settlers in the interior. Taking his own time on the journey, changing his mode of travelling as suited his fancy, now enjoying the luxuries of the bullock wagon, now behind a team of horses flying along up hill and down dale in the usual break-neck Cape fashion, and now riding, he found his tour most interesting. And how he enjoyed the comforts of Cape Town when at length he reached the Capital.

The hotels were not at all of the American type, but Jack had not travelled in America and was therefore ignorant alike of their comforts or drawbacks. He found them clean, and comfortable, the food plain and substantial, with only a general deficiency of good wines! There was quite enough to interest him for the few days that intervened before the sailing of the home mail; the drive to Constantia, the ascent of Table Mountain with some of the officers of the regiment stationed in town and a drive to Simon's Bay which he found too toilsome to be pleasant. The night the steamer left Cape Town was one of the most lovely it is possible to conceive. The vessel was to start at one in the morning, a dinner party occupied the time until eleven; a few of the guests accompanied Jack to the hotel for a parting cup, and to permit him to pick up his last portmanteau, and then they all proceeded to the place of embarkation. Not a pleasant place certainly if the wind comes strong from the sea when the huge rollers fall thundering on the beach.

There is really no harbour, only an exposed road-stead. Indeed a desolate barren-looking shore extends for several hundred miles North along this portion of the African continent. Sailing luggers constructed for the purpose are employed to pass between the vessels and the shore. Passengers who do not feel comfortable when they see the long swell coming in from the sea generally prefer this mode of conveyance. Jack and his friends went off in a row-boat belonging to the agent for the steamers, and enjoyed to the utmost the beauty of the night. The moon was near the full. A gauzy silver haze hung over the horizon and the hills above. It was even more beautiful thus than if the sky had been clear. The great lustrous stars hung out in the dreamy haze, some of them throwing faint gleams on the bay which mingled with the stronger reflections cast by the lights of the steamer. The huge mountain was in garb of silver with a crown of stars. Long did Jack linger on deck to revel in the beauty of the night until the lights of the town grew faint, and there arose before the gallant ship nought but the glittering track into the vast ocean which washes the African shore.

The sensation with which one arrives at home after a few years absence is not always wholly pleasurable. The shorter the absence, the delight is perhaps the greater, for no overwhelming change is feared. Old friends can be greeted just as they were left, perambulating the same streets at the same hour, leaving home and returning by the same trains or bus, and with the old smile or the old frown unchanged. When one has been absent for twelve or fourteen years there is much that is mournful amid the pleasure of visiting the capital of the world. Some of the illusions with which one went out may have vanished, many of the friends one left behind may have gone forever, others may be changed past knowing, and there is always the great mass of people passing and repassing who know not us, and whom we do not know, and with whom it is hard to think we can ever again drop into line and become one of themselves. On one occasion coming up Southampton Water when I was all eagerness to get back after only a few months' absence, for there were those at home watching and waiting to welcome me, and little ones to be awakened out of sleep to get a cuddle from Papa, one who was still young was standing beside me on the poop. He had come from Chile, and like most of us on board had been counting the hours until Southampton could be reached. But now when it was close, when Netley Hospital could be descried and the shores of the Sound were coming out clear – he said "I have made a mistake, I will go back by the next ship."

"Why what's wrong?"

"I know nobody at home. I left as a boy, I have been living a different life out there, and have all my friends and acquaintances, all my pleasures and hopes in that other country. What can I do here sauntering about London without knowing a friend in it. All my relatives I care about are dead."

"Come, come," I said, "You are feeling this biting spring wind to which you are unaccustomed. Stay at Southampton over night. Get a good dinner at the Hotel – go to a theater if there is one, and when you reach London tomorrow you will feel that your capacity of enjoyment has not get been exhausted. Meantime, come and take a cocktail to warm you up."

No doubt many feel as that wanderer felt. And yet how few are the changes after all. The individuals of the crowd pouring along Cheapside may be different, but it is a crowd of men pouring just as it used to pour. If there is any difference in those bus drivers or conductors one cannot see it. The Exchange is in its old place – and the Mansion House. The Bank of England has not taken to itself wings and flown away – although wealth proverbially does so. Nay in less renowned quarters what a touching sameness. So thought Jack, as having taken a room for the night at Paddington Hotel when the train from Plymouth arrived, he passed along Praed Street to the Edgeware Road, and felt all the difficulty which everyone feels of realizing that he had ever been out of London.

There were some new remembrances and emotions within, but the world had not changed without. The same fishmongers shop with the same remnants of fish and lobsters displayed, the same withered vegetables on the greengrocer's window tables, the same little tobacconists', the same old clothes hanging from the same pegs, the same old lady running for the wrong bus, and the same men going the same gin horse round of daily cares,[†] and evening tramps homewards, to eat the same meal of tea and shrimps with stale bread and staler butter. Who would live consistently at home if he had the chance of seeing the world abroad? Where is the sunshine of the tropics with its glory, where the gay clad crowd of swarthy faces, where the jagged peaks of the volcanic hills, where the glittering sea, and the great blue dome of the oer-arching and all-embracing sky, with the calm white cloud gliding in mid-air? Why have I left the flowers and the trees, the morning hours of heat and the evenings of coolness and perfection of beauty, for this scene of care and this clime of cold, for this souless sky and the dust and smoke of these wretched streets?

When Jack had extended his walk to Regent Circus and found himself amid the roar and bustle he felt at least he was in the world and not out of it. The news-boys were spreading out fresh wet copies of a new evening edition, and there on the large bills were the news of all the world for the day. A great debate was taking place in the House of Commons, and while it had scarcely begun the public were being told of what was going on within the House. He dined at a well-remembered Cafe, and here at least was one who recognised him in the waiter who said, "Not seen you for some time Sir. What will you have Sir – fried sole" as in the old times. There was one immense advantage of being in a large City which it took Jack some time to realize, that best of all of blessings, [anonymity]. He could dine where he liked, he could travel in a hansom or a bus, he could go, in the suit he had come out in, to any of the theatres and enjoy the play, he could saunter along looking at the girls, none daring to make him afraid of a scandal being all over the town in the morning. And the world is not so big after all. Here comes swinging up to him on Regent Street an Engineer Officer whom he had met in Mauritius, and with whom he soon made arrangements to spend the rest of the night in a general run through well-known haunts.

View of the harbour of Port Louis

Chapter 21
Canes and Hurricanes

THE BEAUVALLONS HAD REMOVED TO LORRAINE. Many reasons prompted Madame to take this step, but not the least was for the sake of economy. On the estate they had everything which was required for the house except luxuries, and they could venture where few visitors ever appeared, to live much less expensively. The crop had not turned out very well. That fatal drought which threatened to destroy cultivation altogether in that quarter of the island, had been severely felt. The canes had not only been of feeble growth but insects brought into being by the dryness of the weather had been very destructive.

The account at the Bank was coming fast up, it is true, on the right side with the sales of such sugars as they had been able to make, but it was necessary to look ahead, to think of the capital required to carry on the estate through the *entre coupe* or season when the canes are growing, and when the wages of the numerous Coolies must be paid all the same. Madame Beauvallon felt that the head and hand of the proprietor must be on the spot. Managers and employés are all very well. They may be perfectly honest, and their skill not inferior to that of the proprietor himself, but the estate is not theirs, and what they naturally consider is how to do their duty fairly well and enjoy some of the pleasures of life for themselves. With the proprietor the sole question is "will this be for the good of the estate?" with the employé the question may be the same, but there is added to it, "and may it be done tomorrow?" Then not all managers and employes are honest. On great sugar estates like those on Mauritius where the Coolie gets his rations served out to him, a very little carelessness may make a great waste. Some labourers may be favourites who may get too much rice because the employé obtains a quid pro quo and so on throughout the details of the management. The presence of the Proprietor may prevent many quarrels which in his absence get embittered, causing loss to the estate and outlay in appeals to the Magistrate, and loss of precious time at the busiest season of the year. Madame had received some ominous warnings from the Notary that she might find it difficult to get advances of capital next year. She desired both to inspire confidence by her personal attention to the estate, and by the fact that she intended to make the place her home, and would if necessary advance her own fortune for its culture.

The Abbé also resided in the country. Madame Beauvallon felt more and more her dependence on the spiritual adviser whom destiny had sent to her. He was shrewd in business matters as well as devout and attentive to his religious duties. It must be admitted also that if he was thin he was fond of a good curry, or a good dinner generally, and had got into the habit of coming very often to Lorraine when there was not much in the Presbytery. Aunt Clémence had found him not so very ignorant after all of the fashionable literature of Paris. He required to know it only of course to guard the young people of his flock from reading unfit books, and he could thus converse about the chief novels, with many expressions of pity for the writers and of concern for their souls. One thing troubled him, he felt he was making no way with Estelle. She did not seem to enter into the spirit of the preparations for Confirmation, and yet there was nothing he had more set his heart on than having the daughter of one of his leading parishioners to present to the Bishop when he came down for the purpose. It is very odd that the pious man was concerned infinitely more about the spiritual state of this young girl whose sins had not been very numerous or very great, than he was about the condition of Isidore Amirantes who he had very good reason to know was not likely to be numbered among the Saints if he came to die. He had never indeed spoken to Isidore on the subject of his soul, but he was continuously lamenting to Estelle the want of proofs of an exalted spirituality.

But Estelle had mental food to sustain her which the Abbé knew not of. From time to time Mahmoud brought from town those letters which Jack had written from Natal in which he poured out all his fervent love, and expressed his longing for the time when he could again visit Mauritius. It may seem strange that Jack should so take for granted that Estelle did not approve of her Mother's action, but he trusted her so completely that he could not imagine that she could do otherwise than love him as before. He knew of no reason for a change in her feelings, the matters referred to in her mother's letter being much too trifling to separate heart from heart. From time to time, indeed, an unwelcome shade crossed his thoughts. Could it be possible that her estimation of "the cub" had changed? But why should such a thing be when having known him for years she yet preferred another? His self-respect and self-assertion came to the rescue. It was impossible for Estelle to prefer such a man to him, so that he wrote in the full assurance that any resentment she could possibly have felt against him must have been appeased, and the old love be still burning. He had been immensely comforted by Ernestine's saying "Elle vous aime toujours!" He dwelt upon the expression, and inwardly thanked the kind good soul who had given utterance to it. She had always been his friend from the first days of the meetings under the filaos, and why should she deceive him by such an utterance if Estelle were unfaithful and loved another? No, no; he painted her in all the brightness and bloom of her beauty, true to him, and to her engagement whatever attempts others might be making to wean her affections from her English lover.

Such attempts were certainly being made. Isidore had not received permission to visit the family at Lorraine without fully availing himself of the opportunity. He had never been able to repeat the spell of his first visit, but he had a most insinuating manner which would have made him a dangerous rival had Estelle been less true. Always gay, he brightened up the house when he entered it. The other constant visitor, the worthy Abbé, did not do too much in that direction. He was not without his use certainly to both of the older ladies, to Madame from her trust in him, and desire to attend more and more closely to the duties of religion, to Aunt Clémence on account of his literature and his powers of disputation.

Estelle tolerated him and no more, as she felt little inclined to submit her intellect and heart to his teachings, and indeed, for that part of it, infinitely preferred the talk of Isidore. Not only did the latter give them all the news of Port Louis so much better than the relatives who sometimes visited them, but who did not now reside on the estate (rats, it is said, leave a sinking ship), but he was full of information about Paris society. He could tell of the leading politicians, the famous novelists, the young and promising men of science, the actors and actresses, the singers male and female who were making their mark in the musical world, the artists, and the ladies who were starring at Court or flattered for their brief hour in less distinguished but still too well known hearts. He knew the latest fashion of dresses, and could tell the prices which were being paid for the robes which at that time were astonishing Europe. Isidore did not find all these things in the French newspapers because, full of gossip as they were, and giving much information of the persons who were coming to the front in society, there was yet a vast world behind the journals which they never seemed to be able to, or did not care to, touch – like other professions that run in grooves. He got a great deal of information, however, from his correspondents. Some of his friends had gone permanently to France, and there were always some young Mauritians in the French capital each of whom contributed something to the general stack of information. Isidore was a favourite and himself a good correspondent, so that perhaps he knew more than any other man in the Island of what was taking place out of it. What the people of Mauritius look upon as the great world beyond them is simply France. Very few of them care about what goes on in England unless it be something affecting sugar. They are as French now as they were at the time of the capture and will remain so for a generation or two to come.

Madame Beauvallon sympathised with Isidore for another reason. The estate of Pompadour was in the same condition as that of Lorraine. The drought which affected the one had affected the other, and he also had received hints that he might find difficulty in arranging advances for the *entre coupe.** There was much talk therefore of irrigation, of soils, of manure, of the general nature of the vegetable world, of the botanical family to which the sugar cane belonged, of methods of crushing more sugar out of the bagasse, of the most profitable employment for the syrup, and the thousand and one constantly recurring questions as to the best way of getting most work out of the Coolies with least pay. It is to be regretted that this was the department of the management in which Madame Beauvallon excelled. She had been accustomed to Estates from her infancy, and had seen all the methods of many careful managers. She was not unjust, but hard and unsympathetic with the

---

* The low season when cane is not harvested.

alien race. Isidore spoke in the most cynical manner of the many tricks he tried in order to make the monthly pay list less, and his confessions raised a laugh from both the ladies, they were chuckled over by the Priest, and Estelle heard them without the slightest surprise or compunction as it was the kind of talk she had been accustomed to all her life.

Another misfortune was about to visit both estates, and apparently to bind the fortunes of the families still more closely together. It was now the time when *coups de vents,** or hurricanes, might be feared. Mauritius and the neighbouring island of Bourbon are right in the track of those visitants caused by the conflict of the winds from the North and South of the Equator at the hot season of the year. The science of storms had not yet reached that perfection which it has since attained, mainly through the attention which has been paid to the matter by the Mauritius government, and by their having attained the services of a man remarkably well fitted for the post of Meteorological Observer. For nearly thirty years the movements of every hurricane which has visited these seas has been carefully marked on skeleton charts. The Observer obtains copies of all the logs of all the ships which enter the port after having encountered a storm, and from this information he can lay down the course of the hurricane, the direction of the wind, and the state of the barometer. After he has thus watched its progress towards the Island, he follows it up by his own observations while crossing the Island and traces its track into the deep until it has spent its fury. With the knowledge acquired by this careful series of observations and with the aid of the excellent instruments which the Colonial Government has provided the approach, and probable course, and intensity of a hurricane can now be judged of with great certainty.

The Island is very seldom taken unprepared. The science of meteorology has necessarily obtained a great development where such disturbances occur, and where the effect of them may be so great upon the fortunes of individuals and the Island in general. The state of the barometer and the condition of the weather during the months of summer are carefully studied, and whenever it begins to blow in heavier gusts than usual from the South-east, with lulls between, the weather-wise begin their usual predictions. Now that railways have been added to the comfort and conveniences of the population an announcement in the following terms may be read at Port Louis Station when the afternoon trains are going out to the country: "A hurricane is approaching the Island from the North-east. Its present velocity is ten miles an hour with a tendency to increase. Estimated distance 600 miles. We are safe from this particular storm for two days, but it may be better to prepare. Atmospheric disturbances such that it is not improbable two hurricanes may be in the neighbourhood."

The trains are always crowded at this hour, the first and second classes with planters, employés, traders, and people of the middle rank generally who have been in town for business or pleasure. They profit by the announcement and inform their neighbours. The third class carriages are full of Indians, Chinese, and black Creoles or Mozambiques as they are still called

* Cyclones, lit. "gales of wind."

in the Island from the country of their origin, and they carry the intelligence to all the estates, and villages, to which they are bound. Then the sound of the hammer is heard, and of the axe, in order to strengthen roofs or put up supports to rickety walls. The chains which in many houses are kept ready for the purpose are thrown across the dwelling houses, and clamped down to the piles driven deep down into the earth. The Indian who has built for himself a wretched hovel, and roofed it with scraps of galvanized iron, places ropes balanced by heavy stones across the ridge. On the estates the fastenings of the mill windows are looked to, the bagasse shed propped up, the Coolies ordered to make their houses secure, and in general such a preparation goes on as is done on board ship when a careful Mariner knows he is approaching tempestuous [waters], or sees from the barometer that there is stormy weather about. In a well-built home village, or on a farm of the ordinary class, such preparations would be unnecessary as the buildings are so much more substantial. In the Colony all the buildings are of wood except perhaps the mill house where the machinery is and the mill chimney. Mansion, stables, out-houses are as a rule of wood. The cottages of the labourers baffle description. It is thus that a hurricane, often not stronger than a full winter gale at home, plays havoc with an estate and looks so alarming when it is reported in the papers.

The real danger is for those at sea, or rather the real danger was for the passenger sailing ships of the years of which I speak. Now with the first class steamers which perform the mail service a hurricane is no longer a thing of dread. With a full head of steam they can go quicker than most hurricanes, and the barometer never fails to warn them of its approach. Experience has enabled a practical and easy rule to be laid down as to where the centre of the disturbance is at any stage of its approach. To stand with the back to the wind and to hold out the right hand at right angles to the body is not a very difficult rule to remember, but that is all that is necessary to find out where the centre of the hurricane is in the Southern hemisphere. The Captain of the steamer can adjust his course accordingly, he may go faster or slower, but generally he ought to hold such a course as makes his barometer rise in place of fall. All these theories are of modern origin, and are so much more easily put in practice by a vessel whose propelling power is independent of the wind. It seems a cruel thing to force a vessel lying at the anchorage ground called the Bell Buoy of Port Louis, to go to sea at the approach of a hurricane. But the reason is obvious. Lying there she would infallibly go ashore, when the wind changes, as the wind invariably does change in those circular storms from the East to the North. The sea brought in by the North wind mingles with and hustles against the sea which has been rolling before the Eastern gale, and high confused and angry rollers come rushing in upon the land. The only hope for a ship in such a position, when she has not been able to get into harbour in time, is to run for it, and by taking the right course she may, and frequently does, come back again to port after two or three days absence having run in a wide circle round the island without losing a spar.

This was a department of science in which Isidore took a great interest. He had heard so much about it in his boyhood that he had resolved to master all that books could tell him on the subject, and then to observe for himself the cyclones, or portions of cyclones, which crossed the Island every year. The weather was threatening when one day he visited Lorraine, and after the light breakfast he told the ladies all about it, and showed them how to read the barometer accurately so that they could observe for themselves. While he was speaking the head of the mercury began to assume a decidedly hollow appearance, and knowing that to be a more certain sign of a continued disturbance than even the hands moving down an occasional hundredth at a time, he advised the ladies to begin their preparations. It was well that they did so, in fact they had been somewhat remiss for the wind had for two days been coming in those gusts with heavy rain followed by lulls which is a pretty sure indication that the weather would get worse. It was, however, in its ordinary quarter of the South-east, and they had not taken particular notice.

The heavens soon began to be enveloped with a dense veil of mist rather than cloud, for it was without cloud formation. It covered the whole canopy of the sky, as with a garment. Not a fragment of blue could anywhere be seen. The gusts came more frequently and continued longer, lashing the earth with a fierce rain. All the labourers were recalled from the fields, the making of sugar was stopped, and the hands were employed in securing the buildings. Isidore had to return to his own Estate to see that the same preparations were made there. The ladies felt so much in need of some friend to be with them that it was with no small pleasure they saw the Abbé approaching with his portmanteau in the old buggy, showing that he proposed to afford them the comfort of his presence while the hurricane lasted.

The house at Lorraine had an excellent reputation for strength. It was built entirely of Colonial hard wood in the earlier days, when hurricanes had not been deprived of their stings by science, and when they were regarded as dreadful visitations direct from the Almighty. Aunt Clémence, however, happy to think they should have someone with them, could not help making sarcastic references to the strength of the Abbé's faith. The Presbytery had a reputation the very reverse of Lorraine. It was known to be in bad repair, and shaky, and would probably go if the hurricane were a bad one. Unfortunately, as Madame Beauvallon remembered in time, the Abbé made another mouth to feed, and these hurricanes sometimes lasted three, sometime five, days. Ernestine was now in her glory. Lucille was terrified, but Ernestine had had more experience, and looked upon *coups de vents* as ordinary incidents chiefly valuable as allowing her to come out as the good genius and thoughtful provider for the family. She soon had all the small boys in the camp doing her bidding, looking for eggs, bringing in chillies, turmeric, saffron, cocoanuts, coriander seed and all the materials for curries, catching fowls to feed them in a place of safety, and many other details which it would be difficult to particularize. Madame Beauvallon herself went over to superintend the issue of rations for five days to the Coolies, and she saw that the men were busy providing grass and cane tops for the mules and oxen.

The task of providing food for the numerous draft animals was difficult enough every afternoon, but to bring in five days food at once seemed impossible. The employés were, however, all working with a will. Each one had his own department, and his own gang, and in this way a wonderful amount of work was got through in a few hours. It was late before the labourers had finished, and then they had to assist their wives with their own preparations for comfort and safety. The Indians had already lost heart and were shivering with cold. The Creoles were laughing and resolved to make it the occasion for a holiday. The preparations of the latter chiefly consisted in making little refuges of branches and dried sugar cane leaves alongside of their ordinary dwellings, a kind of small hut like roof placed on the ground with the entrance at one end, as experience had taught them that this seemingly frail structure stood better than the firmer and less elastic houses, and were less dangerous to those beneath if they were blown down.

The Abbé turned out to be of great assistance after all. He made the safety of the dwelling house his especial work, and with hammer and nail he more firmly fixed up the hurricane shutters after they had been well barred within. The main house was shingled but several of the outhouses were thatched with cane leaves and these he fastened down by cross pieces of wood so that the wind should not get in under the eaves. It was only necessary to bar up completely as yet the side of the house where the wind was actually blowing, for in a storm beginning as this had done, the change from South-east to East and then to North and North-west where the hurricane generally culminated, would take more than one day. The night was an anxious one. Madame was evidently concerned lest some needful preparation had been forgotten. Although all pretended to go to bed at the usual hour, the older ladies did not sleep, listening hour by hour to the increasing violence of the gale which roared amid the trees surrounding the house. They were kept awake also by having to change the position of articles of furniture as the rain found an entrance through the shingles – *bardeaux* as they called them – which had been shrivelled with the heat.

When morning broke there could be no mistake about the hurricane. The rain driven by the violent gusts lashed the earth with fury. Nothing could be seen twenty yards from the verandah, while every few minutes the wind came on with a roar, bending all the trees in its path, sweeping up every moveable thing into its embrace, shaking the buildings as if by the force of an earthquake, and passing on over the desolate plain to be succeeded by another *rafale* as strong or stronger than the last. It was strange to see the cocoa-nut trees, usually standing up so straight and firm and untouched by ordinary winds, bending double, their crown of leaves streaming out from their heads like ancient hags traversing some storm-haunted Heath. The Banyan trees, to all appearances so strong and massive, were being rent limb from limb, the bread-fruits were suffering still more, and the poor shrubs were torn from the earth, stripped bare, and whirled into the watery waste.

Alas for the poor sugar-canes! The leaves were twitched and buffeted and made to crack like whips, until they appeared a bundle of fibres in place of leaves, and the stalks were shaking in the watery holes which they had made by being tossed backwards and forwards with the blasts. As yet no damage was done to any of the buildings, but the blow had just begun. The spectacle was one which was not pleasant to look upon, but to those who had their all in the fields of cane which were passing through the ordeal the sight was dismal enough. The family had assembled in the verandah to leeward, looking out upon the tempest and desolation, when they imagined they saw two figures struggling along the cane road which led by devious wanderings to Pompadour. "Perhaps it is Isidore sending for assistance," said Madame Beauvallon. "They are even more exposed than we are."

"I believe," replied Estelle, whose young eyes could better pierce the gloom, "that the one in front is Isidore himself."

"Impossible, he would not dream of coming out in such a tempest. He will have too much to occupy him at Pompadour."

"Nevertheless, it is Isidore," re-asserted Estelle, "Oh, see," she cried, "they have both been blown down." It was indeed Isidore, followed by his servant, each of them carrying a packet to which they clung despite of the difficulty of forcing themselves along against the wind and the rain.

"I am glad he has come," said Aunt Clémence, "he will keep us cheerful. He deserves a good breakfast, poor fellow, what have you, sister, to give him?"

"Nay not much Clémence, but as he would not have come through this weather to see either you or me, perhaps Estelle may desire to add something more to what I had thought enough for ourselves, and the Reverend Father."

"That I will, Maman," said Estelle, "although you are too wicked to suggest that he has come for my sake." And she tripped off to consult with Ernestine, as in fact she was not anxious to shew Isidore how much she thought of this visit on such a morning.

When she returned she found the strong young man lying back in his verandah chair almost fainting from the excess of fatigue. Lightly clad, as no clothing could have kept out the rain, he was drenched as thoroughly as if he had swum the distance. Madame Beauvallon had loosened the collar of his flannel shirt, and was wiping the rain from his hair, eyebrows and beard, while the Abbé was rubbing his hands, and Aunt Clémence had run to get brandy and water. The Indian servant had just got inside the verandah and lain down like a dog utterly unable to move one step more. A copious draught of brandy and water revived them both. It was found they had brought over a box of biscuits and a ham to increase the stock at Lorraine, besides Isidore's valise with a change of clothes. The two older ladies could not say enough to thank Isidore for his thoughtful kindness, and after he had had a bedroom assigned to him, and rested an hour, he appeared at breakfast as gay as ever, and determined to do what he could to make the time pass agreeably. Estelle was glad she would be saved from any further attempts of the Abbé to turn the day into a season of tasks. Madame Beauvallon was glad to see Estelle look so pleased, and Aunt Clémence was glad at the prospect of setting the two gentlemen by the ears upon many subjects before their incarceration ended.

The breakfast which promised to be so gloomy thus became the very reverse. The Abbé felt he had to rouse himself or his young friend would utterly eclipse him. He thus began to unfold that wisdom and knowledge of the world which is not infrequently possessed by ecclesiastics: In fact the Abbé had been one of the priests of the Madeleine and knew the world of Paris more intimately than many others who thought they knew more. He had come in contact with most of the Master minds of France and had many stories to tell of their appearance, their conversation, and their bon mots. He knew the ladies of the Court and of the Theatre, he knew others of whose pursuits he only hinted at in phraseology which might be understood by the elders but not by Estelle; he knew those who contributed by their talents to make the France of the second Empire what it had become, for good or evil. This was meeting Isidore on his own ground, and the young Creole was not disposed to yield without a struggle. When the Abbé saw how accurate his information was he expressed his surprise. Aunt Clémence was proud of her neighbour, and even Estelle was peculiarly gratified. It was not that she had as yet any strong feelings in favour of Isidore, but she was pleased to find that one whom she had so long known should prove himself to the French Abbé to be almost as well posted in Parisian affairs as himself. If she had ever entertained strong, very strong opinions against Isidore, they had certainly become much modified. Of course in her relations to Jack she could only look upon him in the same light as any other gentleman whom she might accidentally meet in society. She might admire many for their high qualities without going farther. Isidore had behaved with wonderful thoughtfulness ever since her father died; for that she thanked him, and could not but look more benignantly on him. Besides any friend of her mother and Aunt she was bound to welcome to the house. Did anyone ever hear of such a kind thing as to come over during a hurricane to keep three women from feeling solitary and unhappy?

When the Muse which presides over this branch of literature flew from the house of Lorraine on that eventful morning, Isidore and Estelle were together, laughingly putting the piano in its cover to keep it from the wet and damp. Somehow his lips, with the gentlest and most chivalrous touch, came in contact with her little hand.

Indian workers on Antoinette Estate

Chapter 22
The Innocent and the Guilty

THE MEMBERS OF THE EXECUTIVE COUNCIL felt very much puzzled and humiliated by the position in which they found themselves. Having given their sanction to the execution of Jean LeBlanc, they had afterward been informed by the Governor that he had commuted the sentence. They had then individually approved of the steps subsequently taken to try him for the attempt to murder, for which he had again been condemned to death, and now they were called together by the Governor to consider whether another commutation should not be granted. The section of the population who wished for this commutation were not the powerful class of the island, and if they yielded to their representations which were entirely based, as some of their body argued, on sentiment, they could expose themselves to be attacked by those who clamoured for the execution. Their action if they again commuted would appear weak in the extreme, as, if they had not intended to carry out the capital sentence, why should they have exposed the prisoner to the torture of a new trial. It is very seldom that the Executive Council oppose a Governor.

Indeed as one of them said, the man who opposes will most probably be in a minority of one, and if he attempts to gain his point by dissenting and protesting in order that the decision of the home authorities may be obtained, the chances are they will support the Governor, rightly or wrongly, and the protester be looked upon as an impracticable fellow always making difficulties. But it was apparent that in this case if anyone refused to consent to commute he would not be in a minority but would carry with him the majority of the Council. The Governor felt all the difficulty of his position. The newspapers had not ceased to rave and bellow for the execution, and on the other hand the representations he had received on behalf of Jean were such that he could not venture to treat them cavalierly. That threat to bring the matter to the knowledge of the Queen in Council had made him very uneasy, for although no lawyer he instinctively felt the second trial could not be defended and would appear very reprehensible in English eyes. That was the work of his law adviser, it is true, but he had acquiesced in the course, although as it now turned out without having been informed of the whole facts of the case.

A discussion was in progress which was tending to become acrimonious and painful, when the private Secretary came in and whispered something to the Governor. "Are they in waiting?" he said. On being assured in the affirmative he requested the Council to excuse him for a few minutes and went to his private room. This leaving was the signal for the other members to get up to stretch their legs, and to fight their battles over again, in detached knots, but all of them behind the Governor's back expressed freely their opinion that he was ridiculously weak to make all this fuss about hanging a nigger.

They waited a considerable time before the Governor returned, and when he did it was to inform them that he had just obtained important information which threw doubt upon the guilt of the prisoner altogether. He then detailed what he had heard from Jothee and Lucille – for it was they who had arrived. The former had explained that having been in the habit of watching the men about the camp at Pompadour in order to get information about the murder of one Bhootan, with whom she had lived, she had overheard a plot made by a number of Coolies to murder Amirantes, and that it had been carried out in the way she heard planned. She could not say for certain who the men were who were plotting, but she knew "in her mind" as she phrased it who some of them must have been.

Lucille's story threw light on what many people believed to be the strong part of the case against Jean viz his alleged confession that he had been in the alley where the body was found. She had explained frankly to the Governor her own relations with Jean, and how she had been accidentally mixed up with the matter from having had an appointment with Isidore. She stated that Jean had seen her with Isidore and mistaking the nature of her interview had run hastily from the house and stumbled over the body of Amirantes in the alley, and that the woman could be brought forward who had taken him into the house, and saw him leave in anger not against old Amirantes but against herself and Isidore.

Lucille had tried to command her feelings during the interview with the Governor, but at length breaking down she had thrown herself on her knees before him and besought him to spare Jean's life, for it was all through her fault he had been accused. The Governor was visibly moved. In dealing with questions affecting men's lives we are too much accustomed to keep out of sight the other lives with which they are bound up, and not to be fully conscious of the gap which even the death of one poor man may make in the world. He had scarcely recovered his composure before he returned to the Council, to narrate the curious incident in which he had just taken part.

The Council were wholly incredulous about the truth of the story told by the two women. One member at once very shrewdly suggested that the Indian woman not having been able to find out the murderers of Bhootan, wished to accuse of the murder of Amirantes the men whom she suspected of the former murder, which was quite in keeping with Indian schemes of revenge. As to Lucille, it was the most natural thing in the world that she should endeavour to save her sweetheart. Jean had probably been angry with her and Isidore when he hurriedly left the house, and most likely had murdered the father in place of the son, but that was not less a murder. The Governor could not but acknowledge the strength of these arguments but he was not the less chagrined at the way in which the information he had communicated was received. Evidence which had not been before the jury at the trial, and exactly that description of evidence which the Judge was certain would speedily come out, was beginning to pour in, and yet the members were for hanging the man at once without waiting for more, apparently to save their own consistency at any cost.

The argument was again waxing uncommonly warm, when the Private Secretary quietly entered and placed before the Governor a letter marked "immediate" with a triple underscoring, and with the frank of the Inspector General of Police in the corner. Tearing it open the Governor read as follows: "Understanding that the Executive is now sitting on the case of LeBlanc I think it right to communicate to your Excellency at once the curious fact that an Indian woman has come in this morning to the Inspector of the Pompadour district to say that she knows who the murderers of Amirantes were, that it was not LeBlanc, and that she knows a man who will tell all about it for a reward. I think it is very likely a mere plant by LeBlanc's friends to stay the execution, but the Inspector says he knows the woman and is rather disposed to believe there may be something in what she says."

The woman was no other than Chinacoutee, who had come to the Inspector whom she had seen at Pompadour. She had heard of the discussions over the second trial, and she thought perhaps that the Inspector for whom she entertained a feeling of affection might get into trouble if the wrong man were hanged. She knew a great deal about the murder, and she wished at once to save one who had been concerned in it, and to secure a sum of money for giving information, to do a good turn to the Inspector, and prevent the execution of Jean whom she knew perfectly well as the young fisherman of La Baie.

There was undoubtedly something like triumph in the Governor's voice when he read the communication aloud. This was evidently something quite apart from the story of Jothee and Lucille, and if this new witness could give evidence as to who did the deed, to follow up Jothee's evidence of the plot, it would be quite clear the Police had followed out a wrong track from the very first. Even the most sceptical of the Council began to entertain doubts, and those who had been talking most loudly against the commutation were now the first to suggest that the consideration of the question of affirming or disallowing the new sentence should be postponed. But the Governor had heard enough. He knew that he could not hold a sentence of death in terror over a prisoner while another investigation was going on to endeavour to find out the real murderers. He asked the Procureur General to state to the Council whether it was not the ordinary practice to commute the sentence of death upon prisoners charged with the attempt only. This was acknowledged to be the rule. The Governor then informed the Board that he would not depart from the usual rule on this occasion, especially as so much doubt had been created whether the first verdict, regarding the real offence for which he was to be executed, had been a correct one. He would commute at once to save the prisoner the agony of doubt, and meantime he would direct the police to follow up the new threads of evidence which had been placed in their hands. Returning to his private room he directed Lucille to be sent for, and said, "I am glad to be able to inform you, my girl, that the Council have resolved that the capital sentence shall not be carried out, and if you wish to be the first to convey the intelligence to the prisoner I will give an Order which will admit you at once."

Lucille snatched up his hand and covered it with kisses, and murmured her thanks and her blessings on his head. She gave a few convulsive sobs, making strong efforts to subdue her emotion while the Governor was writing out the Order. "If you would like to compose yourself for a little, you may remain here," he said, as he handed her the paper. "Oh, no, no, I would prefer to go to Jean," she said, and hurriedly left, the Governor, when she retired, himself taking several turns up and down the room in order to regain his own composure before facing any of his staff. He then directed a letter, as in the first case, to be written to the Judge who presided at the second trial, and requested that the Inspector General of Police and the Inspector at Pompadour should be sent for.

With the Order firmly grasped in her hand Lucille walked hurriedly up Government Street to the Supreme Court square in which the public entrance to the gaol is situated. Knocking, a little window was opened to see who was there. It was neither the day nor the hour for visitors and the attendant took some time to think about it before he undid the bars to ask Lucille what she wanted. "I have an Order from the Governor to see Jean LeBlanc," she said.

"Give it" – and having got it the Attendant shut and barred the door, and went to take the commands to the Governor of the Prison.

He returned and with more civility than he had at first shown took the necessary keys and preceded her to the part of the prison where Jean was confined. Poor Jean was seated in the middle of his cell where the light could fall better on the Bible which he was reading. He did not raise his head when he heard the bolts withdrawn, but on the gaoler saying "a young woman come to visit you" he raised his head and beheld Lucille, who stepped forward to embrace him. Jean stepped back looking at her mournfully, but she seized his arm and clung to it, and cried, "Oh Jean – forgive me – forgive me – how much you have suffered for my folly. And how much I have suffered, Jean, I was near death and wished to die, but God saved me to enable me to do you good. Speak to me Jean, forgive, forgive your own Lucille."

Jean held aside his head, but did not endeavour to tear away his hand from the grasp in which she held it.

"Jean, Jean, my friend, my lover, you are not to die."

"Ah yes, Lucille, I am. The whites are determined upon that and they rule."

"No, no, the Governor has sent me to say you are not. I have seen him today."

"You have seen the Governor!" replied Jean, scarcely believing such a thing possible, for Jean in all his life had never seen that functionary and looked upon him as an abstraction rather than a reality.

"Yes, Jean, I have just come from him. I and Jothee, we have both been with him, and he sent me with an Order to say you would not be executed," and as she spoke the word she shivered, and slipping on her knee in the cold cell she again cried "Oh Jean forgive me, I did no evil, but I know you saw me there, and you may have thought I was unfaithful. No, your presence saved me, and I am trying to save you. Have pity upon me Jean, forgive me. O, I love you Jean, and I will die for you – only say you forgive me."

Before he had time to answer her the emotions and fatigue through which the poor girl had passed proved too much for her, and she sunk fainting on the floor of the cell. To raise her up and place her on his bed was the work of a moment, although Jean felt how weak he was compared with his former strength. He ran to the jug of water which stood in a corner, and bathed her brow and temples, and now it was his turn to call upon Lucille, and to implore her to open her eyes, and look upon him, and tell him more about his fate. Slowly recovering consciousness, she sat up on the bed, and pushing back her long locks from her face, for her bonnet had fallen to the floor, she looked around and then at Jean, and in terrified accents exclaimed "My God, where am I, who is this? Am I mad, or am I dead? Great God, oh pity me, pardon me miserable sinner that I am." And then looking more intently at Jean – she seized him and held him firmly. "Jean, Jean LeBlanc, oh save me. I never did wrong. Save me, save me from that terrible thing!"

Jean looked but he saw nothing where she pointed. The poor girl in her weakness and terror had conjured up again in imagination the appearance of the Idiot youth as he came leaping into the garden where Isidore and she were seated.

"My poor Lucille," said Jean, "you are weak and ill. Take a drink of water, it is all I can offer you" he said with a faint smile, "and tell me if you can why the Governor has sent you to tell me what you said."

"To say what, Jean?" she replied, looking at him doubtfully, and then as her senses and memory returned more perfectly she exclaimed, "Oh yes, Jean, now I recollect, the sentence is not to be carried out, I told the Governor what I had done, and what Madame Camille did, and what you did, Jean, and that you did not harm a hair of his head and Jothee she heard them plotting how it was to be done, and thinks she knows who did it."

"But I am not to be let free," said Jean, "and if she does not find out, they will try me again and hang me. They are determined to have my life."

"Oh no, Jean, not so. I saw the Governor, he is a kind good man, he shed a tear Jean when he gave me the Order to admit me. He will set you free too after, but he told me to tell you the sentence would not be carried out."

"I cannot understand it at all," said Jean. "One day they are all for my blood and next day not."

The little window in the Cell door was here flung sharply back. The turnkey speaking in said, "Now then, prisoner, are you to be all day with that young woman. You are wanted down in Court for a commutation again, I believe," said the man gruffly, as if he grudged to hear that there was to be no execution after all.

"One moment, Monsieur," said Jean submissively," and I will be ready."

The moment the window was shut he pulled Lucille close to his heart – and throwing back her hair kissed her brow – saying, "Oh Lucille, if I could only believe that" – but he had not the heart to upbraid the feeble creature who lay in his arms. "I heard you had been very very ill. I see you have, but bless you for what you have done for me. If I am released all may be well."

"Oh Jean, say, say, you forgive me. I am innocent, and I shudder to think how near I was to my fall. The folly is all over now, say you forgive me, Jean, I love you – oh only you – I will live with you, and die for you. Forgive!" – and she buried her face on his breast.

"I do forgive," he exclaimed, "as God may pity and forgive both of us. Lucille, my own, my only beloved." They held each other in a long and close embrace, she sobbing with emotion, until the turnkey again came to the window. They went down to the Court-House together, Lucille clinging to his arm, and it was only when Jean was put to the bar, that she could be induced to let him go. She heard and understood the letter of commutation, and repeated its substance more clearly to Jean in crossing the Court-Yard. In spite of the policeman and gaolers, and the crowd of on-lookers, she kissed him once more as he re-entered his prison-house, when dropping her veil she returned to the Government offices in search of Jothee.

When the Editors heard of the second commutation, and the enquiries which the police had been ordered to open up afresh, they were like the Councillors of the government. The loudest for the execution was now most anxious to make their immediate past be forgotten by going as strongly on the other tack. Indeed some of them had found out that a very dangerous spirit was rising among the Coloured population in regard to the second trial. However much they delighted in mischief they desired to work it with safety to their own skin. They therefore thought it better to go in now and abuse the police for the entirely wrong bent they had given the investigation, and how, so far as could at present be seen, an innocent man had been brought to the very brink of death. Perfectly unabashed they blamed the official for taking exactly those courses which they had themselves most praised and supported, taking care, however, as the Governor said to Monsieur Parquet they would do, to save the Creole officials where possible, and to mention only with approbation those from home. The Governor smiled grimly as he read the articles – muttering to himself "Well of all the places in the world, a Colony like this to observe human baseness!" The Police certainly felt somewhat keenly the attacks that were being made, and it was thought desirable that a victim should be found. The Inspector suggested Stocks as he it was who had persistently led the pursuit after the Creole for whom he entertained a spite. The Governor was not very much disposed to allow the Inspector himself to escape, but as he had sent for all the papers about the original trial before the Magistrate, and found in the "Dossier" as it is called, in cover of the papers, a Memorandum which Jack drew up for the former Procureur General, a flood of light was let in upon the whole nature of the affair, and the conduct of Stocks at least was indefensible. As he had tried to force the hand of Justice to gratify his own malice, as he was a notorious drunkard, as he had purloined public money, and as he had by virtue of his office oppressed the poor in the district where he was stationed, he was permitted to retire from the service upon a handsome pension, and went home "without a stain upon his character!"

With the fresh start which was obtained by the evidence of Jothee and the offer of Chinacoutee, with the knowledge also that the Governor was watching every step of their progress, the Inspector was soon able to get upon the track of the real murderers. They were Coolies, and among them was Carpen who became Queen's evidence at the earnest request of Chinacoutee in order that she might receive the money which was promised as his reward. When the men found they were betrayed they made no attempt to conceal their guilt, but admitted it. They only each and all told a long tale of hardship which they had suffered at the hands of old Amirantes. They detailed first to the Magistrate, and afterwards to the jury when they came to be tried, how for trifling faults their wages had been cut, how when they went to complain to the Magistrate, and were kept waiting about the Courthouse, both their wages and rations were cut for being absent without leave; how for complaining they were set tasks which they could not perform and then punished for neglect of work; how they had to go to the forest to get food for themselves and their children and were punished for absence; how when they became ill and were sent to hospital they only got half rations on which their families could not live and which they themselves could not touch being ill; how they had been struck and buffeted, and imprisoned in outhouses for threatening to go to the Governor; and how the police in place of protecting them always assisted the proprietor in making their life intolerable. They said they knew they must die but preferred death to life under such conditions, but they rejoiced they had first been able to kill the Master who had used them so badly.

The jury, ashamed for once of their Island, and of the conduct of one of themselves, in bringing in the verdict of guilty which was inevitable, strongly recommended the prisoners to mercy on the ground of the cruelties which had been practised against them. The recommendation was duly forwarded and of the eight condemned two only were selected for execution, and the sentence of the remainder commuted to ten years penal servitude. The fit of blood was now over and the community were somewhat ashamed of themselves for the delirium which had passed. The Governor frequently turned sick at heart when he thought of how nearly he had been a tool of the bloodthirsty wretches who had the lead for the moment, and how utterly and absolutely the whole affair of Jean LeBlanc had been misrepresented to him, without his being able to say to any one of his advisers, "here, you lied" or "there you intentionally deceived me." But the whole affair was a lesson to him which he took deeply to heart. Some of the leading black men organised a subscription to compensate Jean in some measure for the terrible ordeal through which he had passed and to this the Governor gave a handsome sum. It need not be said that as soon as the Coolies were committed for trial for the same offence that Jean had received a free pardon. The Governor had not forgotten the young woman who had shown so much interest in Jean's fate and he again chose her as the medium of communication with the prisoner, sending an Order with her first of all to the Office of the Procureur General that the necessary forms might be attended to, and that the Prisoner might leave with Lucille. She had a carriole in waiting at the gate, and with a pride and triumph, tempered with humility, and sanctified by love, she conducted Jean to his father's house at La Baie. The old man tottered to the door, and ejaculating, "Jean, my son, my son," clasped him to his heart, and thanked God that he had not brought down his grey hairs with sorrow to the grave.

Chapter 23
The Three Poplars

A LITTLE SLEEPY AND A LITTLE HURRIED Jack managed to reach the first fast train to the country on time. People in town are always rushing off somewhere, and so the carriages were filled, the platform was encumbered, the newspaper boy and the bookstalls were doing a roaring trade, everywhere life, bustle, movement and activity. The strangers how numerous, the acquaintances how few!

One is obliged to be stiff and formal, curt and self-contained, as we never know who our next neighbour is or may be, whether he has all his wits about him or the reverse, whether he is calm or violent, a fool or a sage. With a few glances at the various types around we unfold our morning paper and try to busy ourselves with the affairs of the world at large. Jack was too restless to read. He took up his *Times,* but found he was scarcely yet in harmony with the ponderous policies it contained. The penny newspapers had not made their mark then as now. They were looked upon as scarcely the thing for a gentleman to buy. How rapidly they grew and became powers in the world, those of us who watched by their cradle well know. He tried the *Standard* but he was driven away from the mass of information it contained by the leaders trying to prove, like Mr Wordy's history,[†] that providence was on the side of the Tories. He was repelled from the *Daily News* by its calm assumption of infallibility – and from the *Daily Telegraph* by its tall talk and exuberance when a little calmness and common sense would have done.

Few probably at this day remember the long and embittered struggle which had to be waged before the House of Lords would give up the paper duties, or the arguments which were used to exclude the public from the benefits of an untainted supply of knowledge. The throne it was contended would be assailed, all our ancient institutions swept away, religion overwhelmed under the torrent of the many foul and scurrilous publications which would appear like flies in mid-summer with the one sole mission to corrupt. The exact mode in which the problem was to work itself out was hardly foreseen. In place of a great number of small sheets living on each other, and on the high priced journals, which it was taken for granted would supply all the news, we have seen a few of the most ably conducted cheap newspapers come gradually to the front and secure a place scarcely second to that of the great organ which for so many years reigned the undoubted King and head of English journalism. It was not the fine writing or the politics of a paper which made its fortune, it was the business management, for what the public wanted was news, early, complete and exclusive and the journal which was fortunate enough to provide these was a success whether its leaders were an embodiment of wisdom or not.

Who does not recollect – alas there are many of this generation who cannot recollect – the effect produced by the letters of the *Times* correspondent from the Crimea. It was a new revelation of power and honesty and bold exposure of the truth at great risk for the sake of a future but assured benefit. Without these bold, searching and graphic accounts our army would have disappeared piecemeal without being replaced, whereas not only was the progress of decay arrested but a fever of recuperation and goodwill established which made the British force at the close of the war double the numerical strength that it had been when the early battles were fought. It was in the same or a similar manner that some of the journals, which now circulate their copies by the hundred thousand, established their position and their fame. And thus it has come to pass that these once despised penny newspapers wield a power which is so vast, and supply information in a manner so complete, as to be marvellous. Nor have we any despotism of opinion such as would have been the result if journals of one set of views only had been able to reach the front. It was feared that as the radicals promoted the abolition of the knowledge, that the most numerously circulated of the new organs would be radical. But the Conservative organ takes the lead in London although the combined press of the divided liberal papers form a sufficient counterpoise. Again, London does not impose its rather weak club-level politics upon the country.

The local organs of opinion are local only in name. They are imperial in their circulation and metropolitan in their influence. Jack was in a humour to criticise. As if he were qualified to judge, or knew what particular line was likely to be acceptable to readers! The less some people know the more they are tempted to dogmatise. If ponderous politics or what one might more justly call the keeping as much as possible to the "golden mean," with just so much of the bow-wow in giving utterance to the thoughts or to impose upon the great mass of the propertied classes in the Kingdom, could at that date keep the *Times* in a marvellous position as a newspaper and bring in a vast income to its proprietors, why should they adopt any other course to please the flying atoms and particles of society who are here today and away tomorrow. Every man thinks he can edit a newspaper just as he can drive a gig by the right of nature, but let him try it and he will find that to deal with the affairs of a vast empire in particular, and the world at large in general, is a complex problem, certainly requiring more brains than to drill and set up a company of yokels and make soldiers of them.

Jack in fact was not in the state which makes a man take to excessive newspaper reading, which is a form of dissipation something like dram drinking, as a refuge from other cares, or from mental vacuity. He was too recently from other lands to enter genially into the curious amusements and dissipations of our own, he had still something to think of from the stores of his foreign adventure, and the pleasure of his homeward voyage, and then he was looking forward to re-entering in an hour or two the old home, to clasp the eagerly proffered hand, to return the impassioned kiss, to revisit the scenes of his youth. What were the affairs of Mexico or Peru, Persia or Timbuctoo to one whose mind was full of themes like these! The paper was listlessly laid on his knee, and Jack began to see the appearance of the country as soon as the train had got quit of the long rambling dullness of the outskirts of the town, where the dreary miles of brick barracks on a poor scale made him miserable. Then the villages appeared, more like to homes, and the people more like to human beings, with human hearts and sympathies, then the frequent villas, and farming equipages, and the distant towns with their canopy of smoke. The swarming multitudes of passengers when they reached the Junction reminded him that he was in an ancient, populous and busy country, in a grand centre of the civilization of the world.

But here is the well-remembered station where he has to descend, and standing by the platform gate, yes, it was, old Simmonds with the dog-cart. The first real touch of home! Harry no doubt will be on the platform, but no, he was not there. The porter who took the portmanteau and the cloaks, was able to give the news that Master Harry had gone to Oxford, and that old Simmonds could not leave the mare's head. To go to the little withered old man, with his ancient coat and top boots which seemed so big for his withered shanks was Jack's first thought.

"Well, Simmonds, how are you? How are they all at home?"

"Welcome home again, Master John! Well you 'ave grown quite a man! You is much stouter Master John, and more like Master Harry, he's agone to the College, and the Squire has a cold, but they is all waiting breakfast for you Master John, they is, and we was not to be long."

"Chuck in the things, then, Simmonds, when Sammie brings them. I must go to the King's Head [...] and see Mrs Pewter for the sake of old times. They are still here I suppose?"

"Yes, Lord bless you, yes sir, they has been here more than handert year the Pewters 'as – and in the same 'ouse."

To run over to the King's Head was the work of a second. To have seen the pretty look of startled surprise with which Mrs Pewter saw Jack enter would have done anyone good. She was quite a young married woman, with a shy smile and pink cheeks, and jet black hair who had known Jack from a boy, and both before she had attained the dignity of being Mrs Pewter and after, she had heard from Simmonds that young master was expected, coming back from foreign parts, and guessing that Jack would not delay before saying good morning she had run off to put on a clean print and a bow to match, and to brush her glossy hair till it was glossier still, and to put on a dainty little saucy morning cap, which said in so many words – "you young chaps may look at me still for it will do you good, but you must draw the line upon the banter, and put a better guard on your lips than heretofore." She was *so* surprised to see Master John; took her breath away people dropping down from India or elsewhere in that sudden and promiscuous fashion. But she had enough left to smile, which was a great thing, for a smile from a pretty woman on a dull morning is the next best thing to sunshine, and to blush when Jack in the warmth of his greeting pressed her hand quite affectionately. It is so pleasant to meet old friends. "Ah it is much nicer to be served by you, Mary" – (oh the rogue, did he forget she was Mrs Pewter, or was it in sheer defiance of the rights of Pewter) "than by the black fellows in Mauritius or Natal."

"Are they all fellows?" said Mary with a malicious smile.

"Yes, all fellows, never saw a female servant all the time I was away, and never was served by a white woman until I arrived at Plymouth."

"A very good arrangement if you are what you were, Master John," she said, referring to certain kinds of lip service given, taken, stolen or tried for in other times.

"And must one never presume to hope again, Mary?"

"Never!"

"What, not when one comes home from foreign service, and of a morning before the business of the day begins!"

"If you speak like that, Master John, I shall call Simmonds to bring the dog-cart to the door," and sure enough she came around the counter, to give effect to her threat, and in the old playful way attempted to push the forward stranger along the passage. It was by mere accident that the door of the parlour opened, and that it shut again quietly, and that a little titter was heard within, and that the pretty cap got awry, and that Jack looked so pleased, and that Mary did not look half so displeased as she pretended she would, and that she did not call up Simmonds with the dog-cart, but watched Jack swaggering up to the station gate with scarce concealed admiration, and went inside and ran upstairs to be quite sure that when he came in Pewter would not see that the cap had been a little crushed.

"All right, Simmonds," Jack exclaimed as he took the reins and kept back the frisky mare until the old man had mounted, and then away between the hedge-rows and the wet green pastures, and the bare plantations, and the frequent hamlets, and the carts of smoking dung, to the mansion where a warm welcome and a good breakfast awaited him.

He who has not felt the joy of returning to a home where all is happiness after a long sojourn abroad has not felt one of the purest and best pleasures of existence. Why need we dilate upon the mother's joy, the tear which sprung unbidden and the smile which chased it away, of the greeting of the sisters, mixed with so much banter, of the cordial grasp of the "Governor," and of his gratified looks when he saw the manlier appearance of the boy. The breakfast, what words could describe the delicate taste of the bacon, cured in the village, of the home-made butter, of the juicy chops, the perfection of the coffee which had always been the strong point of the house, the apple jelly of this years' making! Away ye foolish admirers of things foreign and oily! If ye wish to know how mankind can be blessed, invigorated and humanised, go taste an English breakfast and all may yet be well. And after breakfast there was so much to see, and talk about.

When the girls stood up, to notice which of them had grown most, to go to the drawing room to behold the sweep of view from the new French windows away over the rolling land clad with its plantations, its frequent enclosures, its many residences; to step out to the parterre to note how the seeds had grown which had been sent from Mauritius; to visit the conservatory to notice the struggles of the Frangipani and the Colias; to visit the frisky mare in the stable and the new colt and Master Harry's pony and the hunter, and to hear from Simmonds all the news about the mare which had departed this life, and the foal which was drowned in the pond. Then the fire of questions and jokes, and the pleasantries which Jack had to stand about his engagement. Was she really pretty, or had he only been imagining so? Did she always speak French, if not was her English good, or did she make the funny blunders which foreigners always make with our language. Of course we are not foreigners as regards the other natives, that cannot be, and if we make mistakes in other tongues there can be nothing odd about it because it never makes others laugh as we do! What was the Mama like? Was Jack near the unfortunate Papa at the time of that dreadful accident? How wrong to go to those kind of huntings where there must be so much danger.

"Jack," at last exclaimed his youngest sister, "I do believe she is black!"

Good gracious, why did the boy blush so, she was only poking fun at him. The blush and visible uneasiness of Jack did not escape the father's eye. "It cannot be," he murmured to himself; but concealing the momentary pang of uneasiness he said quietly to him, "Jack, my boy, have you a portrait of any kind of the young lady?" Jack had, and one of which he was very proud. It was a simple likeness done on ivory by an accomplished artist who had visited the island, and left with quite a fortune levied from the vanity of the Creoles.

"I will go and bring it, Sir," he said, not sorry to be able to leave the room for a little to recover himself. All had noticed the uneasiness caused by the remark, and "Baby" as she was still sometimes called was ready to cry for having caused Jack pain the very first morning he was in the house, but all trace of doubt and discomposure vanished when Jack returned smiling trustfully and placed in his father's hands the beautiful miniature. His mother leant over and saw it at the same time. "She is perfectly lovely, Jack," she exclaimed, "if the reality be at all like this she must be considered a beauty."

"Oh that does not nearly do her justice. The portrait gives the beautiful colour of the cheeks very well, but it does not and could not give the soft look of the eyes which is the chief charm of the face."

"And her accomplishments?" enquired the father.

"Well, the usual lot. She plays divinely and sings, and she talks English and French with equal fluency – no, scarcely that perhaps for she does speak English as a foreign language and French is her mother tongue, but that is reserved for *la vie intime*,* and the servants. Parisian French is the talk of educated people."

"How funny it will be to have a French sister," exclaimed the elder girl,

* private life

"we will never want for sugar at all events. Do they keep slaves still, Jack, or what are those people you speak of in your letters?"

"Oh the Coolies, well they seem to have a good number of those certainly, and I am not quite certain of their real position. They cannot leave the estate, that I know, for they are sold with it, but it is the police rather than the Master who sit upon them and make, I should imagine, their life a burden."

Jack had certainly been a more shrewd observer than many of those who had visited the country, including Bishops, clergymen, Colonial Secretaries and many such like. Even then the system of police dragooning of the Indians had commenced which culminated in 1869 in as scandalous a condition of affairs as ever existed in a British Colony. The Coolie under police law had to justify his civil status, as it was called, at every step. He had to carry with him, wherever he went, and at all times, his indenture ticket with his photograph on the front of it, and a pass from his master if he were a new Coolie or a servant, or if an old one his Licence as a hawker, or gardener or labourer or whatever his trade might be, and a permission from the Inspector of Police of his district, who might live miles away, to leave the district in pursuit of his calling, perhaps across the road. If he were standing in his own camp, ten paces from his own door, he could be pounced upon to show his "papers." If he had taken off for the night the tin case in which they were kept, and had not replaced it in the morning, he was liable to be marched off to the police station, and tried as a vagrant at the Magistrate's Court, where the continued absence of his papers might subject him to punishment of days, weeks or months of incarceration. In going along the turnpike road on his Master's business, in coming to town in search of work, in passing from one side of his village to another to visit a sick child or friend, in being present at a marriage or a funeral, or walking to the police office itself to complain of a wrong, the unhappy Coolie might be, and was, seized and treated as a rascal. His children were captured when going with his dinner, his wife was grabbed when at the river for water, and hurried off to prison if she could not show her papers in sight of her own door.

The horrid system, which made life absolutely unendurable for the best and most industrious part of the population, and which sent thirty thousand of them to prison in the year we have named, was then beginning, and Jack had discerned only too clearly that the police and the law which ought to have protected the Indian immigrants were the worst oppressors. To reform the system afterwards required an earthquake. A Governor was sacrificed, two commissions sat amid odium, and reported amid a deluge of calumny, the men who had done their duty in putting a stop to the dangerous iniquity – for it was stopped – were not even thanked, but were left to the mercy of their infuriated local opponents, while all those who had been specially responsible for the worst of the wrongs were promoted and rewarded. Even the defenders of the wrong who had themselves done nothing official bad, but saw how the wind blew, were received into favour and advanced more speedily in the service, but the wrong itself, thank God, was righted, effectually at the time and it is to be hoped forever. They who had to face the local bitterness and the official neglect can at least look back to the incident as one of those beneficial works which it was worth living for to have taken part in, labours which bless so effectively not only the poor who were the oppressed but the government and the rich who were the oppressors, and would soon have become the victims.

Those days at home sped so swiftly. Christmas came and went, the New Year was ushered in with the usual platitudes, and a renewed separation of the family at Three Poplars had to be faced, as Jack must return to his regiment. An official letter came one morning to say that he must go to Mauritius as his Company was to return thither from Natal. It was accordingly necessary to face all those money arrangements which the contemplated marriage rendered necessary. Before going up to town to consult Parchment & Parchment Jack had a long conference with his father and mother. They could not understand how he could be so sure of the marriage going on when the only surviving parent came to be so much opposed to it as to cause her religious confessor to write as he had done. Did he ever hear from the young lady herself? He had got only one letter since he went to Natal but it was all that could be wished being subsequent to the attempt made by the mother to break off the match, it showed that the young lady herself did not approve of that step, and he had other reasons (witness the message delivered by Ernestine) to lead him to the conviction that she would be true to her engagement. The mother, however, being now against him he did not expect to receive letters, and indeed Estelle in her only one told him it would be better if he did not attempt it.

At all events he felt himself bound by every honourable consideration which could have weight with a man to endeavour to carry out his engagement. His answer was approved by the father no less than by Mrs Montmorency who admired the spirit and integrity of her son and to whom indeed Estelle was already almost like a daughter. There was only the one point which had not yet been touched. Jack had not given any indication of the bar sinister which had ended in the old days so many marriages otherwise much to be desired. He would willingly have entirely avoided the subject, but he felt it would not be treating his parents with the confidence and respect which were their due, and they would be sure to hear of it sometime, either before marriage or after, from some of those candid friends with whom all of us are favoured. The subject of difference of religion had already been well ventilated, and the worthy lady almost felt thankful there was such a difference in order that she might have the opportunity of putting her right and showing how superior her own church was to everyone else's church.

The position of the lady of Three Poplars in this respect was an elevated but by no means uncommon one. She felt, as a part of her own being and nature, which therefore never had been and never could be questioned, that the religion she had been taught was the only true one. Not only the religion but the sect, and not only the sect but the particular phase of the sect, that viz of the High Church Party of the English Church. Why the Almighty had especially chosen this phase of thought to be the true Church she never asked herself, but she knew very well that all others were wrong, and that in persisting in their course they showed a spirit of resistance to the light which was deplorable. She did not hesitate to try to bring everyone with whom she came in contact over to her own views. This she called carrying out her religion in a missionary spirit. If a Roman Catholic or a Methodist attempted the same thing they were proselytising and doing wrong. She longed therefore to have Estelle with her when she had little doubt she would soon accept as the true faith the religion in which her husband had been brought up.

But the views of the good soul about the wisdom of all such arrangements were to receive a severe shock. With a countenance the reverse of bright, and in a tone the reverse of confident, poor Jack made his confession that Madame Beauvallon was descended originally but at a distance of time so great as to have practically extinguished the difference of race, from the African blood. But as it was still remembered in Mauritius, and might become known in England when he married Estelle, he thought it right they should know. The pause which followed was a most uncomfortable one. The father, while shocked, did not wish to say anything which if the marriage did take place might cause any feeling of bitterness between his son and himself. The mother was thinking of all the taunts to which they might be subjected in society if it became known that their son, descended from such a pure English stock, had intermarried with one having more or less of black blood in her veins.

Mrs Montmorency was not scientific. She believed that the blood in black people was black. She only continued to be on terms of trust with St Paul when he said that God had made of one blood all nations of the earth by supposing that he meant it in a spiritual and transcendental sense. That there were grades in blackness she knew, but she had hitherto been accustomed to regard them all as inferior beings. Let us pity the poor lady if she would have preferred a swarthy Portuguese or Indian beauty for her son rather than a young lady descended from a good French stock with only such a small soupcon of the African as to add a grace and relish to her beauty. She had been brought up in a land of prejudices and in a prejudiced family. She did not understand that hereditary ignorance, fanaticism, pride and ridiculous notions of family consequence, might be far worse for the mind than any small and faint cross of another breed might be for the body. What she dreaded, it was true, was the ridicule of her country neighbours. "Do you know'" she already imagined she heard them saying, "that poor Jack Montmorency has married a half-caste?" They would not call when Jack brought her home.

There were some old West Indian and still more East Indian officials in the county of whom she stood in great dread, She had heard them talk of the coloured races and of the mixed breeds, and, whether or not they meant it, they seemed to despise both. It is certainly astonishing with what ease a certain weak class of officials from home adopt all the prejudices of the whites in the places to which they are sent, and indeed become worse than they in the utterance of sentiments of contempt. It is thus class hatreds are perpetuated in place of being gradually extinguished by the good sense of society. All this and much more passed through the lady's mind while she thus stood silent and motionless at the confession of her son. He did perhaps the best thing which he could have done in the circumstances. He took out the miniature of Estelle and, smiling as he presented it, said, "Do you perceive any touch of the tar brush there, Mother?"

"Oh no," she replied, looking earnestly at the beautiful face before her, "she is very lovely," and the look had greatly relieved her for she had been reminded that the girl was not only white, but of a perfect complexion which for purity would throw into the shade the cheeks of many English girls. "What like is the mother by this?" enquired Mrs Montmorency again.

"Well, she is not quite so fair, a kind of the yellow of a ripe peach shines through her skin, but she dresses admirably well, carries herself like a lady, and having been in command of six hundred Coolies is perhaps a little bit dictatorial in her tone and manner."

"In every outward respect probably your fiancée will be not only equal but may be superior to ordinary girls – there is only," continued the father, "the chance of compromising oneself with society when the pleasure of a country life might be wholly destroyed, and there is Jack, you will excuse me saying it, the chance of the hereditary taint of disease. Have you made enquiry about that?"

"I have," Jack answered, "and I will show you first of all the genealogical tree of the young lady as drawn up for me by a notary in Mauritius – and then tell you all the satisfactory information which I have obtained about the latter."

The genealogical tree was examined with great interest. It showed that about one hundred and thirty years ago a French General of one of the best families of the French noblesse had to flee from Paris where he had offended a favourite of the reigning monarch. He had settled in Mauritius and purchased considerable estates. His son when he grew up had gone on a slave hunting expedition to the coast of Mozambique, and the daughter of a chief with whom he was in treaty for a cargo of slaves fell in love with him, warned him that her father intended to kill him, and begged him to flee. She fled with him but arriving in Mauritius among slaves taken from another part of the coast she was regarded as one of them and the astonishment and dismay of the slave owners in the Island may be imagined when it was announced that the young man intended to espouse her. He did so in spite of the violent prejudice of the society of the day and it was from the children of this marriage, marrying from generation to generation into the colonial families, from whom Estelle had sprung.

"Bertha," said Mr Montmorency with a smile, "the family almost seems better than our own. I certainly don't feel that the descent of the young lady should induce us to withdraw our consent to the marriage, or to make Jack feel in leaving us that he does not go with our blessing, and our earnest hope to see Estelle as soon as possible among us to become one of ourselves."

"However," said the father with a caution which showed he was not altogether satisfied while little disposed to make difficulties, "we need say nothing about this to the girls or to anybody else. There are some things which, while they involve no dishonour, or anything bearing a trace of it, need not be made a matter of boasting."

The rest of the conference proved to be as amicable and satisfactory, and Jack commenced his preparations to leave with a light heart. No, not exactly with a "light heart,, but with his mind greatly relieved, although not altogether at ease, as he had received a letter from Darcy which informed him that he heard on all sides "the Cub" was making a strong running in his absence and that as Madame la Mère was in favour of the rival he had better come to look after his own interests – unless, indeed, he had abandoned his principles.

Chapter 24
The Results of the Hurricane

IN THE ORDINARY CASE THE FRENCH GIRL GETS VERY LITTLE OF THE FUN of court-ing. Her future is all arranged for her and she is watched as if she were a prisoner on parole whose word is distrusted until she is married. The cus-toms of France rule her Colonies, and those Colonies peopled by the French race, although there is certainly a trifle more freedom where English habits are known if not implicitly followed. The freedom of action which Madame Beauvallon left to Estelle during the days of the hurricane was undoubt-edly unusual, but then Estelle had been wooed and won according to the English ideas, and apparently it was only according to the English ideas the arrangement could be undone. Isidore was left to his sweet will and Estelle was abandoned to hers. The consequence of this permission, the state of the weather, the enforced confinement to the house, the ennui of the situation was that they were thrown back upon conversation and this was Isidore's strong point, and the company of each other, which was the strong point Madame Beauvallon most valued. It was impossible to open the piano for the damp, and if it had been opened the notes would not have sounded. It was impossible to draw for the paper was soft as butter. It was hardly possible to read because of the noise of the elements.

The rain continued to descend as if the windows of heaven had been opened once more and the roar of the blast shook the house, and thundered among the trees. Incidents were continually occurring to distract the atten-tion. Now it was one of the supports of the mill wall which was driven down, again it was a labourer's cottage which was unroofed. Not a servant except Ernestine, and a "chokra"* who slept in the house, came near. Shut up in their huts, and mostly asleep, they awaited the end of the storm if not with equanimity at least without fuss. Perhaps it was better thus as the prepara-tion of food was a diversion, while the eating of it became the only possible pleasure. The Abbé came out magnificently on the occasion of meals, what-ever prayers he said or lessons he learned, and he always pretended to be im-mersed in his Breviary, it did not take away his appetite. Madame Beauvallon feared the claret could not possibly hold out, and the brandy was dwindling with wonderful rapidity. Isidore had also a remarkable appetite for disposing

* boy, young man

of liquors. It is necessary, or thought to be necessary, to drink a great deal in countries where there is a constant flow of perspiration, and when once the habit has been formed it is astonishing how much may be consumed in a day not only without harm but with assumed advantage.

The breakfast on the second morning of Isidore's visit was prolonged till long past midday, but no one knew whether it was mid-day or not. The house was all shut up and the lamps lit. Nervous and excited by the constant roar, the women felt at first they could not do much justice to the repast. Isidore insisted before they sat down they should have some bitters. He compounded with his own hands a mixture as near what is familiarly known as a "cocktail" as he could. The ladies made many difficulties but the Abbé came to Isidore's assistance, and advised them that it was necessary for their health that they should eat, and in order to eat that they should get an appetite. Aunt Clémence was the first to throw aside pretence. She drank the mixture and pronounced a warm eulogism on Isidore's skill, and then the mother and daughter followed. It was hurricane time, the weather was cold and miserable, and if Isidore was so good as to make it, why should Estelle refuse?

"You have a genius for all things, Isidore," she said smiling as she replaced the glass.

"Except for winning her I love," he said in an undertone so as to be heard by her alone. They could not enter into a conversation just then, but he thought it would be an excuse for beginning one after breakfast. A good deal had been done since his lips touched Estelle's fingers when wrapping up the piano. There was a long tête-à-tête after dinner on that day in a sheltered nook of the verandah to leeward, when the older ladies were busy playing cards with the Abbé. There was no love making in the proper acceptation of the term for Isidore was afraid of getting a rebuff, but there was much pleasant talk. They were seated very close together, and as the night was dreary there was a frequent adjustment of wrappers over Estelle's shoulders, and tucking her in generally. It was often difficult to get a shawl to cover the exact spot Isidore wished and an arm was occasionally passed around the shoulders, and rested for just a little while, and then her hand was touched sometimes, and no great fuss was made of accidents. Of course the accidental touch prolonged itself a little into something approaching very near to an intentional clasp, but not quite, for an opening was always left for the most favourable interpretation – *a locus poenitentiae* the lawyers might phrase it.

Isidore, whether he knew it or not, was, by his proximity, his *maniement** and his caressing ways, fascinating the beautiful creature by his side, just as a horse trainer obtains influence over the animal he wishes to subdue. There was no fierce resistance to overcome for more and more Estelle was becoming charmed with his voice and his manner, his bonhomie and natural gaiety. She could talk to him, she could not talk to Jack. With the latter she was always afraid of committing herself, with the former she was at home. He spoke about what she was interested in and understood. He turned his

* "handling; comportment"

phrases happily, and even when they were a little broad, the coarseness was veiled in such a way that she found she could laugh without compromising her position. Indeed they had talked so much and Estelle had occasionally laughed so heartily, that Madame Beauvallon looked at her sister, and smiled as if she quite approved of the charm thus working. It would not be her fault she thought if frequent opportunities were not found for similar interviews while the storm lasted. When the time came for retiring, when the Abbé had gone and Aunt Clémence, and only Madame Beauvallon was left in the dining room arranging and re-arranging she did not very well know what, and Estelle had stood up, and Isidore had taken off the cloaks, and piled them on the chairs, he had said, "May I, Estelle, have one very little kiss, just that I may dream of you when I go to sleep."

"Oh no, Isidore, do not ask me! You know I ought not. I am very grateful for your kindness, and if I could repay it in such a way I would be glad – But you know … mon ami!…"

He put his arm round her waist, and then clasped her in both his powerful arms, she not resisting too much, and took the kiss he had asked for, and gave the embrace for which he had not asked – and she said, as she gave him a look of mingled pleasure and reproach, "you are very wicked, Isidore, and I hope if you dream it will be that I am punishing you for your naughtiness."

Whether Isidore dreamed or not we know not, but Estelle dreamed – a waking dream – and it was all about the man whom she had just left, and only about the absent one insofar as the two were so inextricably bound up together. "I never thrilled so when the Englishman kissed me (it had come to "the Englishman" already). I feel the warmth of Isidore's kiss now and could have returned it. Is it that this is love and the other was but a passing feeling of pleasure because my vanity was ministered to by having such a handsome suitor as Jack? For he is handsome, but Isidore is more so – oh heavens do I love him and have engaged myself to another?"

So when Isidore said in the morning – "Except for winning her I love" – he undervalued his own genius even in that. He was making alarming progress, and might, and perhaps did, imagine as much from the care with which Estelle had adjusted her morning toilet. She was looking beautiful, and Isidore thought it a good augury that when he whispered to her she looked into his eyes, and did not look down or away, and her glance was almost wistful as if she too had something to say and would like the choice of saying it. And so it was not improbable that a breakfast begun with bitters would end in sweets. It did not end soon, for Madame Beauvallon recollected of some champagne which her poor husband had put aside a long time ago. English people do not drink champagne at breakfast, but Colonial French people often do when the occasion calls for it.

A champagne breakfast on Sunday was indeed a very common custom among the planters in the Island. Madame sent Ernestine for the wine. It had been set apart by Monsieur Beauvallon for Estelle's marriage with Jack, but many things might occur before that event happened, and at all events it was

necessary to be somewhat gay with that *diable d'un coup-de-vent** blowing. So
the champagne came, and disappeared, and the Abbé grew merry, and Isidore
became eloquent, and before the brilliant effect had subsided, Madame, with
a great deal of tact, had got her sister and the Abbé to sit down with herself to
cards leaving the young people free to make their own dispositions for spending the afternoon. It was necessary to get to fresh air, and the corner of the
verandah was the only possible place. The rain swept in slanting lines across
the house, dashing onto the earth. When the squalls came the trees were bent
double and the blast swept the place clear of the fallen branches and twigs,
whirling them into the air, and rushing off with them into blind watery space.
Not a soul stirred, not an animal was abroad, the verandah was more of a solitude than if it had been in the heart of a forest, for the ladies and the Abbé
were very busy with their play at the far end of the far away drawing room.

Why did Isidore's hand tremble as he muffled Estelle in rugs and wrappers, why did her eye shine so with an unusual light? The champagne – well,
Isidore had drunk freely but he was not a man to lose control of himself and
Estelle, our maiden who at one time blushed so readily, she had taken very
little, for her ordinary drink was claret and water, and that had been prefaced
this morning by the cocktail. No, no, Isidore felt and she felt instinctively
that their fates were about to be settled for better or worse.

"Isidore! How long you take to fasten the shawl!"

"Would, Estelle, that it would take forever that I might be forever near
you, that I might feel my cheek within reach of thine, that my breath might
mingle with thine."

"If you talk so, Isidore, I must go. You know I ought not to hear expressions of love from you when I am engaged to another."

"Oh, Estelle, why did you engage yourself to another, did you not know
that I had loved you from boyhood, and had laid my plans for life with you
as my wife. Why, Estelle, engage yourself to a stranger when one of your own
countrymen was willing to die for you? Do not refuse me this," he said, seizing her hand and covering it with kisses, "it may be only once, let me enjoy
one hour of the most perfect bliss."

"I knew not that you loved me, Isidore, not," she added, checking herself, "that it would have made any difference, I do not say so, but in truth I
did not know it."

"Oh I have loved you Estelle with a perfect love. No plan have I formed
but you have been part of it. I have worked but for you, studied only for you,
dreamed of you sleeping and waking, lived for you, and would willingly die
for you. Tell me, Estelle, did you never guess that I loved you, did you never
even imagine the possibility of my having thought of you when you were the
light of all around us; oh tell me what spell that Englishman weaved around
you that you should care for him and despise me."

"No, no, Isidore, not despise you, do not speak so. At least not now; I
did not formerly care for you, did not like you, because I did not know you

---

* "devil of a cyclone"

sufficiently, but since my father's death and yours I have known you so much better that I cannot bear to hear you say I despise you. No, no do not say that –" and our timid young lady laid her hand on Isidore's and pressed it ever so gently. What is it that is working this change? She appears much more of a woman, much less of the timid French girl than formerly, the light in her eye is not quenched, and as she looks full in the face of her friend he feels all the witchery of her beauty – to inspire him to renewed efforts for victory.

"Would it have made any difference if you had known me before as well as you do now? Tell me, Estelle, it would comfort me to know it if I have to relinquish all thoughts of you and go out to the wide world alone."

"Why should I tell you, Isidore, if it cannot be now? I did not like you before, I hope you will always be my friend now."

"Nothing more than that, Estelle, ah, friend is a warm word when man speaks to man. It is cold when woman speaks to man. It is cold, cold to me, oh thou who are more to me than life! Thou must be more or nothing, dearest and beloved! But tell me why you did not like me before, Estelle, you may have been under a delusion."

"No, no, I was not – your badly regulated life, Isidore. We hear of those things when men do not think it."

"Mine has not been a good life heretofore, Estelle, I acknowledge it. Not worse than others around us, perhaps, but not the life a man ought to lead, who respects himself. Say you will love me and all the life of the past will vanish like a shadow. All will be regulated by you and for you. I will live and move only for you, Estelle, mine own and only beloved. Oh speak to me the one word and I will become a new man, say – say but that you love me and will have me as your husband."

She paused. A choking, which she could not master, interrupted her voice. Stooping at length to kiss his hand, she burst into tears. "Do not press me, my friend, it is too late."

"Nay, nay, not too late. It may be too late hereafter if you marry one you do not love. Oh, Estelle, think of the terrible sacrifice; why should you give yourself to one when you may only have suffered from a girlish fancy, and with whose people you have no ties in common, and throw over one who loves you madly, if you – oh if you love him even a little – Tell me that you love me and a way will be found out of all difficulties. Estelle, be mine, be my wife, my beloved, and the world itself shall not tear thee from my arms."

"Isidore I fear – I fear – I love you better than him. Oh, my God, what can I do? Pity and protect me, my friend and lover."

Oh the clasp and hug of utter joy and pent up feeling on the one side and the other – The rain lashed and spared not, the hurricane squalls came back and with more fierce intention, the house shook so that the card players in the far corner of the far room stopped frequently to look up at the roof, but no one disturbed that long, long embrace, those murmured words of joy and hope and passionate love, those moments in which the soul itself seems to grow like the gourd in the night and comes out of the ordeal ready to withstand all opposition.

"Shall I tell Maman, Isidore?" Estelle said at length, emerging ruddy and radiant from the hurricane rapture with which Isidore had overwhelmed her. "She will be so pleased!"

"Yes, my beloved, and I will tell Aunt and the Abbé."

The news pleased everyone but Ernestine who did not at all like the alliance with Isidore. She had always been true to Jack and when she found the absent officer was thrown over for their neighbour she felt it keenly and believed her "enfant" had acted wrongly and under some sudden impulse which she would regret.

The event of the day was not to stand alone. The wind had now veered to the North, and the hurricane renewed its ravages with increased power. The barometer was steadily falling. At the height at which Lorraine stood which could not be more than thirty or forty feet above sea-level it was already 28 degrees with a tendency to go lower. The attention of both the ladies and the Abbé had been so much concentrated on the news that they had forgot the barometer and all its sinister prognostications. Isidore, however, who had now a new interest in life and prosperity had been uneasily watching the signs of the evening. "It will blow its hardest tonight," he said, "and I only trust some of the buildings already weakened may not give way when taken in flank." He would gladly have gone out to see that the fastenings and supports were all right, but he could get no help. For better or for worse they must take the chance of the night, as for better or for worse Estelle and he were to face life together.

Dinner passed in discomfort, notwithstanding the new element which had been introduced which in other circumstances would have made them gay and happy. The building creaked like a ship in a gale of wind, the shingles rattled and lifted, and some they could hear were wrenched off and sent flying. About eight o'clock a great branch of the banyan tree which had been such a protection to the house from the sun was wrenched off and driven with so much force against the house that they all started up in dismay. The rain was invading everywhere. Ernestine came in half crying to say that the chambre-à-coucher of Madame was uninhabitable. She had been obliged to take everything out of the room into that of the Abbé for the wind had torn off the shingles and the rain was pouring in everywhere. "Mes diamants!" cried Madame piteously, but they were all safe in the drawer where she had placed them. As they stood looking at the forlorn picture a *rafale** worse than any which had passed over came roaring on its ominous course. It struck the house, and all seemed lost. A dull thud on the ground was heard. "It is the Mill chimney," said Isidore with awe, as he knew all the results which might follow from the necessity for heavy repairs.

"Ah, mon Dieu,"** ejaculated Madame Beauvallon, "we are ruined!"

In the lull which followed the cries and screams of women could be heard through the storm and the shouts of men.

* gust
** "Oh! My God,"

The same blast had levelled nearly every hut in the camp, and the women, half mad with terror, were fishing their children out of the debris. Happy they who in such scenes dwell in huts of mud, or of the stalks of tree ferns, for if a catastrophe comes it doesn't mean death to the inmates.

"I must go to help," said Isidore, "and see what can be done for the people!"

"And I too, "said the Abbé, "I ought not to be in comfort here when these children are struggling with the fury of the elements."

The ladies begged them not to go. They had a rooted belief that a Coolie and a Mozambique could get through every difficulty, even to the extent of living without food. Estelle recollected the night of the shipwreck and her heart sank lest there should again be a repetition of that scene of anguish. It was not without a strange feeling of shame also that she realized what she had done in throwing up that lover whom she then thought she loved, and whom she would have honoured all her days if he had then fallen a victim. But while she was meditating, Isidore and the Abbé were preparing themselves for the expedition, and immediately set out, begging Ernestine to bar the door carefully after them in case of a whirlwind blast coming up. Madame Beauvallon sank sobbing on a sofa. It was now Estelle's time to show herself no longer the weak girl who was a burden, but one upon whom others could rely for assistance and help. She had changed in a night. The moment she had realized in her own heart that she truly loved Isidore, with that strength of woman's love which absorbs all other failings, she ceased to be a girl and rose up a woman. All her previous training which seemed to have so little effect upon her weakness and pliancy, now came into play. Her very figure seemed to expand into more womanly dimensions.

Ernestine felt that her "enfant" had escaped from her, and now prepared to obey her young mistress as totally as she had obeyed the old. Aunt Clémence envied her. She too at a former period had felt the effects of love, and had broken through the thin shell of nursery and conventional girlhood in the same way, but her love was not returned, and she had retired within herself, and become the rather austere, clever, sceptical and novel-devouring Aunt which we have seen here. She alone was able to give Estelle help on the present occasion. Isidore had attained all that her heart had been set upon, but in the very moment of victory this hurricane seemed destined to make paupers of both Estelle and Isidore. Two fairly good properties joined together might make one excellent whole, but two completely ruined estates would only make, if united, a greater and more conspicuous ruin. The poor lady almost ceased to hear the remorseless roaring of the gale as she brooded over all that the morning sun might bring to light.

The voices of women and children were heard in the hills approaching the house. The man conducting them explained that Monsieur Isidore had sent them to obtain shelter in the great house as their own were gone. Estelle, delighted to carry out this first commission from her future, determined to give up the dining-room for the use of the people. The drawing-room would be reserved for themselves. But the numbers who began to arrive threatened to over take the capacity even of the large dining-hall. Two of the pavilions were then placed at their disposal, and finally a third had to be set apart as a hospital for a good number of the older Coolies and children had received cuts and blows from the falling timber, and in one case a woman was brought in with a broken leg.

The hospital was the care of the Abbé with the assistance of the dispenser of the ordinary Estate Hospital which had gone. He set the leg, bandaging it up with all the skill of a professional man. She was equally handy with scissors and lint, but amid all his cares he wondered much to find Estelle coming and going without pretence of being sick at the sight of blood, and administering tea and hot arrowroot to the shivering creatures who had tasted nothing for many hours. The children whispered her name to each other and were kept quiet by the awe they felt that the young lady who they had looked upon as a kind of divinity should go amongst them and help them. The next proof of the violence of the tempest was to find the mules brought to be picquetted under the lee of the house. Their stable had fallen and many of the poor animals had been hurt. But no one could do more for them than to leave them in the pelting rain, as much sheltered from the fury of the gusts as was possible. Then the windowed verandah of the mansion house went. The wooden pillars were let into stone and fastened down with lead, but the roof had not been so securely fastened to the pillars, and the wind having found the weak point had worked and worked until it had wrenched off the roof, twisted the pillars in their sockets and opened a great hole in the front roof of the house itself.

Undoubtedly had the storm continued, the wind having got this advantage, would in the end have perhaps destroyed the whole house, but it was the turning point in the storm. At this point it was blowing with almost incredible violence. Isidore had returned when someone had run to tell him that the house was threatened, and going at once to the barometer he saw it begin to rise and to rise decidedly. Before he spoke he watched for some time very closely, and could see with his own eyes the hand move twice, a hundredth upward each time. He was accordingly able to comfort them with the assurance that the worst was past, although there would still be violent squalls until daylight. It would be necessary to wait quietly for nothing more could be done.

The Coolie women and children in the dining-room, without complaint or wailing, curled themselves up as best they could, and slept, most of them soundly. Beds were prepared for the ladies in one corner of the drawing-room, and for the two gentlemen in the other, and strange as it may seem they were all so tired out by the long tension of the [vigil] that they slept as if they had been in their own rooms on the most quiet of nights. The storm was still playing mischief on a grand scale outside, but its fangs were drawn, it was simply tossing up with furious snarls the prey it had already slain, and before sunrise it had retired, roaring and growling away into its native haunts.

When morning came what a spectacle of desolation! Even Isidore, who was usually so light-hearted, so brave, clever and full of resources, was appalled. If Lorraine is thus, he thought, what will Pompadour be? It would be necessary for him to go at once to enquire into the extent of the disaster, but his friends would not allow him until at least he had drunk his morning coffee, which it was no easy matter to prepare. Estelle awoke and could vividly realize all the peril of their position. Formerly she would have felt crushed, now she went to Isidore, smiled at his gloomy looks, and dismal forebodings, bade him be of good heart as things always looked worse than they really were in the morning after a hurricane. She pointed out that the canes although shaken were still standing and might recover as the rain had so drenched the soil.

After coffee had been obtained she tied with her own dainty hands a handkerchief around his throat, and when he stooped to kiss her who was now his fiancée, she not only held up her mouth but gave him one kiss of her own accord, and returned the pressure of his hand with a brave and cheerful, "Courage, mon ami!"* After he had quitted the verandah she called to him "Isidore!" He stopped to wave his hand, she kissed hers and called after him, "Au revoir et vitement!"** Then she turned and gave orders to clear out the wreck of the house impressing into service, with a tact worthy of Isidore himself, the Coolie women who had shared the shelter for the night.

* "Chin up, friend!"
** "Good-bye, and quick!'

Chapter 25
The Real Dangers of a Voyage

JACK WAS ON HIS WAY TO MAURITIUS. He had booked by what was then the Messageries Imperiales steamers from Marseilles, which were so commodious and well found that a great many of our Indian officials preferred them even to the magnificent ships of the Peninsular and Oriental Company. The Mauritian and Bourbon passengers would leave at Aden where a branch steamer met the trunk line to India and China. They were accordingly in the minority and on their good behaviour. The mass of the passengers, however, were neither for India nor the Islands, they were non-descripts of all kinds going to Alexandria, Cairo, Suez and Aden where French influence at that period reigned supreme.

The Suez Canal had not been made, but its construction was determined on, and already the busy brain of the great Engineer was working out the details of the magnificent scheme. Now that it is completed and so many thousands pass annually through the desert as comfortably as if they were in a well-appointed hotel on shore, looking at the scene through the windows, we are very apt to forget that an Englishman who believed in the possibility of the great work was regarded either as a fool or a knave. The leading organs of opinion united to oppose the idea, not because of its political aspects, but from what they asserted to be the physical impossibility of the enterprise. The English capitalists were debarred from taking shares in the Company, English engineers from sharing in the lucrative contracts, and English traders from reaping the harvest at Ismailia and other places which was reaped by French and Italians. Now of all the vast procession of steam ships going and coming to and from the East, the immense majority are English. No other nation has benefited in anything like the same degree by a work which the leading statesman of the day ridiculed, and the mass of the people, knowing no better, treated as a project of insanity. So it is the same even now with the Panama Canal. When it is spoken of the average American or Englishman smiles a cold smile of derision.

In the West Indies, which will be thrown by its completion so much more in the course of the world's traffic, the progress of the work is known to only a few, while in Jamaica it is looked upon as a public calamity because of the flux of labour from the Island to the Continent. The old system of travel through Egypt was assuredly more picturesque and enjoyable. The Suez Canal is not a work of beauty. Its course through the desert is not marked by any features of loveliness which can stir up enthusiasm. Utility is the one idea which is associated with its whole length, utility from which all the softer influences have fled in terror at the aspect of the waste of sand, and the occasional spectacle of a party of Bedouins unchanged in their customs since the days of Ishmael. The railway from Alexandria to Cairo was luxurious travelling but at the time of which I write the line to Suez was not yet opened. Travellers were accordingly thrown a good deal together. Many friendships, many companion-ships warmer than friendship, date from the day in Cairo and the journey through the desert to Suez.

Jack had found an agreeable set of which he became not the least popular member. It consisted amongst others of an Indian official, who on his way back from furlough had promised to pay a visit to his relative Sir Foolis Foolscap the Governor of Mauritius by running down from Aden and back in a couple of months. His daughter was with him, a young lady who having too early succeeded to the charge of her father's household, had acquired a decision of character not inferior to that of her father himself, who grumbled at his position in having no more than five million of people to govern. It was strange to see so young and beautiful a girl as independent as if she belonged to the other sex and yet without as gentle and womanly as if she had never left a rustic English home. Her orders given in Hindustani to the Indian servants were precise as those of a general on a field of battle, but spoken with a voice soft as that of a woman ought to be. Jack had first noticed her at the railway station at Paris when about to start for Marseilles. He saw the commotion caused by the appearance of the Indian servants and the evident conviction of the employees that they had to deal with a great Milord Anglais, perhaps the Governor General of India himself. The father indeed might have been anything from the grand air of coolness with which he surveyed all the bustle of departure.

The despatch of trains was evidently nothing to one who had despatched armies on trains of thousands of elephants. In fact until he had come home on furlough he had never even seen a train for at least a dozen of years. His post was in a far barbarous district into which railways had not yet penetrated. But then he had mainly from the circumstance of his being the one man of the place acquired the habit of looking down upon the world around him. He had the most decided views upon all questions of Indian politics. There was nothing so great that he could not master in five minutes, nothing so minute that he could not dogmatise about. He had not received that recognition which was his due, but that was the fault of his superiors, not any shortcoming of his own. His one sole notion of government for the Indians was the patriarchal, in which he should be the Patriarch, with infinitely more power than any patriarch in the old world ever possessed, and an unlimited command over the public purse for every public work which he considered of utility whether the possibility of its achievement was approved by skilled engineers or the reverse.

About home politics his views were rather hazy. He regarded them as much beneath attention. The statesmen on both sides were in his opinion only one remove from imbeciles, and their buckling to common opinion uncommonly disgraceful. But his usual talk was more interesting. He seemed to take a thorough interest in the Indian race, he knew all about their agriculture, religion and customs; their difficulties, aspirations and tendencies. He knew the botany of the country intimately and told of the wealth of the forests and the rareness of the plants which lay concealed in their depths. He seldom went out after any game smaller than a tiger, but the haunts of this fierce beast he knew well, and many stirring stories he could tell of escapes from danger when in conflict with man-eaters.

Jack listened attentively to the father because after he was tired, and got up to stretch his legs by walking up and down the deck, or went below to indulge in a snooze, he could continue the conversation with the daughter, who gave him graphic pictures of Indian life. She could tell little about Calcutta society where she had seldom been, although Simla was not unknown to her. Her life after she returned from school had been spent in the remote settlement where her father governed, and which she evidently dearly loved as the home of her childhood, and where they enjoyed for the greater part of the year a delightful climate, and many comforts of which people at home were deprived. She spoke without the slightest effort, yet her words were so choice, and the pronunciation so perfect, and the voice so charming, that Jack could have listened forever. When she wished for a promenade she did not hesitate to say so, and accepted Jack's arm to steady her without the smallest taint of affectation or pretence at reluctance. By the time Alexandria was reached Jack was looked upon and treated as a friend of long standing. He had of course explained who he was, that his regiment was stationed in Mauritius, and that he was on return after a short time home on "private affairs."

It was very odd, but was nonetheless a fact, that he did not allude in even the faintest way to the nature of these private affairs. Was this right? It was surely possible that by paying as much attention as he did to the young lady, she might have been deceived or led into entertaining more than friendship for one who was not free. Jack's heart sometimes, nay often, smote him upon this key point. Night after night, sometimes even hour after hour, he resolved to be more careful, more distant, more candid, more considerate, as an engaged man ought to be in the presence of young and beautiful girls to whom he cannot be anything else than a passing acquaintance. But as often as he made the resolution it was broken. In the morning before breakfast it was not worthwhile beginning to read anything, and it would have been boorish not to say good morning to the ladies. When this was done it was but civil to offer to help them to promenade a little as a "constitutional." Neither he nor anyone else took always the same lady, but there was a gradual tailing off as the voyage proceeded, like taking to like, and dislike avoiding dislike, as was most natural and convenient. The morning when Jack did not have a walk with the Maharanee, as she was called on board, (although she was entered on the passenger list simply as Miss McNeill) did not seem to be so bright as its predecessor. The forenoon when he did not manage to extract at least an hour's conversation with herself out of the flood of talk with which the Commissioner overwhelmed him was not well spent.

The evening after dinner that they did not stand together looking at sea or sky, the faint cloud above Vesuvius, the lights of Messina, or the bold bluffs of Malta had not yet arrived. The Commissioner had always been accustomed to have his private secretary near him, or one of the young officers from the fort, or one of the higher native officials, to whom he could talk and unfold all his great schemes for the government of mankind so that it was the most natural thing in the world that Jack, an officer going to Mauritius where they were to stay for several weeks should be received into the family party, should assist them at the disembarkation, should secure places in the train and should organize an expedition to the Pyramids when they got to Cairo. What more natural and befitting, but what more wrong in Jack? It was neither fair to Miss McNeill nor to Mademoiselle Beauvallon who although far away as yet might hear of it and be as little disposed to approve as the Commissioner would be if he thought there had been any trifling with his daughter. So keenly did Jack feel that he was doing wrong that on occasion a confession of his engagement was just about to be made, when a third person joined them and put an end to the opportunity. On reviewing the events of the day in his cabin Jack was rather pleased than otherwise that the avowal had not been made. "She would have thought that I thought that she thought something of me," he argued with himself, "and would have been offended while I would only have made an ass of myself. We will only be together for the voyage and much is allowed for the sake of making the time pass pleasantly which might not be permissible on land."

Alas! Poor Jack. He was one of those good fellows with a very susceptible heart, who could not resist the fascination of beauty. The sooner such impressibles are married the better, for that is the only thing which is the least likely to sober them. They may have their flirtations afterwards, but they will not be deep or dangerous, whereas so long as they roam about in single blessedness they are always spoiling the peace of mind either of themselves or others. The dilemma in which they find themselves is that they do not know which to marry. Today they are devoted to Mary and think that life should only be endurable with her by their side, but a little spell of absence cools their ardour, and Louisa or Kate rise above the horizon of their hopes. They worship women as some nations do the stars of the firmament. Venus may today be the morning or the evening star; but all the stars in turn would assume the same lustre and beauty if life was long enough, or the course of Creation benevolent enough, to bring each in succession as near the rapt vision of the enthusiast.

It is a remarkable effect of absence that although it is said to make the heart grow fonder the usual result is to weaken so much the strongest feelings that the very faces and figures of loved ones are forgotten. Jack had not looked at his miniature of Estelle since he had shewn it to his father and mother at home. There had been a few days in London which were very busy ones, and nights wherein the leading actresses occupied the first place. There had been a few days and nights in Paris, and a young officer passing through Paris can surely be excused if he forgets father and mother, fiancée or any other dear and intimate friend, while tasting the latest novelty in the Capital of pleasure. He took it out the evening they arrived at Cairo. It had been such a pleasant day; she had been so charming, there had been so many opportunities for little bits of conversation, little services tendered and received, little touchings of hands to give help, or offers of help that were so touching that when the young man retired, he took himself severely to task.

It was to aid his self-abasement that he produced the image of his beloved. A face as beautiful as could be desired, but beautiful and nothing else. Will it be believed that for the first time Jack found it singularly devoid of expression. Of course because it is only a miniature; the expression is a fleeting, passing, evanescent thing, which if a painter can seize and place on canvas he has reached the height of genius. Why should the youth begin now to find fault with what he had always hitherto regarded as a faultless likeness? But it was not with the miniature alone that he found fault. "That," he murmured to himself, "was always the weak point of Estelle – the want of expression. There is no character in her face. She has a mode, a very pretty mode, of using her eyelashes, but one must have something more than that for the journey of life." (Oh, Jack, you hypocrite.) "Then, of course, as I knew very well from the first, but I thought she would get over it, there is that disturbing want of conversation. That might be excused when she is speaking English, but she cannot say anything sprightly or nice even in French. She looks as if she has nothing in her. But she plays certainly splendidly. I wonder if Agnes can play." So, so, the rogue had got hold of the Christian name, and already thought of her by that. He had read it in her prayer-book when she sat devoutly poring over the service on a fine breezy sunshiney Sunday. She allowed him to take it up, and to look at the fly leaf for the very purpose of finding out the name, and she smiled an affirmation when in their usual tête-à-tête after dinner, he asked her if the name written there was hers. What a beautiful combination, he thought, of softness and masculine power, just like herself, and he remained at her side, pensively looking at the stars, with just an occasional half suppressed sigh until she held out her hand to say goodnight, when they parted with a – no, no, it cannot be, there must have been some mistake, or accident, or it must only have been imagination, *without* – yes that is the word which cannot but most nearly express the truth, *without*, we think it right to emphasize it again, any, even the faintest, pressure of the hands. It was not that which raised the colour of Miss McNeill's cheeks, it was only the fresh evening air which was so health-giving and nice, especially away near the stern where most passengers seldom came. But we fear it was a suspicion that he had approached to within a measurable distance of an ever so gentle pressure, both then and the night of the arrival in Cairo, although he was mistaken and it was only a mental illusion, which induced Jack to take out Estelle's portrait and pronounce over it the monologue we have already given.

There was a hurricane blowing in Mauritius that night, and two figures sat close together in a cosy corner of the verandah. Ha, ha, Master Jack, others can play at the game of hide and seek as well as you!

And so the Pyramids were visited, the desert crossed, the passengers embarked at Suez, the Red Sea traversed and Aden in sight. The Commissioner had decided views about Aden as of everything else. He had only seen it once, his former trips out and home having been round the Cape, but Aden is certainly a place which if once seen may be easily remembered. It was with something like dismay therefore that the Commissioner heard that the Mauritius steamer had not arrived. There was no help for it, the passengers bound for the two Islands and Seychelles had to disembark, and make the best terms they could with the hotel keepers on shore. Nearly all the French passengers went to the French hotel, while the Commissioner and his daughter, Jack and one or two English employees of the Mauritius Government going back to duty chose the rival establishment.

The outlook was not cheerful, as the heat when landing was something more than Indian at mid-summer, and there was nothing in or about the hotel which promised to make a stay agreeable. There had been no rain for three years. Not a blade of grass could be detected on the bare and burnt hills which encircled the town and separated it from the desert of Arabia. Every drop of water for cooking and washing purposes had to be brought from the tanks some miles from town on the backs of camels. The scraggy horses of the many cabs which plied between the town and the Tank looked as if they had been buried and risen again. The white soldiers who came into town from camp looked pale and fear stricken. The Sepoys and their wives and children were dirty, water being too precious to admit of the usual cleansing of robes in which the Indians delight when they are to appear in public. Long strings of camels were seen coming in from the desert to purchase supplies in the town, but above all to take back with exceeding care water in the leathern bottles of which the Scriptures speak as the custom then as well as now.

It happened, however, that the few days spent in Aden were about the happiest of the whole voyage. Not only did all the English officers of the regiment in garrison come to call immediately they heard of their arrival, but the Colonel of the Sepoys was found to be an old friend of the Commissioner and the place gave itself up to all descriptions of gaiety. Dinner parties, dances and picnics to the Tanks filled up the days and nights so that when the Mauritius steamer arrived and transferred her passengers to the home-going mail, it was with something like regret that all our party bade adieu to the treeless waste of Aden.

On their renewed voyage Jack and Agnes MacNeill were now on a different and better footing. One evening when returning from a dinner at the Fort, it was suggested that as the night was so beautiful they might leave the carriage and return the remainder of the way on foot. The Commissioner declined, the moon having no such charms for him as for the two young people who were however allowed to have their own way. With one of the Indian boys following to be the bearer of wraps which could not possibly be needed, the two walked slowly homewards along the excellent road. All the features of the scenery were shrouded by the gauzy splendour of the moonlight. The deep rifts in the mountainside caused by the torrents when the infrequent rain does fall seemed lovely sequestered valleys. The hills themselves so gaunt and bare, so destitute of all the softness of outline and beauty of verdure which under the hills and mountains of other lands are conspicuous and picturesque, were lit up with a light which transformed their massive rudeness into sublimity. The sea shimmered before them. The masts of the native craft lengthened themselves in the broken brilliance of the moonlight, which mingled with the reflection from the port-holes of the steamers waiting for the dawn. All was peaceful, beautiful, heaven-like. A few of the greater stars shone amid the splendour and lent the influence of their rays to beautify still more and glorify the mirror-like sea.

Who could walk amid such a scene, with a companion such as Jack had, and with whom he had been on terms of friendship and confidence for so many days, without making a clean breast of his hopes and fears, his dilemmas and difficulties, his yearning and self-upbraiding, his love and his folly, which had made him compromise his future before he had met the one for whom he felt Fate had destined him. It was better thus to be honest than to steal a heart with false promises which could never be fulfilled.

Agnes listened with deep and absorbing interest. Perhaps the conference had come too late to prevent anguish, but it had come before it was too late for her to keep to herself her own emotions. She admired the young officer for his frankness while she pitied him when she heard that he must espouse one from whom he feared his heart had become alienated. It was strange to hear for the first time the words of love from one who declared that he was bound hand and foot, in honour and in duty, to another, from one who did not venture to ask her the state of her heart as he was not free to dispose of his own, but who did not disguise, if he had been free, where he had all his affections, and from whom he would have asked a return. "You must be true to your promise," she whispered, "and send me a newspaper to show me when you are married." Jack groaned in spirit. The prospect was not a cheering one. The open road and the servant behind prevented any of those convulsive claspings which are the best language of stormy loves and hopes, and Agnes besides was much too self-possessed to permit any such manifestations of feeling. However deep the wound might have entered, she at least would not exhibit any symptoms of pain. She did not hesitate to show to her friend that she pitied him, but gave no indication how it had affected herself. Nor did she during the remainder of the voyage alter her manner towards him. The Commissioner, who knew all things so well never suspected the confidence which had passed between them. His daughter did not think it necessary to communicate anything, and thus as the vessel steamed to Seychelles, and afterwards bore down on Bourbon, she appeared outwardly to go on as before. There was a difference, however, to the two persons chiefly interested. Their conversation and intercourse had a graver and riper tone. It was that of friends rather than that of possible lovers, but of friends whose thoughts were steeped in sentiment rich as lights of dawn or sunset. These two, as the steamer beat down the Indian Ocean, in the hot days and matchless nights seemed to be standing among shadows mingled with hues not of the earth but freer and more ethereal the nearer they came to the end of the day which was to separate them forever.[‡]

[‡] It would appear that Gorrie intended there to be an intervening chapter between this one and the next.

Chapter 26
In the Hands of the Bankers

THE VERY STEP WHICH OLD MONSIEUR AMIRANTES TOOK with a view to the joining of the two estates of Pompadour and Lorraine was now turned into a weapon against the two families. The estates would in all probability be made one but in other hands. M. Amirantes was so suddenly removed it was necessary to provide money for working the Pompadour as the Bank took the opportunity of stopping the credit. Others much stronger in capital were on the outlook for estates, and it was thought that it would be "better for all parties" if the present holders were gently forced out. The parties to be benefited were the Bank themselves, a commercial Firm which was in search of imports and accommodation, and the Notary who would have the fees of the business, which in the case of two such estates would amount to a fair year's income.

People have often wondered how commercial Firms at home could enter the risky business of supplying money to sugar estates merely for the sake of receiving the monopoly of the sugar. But if it did not pay them it suited their books in many ways. It would not do for a Bank to advance money directly on mortgage to a sugar estate for that would not be "banking business," but there was no objection, on the contrary there was great competition among the Banks in London, to discount bills for merchants doing a large trade in imports and necessarily also in exports, since all trade is barter. The nominal owner of the estate draws for his supplies on the branch of the mercantile house in the Island, and they endorse the Promissory Notes and have them discounted by the Banks of the Island. Their credit thus supplies them with local capital. The house at home in sending out machinery or great supplies to the estate, and the estate must deal with the fatherly establishment which charges advances at the rate of 12 per cent with commission to boot, draws against the estate for the amount and gets the bills discounted at home, at a third of the rate which it charges the estate. The Firm in place of advancing actual cash thus makes a profit of borrowing it.

When sugar is on its way home the branch house in the Island draws against the Bill of Lading which goes home by the mail to keep its accounts full with the local Bank, and long before the sugar reaches home it has been sold and the bills given for the price are again discounted to meet the bill of the Branch house when it comes due. Thus the ball is kept rolling and the secret explained why enterprises which seem to require a constant outlay of capital come really to provide capital by a bold and unsparing use of credit. The system was never so extensively followed in Mauritius as in the West Indies, because in the former colony there was always more local capital seeking investment, and the merchant had no security or privilege greater than he could obtain by taking a mortgage over the property or purchasing it in the name of another.

In the West Indies, or in some of the islands at least, the mere fact of advancing money to an estate gives the merchant a privilege which comes in before all mortgage. The consequence has been that the credit of the land has been extinguished, and will never be revived until this unnatural state of affairs has been remedied. The advances to estates in Mauritius at the present day are arranged almost entirely by Land Credit companies, or combinations of estates have been made into limited companies with sufficient capital of their own. In the earlier days however one European Firm in particular, which no more exists, went in largely to obtain a monopoly of the supply of sugar. It accomplished this thing because the owners of estates which they put in were the names of men of straw. They found the easiest method was to work through one of the old and thoroughly respectable Notaries of the Island, who knew the affairs of everyone, and who at the right moment could make a suggestion where the screw could be applied with advantage. M. Notary Soussigné was the man whom they selected. The firm had also a powerful auxiliary in a Bank which discounted all its bills, and which was not unwilling with a view to the extension of business to lend substantial aid when wanted. When Amirantes was murdered the representative of the Firm had a long interview with Soussigné, and a long interview afterwards with the manager of the Bank.

After a due interval the Bank pulled up Isidore, and requested him to regulate the estate account. Isidore had accordingly to consult his Notary, who had already been consulted by others, but a Notary being able by law to act in the drawing up of deeds for two parties having different interests, never hesitated to act for any number of parties who all came to consult him as a man skilled in affairs. Soussigné advised Isidore to sell the Mortgage over Lorraine which his father had lately bought. Isidore thought he could now do without any aid of that description, but indeed there was no choice. His father had overdrawn his bank account considerably in order to make up the sum to purchase this mortgage, and it was to legalise this overdraft that the mortgage must again be sold. It was bought directly by the Firm which desired to get hold of the estates, in the name however of a man of straw in their interest when they intended to put in a nominal owner. They had a perfect control over him, for not only was he attached to them by the prospect of being made nominal proprietor of two fine estates, but every half-penny had to be advanced to him, and on the least symptom of independence or treachery he could be at once squashed.

The next step was to purchase a mortgage over Pompadour. That was not difficult as the death of old Amirantes had made the mortgagees anxious about the position of affairs. One of the first mortgages was easily secured. On this occasion Soussigné could do a good turn to an old friend of his own. He intimated to her that there would probably be great changes in the proprietorship of the estates before long, and as he doubted whether a Firm which could go so extensively into transactions of this kind would last, he advised her to transfer her money to one of the old estates held by a good Island family, which had always made good crops and was in a sound condition.

This mortgage was not transferred to the same man of straw for Soussigné dearly loved mystery. He found it paid in the long run. The reason he gave to the Firm and the Bank for putting it in the name of another man of straw was to give an appearance of a combination to sell the estates as there was no saying what view of such a transaction might be taken by the Supreme Court. But he had another reason and that was that two transfers of the mortgage would be required instead of one and he would thus have two fees calculated by a percentage on the amount of the mortgages, probably even two Partitions, as they are called, when the whole nominal amount of the value of the estate being in question the fee of the Notary could come up to several hundreds of pounds. It is thus that clever lawyers feather their nests when dealing with clever rogues, or too enterprising men who covet the possessions of others. The "stamped paper" which Isidore got on the day he shot at Julius Citron was the demand for repayment of the mortgage over Pompadour which had been so purchased.

Lorraine was not so easy to attack with safety. The hurricane had done more damage to it than to Pompadour but Madame Beauvallon as we have seen had rights over it which placed her in a somewhat commanding position. Estelle also being a minor her rights were well protected by the law. Any partition of the estate which might follow upon a forced sale would require to be laid before the law officer of the Crown who would give his opinion upon the propriety and genuineness of the transaction before the Court would give its consent to the terms. Much of all this was usually done as a mere formality, but from time to time law officers cropped up who did not take everything for granted and who had good noses for sniffing out conspiracies and combinations. The whole aim of the Firm, however, would be frustrated if Lorraine was not brought to the hammer at or about the same time as Pompadour. They intended to raise money and go into planting on a large scale if they could only join the two estates, which would give them a territory of not less than 3,000 acres to which it was their intention to apply irrigation on a great scale. Isidore was at Lorraine some days after the events narrated in the last chapter when the same huissier was seen approaching. Having no doubt as to his errand he warned the ladies what was likely to happen, so that they had time to master their emotion, and to receive the visit of the officer of the law with apparent composure. But after he had gone the nerves of poor Madame Beauvallon completely gave way. Ever since the hurricane they had been in the midst of difficulties which might have appalled the stout heart of a man, and which could scarcely be tranquilly faced by any woman.

The losses and repairs necessary were very great. The estate was thus without credit. The Bank had given warning that the account must be kept full as no overdrafts would be allowed. The source from which the account could alone be replenished was from the sale of the sugar, then on the ground which the hurricane had destroyed, to the extent of at least one third. The Coolies had to be paid and the enormous amount of their rice and other rations had also to be purchased. The proprietors could go on for a few weeks with the money they had but the outlook for the future was a dark one even if the creditors had been willing not to press their claims at such a moment. But here was one who had begun to press and who had doubtless purchased the mortgage over Lorraine for the very purpose of forcing a sale. They did not know all the details of the combination but they felt someone wanted the estate for himself.

Even Isidore was fairly overwhelmed. He could not give undivided attention to the affairs of the estates as he had his own trial on his mind which was of even more importance as it affected his personal liberty. The Magistrate had made the usual investigation, and had committed him on the charge of wounding with intent to commit grievous bodily harm, so that it would be left to a jury to decide whether he had any justification in consequence of the menace by Julius or not. Counsel had to be retained and paid which was not easy in the straitened circumstances of the time, frequent consultation had to be held with him and his solicitor amid much trouble and worry in working up points of the evidence. To have the forced sale of both Pompadour and Lorraine on his hands at the same time was too much for him, and he could not bring his mind to work out those combinations by which alone they could be saved.

Estelle happily had the necessary courage to face the difficulties, possibly because not being able completely to comprehend the dangers she undervalued them. But at all events her suggestions and bold proposals were most opportune. She became as we have already seen a new being when she found that she really loved Isidore. So long as she believed she was to be married to Jack she remained perfectly passive contemplating her future not without pleasure, thinking often of him whom she believed she loved, and with whom, had she married him, she would doubtless have spent a pleasant, comfortable, hum-drum life. There would have been nothing in her existence to stir up the deeper feelings and higher intellect which she really possessed. But Isidore having found the way to her heart, and she in turn having found what it really was to love, her whole nature was stirred up and the latent strength revealed. Indeed a careful student of character might have guessed there was strength somewhere from the wonderful musical power she developed. Not only could that not have been acquired without talent, but it necessitated also a constant practice which a strong resolution alone enabled her to give.

Madame Beauvallon on one occasion told Isidore that she had frequently found Estelle in tears because she could not render a piece to her own satisfaction. But she did not on that account give it up and leave in disquiet or disheartened with her want of success. She would only panic for a little, playing something she knew better, and then returned to the difficult pages with a determination to conquer. She had thus both intellect and resolution, and no doubt it was that combination which enabled her to take the bold course of accepting the offer of Isidore when she found she really loved him. Many would have allowed themselves to drift and marred the happiness of their life.

"Who is this M. De Lapaille?" she said, laying down the formal paper she had been reading.

"He is the man who has bought the *créance** over Lorraine," Isidore replied, "which my father bought, and which I was obliged to sell the other day."

"But to what family does he belong? Do we know anything of him? What is his profession that he is able to purchase the créance? I never heard of him among the families in easy circumstances in the Island."

"Oh no, I don't suppose it is his own money."

"Then who can be advancing it?"

"Ah, that is the question and the puzzle! If we knew that we could perhaps take measures to circumvent their designs."

"But can we not take steps to find out? Could Monsieur Soussigné not tell us?"

"Perhaps – if he chose," said Isidore, who knew pretty well that it was Soussigné who had assisted his father in purchasing the Mortgage over Lorraine with a view to the gentle pressure which was no longer necessary.

"Surely our own Notary would assist us!" she argued.

"Only if he is not assisting someone else whose purse is longer and whose business holds out the prospect of more fees."

"That is shameful," exclaimed Estelle. "Is there no one else who could get the information for us? Surely if a man is taking steps to crush us we are entitled to defend ourselves by crushing him?"

Aunt Clémence looked up with a little laugh. That, she thought, was Isidore all over. She had often had cause to wonder of late where the little lady had drawn her courage and resources, but that she had become a new being was manifest. Every trace of feebleness seemed to have left both body and mind. She stood erect, she ordered servants about, she inspected and checked the Coolie rations, she handled the pass books of the stores, ordered supplies for the house, and all this with an even greater regard than before for dressing and adorning her person. She even talked of learning to ride that she might take a turn through the estate occasionally, or perhaps it was because Isidore in looking at the pictures in *L'Illustration Universelle* had praised the appearance of a lady in riding habit following the hounds in England. When she spoke of crushing the person who was attempting to crush them there was a decision about her tone which showed that she meant what she said.

"Mama," she continued to Madame Beauvallon, "this is no time for family quarrels. I will write to invite Uncle Jules and Aunt to stay with us from

* mortgage

Saturday to Monday. Uncle must know about these people better than we do, and as he is the Attorney of the Estate he is bound to help us."

"I doubt if he will be able to circumvent that old fox Soussigné," said Clémence, "but Jules will assist us, and I think Estelle is right, Marie, he ought to be by our side."

Madame Beauvallon had offended her brother by not inviting him to the picnic at the Tamarin Falls, and she did not do so because his wife was a shade darker than himself, and belonged to a family a considerable proportion of whom were well-known scamps. But the reason for all this excessive care had passed away when the alliance with Jack was no longer considered desirable. Madame, fairly broken down in spirit by her misfortunes, was glad to acquiesce in the proposal. Estelle did not wait for Saturday to commence her researches into the history of M. De Lapaille, who in one evil hour for himself had become a tool in the hands of others.

First of all she applied to Ernestine who knew every Creole family, and they then called into their aid the clever Lucille. She being obliged to walk circumspectly was very willing to distinguish herself in other directions. Estelle told both the whole story, how someone was trying to force them out of the Estate, and were using this M. De Lapaille for their purpose. Ernestine knew two families of the name, but Lucille had no doubt he would be the same person whose name was used in the sale of Mon Repos, but it had fallen through and the estate had to be taken over by the Bank. If it was the same he was a mere adventurer of no profession whose name was used by the Notaries and attached to transactions which were too disreputable for their own to be seen. But Lucille could give more practical hints than that. She knew that the place to learn everything was the office of the Registrar General, and she knew a young clerk there who might have told her something, but now she would have to ask Jean LeBlanc to go to see him.

Ernestine and Estelle both laughed as they well knew how recently it was that Lucille had become so careful. "I am afraid," said Estelle, "your influence cannot be transferred to Jean when it affects another man. How would you have found out anything Lucille, tell me, and I may try it myself."

"No," said Ernestine, "you could not employ exactly the same methods as Lucille. M. Isidore might object."

"Ernestine!" exclaimed her fellow servant, "have you no respect for Mam'zelle? I would have employed no methods but honest ones."

"Oh, no one ever doubted your honesty, Lucille, it is not that!"

Upon which Lucille got hold of a towel and chased Ernestine from the room. Estelle begged them to return to give her their advice seriously as the business was not one which admitted of delay. They returned and with much talk at length determined on the persons to whom to apply who would be most likely to give them information. Ernestine had thought of a relative who was a huissier and Lucille undertook to enlist Jean LeBlanc in the prosecution of the enquiry giving him the hints which occurred to herself.

It thus happened that when the attorney Uncle arrived on Saturday Estelle had a great deal of information to give him as to the man of straw who had been employed to turn them out of the estate. Some of the information was of little value and indeed at first sight the attorney thought that none of it would be of any use. "He is not the real mover," he said, "so that at the most we can only get one man of straw out and another is put in."

"Not so," said Estelle, "if you push the man of straw hard he could fall back upon those who employ him, and some paper or deed may be drawn up which may show us who they are and then we can see whether we cannot say something to the principals."

"It is a shrewd suggestion, Estelle," said the attorney who looked at her with some surprise. He had not seen her since the time of the visit of Jack, but she had changed wonderfully since then. He saw he had now to deal with a woman not a girl, a woman remarkably clever and resolute, one who seemed rather to court the struggle to which others had challenged them – and who would not easily be defeated.

He had learned that the English officer had been thrown over, and that Isidore was in the ascendant, but had not been initiated formally into any of the family secrets. Isidore was coming to dine and he thought he would observe Estelle a little more closely. He confided his views to his wife, as the observation of two might be better than the deductions of one. But no minute observations were necessary. Estelle had dressed herself with care. Her eyes were radiant, her beautiful hair done up to perfection, her neck and bust not too much covered – and they saw now better than before how she had grown. Formerly she was thin and supple, now she was still supple but no longer thin. Her body was full and rounded, her arms plump, her whole appearance more that of a woman of eight-and-twenty than a young lady of eighteen. Taking her aunt into a corner she told her that although the *faire-part** had not been yet sent to their friends because of the circumstances of the time, that she was going to marry Isidore.

"But what about the young English officer?" her aunt innocently enough enquired.

"Mama had already forbidden him the house," said Estelle "but as time went on I felt I did not and could not love him, that the whole engagement had been too hastily made, and I believed I would never be happy if married away from Maurice and having to live with people who know us not, and with whom we have not two ideas in common."

"And I suppose," said the Aunt, "that Isidore helped you to come to these conclusions."

"Indeed he did," she said. "I found I had mistaken him altogether. My father's death and his seemed to draw us more and more together. I found him so kind and good, so dear, and he loved me so much, that I could not refuse him."

"We always knew Isidore to be dear and kind, and that he professed to love you, Estelle, but we never heard him called "good" before."

"Hush," said Estelle, "here he comes. He has promised me to be good in future, and good or not," she added, "I love him so that I will go with him to

* announcement

a cottage on any estate and live on salt fish and margoze if we are put out of our home."

"There, Estelle, all is finished with you. I wish you joy, and sincerely hope he will make you a good husband."

Isidore entered draped in a suit of Paris-made clothes, looking certainly a fine handsome specimen of a man. His counsel had informed him that afternoon that he was in great hopes of getting him off at the trial. Pecuniary cares sat lightly upon his broad shoulders and having that assurance all his old gaiety had returned.

He let his eloquence have its natural course at dinner, Estelle listening in silence, and as none were present but relatives and the Abbé, regarding him with undisguised love and admiration. It was her turn when they came to the drawing room. She eclipsed herself in the brilliance of her performance and the excellence of her singing. The servants clung and clustered round the door to hear her. She seemed in playing to throw her whole soul into the music. She could not speak as Isidore could but she could make the piano speak for her. She made it pour forth raptures, now strong as the torrent of a rushing river, now gentle as the voice of spring, now rising to heights of sentiment and passion which made her hearers feel as if the girl were inspired. She felt herself amply rewarded when Isidore bending over her, his sparkling eyes meeting hers which rayed back, love passionate and overwhelming, he whispered, "It is thus Estelle, Venus would have played if she had been Queen of Music as well as of Love!"

Chapter 27
The Discarded Lover

EVERY OFFICER IN THE REGIMENT WAS READY TO FIGHT in place of Jack or to be his second. The way in which the "Cub" had supplanted him in his absence had become known, and as Jack was assumed and known to be definitely in love with Estelle, it was taken for granted that he would have something to say to his rival. Jack certainly did not hear of what had taken place without chagrin. His self-love and importance were wounded. He would have preferred that Estelle had seen him and received his permission before she abandoned her engagement, as he had come prepared to keep his, notwithstanding his preference for Miss MacNeill. But withal he felt immensely relieved and his brother officers could not understand the calmness with which he heard the announcement. They had expected that he would be so cut up, and that there would be such a "devil of a scene," that Darcy had been deputed to break the news quietly, and he had done this with wonderful tact and kindness, offering at the same time to carry any message to the "Cub" which might be necessary. Jack's calm rejection of such a prospect was considered inexplicable, for of his courage they had no doubt. "If," he quietly said to Darcy, "If after all that has taken place she prefers the "Cub" why then she must have him. All I will ask is that she tell me so with her own lips, and that it is her own free choice."

"There is one thing at all events," said Darcy. "They are all absolutely ruined."

"How so?" said Jack quickly, to whom the announcement brought no pleasure.

"Oh, the hurricane, the death of the two fathers, and one thing and another. Both estates are understood to be in the market, and are to be sold for debt or something of that sort."

"I am very sorry for that for Estelle's sake," said Jack, and he wondered who could give him exact information on the point.

"Oh the Bank I daresay, or old Soussigné. What do you intend to do, Jack, will you call on the Beauvallons?"

"Are they in town?"

"I believe so, because the Cub has been shooting some relative of his from France, and there has been a great row about it. He is to be tried one of these days. By the way," he continued, "did I or anyone ever write you of the narrow escape of that young fisherman who saved you the night of the shipwreck."

"No," replied Jack, "I would be so glad to hear something about him as my heart has often smote me for not doing more for him, but our departure to Natal was so hurried. My father, when I was home, severely blamed me for my lack of generosity to the noble fellow and I have got something substantial for him from my parents."

Darcy then told the whole story of the murder of old Amirantes, Jean's narrow escape from being hanged, and of the discovery of the true murderers by the exertions of Lucille.

He had scarcely concluded when Mahmoud, the former Indian servant of Jack, appeared, desiring to be at once taken back into his service. Jack would not hear of this until he had obtained the consent of his mistress who had kindly provided a place for him immediately his former master had left.

"Sahib," he said with deep sorrow, as if he were himself partly to blame for the result. "Massa Isidore come every day. Mam'zelle she cry at first over your letters. Then she not cry. When letters not come she not ask for them. When Captain Dassy he tell me Sahib had gone to England Mam'zelle laugh and say, "Capt Jack will take an English wife, Mahmoud." I look and I say Mam'zelle Estelle wife of Captain Jack. "No, not now Mahmoud," she said, "Sahib!"

"Very well, Mahmoud, you get Madame Beauvallon's consent and I will be glad to take you back."

Jack could not affect to disbelieve all he had heard, but to make quite sure before he took any step he requested Mahmoud to say to Ernestine that he would be glad to see her if her duties would allow her to be near the monument in the Champs de Mars at four o'clock.

She came, and with tears confirmed all that Jack had heard. "Is it of her own free will, Ernestine?"

"Oh, Massa, she be like one out of her mind. Believe Massa Isidore hab *Ti Albert** on him side,[†] she lub him so."

Jack winced even when he rejoiced to find himself free as he had thought that certainly Estelle loved him, and believing so would have carried out his engagement at any cost. It was not pleasant to find that after all she had never really cared for him.

There was nothing now to be done except to solicit an interview and be loosed from his vows by the lady herself. He accordingly penned a few lines to Estelle saying he had returned but he awaited her Mother's permission to call for her, to learn from herself whether they were still the same to each other as before. The question necessarily implied a doubt, but it would have been mere pretence to have assumed that there was no cause for it.

This done Jack asked Darcy whether he would go with him to La Baie to find out Jean LeBlanc. Darcy consented, and as it was a fair drive they got a good pair of horses for the mail phaeton and started. "Jack," said Darcy on the way, "you take your bad fortune very philosophically. Were the old folks against the marriage?"

---

* Petit Albert, a popular textbook of magic.

"On the contrary, they will be very much astonished if next mail does not bring them news of the wedding."

"Well, by Jove, I cannot understand it, except on the supposition that you have got another charmer."

In place of replying Jack pretended he saw something wrong with the traces and then asked some questions about the trial and nearly accomplished tragedy of Jean LeBlanc.

"What beasts these Mauritians are," he said to his friend. "Do you recollect how they abused us about their beastly quarantine laws because we saved some men from shipwreck?"

"They are so cursedly excitable," replied Darcy, "they cannot listen to reason when they take up any cry and indeed there is no one to suggest wiser courses to them for their journalists are infinitely worse than themselves. They are the leaders in every bad movement and they never initiate anything good."

"But surely that must be accidental. There may be a bad set at present. Some of the papers are not so bad as others. It depends I presume upon whether they have a scamp as a writer or not."

"Well that is partly true. But for the emoluments they receive you cannot expect to get men of wisdom or principle and I have seen in other colonies that papers which are devoted to the interests of planters are as a rule rowdy and violent. The questions of labour and so on touch their persons so nearly that they rejoice to see anyone who deals with these questions in a way in the least degree favourable to the labourers furiously abused, and the base rascals who write for them seem to know always what is required of them."

"Don't you think that the planters have above all things an interest in public order which may be disturbed by violent writing as well as by violent acts. When they set the example of violence on one question, other portions of the community will follow their example on another occasion."

"So they do – the public life of colonies like these is divided into intervals of deadness varied by fierce outbursts; like the calm and hurricanes of that climate."

"Do you think it affects the position of the Governor at home these bitter attacks upon him constantly renewed."

"Well it does and doesn't. Of course the Colonial Office knows very well by this time the worth of editorial attacks – but then a number of people in England get the papers who know nothing of what is really going on, and they take it for granted the Governor has done something wrong. They talk in society and go to the Clerks and the Under Secretaries of the Colonial Office, and Members of Parliament talk to the Parliamentary Under Secretary, and they shake their heads and say "that fellow is getting the Colony into a fine mess," pretending to have exclusive information, while all the while they are merely echoing the vile *rodomontade** of ruffians who glory in the violence with which they can attack an official who by the rules of the service cannot defend himself."

* boastful behaviour, bragging

"What would you do then? Would you establish censorship of the press? Or would you keep prosecuting the fellows for libel?"

"Oh it is not necessary to do that. You recollect the attacks upon the venerable old judge; oh no, you had left the Island! But that was done by a paper which was almost wholly supported by the Government. It printed the Government Gazette, and the editor was never out of the Government Offices, and encouraged in every way. The Governor was afraid to tackle the question as most probably he would have had the Colonial Secretary and the Governor General supporting the paper which always praised them up. What is often wanted is not prosecution but information. I have sometimes seen a public clamour completely stopped by a few words of official explanation. But even that is against the absurd traditions of the service. You recollect how the tables were turned in our case by the two letters authoritatively explaining the whole affair."

They had now arrived at La Baie and created a great commotion among the little community. They were led to the house of Jean's father, who repeated to them more clearly than they had yet learned why it was that Jean had been suspected. He passed very lightly over Lucille's share in the transaction as he was aware of Jean's love for her and that their marriage was determined on as soon as both could save the necessary money. This was the point which Jack most of all wished to bring them to. He had money to give, and he was anxious to know how he could give it so as to be most satisfactory to Jean. The latter explained that he had recommenced his vocation as a fisherman but at the best it was poorly paid and the chance of losing their boats and nets for some trifling infraction of police laws was so great that at any moment he might, after many months of toil, be thrown back stripped of every farthing. He was therefore anxious to change his métier and thought the best thing he could do, if he had money to start with, was to keep mules and carts to let them out for hire. These are so necessary for the estates and the merchants in town that the law would protect in place of oppressing him.

This was exactly the point to which Jack wished to bring him. Four carts and eight mules would cost about £140, and he would require to pay the rent of his stable and yard in advance. The sum which Jack had in commission to give him from his parents was £200 and he proposed to add £50 from himself to be given to Lucille for the purpose of the marriage. As it would have been unwise to have given so large a sum to Jean at once – not that he was not shrewd enough to make his own purchases but because he might be tempted to share part of the money among his relatives and cripple himself – Jack informed him that in proportion as he was able to arrange for his premises and the purchase of his animals he would provide him with the money from time to time up to the amount named. Poor Jean could barely believe his ears. As he had already a considerable sum by him, the proceeds of the subscription in his favour, he saw as he expressed it his fortune made, and Lucille a "lady," which she always aimed to be considered.

Jack thought that evening drive home one of the finest he had ever enjoyed in the Colony. Away out to the West rose-coloured clouds floated in the amber sky. Star after star stole out from the rich heavens expanded above their heads. The fantastic peaks of the volcanic hills stood out in the calm air, with a dreamy light about and above them. From every cottage and hut the smoke rose slowly, curling upwards as the females prepared the evening meal. The laughter of children was in the air, the light of outdoor fires lit up their gambols and shewed their gleaming merry eyes as they came running to see the Sahibs pass. Not a breath stirred the repose of the trees, while some of them had closed their leaves and retired to sleep for the night. In the distance the twinkling lanterns of mule carts could be seen on the highway, the light of the beacon at the Bell Buoy, and the gauzy illuminated curtain which hung over the town.

But what added most to the young officer's enjoyment of the return drive was the consciousness of having discharged a duty, and of having brought happiness within the reach of one to whom he owed much. As he smoked his cigar he thought too of Estelle. His thoughts of her had never been but gentle and loving and kind. Most willingly would he have sacrificed even his own happiness to have kept his engagement with her, but if she willed otherwise his thoughts could not become soured or bitter. He planned how he would benefit her, as he had been able to benefit Jean LeBlanc, but he knew too little as yet to form any plan.

"Do you think she will see me Darcy?" he at length observed, breaking a long silence during which the horses had trotted briskly along the admirably kept highway.

"No, I don't, and it would be better not – What would be the use? You could not meet without embarrassment, she as the breaker of vows would scarcely like to meet you in private, and as engaged to another she could scarcely do so either with propriety."

"And yet I should like to meet her and say goodbye at least, there need be no scene. I am prepared to forgive her, if she is prepared to look upon me still as her friend."

"By Jove, I can't understand it," broke in Darcy, "if a girl whom I loved had jilted me in that manner I would have gone and cursed her by bell, book and candle. I would have threatened to haunt her by day and night, and to spoil her every pleasure in life, and to curse every child she might bear."

"You would do nothing of the kind Darcy. The more thoroughly you loved her the more would you be disposed to sacrifice yourself that she might be happy. How better could you show your love than by holding aloof, and saying to yourself "if I love her let me at least do this much for her – to leave her in peace to love whom she pleases." There is a feeling of satisfaction in sacrificing ourselves for others, at least for others to whom we are tenderly attached, which makes up in some degree for their loss. Often and often in after life the thought might recur – "ah how I wish I had won her, but at the moment there is a feeling of exaltation that one can at least immolate our own cherished hopes that she may be happy."

"You speak so eloquently, Jack, that you might win back the heart of any woman even if she were estranged from you."

"Ah, Darcy, that is exactly the point in which I have failed. I am con-

vinced of it. With a pretty girl of any nationality you can spoon and be senti-
mental, and if she be beautiful even fall in love with. But you can never know
her, and she can never know you except in very rare cases unless you are able
by superior genius or in some other way to surmount the barrier of difference
of language, and thus enable you to converse soul to soul. I could never say
to Estelle what I wished to say. I always broke down into commonplace – and
the poor girl was much the same with me. In fact she seldom spoke at all,
although she did a fair amount of the eye and sigh work. Poor thing I think
she loved me once."

"Nay that cannot be, Jack, or she would love you now. I suspect there
are a good many times illusions of the heart with a man or woman as well as
illusions of the brain. I have passed through a few myself."

"Are you passing through one now, Darcy, or are you disengaged just at
present?"

"Free as the air we breathe, my boy, and what is more I intend to keep
so until I get back to dear old Ireland when I shall marry some sweet sprig
of shamrock."

"But here we are in town – faugh – how it smells! There will be some
nice outbreak of disease here someday. I wish our barracks were up at the
Tamarin Falls."

"Where then would be the danger of foreign service?" replied Darcy as
he jumped out – "A precious pleasant idea but I believe we are too late for
dinner."

Next morning Estelle's answer to Jack's note arrived. It was no mere formal yes or no to his proposal to call but it was an impassioned defence of herself for the course she had taken – begging forgiveness if she had caused him
sorrow or suffering, hoping that friendship might remain although love was
impossible, bespeaking kindly feelings for her future husband whose character she had at one time so strangely misapprehended, and enclosing the few
remaining letters of his which Madame Beauvallon had not already returned.

"Can this be Estelle?" was Jack's first reflection. He read and re-read the
letter but was fairly puzzled. It was a woman's hand but a masculine mind.
There was nothing of the old namby-pamby character of her notes about this
letter, there was a depth of feeling and decision of character more like what
could have been expected from Isidore himself than from his fiancée. "Can he
have written it?" But no, it was impossible to believe that. The letter was too
genuine, and the force, if hitherto unexhibited, must be the natural outcome of
the girl's own intellect. "Ah, if it had been always thus," was Jack's next reflection, "how much more ardent would my feelings have been, how much more
lasting, so that my short absence, and the seeing of my countrywomen would
have made no impression on me." But then if it had always been thus Estelle
would not have so easily imagined herself to be in love with the young English
officer. It was simply because her character was unformed and her disposition
too pliable that she had listened to his suit, mingled undoubtedly with the
desire to take a good place in society, and to be spoken of among her fellows
as a fortunate *Mauritienne*. Her mother, too, certainly encouraged her at first.

The offer of Jack was thought to be a great thing for all of them, and it was only after the death of her husband that Madame Beauvallon began seriously to doubt whether she was doing the best for her daughter. She had entirely forgot about all those differences of language, customs, religion, occupation, and turns of thought which are not merely things outward and accidental to the man, but which really go to make up the greater part of his being. It was the religious difficulty which first presented itself vividly to her mind, but it was not the greatest. In these days of tolerance there are many happy homes where the husband and wife have separate religious instructors. But it is difficult to make a home in the true sense of the word where the bent of mind, the training, the customs, the traditions of country, the longings and likings of race are essentially diverse. What would a young English woman, brought up as our young ladies are, do amidst the squalor and vice, the squabbling, the illnesses, the dirt and destitution of a Coolie camp? But to Estelle that had been her surroundings from infancy. To a young English lady the story of Jothee with her six husbands would appear only as a height of sin which she could not comprehend. Estelle comprehended it perfectly, and would probably only have ejaculated *cochon!** had anyone spoken to her of the woman.

The French law of lien** property and inheritance would appear to an Englishwoman to be something repulsive. Estelle was already deep in its study determined to guard at all hazards the family estate from being wrecked. She liked the Code,† she had no great love for the Bible. In fact she never read the latter, and only knew as much of the mysteries of religion as she could pick up in a general and desultory way by going to Mass. A young Englishwoman would shrink from hearing the least reference to the material view of marriage from servants or dependants. Estelle heard of it without flinching from Ernestine and Lucille who bantered without agreeing. In place of the cold Teuton self-containedness, the hot blood of Gaul, and the still hotter blood of Africa, was coursing through her veins, impelled as it were to more throbbing flow by the sudden bursting of the reservoir of her deep feelings and ardent nature. If that welling up of the fountains of the great deep had not come in time, and Jack had married one that he believed to be a simple, devoted, pliant creature, and she had after marriage found out her strength and her weakness, what a wreck it would have made of home and happiness! A thousand times better as it was, and this was the conclusion to which Jack came even before he had called to bid her adieu.

He was determined to do this as he had done no wrong, and he did not wish Estelle to believe that she had wounded his feelings past recovery. He was anxious to assure her of his sympathy, and friendship, and to hope that he might have the pleasure of continuing the intimacy with herself and her family. Ernestine uttered an exclamation when she discovered him in the sa-

* pig!
** A form of security interest granted over an item of property to secure the payment of a debt or performance of some other obligation.

lon, after the chokra had taken his card. She feared Isidore might come at the same time and that the two men might quarrel as they had done once before. But Estelle apparently did not fear anything of the sort, nor was she afraid of meeting Jack alone, as she neither requested the company of her mother nor aunt. They cordially shook hands. In other circumstances there would have been a warmer meeting. Both smiled just as if they had been ordinary acquaintances who had seen each other a week ago.

"I do believe, Mam'selle Beauvallon, you have grown taller."

Estelle winced at the "Mademoiselle." But she speedily recovered herself as how could it be otherwise?

"They tell me I have grown stouter of late, Captain Montmorency," she replied, "but I am not a good judge of any change in myself. I am glad to see you in good health, and I hope you found your parents well when you arrived in England."

"My parents were both well, and I had many messages from them especially from my mother which I presume I dare not now offer in their name?"

Estelle blushed – a habit she had almost entirely conquered, except on some of those rare occasions when Isidore in the outflow of his talk occasionally made an allusion which he ought not to have made. It was the first direct reference to their former attitude, and however much she felt herself justified in what she had done she could not help the tell-tale blood mounting to her cheeks.

Jack had not intended in the most remote degree to reproach her. So hastening to reassure her he said, using this time her own name, "Estelle, I have read your kind and most frank letter. I hope you will allow me to keep it that I may frequently read it over again and admire it, and I wish to say that your feelings having undergone the change you mention you were quite right to do what you have done. So far as I have any claim upon your promise I entirely and forever release you – and wish you joy with all my heart and soul."

"Oh how good you are, Captain Montmorency!" she replied, her lips quivering, her eyes moist with tears ready to flow, and with her cheeks burning with the shame of having on her part broken the troth she had plighted in the early days of their acquaintance. Taking the engagement ring from a little box which she had brought with her she added, "here it is. I refused to give it up to Mama formerly, but I ought not to keep it now. May you find someone to give it to, more worthy to wear it than I am, and who will make you more happy than I ever could have done."

"I will take this, Estelle, as you wish to return it. I would however like you to keep something to remember me by, but I may have a better opportunity of asking your future husband and yourself to accept some little gift on the occasion of your marriage."

"Oh I hope Jack – Captain Montmorency," she added hesitatingly, "that you and Isidore may be friends. I am sure I did him an injury with you formerly for I did not like him, but he has altered so, and has had so many trials to bear. May I assure him," she said offering her hand to Jack, "that there is no – no – feeling of anger against him. Dear Captain Montmorency say there is not, and complete your generosity."

"Estelle," he said, holding her hand, "when he was the suitor for your love which I thought I had secured it was not in human nature that I should look upon him with very friendly feelings, but as your chosen husband, I think no longer of him, but of you, and for your sake, I wish him every happiness, and will be glad to meet him at any time as a friend."

"None but an Englishman could deal so generously," Estelle replied, radiant with joy that there was no fear of duels or angry recriminations. "Oh that I could do something to make your life happy!"

"You can, Estelle, by being happy and prosperous yourself. I can have no greater pleasure than to hear that you are so."

"But you will not think of me any more," she said, "you are not to grieve for me. You will seek out someone who will love you. Ah perhaps you have already found one at home," a jealousy in spite of herself rising in her heart, at the thought of any one possessing what she herself was throwing away.

"I will not deceive you by saying that such a thing is not possible, Estelle. Now farewell forever as one dear to me, although I hope we may often meet as acquaintances and friends."

So saying he wrung her hand with a grip which almost made her cry out. It was quite impossible for her to return it but her eyes showed how grateful she was that all had been ended satisfactorily, and murmuring, "Thank you, thank you, adieu," she ran off to bring Madame Beauvallon and Clémence to meet him no longer as an accepted lover of the daughter, but as a "friend of the family." The girl felt perfectly that his love for her had undergone alteration also, and all the remainder of the day and night she felt angry with herself for harbouring a feeling of dislike to the new object of his affection whosoever she might be. So strangely are some women formed by nature that even when they care not for an individual themselves, and have discarded him for another, they cannot bear the thought either that he should love another or that another should love him.

Chapter 28
In Search of Consolation

IT HAD BEEN KNOWN IN SOCIETY GENERALLY before Jack's arrival that Isidore had been making great running in his absence, but it was not until his return that it became absolutely certain he had been thrown over. There were some who doubted, and thought that the gay Captain had formed other ties in England, or that his people had forbidden the marriage, but these views disappeared before the reality. There was no boasting on Isidore's part. Among his most intimate friends he had already made known his success, but he had become much more staid, and less disposed to make every act of his life an occasion for feasting and bravado. As in a small society everything is known the interview Jack had had with Estelle could not be concealed. What had passed could not indeed be repeated, but from the servants, from the elder ladies, and in various other ways, it was found the lovers were no longer anything to each other. The only persons to whom it gave unalloyed satisfaction were the older and higher officers of the garrison, men hardened to all kinds of partings and especially opposed to foreign matches. Some of the civilians also were pleased, those who had got out of sympathy with the population of the Island and did not like the notion of the alliance.

The General in command, who it may be recollected sent Jack down to Mahebourg, and kept him there as Musketry Instructor, in the hope that absence would have a good effect, took all the credit to himself. It would be a little hard to explain how the absence of Jack on that occasion had altered Estelle's views of Isidore, but the General did not go into minute particulars. He told the Governor and the Commissioner next evening at Réduit, where Lady Foolscap gave her first dinner in honour of her visitors, that he had saved the boy and that it was "a d— good thing too." Several of the younger officers were at the same dinner and the topic of Jack's release, in default of something better, became the general theme of the discourse. Miss MacNeill to whom as a new-come English lady they were all paying court, heard it with a beating heart, but none of them having even suspected that the news could be anything to her, she was easily able to conceal that she had any special interest in the matter, and to hear, what was more pleasant, the praises of Jack as a good fellow lavishly bestowed on all sides.

"You must have been his fellow passenger," said the Colonel to the Commissioner who was in his element among a party of strangers to whom he could develop all his theories about the government of mankind.

"Captain Montmorency! Oh of course he is one of yours. He was quite one of our party coming out. Agnes," He said to his daughter, "it is your friend of the Pyramids who has been jilted by some French woman. The sly fellow did not tell us anything about that coming out."

"I am very sorry to hear of his disappointment," replied Agnes meekly.

"If we had known you had been fellow passengers we would have had Captain Montmorency here tonight," said the Governor, "Johnson," he added to his aide-de-camp. "All right sir," which meant that Jack would be invited to the next dinner party, that indeed was to take place the evening after next, as it was resolved to make the visit of the MacNeills as agreeable to them, and as noteworthy in the Colony, as possible.

Jack had intended to pay his respects at Réduit as soon as possible, and had only deferred doing it for a single day because of the more important business on hand. He borrowed Darcy's trap and saw that it was got up to perfection, that the groom was spotless, and the horse's coat sleek and shining. In all probability, nay almost for a certainty, the ladies would not see his arrival, but still it gave him pleasure to have his turn-out as it should be. On his own person Jack had bestowed more care than usual. For a jilted lover he certainly looked smiling and happy. Having got the scene over his natural spirits made him, at breakfast and at lunch, the gayest of the gay. The health which he had gained by the run home predisposed him for merriment, while all those who had remained on Mauritius were more or less suffering from bile, languor, discontent, and quarrels with each other.

Jack's arrival was in every way a fortunate thing for the regiment. Up the long Moka Road he drove at a walk, thinking and wondering whether if he got a chance he might dare – but such thoughts do not usually come to any definite conclusion. He stopped to give his horse breathing time, and in order that he might look back upon the scenery which from that point was exceedingly lovely. The Valley of Les Pailles at his feet then full of residences stretching out onto the plain which bordered the sea, the ravines of Grand River at his side whence he heard the sound of waterfalls, the noble mountains all around with the unutterable blue sky, fleeced with vapours overhead. It was a scene to have charmed him even if he had been crushed by the disenchantment of yesterday. As it was it made his heart bound with enjoyment and hope.

Thinking it possible that the ladies might be out walking, Jack went down the long avenue at a fine pace, and drew up at the door without anyone having seen him except the sentry, one of the soldiers of his own regiment. He dreaded he would find everyone out, but when in the act of writing his name in the Visitor's Book a servant appeared who took in his card. Jack was ushered into the Drawing Room and found the wife of the Governor and Miss MacNeill. They had been talking about him, and when the lady looked at the card she said to her young friend "speak of the —" Miss MacNeill looked up with somewhat of a startled look, and would if she could have run off just for an instant to be quite sure she looked composed, and to see for herself whether she was all comme il faut in the way of dress. But there was no chance, Jack followed his card so closely. She was outwardly quite composed, and it need scarcely be said that not a word was uttered of what had been the topic of conversation before his arrival.

The Governor and Commissioner were out. Lady Foolscap remarked that the Commissioner had taken quite a fancy to the dells and ravines about Réduit, and she was quite sure the Governor had already seen more of them than he had ever done before. This was a topic upon which Jack could be eloquent, having often visited them, and always with a fresh impression of their beauty. The incidents of the voyage also formed a never failing fund on which to draw. He so painted for the Governor's wife the scene when they passed through the straits of Messina in the early hours of the night that she declared it made her determined to go home by the first opportunity. It was the first occasion when Agnes and he had had a long confidential talk together, the first time she had found him to be anything more to her than the ordinary run of young men, and the first time that he had allowed himself to think even for a moment "Oh for a companion like this on life's long voyage." There were reasons therefore why he should be able to reproduce the scene with artistic effect, and as he spoke Agnes ventured to look up and meet his eyes, as they were lit with the rapture of the remembrance. She speedily looked elsewhere, and the conversation had sunk again to the ordinary level when the Governor's lady begged to be excused until she went up to the nursery to send the children out for their evening walk. Jack and Agnes being thus left alone she proposed to go into the garden which was reached by stepping out of a French window, almost level with the parterre.

The flower beds had been laid out with much care, the broad walks had all been newly attended to in expectation of the visit of the MacNeills, and thus the place was at its very best. Situated some eight hundred feet above the sea level not only is the prospect extensive and grand but the air is pure and invigorating. Whatever evils and hurtful chances to human life there may be living down on the sea level in tropical countries these elevated spots are quite as healthy as England, and with many many charms of which England cannot boast. The sun was still a little strong, so that Jack had to run back for Miss MacNeill's parasol. Again he wondered whether he dare venture, but he feared their acquaintance had been too short. On the other hand if he did not make use of his opportunities, she would so shortly leave again to return to India that they might never meet in this world. He resolved at least to approach the confines and take his chance—

"Miss MacNeill," he said, after they had admired the flowers and she had picked out all her favourites, "you recollect our conversation at Aden. I am now free. My fiancée had been beforehand with me and had engaged herself to another."

"I am glad of it for your sake if you felt you could not love her. Neither of you seem to have known your own minds."

"The reason is that we have both changed. She especially has changed wonderfully. I left her a girl and found her a woman."

"And having got the strength and sense of a woman she rejected you,

Captain Montmorency," said Miss MacNeill with a bit of good-humoured raillery which Jack only half appreciated.

"I suppose she naturally preferred one of her own countrymen. It was a mistake in me ever dreaming of such a thing."

"How beautifully these begonias match with the dark brown colias," said Agnes.

"Contrast," Jack ventured to say, "each has his own part to fill and I imagine it is the happiness of the contrast which gives us pleasure."

"Perhaps so," said Agnes, "yet flowers match as well as contrast, and there is pleasure from both harmonies. Look at that bed of phloxes, you could not say that the colours contrast, they only so match and mix well together that we love to look at them."

"Quite true. That I would say is like shades of character in the same class and race of individuals. There is variety without contrariety, distinctions without differences, subtle marks by which individuals are known while the family remains intact, moulded on the same general plan, and obedient to one general law."

"You mean a phlox is always a phlox which is undeniable. But unless there were all these differences, which we see, do you think there would be the same beauty among plants?"

"Did you ever, Miss MacNeill, see a field of coffee in flower?"

"I do not think I have ever seen a coffee plant at all except in botanical gardens."

"Come then," said Jack, "let us search for them. I know there are some here and if they happen to be in flower they will illustrate better what I wish to say, which is simply this, that although every flower of coffee is like its neighbour in colour and shape, and although one cannot see any difference except that some are not yet opened, and some are full, and some decayed, that the harmony of the whole is perfect. We feel even more impressed, and feel a higher pleasure, because of the unity, homogenousness, and sameness if you will, of the mass of snow white flowers, than we could possibly have done if colours and differences had been well marked. Oh there they are, four trees planted together!"

"How beautiful," exclaimed Agnes, "the flower is a most delicious white and the leaf, how glossy and rich. Now, Captain Montmorency, there is a contrast for you, since you like the word, between the dark green of the leaf and the purity of the flower."

"Yes, and a contrast which gives infinite pleasure. It is the distinction between two organs of the same plant, each perfect in their kind, and one never by any chance passing into the other."

"No, indeed is it so? My father you know is an enthusiastic botanist, and as I am frequently his only companion he tells me much, which I could never have comprehended if I had only read botanical books. He has told me often that the flower is only a modified leaf, that the whole plant indeed is made upon one general plan, and although this part was devoted to one function and that to another, we ought not to think of the parts as essentially distinct, but as one harmonious whole."

Jack found he was not likely to gain anything by this kind of discussion in a field in which the lady probably knew so much more than himself. So to try to hark back to his point he added:

"You know what I mean. Flowers which don't belong to the same family may form good contrasts when they are planted together – but they don't harmonize well in the best sense of the term. Because there can be no perfect harmony without perfect accord in all the essential elements."

"Ah, but we were only speaking of the harmony of colours not of anything deeper. Of the pleasure to the eye of the grouping of that which assimilated well, not of the inner harmony of that which was concealed."

"Well, of course you're right, I was thinking of one thing – you of another. I was thinking in fact that as you never see two families of plants running into and mixing with each other, it is much better to take their example, and for the families of mankind to keep separate from each other."

"But what are families as regards the human race, Captain Montmorency? There may be great differences with fundamental unity and agreement. Is that Banyan tree not a Fig, and yonder Camellia is it not of the same family as our Assam Tea?"

"Well but you could not graft tea upon a Camellia so that both would either produce wholly the flowers of tea, or wholly the flowers of Camelia."

"There might however be a good mixture of both. Look at those roses, all grafted upon the dog-rose stem."

"Ah, there you have not only the same family but the same kind – and that is what I meant to say that supposing races of men were of different families there need be no attempt at mixing them for things will not go well."

"In short you mean to say," said Miss MacNeill, who had seen the poor fellow's drift all along but could not help teasing him, "that since Mademoiselle Beauvallon..." But she had not the heart to finish the sentence, as she feared it would give him pain.

"Exactly," said Jack, getting somewhat desperate, "do you not agree with me that it is better men should marry one of their countrywomen?"

"I daresay, as a general proposition, that is unobjectionable," she replied.

But in search of the Coffee trees, and in search of this truth, which Jack saw clearly before him, but did not very well know how to express, they had wandered out of sight of the house, the opportunity was one which might never recur, so swallowing something which rose in his throat, and with a voice tremulous with emotion, strong man as he was, he stopped and said,

"Miss MacNeill, my comrades cannot understand why I take the loss of Mademoiselle Beauvallon so easily, but it is because I had met you, and felt how immeasurably superior you were to anyone else. I would not now offer you my love if there was any chance of being able to prove my devotion to you during weeks or months of acquaintance, but you will soon leave, and we might never meet again. Will you be mine?"

She spoke not. He took her hand, which she did not withdraw. He sunk on one knee and kissed it respectfully, and holding it, again said, "Will you be mine – oh say that you will, and I will be yours till death."

"Rise," she said at length with difficulty. "Rise Captain Montmorency, I know not what to reply. My father would be alone in the world; he has no one but me. I had never thought of marriage until" – nor did she finish this sentence for if she had the ending would have been "I saw you."

Jack thought it meant "until now." So he added, rising, "you need not separate from your Father. I can easily manage that. Say, Agnes, that you will be mine," and he gently put his arm around her waist.

She did not refuse permission, nor did she give any answer. Her cheeks were burning, and her fingers were convulsively pulling to pieces some of the flowers of the coffee tree he had culled for her. She did not wish to refuse to hear him. She did not wish to give an affirmative reply without having heard her father's wishes whom she had been accustomed to obey in all things. Nor could she give a negative. She could not indeed find words to frame any reply.

Was this then the decided, clear headed, commanding young lady who was already at the head of a large establishment, and could have given in a few minutes the necessary orders to feed a score of guests and a hundred attendants in the jungle? Ah yes, there are times and seasons in every life when men and women find themselves equally weak. When disease comes and makes the strong man as a little child, when death comes and unlooses the fountain of grief, when love comes and says "will thou be mine till death doth us part," then the bold and manly who utter the words, and the shrewd, clever, self-contained, and most firmly knit who hear it, trembling and halting in speech, and ready to throw themselves down to weep their fill, all acknowledge the common frailty. There is, it is true, a pleasant side to such a picture as the last. The fount of laughter is near to that of tears, and we who look on upon the representation of such a scene have a tendency to look at one side only. But what a supreme moment it is for those who act. Happiness or misery for the two sides if they are to be united, the opening up of other fountains of being to flow on until time shall be no more, the one moment which is to consecrate or desecrate all things, the moment which is the true beginning of the higher life on life, even to death, is the beginning of the higher life beyond death.

She was not easily conquered. Not since her mother's death had she shed a tear, not since her father was brought home wounded by the man-eating tiger had she trembled – but she trembled now, and she strove hard to keep from weeping, too hard, for nature can only stand a certain pressure. "Speak to me, Agnes, speak to me, wilt thou be mine?" he pleaded gently, mournfully, dreading a refusal.

"Oh I cannot – I cannot," she gasped, and he thought it was a refusal.

"Oh God," he cried, "wilt thou not be mine?" A space of silence followed when the beating of both hearts might have been heard.

She saw he had misunderstood but she could not articulate – "No, no," – she again gasped – for her throat was parched, and the words refused to come.

Again a negative. He threw himself once more on his knee. "Agnes, Agnes, I beseech you hear me, do not, do not kill me by a refusal."

She dragged him up to his feet – "do not – do not – Oh I cannot – speak. Forgive me."

His arm was again round her waist, and with the other he had clasped her hand. "Wilt thou be mine, Agnes, in very truth – "

She turned her face to his shoulder and the welcome tears came at length, in a deluge, and with sobs, hysterical in their violence, from that bosom long pent up, and where the softer emotions had been so sternly repressed.

"If – if – yes, Jack, I am yours," she at length managed to ejaculate, and their lips were sealed in the solemn pledge of accepted love.

How long they thus stood they knew not. They were awakened by the voice of a Scotch-negro gardener exclaiming.

"Oh – that's a nice way to behave in a garden walk – and the Governor's garden too."

Agnes felt unutterably guilty. "Here my man," said Jack, chucking him a sovereign, "this is to be my wife, but these are things that are not to be blabbed about until they are ripe."

"Oh if that's hit," said the cunning fellow, groping for the gold among the grass, "I can be as close as anybody. But my Leddy's looking for you everywhere."

They had forgot my Lady, and everything else. Jack had certainly made a long call and done a good deal of execution. They both felt somewhat the awkwardness of the situation. If the Governor and the Commissioner had returned!

"Shall I stay and see your father at once, Agnes," whispered Jack as, she reposing on his arm, walked slowly beside him in the direction of the house.

"No, I think I know Papa's ways better. But are you quite sure Jack that I need not part from my dear father?"

"Quite sure. I am independent, and I can manage an exchange – anything that is necessary."

"Then I will tell him first, and you can see him tomorrow."

"I am to dine here tomorrow – but I had better see him in the morning."

"After eleven, Jack, if you please, we are not early people!"

"And what about Lady Foolscap. What shall we say to her?" said Jack laughing. "You see what scrapes we get into with making love, my Agnes," he said tenderly.

"I will tell her at once," she said, "all women like to know about match making and that will get her on our side."

"Then adieu till tomorrow, Agnes. If your father listens to me we can have an hour together in the morning."

"Yes, yes, goodbye darling, at present, I cannot face Lady Foolscap until I have dried my eyes. You must storm the battery alone, Jack," she added, tripping off, while Jack entered the French window again and found the room deserted. No, not deserted for Lady Foolscap was fast asleep on the sofa, and Jack slipped away, and Agnes looking down when she heard the noise of wheels saw her lover drive off.

She went to Lady Foolscap's room and knocked but there was no one there so returning to the Drawing Room, the noise of her entrance awoke the hostess.

"Has Captain Montmorency gone?" said Agnes, not knowing very well what to say.

"Has he not been with you?" she replied, rousing herself and then sitting upright. "I believe I have been asleep. I thought you had gone for a walk together."

"Oh we merely went to see the flowers, but after we had gone out Captain Montmorency said he wished to speak with me and we went a little farther."

"You knew him coming out?"

"Oh yes, he was always with us. Papa liked him so much – and – and – do you know Lady Foolscap he has – he has –"

"Goodness gracious! Not proposed!"

"Yes indeed he has, dearest lady, and I have accepted him," said Agnes, going up to kiss her, "and I hope you will give me your counsel and advice so as to break it to Papa!"

"My dear child," said the good-hearted lady giving her a hearty embrace, "a proposal in Réduit garden is something new…"

To obtain the Lady's promise of silence for one night was easily got, but for Lady Foolscap it was not easily kept. She rushed to her husband and told him the moment he came in. That great man was at first inclined to take the gardener's view of it, that for a Captain to propose to a visitor of his in his own garden was an infraction of the articles of war, but his wife soon laughed him out of it. If the Commissioner had been gifted with ordinary penetration he would have seen that something extraordinary had happened for Lady Foolscap notwithstanding her promise could not restrain at dinner her jokes and allusions, so that the Aide-de-Camp before the meal was half over had made a shrewd guess at what had happened. He felt rather small as he had been revolving thoughts in his own mind with the same general object in view. But he would never in any case have made up his mind before Miss MacNeill had left so that no wrong was really done him. The hardest part fell to the lot of poor Agnes and that was after she had got her father to retire early to go with him and tell him the momentous occurrence of the day. The poor gentleman was very much cut up. He knew of course that his daughter would in all likelihood follow the course of those before her and accept a husband some day. But that day he believed was in the far future, and now to see it suddenly so near him unmanned him. But he conquered himself so far as to enter into a minute cross-examination of Agnes as to the state of her own heart and being satisfied on that point, made no other objection. He sent her to bed happy with his warmest blessing.

When Jack arrived next morning he was met at the door by one of the Indian servants who placed a dainty little note in his hand with the instruction it was to be read at once. The memorandum was from Agnes and simply said "All right" – and thus the dreaded interview with the stern parent was not so formidable as it was feared. When the result became known Lady

Foolscap would not allow Jack to leave for the day, so sending back by servant for his evening clothes he had a long glorious day of love, with Agnes all to himself, except at luncheon, and a drive with Lady Foolscap and her along the Moka Road towards the Deux Mamelles in the cool of the evening.

The dinner party that night was a large one. The cream of the military and civilians were present, and it so happened that a man-of-war from the East India station had come down for a few days. It was an ordeal for both Jack and Agnes to come down amongst all these uniforms and "heavy swells" as Jack rather irreverently termed them, knowing very well that the chief talk before dinner would be of their engagement.

The General, who had taken so much trouble to prevent Jack marrying the Frenchwoman as he called her did not at all approve of his proposing to Miss MacNeill. He had no particular objection but he thought it was "d—impertinent." He did not say this to the Commissioner, nor to Jack whom he complimented quite warmly on his success with the fair sex. Jack sat next the Procureur General at dinner, the same who had strenuously striven to hang Jean LeBlanc. In the course of conversation he said carelessly, "I think my friend Estelle Beauvallon has made a mistake becoming affianced to young Amirantes for he is just about to be sold up and most likely Lorraine will follow."

"Are things so very desperate then?" said Jack.

"As desperate as they possibly can be. I think the sale of Pompadour takes place this week."

Jack heard the tidings with real concern, but resolved to make himself more acquainted with the position of affairs on the morrow.

Chapter 29
Something Lost and Something Won

M. DE LAPAILLE WHO IN AN EVIL HOUR FOR HIMSELF had been put forward as the wrecker of Lorraine was having a bad time of it. As a penniless adventurer his *bons*,* which may be translated by his I.O.U.s, were in numerous "dossiers" in the town. He had been mixed up with several sales of estates, and on one occasion at least a *Folle Enchère*** had been sued out against him for failing to comply with the conditions of his pretended purchase. Before it came known that the Firm of which we have spoken had taken him up it was not difficult for Uncle Jules to ferret out, and purchase at a mere nominal price, a couple of handfuls of Lapaille's obligations, and he was diligently working up, under the able direction of Estelle, the *Folle Enchère* business in order to be ready to hurl the legal stone on his head at the proper moment.

It would be too technical to explain the many and devious ways which had to be followed, and the curious corners into which they were led in tracing the recent cases of Lapaille by the "bons" he had left behind him. It was like the amusement of a paper chase when horsemen follow the track of the "fox," turning and twisting across country, following the numerous paper indicators he leaves as he runs. The Firm were quite aware of the pecuniary condition of Lapaille and they expected they would probably have to advance him a hundred pounds or so to stave off importunate private creditors who were likely to start up when they heard he had a job in hand. But they little expected the stirring up of chaos which did take place. The Attorney for Lorraine was in full cry when happening one day to be in the Bank he saw Lapaille leave the Manager's Room, and before the door could be closed he saw also inside the representative of the Firm, and the Attorney who did the dirty part of their business. They might have been arranging for the sums which were necessary on the sale of Pompadour which took place immediately, but Jules thought it not improbable they were consulting Lapaille about his affairs, to see whether it would be safe to go on with him as the nominal purchaser of the Lorraine mortgage. At all events, having had this glimpse the

---

* Lit. "make-good"s, thus I.O.U's.
** boastful behaviour, bragging Lit. "mad auction," a legal procedure of adjudication on resale (after bidding) of an immovable property.

Attorney did not any longer doubt what he had already suspected, that the Firm were the moving parties. He immediately betook himself to the Office of the Registrar General where every Notarial Deed, and every deed affecting land in any way, was registered, and in a few hours he had put his finger upon four cases where the Firm had been the real purchasers of estates through the agency of men-of-straw. The object of the Attorney then was to ascertain the condition of these men as to their liabilities in other transactions, to discover the state of the proceedings in the sales to the Firms, and generally by means of every possible and plausible handle which an intricate law, and a loose style of procedure, gave him, to attack them right and left and thus make them desist in terror from harassing the proprietors of Lorraine.

Estelle did something even bolder, and for a young lady of the Colony unprecedented. She went to the office of the Firm and demanding to see the chief partner taxed him with endeavouring to turn their family out of Lorraine in order that they themselves might buy. It was in vain for the gentleman to protest his innocence and for the junior partner to be brought, and the chief clerk. She told them it had been satisfactorily discovered that they were supplying the means to De Lapaille, and a happy thought struck her, in the excitement of the interview. She threatened to write to the Bank of England to ask for their protection. It was a mere random shot, but it was an effectual one.

"What the deuce can she know about the Bank of England," said the senior partner after she retired. The Firm had very good reasons for not wishing to draw the attention of the Bank in any special way to their transactions in Mauritius.

"There is a most extraordinary change in that young lady," replied the junior partner, "when I first knew her she would have fainted at the very thought of entering a merchant's office. I suspect Amirantes will feel by and by he has met his match."

"We have, I suspect," mumbled the senior.

Things were getting decidedly too disagreeable to permit them to go on with the attempt to wreck Lorraine. Their own Attorney came to them in the afternoon with the intimation that steps had been taken in five different actions aimed against them or Lapaille, and the Folle Enchere business against the latter would make them look very foolish and he very dangerous if he purchased Lorraine. Severe recriminations passed between the partners and the Attorney. Soussigné was sent for and was blamed for leaving so many matters in a condition to be opened up and impugned, and before the afternoon had closed the Manager of the Bank had sent for the junior partner and said, "This will never do, it may involve your credit as Merchants." "They tell me it is very likely the sale of *Allezaudiable** will be upset and the very deuce to pay. D—, stop it all." And so they did. The brilliant scheme of uniting Lorraine to Pompadour and irrigating the plain on a grand scale with other people's money had to be dropped. Soussigné was ordered to sell the

* "Gotothedevil"

mortgage over Lorraine and to be done with the whole affair. But they could not get out so easily as they thought. The sale of Pompadour was too far gone to be stopped, while the proceedings against Lorraine having become known (indeed everything is known in Port Louis the moment after it is done) the mortgage was no longer saleable. It was purchased by Jules (by means of a man-of-straw also) at one quarter of its value, so that the enterprising Firm lost a thousand or two by this *coup manqué*.* All was due to the spirit and determination and knowledge of Estelle. The manner in which she learned what ought to have been done, and what ought not to have been done, her boldness in attacking the enemy with his own weapons, and her unheard of proceeding in bearding the lions in their own den, became afterwards the talk and admiration of the town. "That is nothing," said the wife of Jules to a friend in speaking about the events of the last few days. "She says she would live on rice and margoze with Isidore Amirantes rather than have that handsome Englishman and ten thousand pounds."

"Notre belle Mauritienne,"** exclaimed the neighbour.

The prospect of rice and margoze was certainly unpleasantly near to Isidore. There had been no time to save both estates, Isidore's attention had been taken up with his trial and the sale of the estate came on. The Firm it was supposed would be obliged to take measures to buy in order that they might afterwards sell at a profit, as they had severely burned their fingers over Lorraine. All such sales by the law of Mauritius are conducted before the Master of the Supreme Court. There is not much space for the Attorneys and the public in the little court room and in this case a larger attendance than usual of both had mustered. Some had come with a view to business, some as friends of Isidore, a few in the hope that something piquant would occur as everyone knew his boldness, and the success of Estelle with Lorraine had been already whispered abroad. Something unusual did happen but not of the kind the lookers-on had anticipated. One or two bids were given for the property and duly signed by the bidders, but the competition was very languid. It was hoped by his friends that Isidore had made arrangements to buy the property in by means of an alter ego and that the price would be *pro forma* run up to a sum which would enable the leading mortgages to be reinserted at the old value. But no such arrangement had been made in consequence of the first mortgage being in unfriendly hands. No one except the Attorney for the Bank knew that that mortgage had been purchased the previous afternoon, at something considerably less than its value so anxious were the Firm now to have nothing to do with the sale, and so scared had the Banker become at the risks which had been run.

The next bid was made by Jean LeBlanc! A laugh of derision ran around the hall, but Jean with perfect sang-froid signed his bid as he had seen the others do, and awaited calmly the conclusion of the affair. Several bids were made in succession, the attorneys who made them for their clients looking

* "a missed opportunity."
** "Our beautiful Mauritian."

angrily at Jean as if they thought his pleasantry had gone too far, and that if he was going to trifle with them it was a pity he had not been hanged. But after this little spurt was over Jean capped the previous bidding by another from himself, and so shook the confidence of the habitués of the court that they could no longer see their way to proceed. There was evidently some mystery behind it of a new and unusual nature which they could not fathom. While they still discussed in whispers the hour-glass had run out and Jean was declared the last bidder and purchaser of the property, and in reply to a question offered to deposit the whole price if necessary there and then. It was seen someone with money was backing him and nothing further was said.

Isidore knew nothing about the arrangements so that his friends condoled with him, believing he had lost the estate which his father and grandfather had both held before him. The peons ran round the offices spreading the news that Jean LeBlanc had purchased Pompadour. An Indian owned one of the sugar estates in the colony, but it was a thing unheard of that a Creole fisherman, or carter as Jean now was, should presume to do such a thing. When the news got wind in town most people laughed, some said his head had been turned by his having been too much made of after his second trial, his own fellows who had subscribed a sum of money for him were most indignant, while when it was mentioned to the Beauvallons they were thoroughly disgusted and Lucille felt so ashamed of her lover that she cried bitterly.

However hard soever it was for Isidore to lose his property he had something harder to face in a few days which required him to summon up all his nerve. Estelle encouraged him nobly. She had made light of the loss of Pompadour for she said they could not work the two estates so satisfactorily as one. Lorraine was better supplied with water, and when Isidore could apply his knowledge and genius to it, the temporary difficulties under which it laboured would soon be surmounted. The Coolies on Lorraine were a better set, the stock was better, the yield per acre larger. "Who the deuce can be backing Jean LeBlanc?" was Isidore's frequent question or reflection, but as yet he had found no satisfactory answer. The Assizes were near, and it was necessary to turn to the preparations for the trial. The first thing was to be quite sure they would have a Judge likely to be favourable to them. One Judge had one set of views, another looked at the affairs of life differently. One was very severe about any act of violence, another allowed a good deal for hot blood, for hot French blood, and rash Indian and Mozambique acts done in passion. The second would be certainly preferable to the first. Estelle who was rapidly qualifying as a lawyer asked how the cases were divided among the Judges.

They sat alternately but no one could give her very exact information as to how the cases were divided. A friend of hers who had been at the same Convent school had married very young a clerk in the office of the Procureur General. She took care to call for her one day when the husband was likely to be at home, and from him she easily learned that the list of cases was made up in the Procureur General's office and very seldom changed, while the Judges took the Courts on successive days in the order of their severity. The Judge for the third day was the one whom they regarded as specially favourable, and Estelle threw herself sobbing into the arms of her friend, and wondered if it were possible to get Isidore's trial set down for the third day. Marie was likewise deeply interested in the trial. She not only was a friend of Estelle but of Isidore, and many a delightful dance she had had with him. "These other men are such horrid wretches they would take a pleasure in consigning Isidore to prison for life," said Estelle.

"But is there any fear that Isidore may be condemned, Estelle?"

"Fear! He is certain to be sent to prison for years, and chained in the gang, if any of those others try him."

"You did not tell me anything about this, Alfred," she said upbraidingly to her husband, "everyone knows of what is going on but me. Is it possible that Isidore can be sent to prison for anything like this?"

"Oh yes, he may," the husband replied, "it depends upon what view the jury take."

"And the jury are apt to be led by the Judge," remarked Estelle.

"Certainly."

"You see, Marie, what an immense thing it would be for us to have a Judge who knows and understands us Creoles. O I wonder how it could be managed!"

"Alfred will be able to manage that I am sure," said Marie quite simply.

"Oh, Alfred, do," broke in Estelle, "do and we will be ever grateful to you. It is only in these little things we Creoles can assist each other. Promise me, Alfred, make him promise Marie, and it will remove a lead from my heart."

"It is of course much the same in what order cases are tried," said Alfred sheepishly, having a notion he ought not to promise, but the thing looking a very small favour to do for his wife's old friend, "All Judges will do what is right I fancy. I can't guarantee, you know, that the order will not be changed, but I have never seen it changed and in writing out the list there is no reason why I should not put Isidore's trial for the third day and let it take its chance."

"Oh thank you, Alfred, so much. Thank you dear Marie. May the good angels bless you. Will you let me run to tell Isidore, he is so anxious!"

But Isidore had secured something better than even a supposed friendly Judge. He had got a popular Counsel, the crack orator of the bar, one who could generally extract a verdict in his favour if it could be got at all, and one who was sure on this occasion to do his very best to raise his fame – the Mauritius bar had long been famous for the talent and eloquence of its members. They had to be called at home, and this necessitated the acquiring of a competent knowledge of English. They spoke both languages indeed with equal fluency. Not infrequently they had been successful students at the Royal College and been sent home with the Government scholarship of £200 per annum for four years. But none of the young men, or only one or two at rare intervals, left the Island permanently to push their fortunes elsewhere. There was a glut in all the professions. The bar in particular was crowded. It was the profession most in favour with the colonials for a variety of reasons. Gauls by descent they liked oratory, and Frenchmen to the hearts' core they were all lawyers by nature, knowing the Code, as has already been said, better than their Bible.

Every considerable person in the community had been a litigant over and over again, and thus knew the good points of the various counsels. The Colony moreover not having free institutions, the bar was the only field where the younger and more able men could assert themselves and show what they could do if they only had opportunities to eclipse the foremost men of England.

Isidore had another point in his favour which was perhaps the strongest of all. He was a white. Important as was the trial of Jean he was only after all a "noir," a man who was nobody, and whether he were saved or hung was of little consequence to most people. But to see a white at the bar, and his liberty in peril, was a very different thing. Penal servitude, that is, the working of prisoners in gangs on public works, is very good for black Indians or Mozambiques, but when it comes to the chance of whites, the whole moral sense of (one may use the expression of the community) revolts against it. The white prisoner would require to associate with and work among the blacks, and this is considered too degrading for the superior race to witness. The punishment of whites is almost invariably confined to imprisonment without hard labour, or if hard labour be specified it is not enforced. The juries drawn from the ordinary class of the population are all animated by this feeling. In any doubtful case, that is, any case where the Counsel can by his ingenuity manage to conjure up a doubt, the jury will return a verdict of not guilty in order that there may be no punishment.

In a well known case where a white employee had killed a Coolie in the field by knocking him down and jumping upon his body with the result of driving one of the ribs into the lungs, the jury found a verdict of common assault. Another case where the verdict ought to have been one of murder against a coloured Creole, where the witnesses deposed most distinctly to seeing the accused deliberately shoot his brother, the verdict was "not guilty" in order that the Colony might be spared the pain of seeing a light coloured man hanged. There was every hope therefore that with these feelings to work upon, of the hasty nature of the act and the threat of Julius, with the public sympathy created by the purchase of Pompadour over Isidore's head, as it was thought, and his impending marriage to a daughter of the soil who had refused a highly born, wealthy, and gallant Englishman to take the noble young Creole, there was every hope of success!

The trial was taken on the third day as had been so cleverly arranged and the supposed favourable Judge presided. The jury list had been most closely scanned by all the intimate friends of the two families, and all those supposed in any way to be unfriendly and antagonistic marked to be challenged if called. There was a considerable number of those who were more French than Creole who thought Isidore's action most rash and worthy of some punishment. They did not believe that Julius had threatened him, and they feared the charge against Isidore may have had some foundation. The fate of the poor girl had met with great commiseration, some who did not know the facts pitying the husband because of his bereavement, and their sympathy with the husband took the direction of strong feelings against Isidore because he had rashly used his pistol. The incident had been so much canvassed by the whole town that the opinions of nearly everyone were well known, and thus the jury list could be surely manipulated.

After the challenges were exhausted there was only one man called to the box of whose opinion they were not certain. Much of the subsequent eloquence of the Counsel was therefore poured forth to obtain a triumphant acquittal by unanimity rather by a majority. No sooner was the jury drawn than the names were sent up to Estelle, who had organised a corps of messengers out of their own servants and the chokras of their friends, to bring intelligence of every movement. The town house of the Beauvallons became like the Committee Room at the election. People who could not get to Court came for news, others who had been in Court ran up to mention any incident of importance which had occurred, wine and cake were on the table all day, and a grand dinner was in course of being cooked in the assured confidence that Isidore would return a free man to eat it with them.

The counsel for the accused made mincemeat of Julius Citron. Julius had somehow denied before the Magistrate that he had pointed his revolver at Isidore, but he was compelled on cross examination to admit that he had. He had denied before the Magistrate that he had made a charge or insinuated that Isidore was himself the cause of Rosetta's misfortune but he was forced to admit that also. These were the two points upon which the case hung, and although the rest of the evidence took much time it did not alter substantially the aspect of the case. Isidore's Counsel began to speak about 4 o'clock in the afternoon and for three hours poured forth a torrent of invective and eloquence such as had seldom been listened to.

According to English ideas much of his speech had no connection whatever with the case but the Counsel knew his fellow countrymen, and it had connection with the case if it enabled him to bring his client off. He represented Isidore as taking a more than paternal interest in Rosetta, caring for her reputation and the reputation of the family in putting her to school in France. He represented Julius as a petty adventurer, perfectly satisfied with his wife so long as the interest on the hypothèque was paid, but turning round to endeavour to make merchandise of her early frailty when he found his own pecuniary interests affected. He described him as attempting to bully their countrymen into going away to compound the monstrous charge which his assailant threatened to make against him, and when that failed had threatened his life with the revolver carefully concealed on his person for the purpose. And this enabled the counsel to refer to the manner in which Isidore had shown himself capable of standing fire in his duel with Montmorency, of the way in which he had won the fair [lady] who was threatened to be stolen from him, of the perseverance, the talent and the courage with which he had battled against adversity, of the terrible ordeal of his father's murder, and now at the key moment when he was about to wed her whose love he had conquered by his nobleness of character and the rectitude of his conduct, would they give a verdict which would consign him to a felon's cell, a verdict which to one of the high spirit of his client would mean consignment to his grave, and a like fate for her who now stood on the steps of that dwelling they all knew so well straining to hear the [inescapable] announcement of the verdict of not guilty.

Every word of the orator could be distinctly heard outside the Court House as well as in, and when he sat down the buzz of gratification and appreciation prevented for some minutes the Judge proceeding with his summing up that although less favourable to Isidore than his friends fondly hoped, was certainly not against him. When the jury retired it was expected that they would at once return a verdict of not guilty, but they did not immediately return and speculation began, the feeling being one of surprise that there could be any doubt in their minds.

The party which had become very large at the town house of the Beauvallons had heard of the success of the speech and were expecting the verdict every minute, when first one messenger arrived and then another with the information that the jury were still deliberating. What could it mean? Was it possible that they would convict – perhaps not of the aggravated offence but of one of the minor charges which were contained within the greater, and thus Isidore might be punished with from three or four months to two years imprisonment. The tension was great. Estelle could not rest, nor could she pretend to pay any attention to the guests. She watched everyone approaching to guess, even when he was at a distance, whether he came with good news or bad.

At length an Indian peon of Isidore's solicitor appeared with a scrap of paper for Madame Beauvallon. It simply contained the words "come down immediately to the lane which runs by the side of the Court House." Madame hastily attired herself and went, and when she got there to a door opposite to the room where the jury were confined during their deliberations, the solicitor himself opened it and as he took her into a little garden whispered "they are in a majority of seven to two for acquittal but we wish to get a unanimous verdict. It is Rougecanne of Moka who is standing out and a friend of his follows him. You know Rougecanne, he is a distant connection of the Beauvallon's, but we believe he has some grievance against Amirantes. If you were to use your influence with him we might get a unanimous verdict of not guilty. I have only to tap at the door and the huissier, who is one of ours, will say to him that his wife wishes to speak with him a few moments, and will bring him out." This was done and Madame plied the recalcitrant juryman so well with arguments, promises and appeals to his friendship, that after he returned he only stood out a little longer for form's sake and then got his friend to join him in yielding. The verdict of not guilty was given amid a storm of cheering which was heard in the still evening far and near and Estelle knew that all was safe. Isidore was escorted home by a crowd of his admirers, and by the time dinner was on the table, his Counsel, his Attorney and even some of the jurymen were at table, drinking toasts, making speeches and generally conducting themselves like madmen.

However delighted at his escape Isidore still felt humiliated at the position in which he now stood. Deprived as he was of his estate when the

"Ordre," or the regulating of the claims against it was opened, he would be found to have much less than nothing, and in such a position could he dare to propose to Estelle to name a day for their marriage? There are some things much more absolutely necessary according to French customs than to English, and one of these is the Contract of Marriage in all cases where the families of the contracting parties belong to the lower middle class. A sum whether real or nominal is inserted by the obliging Notary as the lady's lot, the Contract is recorded, and the young people feel that they begin life in as good a position as their neighbours.

Isidore had that honourable pride which distinguishes his countrymen. He could not bear to leave himself open to the charge of being taken by Madame Beauvallon to manage her estate and wedding the daughter. Estelle who did not see things in the same light, and was now all radiant with the double triumph of having saved Lorraine and getting Isidore out of his trouble, could not understand why he should become so moody, silent and preoccupied. Was it possible he regretted the nearness of the day for their marriage? Knowing full well his former character she could understand how he would find some difficulty in arranging all his affairs without money, and she was resolved to get some for him, even by increasing the indebtedness of their own Estate.

But such a course she knew would be opposed by Isidore, would hurt his pride, and that at present it could not be accomplished. What then could be done? It was with something like dismay she heard him hint that probably the best course for him would be to go to Australia where the working of the gold mines was then proceeding with great vigour, and where sugar estates were talked of in Queensland. After all the excitement of her triumph, Estelle felt deeply mortified that it should come to this. "Would you take me with you, Isidore?"

"No, Estelle, I would go to provide money to return to wed you as you should be wed, by a man of means, and not a beggar!"

Chapter 30
The Final Arrangements

IT WAS JACK WHO HAD PURCHASED THE MORTGAGE over Pompadour which had been used to sell up the Estate. He had gone to his friend the Banker who knew he could draw for his ten thousand pounds at any time, and asked him about the difficulties of Lorraine and Pompadour. "As to the former," said the Banker, "that is safe for the present. But the sale of the other takes place tomorrow." Jack explained that he either wished to prevent the sale or purchase the property with the view of handing it back to Amirantes. "To the man who injured you!" the Banker could not help exclaiming, but Jack told him that not only had Isidore not injured him by carrying off Estelle but had opened to him a path of happiness. But he said that while he was anxious to prevent Amirantes being ruined, it was chiefly for the sake of Estelle to whom he had been engaged, and in whose welfare he should always take the deepest interest.

The Banker was unwilling to permit Jack to put his money in for such a purpose. "It is a very risky business," he said, "and I might be blamed for allowing you to do so." But Jack having pressed the point, the Banker came to see that it would not be a great risk to purchase up the first mortgage, especially as it could be got most probably at a less sum than its full value, or to purchase the estate for himself in order to have the lead in the adjustment of all the questions arising out of the sale. On the Banker explaining that all this could easily be done in name of another as he wished his own share in the business to be concealed, Jack at once thought of Jean LeBlanc. The Banker was aghast. "That black fellow whom they wanted to hang for Amirante's murder?" Yes, even he. Jack was inexorable on this point for he thought that a great reparation was due to Jean. "He saved my life," he said, "and he was perfectly innocent of the charge laid against him as to taking the life of old Amirantes, and the poor fellow must have suffered much. Besides," added Jack, "I know from what I formerly found out that it was a trick of Master Isidore's which led him first of all into the difficulty with Serjeant Stocks, and while most unwilling that Estelle's future husband should be driven to the wall, I am not sorry to be able to give him a lesson, which he may take to heart after Jean has held his property for some little time."

This conversation will explain what took place at the sale. The Firm were only too glad to get good money for the mortgage even if it were somewhat less than they paid for it. The money really went to the Bank which had advanced the sum. The mortgage was originally for $30,000, the dollar being the monetary unit in Mauritius, although it has since been changed to the Rupee. It was purchased by the Firm for $22,500, the holder having got it several years before at a reduced figure also, during a season of panic. Jack purchased it for $20,000 and thus the Banker explained to him that while he risked something he would also stand to gain, as if the next crop was a good one he would probably be able to sell the mortgage for its full value and at all events would in the meantime draw nine per cent interest on $30,000 or thirteen and a half per cent on $20,000. The Banker's surprise was quick when Jack told him that if he bought the mortgage cheaper he would give Isidore the benefit by reducing the nominal amount to the real sum he had paid. This would both lessen the annual charge on the estate, and give Isidore a little margin of value on which to arrange for the advances of the *entre-coupe*. Indeed the two estates had profited by the attempts which had been made to wreck them by $25,000, the first mortgage on Lorraine having also been bought in by the family at a greatly reduced price. The effect of the hurricane had thus not been wholly disastrous. The Banker indeed, when he looked at the other side of the picture, began to regret that the larger arrangement of uniting the two estates, with the intention of irrigating on a great scale, had not been carried out. And then when he came to reflect afterwards he saw that if Jack [reconveyed] Pompadour to Isidore, and the latter married Estelle, that the estates would be practically united, and so far as the Bank and its profit were concerned it might be the same, or perhaps better, to deal with Isidore in carrying out the idea which the Firm contemplated.

He was full of this idea when he returned to his office in the morning. Isidore called to confer with him about his contemplated journey to Australia. The Banker laughed and treated the proposal very cavalierly. "What, and leave the clever Miss Estelle who has outwitted all these Notary and Attorney fellows so nicely? Why man, she is worth as she stands much more in Mauritius than any amount you could make in ten years in Australia, even were you to save every penny you make which with your habits is impossible."

"But what am I to do? I cannot marry Estelle so long as I am not a person of property. I cannot degrade her and her family."

"No, but you can raise both. How are the young canes looking on the two estates?"

"They are looking splendid. Oh what a shame it was to come upon me when my mind was so much occupied with my trial that I could not make the combinations desirable!"

"It is better as it is. You could not have done better for yourself than others have done for you."

"How for me? Is it for me to buy my estate over my head, and leave me penniless?"

"I am not at liberty to explain everything at this stage, but to prevent you talking or thinking any more of Australia I may at least confide to you that the object of the purchase of Pompadour was not otherwise than friendly to yourself and that the result may be extremely beneficial," and then he added:

"How about the water on Lorraine? Is there not some good spring or

some canal head which lies well up the hill, and from which the plain could
be irrigated?"

"There is a splendid spring which forms a *ruisseau,* but before it has gone
a couple of hundred yards it disappears again in the earth, and is no more
seen. It is I imagine the beginning of a subterranean water course, which will
come out below the sea-level."

"Well, Isidore, could not something be done with that, infinitely better
than by going to Australia."

"But Lorraine is not mine. I would willingly do all I could as a neighbour for
Madame Beauvallon, but I cannot talk and act as if her property were my own."

"Yes, yes, we know all that," said the Banker somewhat impatiently, "but
on the assumption I was making that Pompadour somehow might be got back
for you, and that you married Miss Beauvallon, who in the course of nature
will inherit Lorraine, could not the two estates be worked together, and both
be watered from that spring in the event of drought, if the requisite reservoir
were built for the water?"

"It could be done but it would require a large capital."

"Where is the great difficulty? It could be built of concrete, and you have
the lime on the seashore. You have on the two estates more than a thousand
Coolies, and abundance of carts and cattle for carrying materials. The estates
are extensive and excellent, all they require is to be protected against the
chances of a very dry season. This season promises rain enough, and you tell
me the young canes are looking well. If so I think there will be no difficulty
about the capital, either for the ordinary working or for the extraordinary
expenditure like a tank. By Jove, Isidore, you ought to take a run up and see
the great tanks at Aden. That will open your mind better than anything else.
I would advise you in place of thinking about Australia to begin at once to
study the construction of concrete reservoirs – Good morning, for I am busy."

Isidore, thus bowed out, had to leave, and as it was near breakfast time
he went up to the Beauvallons'. He had cut Estelle to the heart the previous
night by his wild talk of leaving, and the least he could do was to inform her
of the conversation he had just had with the Banker.

She, with more acute penetration, at once saw that while the purchase
by Jean LeBlanc was with a friendly motive to Isidore, that the Banker was so
satisfied that things were likely to come round that he was anxious to retain
the business, and even to assist with capital for a great extension of the cultivation. Who can be behind Jean LeBlanc? This was the question of the hour,
and several well known rich men were suggested, but thrown aside almost as
soon as named, because they never could have done a generous thing, being
only pushing enterprising men working to make themselves rich.

"You will not now think of Australia, Isidore," Estelle said in imploring tones.

"All I can do is to suspend the project until we see what the next few
days will bring forth."

While they talked a mounted Orderly stopped at the door, and delivered
two letters with the Royal arms at the seal of the envelope. They were addressed to Madame Beauvallon and to Aunt Clémence.

"Can you tell me where M. Isidore Amirantes is to be found in town?" said the Orderly.

"He is here now," replied Estelle who had taken the letters wondering what it could all mean.

The letter for Isidore was handed in, and the others were sent up to Madame Beauvallon in her own room. Estelle said to Isidore, "Oh I hope it is nothing about the trial. Poor Isidore you have had enough of worry."

"On the contrary, Estelle, it is something much more pleasant, it is an invitation to dinner at Government House on Saturday evening."

"To Réduit?" exclaimed Estelle, "Then Mama must be invited also." Not only was Madame Beauvallon invited but Miss Beauvallon, and a conference was instantly held as to what it meant, and what the answer should be.

After reflection, all the invitations were accepted, as the design could not be anything but friendly. It was in fact a happy thought of Lady Foolscap. She recollected that Madame Beauvallon and her daughter had been at dinner at the time Estelle's engagement with Jack was first talked of, and the poor lady had since then had no end of trouble, what with her husband's death and the attempted sale of her Estate. Lady Foolscap and Miss MacNeill were very curious to see how she looked, and were no less anxious to see Isidore, who, after so many adventures, had carried off the prize. The lady had an eye to effect. Réduit dinners were usually a little hum-drum. The same people over and over again, the same talk, the same dreary music in the Drawing Room afterwards. It would be something piquant to have the lovers who had been playing at cross purposes, and then Miss Beauvallon as well as Miss MacNeill was famous for her music. Moreover both the Governor and the Commissioner were very anxious to see the young lady who had out-manoeuvred the attorneys. "By Jove," exclaimed the Governor who knew the manners and customs of the Island in these particulars in a vague kind of way. "She must be a brick, and a clever brick too."

The party was uncommonly well selected. A sprinkling of the military, and civilian officials, a few of the leading merchants, and two or three of the leading planters, together with the Banker upon whom so much depended. Jack had been staying at Government House for some days, acting, as the Governor kindly told him, as an additional aide-de-camp while the festivities were going on of which the arrival of the MacNeills had been the occasion. He was accordingly early in the Drawing Room to be ready to receive the Company on their arrival. It so happened that the Beauvallon party were the first to arrive. Isidore came with them in the same carriage. Poor Madame Beauvallon winced a little when she saw who it was who received her, when she thought of the saucy way in which she had thrown up Jack after her husband's death. But she had already been assured of his pardon, and entire forgetfulness of the affair, on the occasion of his visit to Estelle when he had released her from her engagement. He led Madame with the utmost courtesy to a seat beside the fire which was not ungrateful on these heights in the cooler nights, and then turned to shake hands with Aunt Clémence and Estelle. The latter was looking so lovely and so queen like that Jack almost started back from her. It was not his Estelle, not the shrinking beautiful girl whom he had petted and patted, and thought he loved, but another Estelle more womanly, more commanding, more overpowering in the grand outlines of her figure, the perfection of her features and brilliance of her glance.

"Did you not expect to see me, Captain Montmorency?" she said smiling, holding out her hand.

"Yes, Mademoiselle Beauvallon, but – but – you are so changed."

"For the better I hope," she said as he led her over to the sofa.

"Better for him," whispered Jack, "but it was the old Estelle I loved."

"Oh Isidore has been telling me," she added, turning to the place where she left him, "that he ought perhaps to be introduced to you, and he has only made his bow to His Excellency at the Levee. Will you allow me to introduce him?"

"Isidore – Captain Montmorency."

Isidore hung back for a second, waiting for the movement to come from his old opponent. But Jack held out his hand frankly and said, "We scarcely needed this formality. May I be allowed to wish you joy with all my heart."

"You are generous and noble-hearted," said Isidore warmly. "I ask your forgiveness for any incidents in the past which were not of that character on my part towards you."

"Let it all be forgotten," was the reply, "and let there be friendship here-after between us for the sake of her who will always allow me, I hope, to be her friend."

Estelle gave a convulsive sob, and Jack remembered that this was scarce-ly the place for a scene. So handing her to Isidore he said gaily, "Get Miss Beauvallon a chair, Amirantes, I must go to my duties, or there will be the devil to pay."

And off he ran. The carriages drove up in quick succession. The room soon became well-filled and all were talking volubly when a vision of beauty made them all pause. It was Miss MacNeill led in by her father. She had taken particular care with her toilet, as Lady Foolscap had of course let her into the secret of the dinner party. Her dark hair, clear hazel eyes, and a forehead of perfect purity, which a sculptor might have gazed on with rapture and rev-erence, her features all beaming with intelligence and the pride of love were set off to admiration by her rich dress of Indian stuff which all the looms of Manchester or Lyon could not match. She had only one jewel (Estelle was blazing with them, her mother having insisted on her wearing her own) as a brooch. It was a beautiful stone which flashed from time to time but did not withdraw attention from the superb neck and throat which it adorned, or from the pure dazzling whiteness of the shoulders. Jack himself did not imagine Agnes could look so perfect a picture of loveliness. How different it was from the beauty of Estelle. Seldom in one room could be seen at one time two wom-en so conspicuously lovely, and of styles of beauty so completely different.

The younger ladies, and Estelle among them, were standing talking when Lady Foolscap entered a little late. She also had been attiring herself with more than her usual care. She recollected that diamond brooch of Madame Beauvallon's at her first dinner, and was resolved she would not be outdone.

This was, besides, a full dress dinner and she had put on her jewels with lavish hand. Her open bosom and throat bore a necklet of priceless gems, in her hair was a tiara of diamonds, on her fingers rings of all rare and costly stones. Madame Beauvallon felt for a moment somewhat overwhelmed, but when she looked round at Estelle as Lady Foolscap spoke to her she felt reassured. Her daughter, she felt, could take her place anywhere – and so thought Lady Foolscap, amazed at the change which had taken place, and wondering how on earth Jack could have allowed her to slip through his fingers.

Jack took care at the earliest opportunity to bring up Isidore to Lady Foolscap and the Governor. Both were pleased with his appearance and style. The more indeed Lady Foolscap looked, and she had a sly way of looking without allowing people to observe her, she thought that Isidore was after all the best match for Estelle. "She is much the finer animal of the two," she said to herself, meaning the contrast between Estelle and Miss MacNeill, "but Agnes could no sooner marry that man, than Jack could have long pleased that imperious Queen of Love." Part of the fun of the evening was to separate the lovers. The Beauvallon party were yet ignorant of the acceptance of Jack by Miss MacNeill, but all the official circle knew it.

There being too few ladies as is not infrequently the case at such parties, Isidore was directed to follow the Governor, who took Miss MacNeill, and to place himself at her other side. The Commissioner took in Madame Beauvallon, the General had already gone with Lady Foolscap, while Estelle was reserved for Jack, on the opposite side of the table from Isidore and Miss MacNeill, and with Estelle on the left of the General. The table was a wide and massive one so that while the couples opposite could see each other perfectly there was little chance of passing a remark. Lady Foolscap thought at first she had made a mistake, and that there would have been more fun for her in watching Jack and Estelle who were on the same side as herself. But she was soon attracted both by the manner in which Isidore had engaged the attention of both the governor and Miss MacNeill and of the way in which she herself was being neglected by the General for Estelle. It was the General, she recollected, who had prided himself on having saved Jack from the "Frenchwoman," but no sooner did the old warrior, whose breast was covered with decorations, gained in every quarter of the Globe, see her in the Drawing Room than he had fallen completely under the spell of her beauty. He was all but rude in his neglect of the Hostess, and when she turned for sympathy to the Commissioner she found he was busy with Madame Beauvallon. She was thus left free to watch with more ease what was transpiring around her. She was somewhat mollified by observing that more than one of the younger men were regarding her with admiration. She had still the remains of her good-looks, and when she was draped as she was tonight she was of a style of matronly beauty worthy of her place.

"What can they be talking about over there," she said to herself, for the Governor, which was a fault very unusual with him, was talking across Miss MacNeill to Isidore, and taking very little notice of the wife of the Procureur General who was at his other side. It was in vain to attempt to catch his eye.

It was always the custom at the dinners of Sir Foulis Foolscap to bring up the champagne early. Dinners of this kind are so apt to be stiff, and the only thing to save such a calamity is to bring in champagne to loosen the bonds of the tongue. We have seen many dinners where French and English people were mixed where at first the most awful silence prevailed, the English fearing to speak French, and the French positively declining to speak English. But after the champagne had gone round once or twice the Englishmen would not even speak English to their French neighbours when the latter wished them to do so, but dashed in to French with an utter disregard to the gender of the nouns or the gender of the person whom they addressed. The dinners of Sir Foulis also were always admirably served. Having a good butler, and a sufficient number of servants, together with those of the General, who was his next neighbour, to fall back upon on guest nights everything went smoothly and swiftly.

The white clad Indians flitted about noiselessly without any clattering of plates or knives, and filling up wine glasses assiduously they were especially attentive to the Commissioner – the Burra Sahib from India who could speak to them in Hindustani.

Estelle having been forced to desert Jack for the General, who talked to her incessantly, he made up for it by canvassing the guests on behalf of Jean LeBlanc.

"What is your interest in him, Captain Montmorency," said the Colonial Secretary, "we have a good deal of Government work and he may as well have a chance as another."

"Why it was he who saved my life on the night of the shipwreck," replied Jack.

"The deuce it was," said the Banker, "and these gentlemen (referring to the Colonial Secretary and the Procureur General) were going to hang him."

"Well we must make it up to him somehow," said the Colonial Secretary.

"It would be a great thing to have some really intelligent honest fellow in a business of that kind upon whom we could rely," said the Banker, "and I will tell you what, if you give him the Government business I will throw the Bank's influence into the scale and that will give him a good lift."

"Thank you, gentlemen, on behalf of my protégé. I have sent home for a wedding dress for his wife that is to be, and I hope it will arrive in time."

"And who is to be his wife? A sable beauty like himself?"

"Why it is Lucille, Miss Beauvallon's maid."

"Bless my soul," said the Banker, "you are all getting married together, mistress and maid," and then recollecting that it was not Jack who was to marry Estelle, but Isidore, he stopped, thinking he had put his foot in it. But Jack did not appear in the least disturbed.

Estelle, however, who while pretending to listen to the General, had been hearing what was going, turned at last resolutely from her gallant admirer and said to Jack – "You are always thinking of doing good to somebody. May I tell Lucille what I have overheard?"

"Oh yes. You know," he added rather incautiously, "her husband will not be a grand proprietaire for long, and we must take care of his success in his own career."

"Can you tell us to whom were are indebted for Jean's purchase of Pompadour, which we hear is not intended to hurt Isidore?" And then, the whole truth seeming to dawn on her mind at once, she exclaimed: "It is to you, Captain Montmorency, how foolish I have been not to have thought of that before. It is to you is it not," she repeated, "how true it was what I said just now that you were always thinking of doing good to someone."

Jack did not reply and felt rather foolish. But the Banker thought the chance too good to be lost. So to relieve Jack and to calculate good advice with a view to business, in a jocular way he said, "Yes, Miss Beauvallon, it is the Captain. Isidore's future is assured so soon as the Estates are joined by the joining together of their proprietors by the Church so that no man shall put them asunder."

"Oh Jack," she murmured, "and we have not known it in order to thank you."

"How will Amirantes take it if he knows?" asked Jack.

"Perhaps this morning he would have refused to accept anything at your hands, but after the meeting of tonight I am sure he will be deeply grateful. How can we repay you, Jack. I must call you so when you act so like your old self."

"Repay me!" said Jack, pretending to speak austerely, "you must repay me – and meantime remit me to India interest at the rate of nine per cent."

"To India," exclaimed Estelle. The truth having again slipped out, she looked for an explanation, and Jack with some shame-facedness gave it her in a whisper. "I am to marry Miss MacNeill, Estelle."

She paused for a moment without speaking, looking towards the place where that young lady sat turning towards Isidore and speaking with evident animation and pleasure. Isidore was looking at no one else but her, and presently struck in with his reply in his full sonorous voice which he was toning down so as not to interrupt others.

"I don't know of whom to be most jealous, Jack, of you who forgot me so soon, or of my faithless lover who has forgotten me for that beautiful being."

"I will not forget you, Estelle, and I hope you will not forget me. Do you approve of my choice?"

"She is beautiful as an angel," said Estelle with heartfelt admiration. "I do wish Isidore would not look into her eyes so!"

"He is so accustomed to look into yours, Estelle, he must gaze at something beautiful."

"Oh that is so nice Ja... Captain Montmorency, I ought to say let us get up a good flirtation for I feel quite savage. Isidore has not looked across to me once since dinner began. I don't believe he knows where I sit."

"Then he has deprived himself of a real pleasure, Estelle, for I never in my life saw one so well worth looking at as you are tonight."

"Not even Miss Macneill, Jack – come now?"

"Well you are at the opposite poles of beauty – each perfect in your kind."

"Everything I suppose is permitted to us, Jack, in the way of talk. But don't you think Miss MacNeill ought to look at you occasionally, just to recall you to your duty. I feel if Isidore does not look soon I will be ready to elope with the General."

"He is quite ready I am sure, Estelle. Just give him a glance or two more and he will be kneeling at your feet. Whether he will be able to rise again is another question."

"Poor man, is he married, or has he ever been married?"

"He is free from bonds as yet. But tell me, Estelle, we may not have another opportunity, when did you think of accepting Amirantes?"

"The 15th of January," she replied without hesitation, "during the hurricane."

"The very night we were passing the straits of Messina, when I first thought of Agnes" – (she winced like a young horse at the spur when she heard him call the young lady by her Christian name). "So, Estelle, we cannot reproach each other. If we have done wrong we did it mutually."

"I never thought I had done wrong till now, when he seems to ignore my existence and you have been thinking so constantly of me and my happiness."

But Isidore did at length look. He had in fact looked across frequently, but Estelle was so busy either with the General on the one side, or Jack on the other, that he could not catch her glance. And Miss MacNeill looked also towards Jack, and the smile of Isidore was so open and sweet, his eyes glanced so tenderly, and so full of the infinite yearning of love, that Estelle was appeased, and in her turn gave him one of those flashes of hers which make a man feel giddy with all that it revealed. The smile of Agnes to Jack was bright, clear as crystal, and full of trust and hope. And she also was satisfied with the look she got from him in return.

The table was cleared and the Governor having seen that all the gentlemen had been supplied with claret was about to give "the Queen," when Isidore thinking of something else, and seeing a glass of claret before him which was probably exceptionally good, emptied it at a gulp.

"The Queen," said the Governor immediately after, and Isidore seeing all the gentlemen drink the toast, saw he had committed a "betise" as Aunt Clémence, who had been thoroughly engaging herself watching others, called it afterwards.

"I beg your pardon," said Isidore with perfect self-possession, "I ought to have awaited your Excellency's toast. May I ask for another glass of claret to drink it," he added, half turning to the servant behind him.

"We can readily excuse you, Monsieur Amirantes," said the Governor, "you were thinking doubtless of another Queen."

"Of the Queen of India," replied Isidore, bowing to Miss MacNeill, giving her a covert compliment, while professing to have been thinking of Her Majesty in another capacity.

Lady Foolscap soon after rose, while the gentlemen remained to empty a bottle or two of claret.

No sooner did Isidore come into the Drawing Room than Estelle ran to him, and said, "who do you think is our unknown benefactor in the matter of Pompadour?"

He looked at her but did not reply.

"Come Mr Bullion," she said to the Banker, "tell Isidore all about it while I go to play something. Lady Foolscap has asked me."

She played, and with an ease and grace and power which astonished all who heard her. Perhaps a trifle too much expression, but it was not affectation with her, it was the natural style of the woman – full and rich, as the almost too Venus-like neck and breast which shewed above the piano, easy, supple, dexterous, and capable of all emotions. As she approached the conclusion of the piece she seemed to make the piano leap under her masterly touches, and then when she finished stood up with her eye flashing the light of genius that told whence all this power came. Miss MacNeill sang after. It was like coming into the calm still pool, after the dash and froth, the foam and sparkling power of the waterfall. Calm and smooth and deep, for this lady also had been touched by the fire from heaven; but her strength lay in other zones of feeling and art. Isidore also sang, his powerful voice ringing out in the old Drawing Room tones such as its roof had not re-echoed for many a long year. Estelle played the accompaniment, and to please her he exerted himself to the utmost. The song was received with a murmur of appreciation by everyone. Estelle forgave Miss MacNeill her apparent flirtation with Isidore during dinner, when she came up and expressed the very great pleasure with which she had heard him sing a song which was a favourite of hers, and which he had given more to her taste than she had heard it in the opera at Paris in coming through.

More music followed, and while it proceeded the Banker had brought Jack to talk to Isidore about Pompadour. "To any man but yourself, Captain Montmorency, I would have felt the reverse of grateful," he said, "but now what can I do to show my appreciation of your goodness?"

"Treat your labourers well, Amirantes, and you will see it will repay you in a thousand ways."

When Jack handed Estelle to the carriage they had to wait some little time while other vehicles cleared out. The full moon was shining through the tall dark trees of the avenue and lighting up the lawn in front with soft patches of light. "We will not meet again, it may be, for long years Estelle. I go home by the mail to try to arrange an exchange to India that I may marry Agnes without delay. But wherever and whenever we may meet, be it ourselves or our children, let us pledge an everlasting friendship."

"May God bless you, my dear friend," said Estelle. "Bless you and keep you forever. Come and receive Mama's blessing too."

They bade each other a warm adieu, and Isidore, taking Estelle in his arms after he got into the carriage as she was sobbing with emotion ejaculated, "Estelle you have made a poor choice in rejecting that able fellow for me."

"No, no, Isidore," she gasped, "Respect, honour, warmest friendship are not love – and my love is for you!"

"Let us shut our eyes and go to sleep, Marie," said Aunt Clémence, "we are *de trop!*"

Epilogue
The Colonel and the Knight

It was many years after that Colonel Montmorency with his wife were at a great gathering in the Salons of the Countess of Birkenhead whose husband was then the Secretary of State for the Colonies. They observed a tall, dark handsome man enter with a most beautiful woman beside him. Every eye was at once turned on her as she was one of those women whose commanding beauty attracted attention in spite of themselves. "By heavens, it is Estelle," said the Colonel to his wife. They had not heard the name announced. "Who is the couple who have just entered?" he said to a friend. "One of the new K.C.M.G.s[†] I believe. Sir Isidore Amirantes from Mauritius and Lady Amirantes. Isn't she handsome?"

"Yes, I knew them long ago and must way-lay them. How did he get knighted?"

"Oh there has been some great outcry in Mauritius about the ill treatment of Coolies, and this man who is the largest sugar planter in the Island was found to have treated his labourers so well that the Government of India suggested he should receive some mark of the Royal favour. Do you know a person has just been appointed Member of Council in that Colony who is almost a pure negro. He is said to be rich and very well educated and intelligent. The fun of the thing is that they call him LeBlanc."

Notes

Chapter 1

"The great fever of 1867" — The devastating malaria epidemic of 1866–68 which wiped out tens of thousands of inhabitants.

"where any conflagration had broken out" — Gorrie is referring to a fire that broke out in 1816.

"an officer was on watch in the Citadel, a commanding position whence the whole streets could be scanned" — British soldiers garrisoned at the Citadel operated warning systems using lights and cannon fire to announce a fire or a cyclone.

"You will find scarcely one of these *jeunes gens* will have the courage to dance with the girl" — It was customary for balls to be organised by different social groups, typically *pères de familles* (heads of household) and *jeunes gens* (young bachelors).

"was a strong dose for a white Creole to swallow" — The term "Creole" at the time Gorrie was writing simply designated a colonial-born person and did not specify ethnicity, although here Gorrie does uses the epithet "white" to clarify what kind of "Creole" is meant.

Chapter 2

"tiffin" — An Anglo-Indian word used by the British in India to describe the light meal that superseded afternoon tea.

"The Articles of the Capitulation guaranteed to the inhabitants the free exercise of their own religion and their own laws and customs" — When the defeated Governor Decaen agreed to surrender Mauritius to the British in 1810, he successfully demanded that the British allow the French language and Catholicism to be practised.

"enquired the Procureur General" — The highest ranking member of the judiciary when Mauritius was a British colony was still designated by the French term Procureur General. Gorrie himself explains this title, and also the justice system, in chapter 17.

Chapter 3

"The Coolie boys" — Indentured, unskilled labourers from India, brought in by the British to work the cane fields.

"Mozambique" — Slaves and some later contract workers were imported from the east coast of Africa and Madagascar to Mauritius in the 18th and 19th centuries. The term 'Mozambic' or 'Mozambique' was often applied to Afro-Creoles as a general term irrespective of their ethnic identity, but especially to those considered to be of 'African appearance.'

"they were fed, from day to day, from year to year, upon manioc and *margoze*, a bitter creeper which grows by the wayside" — Margoze, or bitter gourd, mentioned several times by Gorrie, is associated with hard times in Mauritius. After abolition ex-slaves referred to the period of slavery as "le temps margoze," "bitter gourd days," a reference to the cheap food and the bitterness of those times.

Chapter 4

"it is a Coolie ship" — A ship bringing indentured labourers from India to the island

"Chouxfleur" — A mispronunciation of "Le Souffleur" (from French "souffler", to "blow"), the name given to the blowing sound made by waves crashing against rocks in certain parts of Mauritius.

Chapter 5

"having been cared for without having obtained *pratique*" — "Pratique" was a term used in Mauritius to designate the formalities through which a ship gained admittance. Because of several devastating epidemics (e.g. smallpox) introduced from ships coming from affected areas, stringent quarantine measures were strongly supported and followed.

"that he sent secretly to the shop of the Chinaman" — During the second half of the 19th century, the expansion of sugar cultivation in Mauritius and the development of villages around the estates provided opportunities for the opening of shops in these rural areas, many of which were owned/operated by Chinese immigrants.

Chapter 6

"*The Fisherman's Pride*" — Gorrie had not made up his mind about the title of this chapter and provides several alternatives: "Twice Reprieved," "In the Jaws of Death," "A Lowly Hero," "Who Did the Deed?" "Was it He?," "The False Scent," "Who Did It?"

Chapter 7

"One epidemic in particular had come like a plague" — The earlier epidemic to which Gorrie refers is likely the cholera epidemic of 1854.

"In this last plague, fever took the place of cholera" — The second epidemic of "fever" is another reference to the deadly malaria outbreak of 1866–68.

"*Beauty and Terror – children of one birth ...*" — Apparently a poem by Gorrie himself.

"Quarantine Island" — This is presumably Flat Island and the neighboring Gabriel Islet, where a quarantine station was set up; the ruins of the stone quarantine buildings can still be seen there.

"Mofussel" — The name used resembles that of the 'Mofussilite' which made several voyages to Mauritius carrying labourers from India between 1879 and 1883. The name literally means "interior provinces."

"The Executive Council which had been hastily called together" — Mauritius was a crown colony at the time, without an elected legislature. An Executive Council composed of notables of the colony and senior British officials made policy decisions.

Chapter 8

"He had become a Colonial Governor no one very well knew why" — Gorrie was in Mauritius between 1869 and 1876. During this time the Governors were Sir Henry Barkly (1863–70), Sir Arthur Charles Hamilton-Gordon (1871–74), and Sir Arthur Purves Phayre (1874–78).

"Flore Mauritienne" — The Flore Mauricienne was a popular café-restaurant in Port Louis, still in business today.

"Let me first send this poor girl to bed" — Two chapters in which the "tale of the idiot" were recounted are lost. (The chapters have been renumbered accordingly.)

Chapter 9

"when as old immigrants they would choose their own field of labour" — The term "old immigrant" was given to a man who had completed his engagement as an "indentured labourer" and was technically free to work on his own account. The harassment of "old immigrants" was rife at the time Gorrie was on Mauritius and caused such a scandal that a Royal Commission was sent to the island in the early 1870s to investigate conditions.

Chapter 10

"To these glades the Solitaire, driven from the coast may have fled for shelter from the unwelcome presence of man" — The now extinct Solitaire was a bird only found on Rodrigues, an island 350 miles east of Mauritius. Gorrie has confused the Solitaire with its closest relative, the Dodo, indigenous only to Mauritius.

"the posters waited with eager expectation" — Gorrie uses the term "poster" and "chasseur" interchangeably.

Chapter 11

"The Trials of Widowhood' — An alternative chapter heading, crossed out by Gorrie, was "The Course of true love never did run smooth."

Chapter 12

"the most horrible scourge ever sent to afflict the human family" — This may be a reference to leprosy which at the time was believed to be a communicable disease. In Mauritius lepers were sent to the Chagos archipelago and later to Curieuse Island in the Seychelles

"to endeavour to distinguish the wreck of an English ship which was sunk there by the French in 1810. The lighthouse was inspected, standing up grimly facing the great Southern ocean" — Gorrie is referring to the wrecks of British ships destroyed during the battle of Grand Port. This famous French victory is inscribed on the Arc de Triomphe in Paris. The lighthouse is on the nearby Isle aux Fouquets.

Chapter 15

"visit Isidore in his pavilion" — French country residences in Mauritius consisted of a main house and several smaller independent buildings known as *dépendances* or *pavillons*.

Chapter 20

"the weak points and vanity of the French policy when they go swaggering to Tonquin and elsewhere" — Gorrie is likely referring to the Sino–French War, also known as the Tonkin (or Tonquin) War, of 1884–85, fought between France and China over control of Tonkin (northern Vietnam).

"and the same men going the same gin horse round of daily cares" — Horse gins were commonly used in Scotland in coal mining. Gorrie is referencing the drudgery of the horses who worked the gin by circling round and round the pit shaft.

"like Mr Wordy's history" — Mr Wordy is a character in Disraeli's novel *Coningsby*.

Chapter 27

"Believe Massa Isidore hab *Ti Albert* on him side" — Ernestine is referring to "Petit Albert," a nickname for local magic beliefs. She is saying that Isidore must have enlisted the help of "Petit Albert" in order to have so bewitched Estelle.

"The French law of lien" — a lien is a form of security interest granted over an item of property to secure the payment of a debt or performance of some other obligation.

Glossary

Arago
Dominique François Jean Arago (1786–1853), French mathematician, physicist and astronomer, and a famous and successful abolitionist.

Beau Bassin
A town established by the French in 1759, 3 miles south of Port Louis; the elevation is approximately 500 ft.

Bernardin de St Pierre
Jacques-Henri Bernardin de St Pierre (1737–1814) was a French writer and botanist, and author of the very popular novel, *Paul et Virginie* (1788), set on Mauritius.

Black River
A district on the West coast of Mauritius.

Blue Bay
A town, and bay, in the Southwest of Mauritius, near Mahebourg and Pointe d'Esny.

Blue Book
An official report produced by the British Parliament or Privy Council.

Botanical Gardens
The Royal Botanical Gardens at Pamplemousses, in the north of the island.

Bourbon
Present day Île de la Réunion, the sister-island of Mauritius. Like Mauritius, it was conquered in 1810 by the British, but handed back to the French in 1815, and remains a French *département d'outre-mer*.

Champ de Mars
A French military training ground, in the capital Port Louis, converted by the British in 1812 into a race-track. It was a popular meeting spot and included a kiosk where the military band played.

Chaussée
La Chaussée, one of the principal streets of the capital Port Louis.

Citadel	The Citadel, officially named Fort Adelaide was built by the British around 1840 and overlooks Port Louis town and harbour.
Constantia	A southerly suburb of Cape Town.
Coolie line	The name given to a row of houses built by or for Indian labourers on Mauritian sugar estates. These were initially little more than thatched huts, often put up by the labourers themselves, but over the course of the 19th century purpose-built blocks were constructed using more durable materials. Several examples remain.
Curepipe	A town 10 miles SSE of Port Louis at an elevation of 1800 feet, founded by inhabitants fleeing the malaria epidemic of 1866–68.
Deux Mamelles	Lit. "Two Breasts," twin peaks in the Moka range, about four miles SE of Port Louis.
En Avant	The name of a fictitious newspaper published in Mauritius. Gorrie would have been familiar with the French-language newspaper *Le Cernéen*, as well as English language media then in circulation.
Fort George	A fort on Île aux Tonneliers, just off the NE of Mauritius.
Graces	According to Greek mythology, Hera and Zeus were the parents of the three Graces, the attendants to Aphrodite, the goddess of Love. Their names reflect their attributes: Aglaia (Splendor), Euphrosyne (Festivity), and Thalia (Rejoicing).
Grand Bassin	A crater lake situated in the southern district of Savanne, believed to contain eels of enormous size. In Gorrie's time, it was known as a popular excursion spot. It is now known as Ganga Talao and is a site of Hindu pilgrimage in Mauritius.
Grand River	A river on the western edge of Port Louis
Île de la Passe	An island off Grand Port on the East coast of Mauritius, site of a naval battle between the British and the French.
L'Illustration Universelle	*L'Illustration – Journal Universel* was a popular weekly newspaper published between 1843 and 1944 with news, travel and literary articles and engravings.
Jardin de la Compagnie	A garden in central Port Louis. It began as the vegetable patch of the French Compagnie des Indes.

Jemappes Street	A road that runs North-South in Port Louis, just east of the Barracks ("Casernes").
K.C.M.G.	Knight Commander of the Orders of St Michael and St George.
La Baie	An unspecified settlement in Mauritius, by a bay.
Lascar	A term used to designate anyone of Muslim faith, often applied to Muslim seamen. Still in use in Mauritius, it is sometimes viewed as pejorative.
Madeleine	An important and imposing Roman Catholic church in the 8th *arrondissement* of Paris.
Madrassee	Literally a person from Madras, it refers to people of Tamil origin (or appearance).
Maharanee	The wife of a Maharaja.
Mahebourg	A city on the SE coast of Mauritius, eclipsed when the capital was moved to Port Louis.
Malabar Coast	A long, narrow coastline on the southwestern shoreline of the Indian subcontinent. In the Mauritian context the term 'Malabar' was used to designate a south Indian whether from the Coromandel or the Malabar coastal areas.
Messageries Imperiales	The French company that carried the mail from Europe to the Indian Ocean.
Moka Road	The main road leading out of Port Louis toward the South. The easiest access to Le Pouce is from the village of Moka (elevation 650 feet).
Moka Street	Main thoroughfare in Port Louis which becomes the Moka Road.
Netley Hospital	An enormous military hospital built in Netley, near Southampton, shortly after the Crimean War.
Pamplemousses	A district in the north of Mauritius. Pamplemousses church and graveyard, near the botanical gardens, still stand.
Pas Géométriques	In the Napoleonic era, a coastal strip of land designated primarily for military and defensive purposes, and over which the state retained control. The term remains in use in Mauritius along most of the coastline, covering the high water mark of the spring tides to at least 81.21 metres inland. This area is state land and buildings located there are "leased," not privately owned.

Petite-Rivière	A fishing village in the west of Mauritius.
Piqueurs	A whipper-in, or huntsman's assistant, in charge of keeping the dogs in check. The piqueur can be mounted or on foot.
Pointe D'Esny	An area in the SW of Mauritius, north of Blue Bay and south of Mahebourg.
Pouce	Le Pouce, lit. "thumb," a mountain visible from Port Louis and, though the third highest mountain, relatively easy to climb. It has an elevation of 2600 feet.
Réduit	Réduit is the name of the Governor's official country residence, located in the central uplands of Mauritius near Moka.
Revue des deux mondes	A French-language monthly literary and cultural affairs magazine first published in Paris on 1 August 1829.
Roland	The hero of the 11th-century French epic, *La chanson de Roland*.
Royal College	The former Lycée Colonial, still the premier state school in Mauritius.
Sepoy	A term used to designate a soldier, usually associated with India.
Simon's Bay	Located on the eastern side of the Cape of Good Hope, the naval base and harbour of the British navy.
Southampton Water	A tidal estuary with Southampton at its northernmost point.
Swizzle	Any of various tall mixed drinks usually made with rum.
Table Mountain	A large flat-topped mountain overlooking the Cape of Good Hope.
Tamarin Falls	A series of seven cataracts on the Tamarin River, on the west coast of Mauritius.
Terre Rouge	Lit. "red earth," a village just north of Port Louis.
Valley of Les Pailles	An area south of Port Louis.

Biography of John Gorrie

John Gorrie[1] was born at Kingskettle, Fife, Scotland, on 30th March, 1829, the fourth child and second son of Daniel Gorrie (d. 1852), a popular and impoverished Minister in the Relief Church, later the United Presbyterian Church, and Jane Moffatt (d. 1863). John Gorrie read law at Edinburgh University, making a modest living as a journalist and simultaneously working in legal offices. At one point he was Editor of the *Stirling Observer* in Edinburgh, associated with two other Edinburgh papers, as well as a Captain in the Scottish Volunteers; he later became an Advocate-Depute for Scotland. On 6th December 1855 he married Marion Graham (d. 1884), when he was 26 and she 18. Their first child Marion (Minnie) was born two years later and Isabella Jane (also called Charlie) four years after that. In 1859 he travelled to the U.S. and became interested in the problems of slavery. After his return he involved himself with the British Union and Emancipation Society and spoke at meetings with John Bright. In 1862 he moved to London as a barrister and leader writer for the radical *Morning Star and Dial Newspaper.*

Gorrie and his family – there was now a son, Malcolm, and a third daughter, Jane (Jeanie) – began colonial life on Mauritius in 1869, where he was posted as Substitute Procureur-General. He rose to be third then second Puisne (Junior) Judge on the island; was called to Fiji as Chief Justice in 1876; became Chief Judicial Commissioner of the Western Pacific High Commission in 1878; was knighted in 1881; was Chief Justice of the Leeward Islands in 1882; and Chief Justice in Trinidad from 1886 to 1888, and of the united Trinidad and Tobago from 1889 to 1892.

The attitudes which made him dangerous enemies among some of the white planters and other capitalists, and which won him immense affection among the black, coloured and labouring island populations, were formed early on,

1 For a full biographical study, see Bridget Brereton, *Law, Justice and Empire: The Colonial Career of John Gorrie, 1829–1892* (Barbados, Jamaica, Trinidad and Tobago: The Press University of the West Indies, 1997).

Marion Graham Gorrie (1836–1884)   Sir John Gorrie (1829–1892)

but were confirmed and hardened at the time of a Commission of Enquiry into
something which eventually came to be known as The Jamaica Case.

In 1865 the simmering resentment felt by the black population of Jamaica
against certain elements of the white administration flared into a violent rebellion in the eastern district of the island. Martial Law was declared and
the rebellion was quashed with extraordinary, and apparently uncharacter-
istic, ferocity by Governor Eyre. Nearly five hundred locals were killed, frequently without trial or after the most perfunctory of Courts Martial. The
Militia burned down houses and administered torture and severe floggings
with whips made of piano wire. The charge was almost always treason, and
although there is no doubt that atrocities had been committed by the insur-
rectionists, the majority of those who suffered during the month-long reign
of terror had had no personal involvement in the uprising at all.

Finally, Governor Eyre engineered the Court Martial and execution by
hanging of George William Gordon, on the grounds that he was the instiga-
tor of the revolt. Gordon was a mulatto planter and member of the Jamaica
House of Assembly, who had made himself into the articulate voice of the
down-trodden of the Colony, and who was therefore regarded by Eyre as
a personal and political enemy. Gordon, outspoken and injudicious as he
might sometimes have been, had in fact always used the proper channels to
press for reform. When he commented publicly that continued disregard of
grievances would lead to bloodshed, the majority understood that he was
warning against possible violence not advocating it. It seems, so far as can
be judged, that Gordon's character and approach to reform were not unlike
Gorrie's own.

The Jamaica Affair became a cause célèbre in Britain, with debates in the Houses of Lords and Commons and emotional articles in the press continuing for three years. Opinion was almost entirely polarised. There were those who thought that Governor Eyre's prompt, decisive actions had saved the lives of virtually every white on the island and had preserved the Colony for the Crown; chief among these were Lord Cardigan, Charles Kingsley, Thomas Carlyle, John Ruskin, Charles Dickens and Tennyson. On the other side were those who saw Eyre not only as a panicky incompetent who had over-reacted with tragic results, but quite specifically as a murderer. These latter formed themselves into the Jamaica Committee (denigrated by Carlyle) and included John Stuart Mill as Chairman, Thomas Huxley, Thomas Hughes, John Bright and Herbert Spencer.[2]

The image of the hanged man threw a shadow overall, and this shadow was darkened and strengthened by his supporters who circulated copies of his last letter to his wife, written under the eye of the soldier waiting to take him to the gallows, and quite obviously spun out in an attempt to put off the inevitable moment.

In January 1866 a Royal Commission of Enquiry arrived in Jamaica and sat until nearly the end of March, listening to grisly evidence from both sides. With the Commission were four Counsels: Mr Walcott of the Jamaica Bar acting for Governor Eyre; Mr Phillips of the Colonial Bar representing the Baptist Missionaries whose conduct had been impugned by Eyre; and Horne Payne of the English Bar and John Gorrie of the Scotch Bar, representing the Jamaica Committee and Mrs Gordon.

The Commission's findings struck a middle ground between the extreme positions taken up by virtually everybody else. The shortest way to simplify their conclusions is to say that they praised Eyre for the speed and skill with which he put down the insurrection, but censured him for overuse of Martial Law and for excessive punishments. The words 'reckless', 'cruel' and 'barbarous' appear in their report. Eyre was recalled and pensioned off, and although the Jamaica Committee succeeded in bringing a private prosecution, he was acquitted of the charges.

In the course of the Inquiry, Gorrie encountered the blackest humour on a grand scale. A twenty-four year old Lieutenant Brand, who had presided over Courts Martial where upwards of a hundred people were condemned to death, was asked at one point why he ever stopped the hanging. He replied, 'When I found that someone was coming to accuse someone else of stealing a pig, I thought I would stop.' This was taken at the time as an inappropriate joke, but it later transpired that two men had been executed on the Blue Mountain Valleyside at the request of an English Justice of the Peace who had accused them of treason against the Queen because they had stolen his sow. The men were buried that night and the sow came out of the bush next morning with a litter of piglets.

2   In what follows, I rely on Gorrie's letters and papers, housed in the National Records of Scotland (GD1/1441), and on the papers of Sir Arthur Gordon, Lord Stanmore, housed in the British Library (Add. MSS 49199–49285).

On another occasion the Maroons – descendants of the old Spanish slaves – were ordered to execute a man of the name of Williams. They seized the first Williams they encountered, the head of the local Wesleyan Church and one of the best known and most respected men in the area, and shot him. When the local police told them they had got the wrong Williams, they are reported to have said, 'Very well, we will go and shoot the right one', which they then did.

As the Inquiry grew increasingly surreal, Gorrie asked one of his opponents, 'Suppose I bring before you a man who has been executed could you tell us what you had him executed for?' He then produced a man who had been roped in a line with nineteen others before a firing squad and who had fallen with no more than a musket ball in the shoulder but, since he was last in the line, had been presumed to be as dead as all the rest. He had managed to escape while the pits were being dug for the bodies. This man stood before the Commission – and no evidence could be found against him.

In 1867 John Gorrie published a paper on the Inquiry. The final paragraph reads:

> These are samples of the scenes enacted in the beautiful island of Jamaica given under pretence of repressing disturbances. My task has not been undertaken in vain if it tends to deepen the resolve of my countrymen to resist at all hazards the preposterous pretensions of Colonial Governors and military officers to deal with human life and property as they please, without responsibility to the laws which bind society together or to the Nation which places the sword in their hands for the purposes of justice and mercy.

———◆———

In 1869 John Gorrie was appointed to Mauritius as Substitute Procureur-General and sailed there with his family. The Gorrie daughters, especially, loved their time on the very beautiful, though cyclone-afflicted, island where the social life included balls given by the Regiment in Garrison, at Government House, and on board ship whenever the British Navy visited.

Sir Arthur Gordon (later Lord Stanmore) who took over as Governor of Mauritius in 1871, thought less well of the place. His diary records problems with sewage, fouled water, malaria and poisonous centipedes which 'have a horrid secret way of lurking in unexpected places.' He complained that even the canaries were dingey, 'like sparrows that have flown up chimneys.' Lady Gordon recorded in her own diary that her dresses suffered from cockroaches, mildew, rats, moths, caterpillars and 'the launderers who beat them violently on the sharp stones in the river bed.'

Gorrie, who had instantly been confronted with abuses and corruption, especially in the police force, swung into action immediately. 'The papers give the credit for reforming some abuses already since I was placed on the bench,' he wrote from Port Louis in June 1871, 'but the French organ complains that I am severe and harsh in language to those who require to be rebuked. My hand is rather heavy on the snaffle, I suppose, for a horse not accustomed to be ridden much. We will understand each other better by and by.' Some did, some didn't. Those with vested interests were already beginning to bristle at reforms that limited their privileges and at judgements that affected their prestige.

Sir Arthur Gordon was at first wary of Gorrie; later he found that most of Gorrie's views tallied with his own and the two families became friends, although it is clear from Sir Arthur's journals that there were occasional tensions and clashes between the two men. When, in 1874, Sir Arthur was posted away from Mauritius to become the first Governor of the newly acquired Fiji, he wrote in his diary, 'There is a sort of conspiracy of the newspapers against Judge Gorrie which annoys him greatly, and I can see that when I go it will fare but badly with him.' Early in 1876, Gorrie wrote:

> Now, just when I was very comfortably situated with my family, and with a lot of friends around me – the mail had just come in and we were reading our letters – I saw an orderly approaching. I said 'There is some horrid bore on business' and business it was, and no mistake. It was a telegram from home telling me to go to Fiji at once. Here were all our arrangements and family broken up, and we did not meet for some eighteen months afterwards.'

The whole family were sad to leave Mauritius, but especially Minnie who, having turned down one proposal of marriage, had met someone she really cared for; they never met again and she never married.

Sir Arthur Gordon had asked that Gorrie be appointed Chief Justice under him in Fiji, a group of islands which was then still known as the Cannibal Isles. Gorrie went to Fiji via Australia and his family sailed back to Britain to stay with relatives until he should be sufficiently settled to send for them. Because of the slowness of communications it was more than four months before they heard from him again. When his first letter broke the anxious silence his eldest daughter, Minnie, wrote apprehensively in her diary, 'Fiji … seems a very wild sort of place. The houses are not very good, and very dear. In some parts the people are still cannibals. At dinner only Sir A Gordon and Papa sat on chairs, the others on mats. There are no roads and altogether it seems a very rough sort of life. I don't think I shall like it.'

'A rough sort of life' was probably a fair description. During that summer Arthur Gordon mentions an internal trip taken by Captain Knollys, one of his military commanders, during which he disturbed 'a breakfast party who were just preparing to feast on a roast leg of man which was already cooked for their meal.' Captain Knollys seems to have been more intrigued than horrified by the cannibal feast. On July 31st of that year, Lady Gordon confided to her diary, 'Captain Knollys says he has got the real fork and dish with which the missionary, Mr Baker, was eaten some years ago and the man who ate him is one of his prisoners.' This fork and dish are among the exhibits at the museum in Suva, and a school has been named after Mr Baker.

———◆———

Judge Gorrie arrived in Fiji at a turbulent moment, in the midst of an outbreak of rioting, murder and village-burning in the Sigatoga Highlands. These outbreaks were eventually suppressed with the use of native rather than European forces, Sir Arthur noting in his journal that 'it was of the utmost importance to avoid a war of races.'

Shortly after Gorrie's arrival Sir Arthur set out by sea on a tour of inspection which culminated, as it turned out, in the trial of some of the perpetrators of the troubles. He took several members of his staff with him, including Charles Eyre, son of Governor Eyre, and 'the new Chief Justice, Gorrie, who … wished to see something of the country before his predecessor departs and he sets to work.' Later in the journal Sir Arthur comments, 'Is it not a curious thing that Gorrie should have been with me on this expedition and also a son of Governor Eyre? I sent them both away, however' – with an interpreter and the boat's crew for a protracted walk-about – 'before these events.'

This was just as well, because although Sir Arthur was respected as a liberal – some said too liberal – and fair Governor, retribution was savage by today's standards, and almost certainly by Gorrie's standards even then. Sir Arthur wrote: 'I had hoped to keep the number to be executed down to ten or twelve but found it impossible to bring it below fifteen. … The two high upright posts of an old house remained there, standing on its terraces, and across this a cross beam was put. Halfway up another beam was put across, lashed with a sinnet, and on this the convicts were seated, the ropes put around their necks, and they were pushed off by Solomoni. The first was Matalau. The fall in his case was too great and the rope broke. He fell on his face on the ground and Solomoni shot him through the head with a rifle…. During the night a woman outside began talking to the ghost of Matalau – very weird and ghastly.'

The essential support of Lord Caernarvon and the Colonial Office for Gordon's policy of upholding native law and encouraging native councils had been given – despite it being 'rather a large pill to swallow' – 'in order to give you the chance you desire of proving that you can govern the natives instead of killing off', and this, despite the foregoing, is what he strove to do. Nevertheless, the care with which he got Gorrie out of the way first says something about the reaction he would have expected from that quarter. Certainly Gorrie's reaction to a later, more questionable retribution was vigorous enough.

Gordon wrote: 'Just before leaving Fiji I was engaged in a very troublesome business which threatened to bring me and Gorrie into open and violent collision. In the early part of last year some of the natives attached to the Wesleyan Mission in New Britain were killed by the natives of the island, who, elated by their success, threatened to wipe out the rest of the Mission and the white traders. Mr Brown, the head of the Mission, in these circumstances thought it right to organise and lead a punitive expedition, in the course of which I believe a good many natives were killed, and they were effectively taught that they could not murder strangers with impunity. Mr Brown sent an account of these proceedings to his superiors, in some not very discreet letters, which were published in the Australian newspapers. Gorrie, who was acting for me as High Commissioner in my absence, and who hates the Missionaries, took fire at this, and as Chief Judicial Commissioner issued a summons to Mr Brown on a charge of manslaughter, and asked the Commodore to give him a ship in which to go down to New Britain and try Mr Brown on the spot. I could not trust his impartiality where Missionaries were concerned, and being in England when this news reached us, got the Commodore telegraphed to, not to give him a ship, and to leave the whole matter in abeyance until my return. I as High Commissioner could only treat it as an act of self-defence on the part of British subjects threatened with annihilation by savages. But I knew that if Gorrie once got him into Court he was sure to condemn him. Here there were the materials for a very pretty quarrel. However, we at last hit on a satisfactory solution of the affair, and I must do Gorrie the justice to say, that when he had once caved in, he behaved well and handsomely in facilitating an arrangement. I am very glad it was so clear to me, for had Brown been sent to prison we should not only have had all the Wesleyans both in Australia and England up in arms, but also all the settlers usually most opposed to Missionaries, who would have resented the interference with a white man's right to protect himself from the attacks of natives. I find it difficult enough as it is to carry out my policy of maintaining native rights without raising up a fresh host of formidable enemies. Personally, I think Brown would more have resembled a Missionary of the first few centuries if he had allowed himself to be massacred, but that is for his spiritual superiors to consider.'

Gorrie's dislike and distrust of Missionaries had built up gradually during his time in the colonies. He was in sympathy with their religious views but experience suggested to him that they neglected the health of the indigenous peoples they had chosen to take under their wing, and positively blocked their secular and social advancement.

Gorrie held other posts on Fiji, as well as that of Chief Justice, including Chairman of the Land Claims Commission. Occasionally, as well as his official report on cases heard, he was moved to send Sir Arthur something lighter, such as the following:

> 'We sat in Adi Kuila's house,
> We slept upon her mats;
> But, oh the swarm of mosquitoes,
> And, oh, the rush of rats.

The planter came with his land claim,
He swore that white was black;
The pious Missionary, too,
Swore black was white – alack!

And when these oaths had all been sworn
The lies in form recorded;
What could we do but make report
That men were mean and sordid!'

In the summer of 1881 Gorrie wrote to a friend:

> I wish I could give you an idea of the nature of the work we
> are doing in the Lands Claims Court. I am sure it would give
> you satisfaction. We have the native owners represented
> and they are regarded exactly in the light of white persons
> having land rights of the same nature. The claimant must
> prove that he has got a good title (meaning by that not a
> technical bit of paper) from the actual owners before we will
> give a decision which may dispossess them. Last evening we
> threw out a claim to 30,000 acres which is covered by native
> towns and would probably have required force to turn out
> the people if we had granted the claim. On the other hand,
> as the claimant is a Queenslander who cannot comprehend
> the first principle of fair dealing with a native race, he will
> probably make a great howl.

Great howls sometimes had wider implications than that one. Gorrie's settlement of some German land claims had political reverberations; Bismarck
himself lodged formal complaints about the results which were not in his
countrymen's favour. The British Government had to pay large sums of compensation because the Germans had acquired their land on a 'misunderstand-
ing' and did not see why they should lose out financially when the misunder-
standing was cleared up.

◆

In 1880 Sir Arthur Gordon became Governor of New Zealand and Sir George
des Voeux – who had already acted as Governor of Fiji in 1879 when Sir Arthur
was on extended leave of a year – formally took up the Governorship. Gorrie
and des Voeux had clashed during des Voeux's first term of office and didn't
find themselves any more in accord during the second. Des Voeux wrote, 'My
experiences with Chief Justice (Gorrie) in my first administration caused me
to return to Fiji with a fixed determination to make any sacrifice consistent
with my duty to the public to maintain friendly relations with him; and I

hoped that this would prove more easy than before, because except as Judge he would have nothing further to do with the High Commission' (Gorrie had been acting High Commissioner to the Western Pacific during Gordon's absence) 'The task, however, proved more difficult than I expected. Having but very little of obligatory duty, he had abundant leisure for the indulgence of *cacoethes scribendi* (an itch for scribbling) of a very severe type; while having been sometimes useful to my predecessor for the drafting of necessary laws he seemed to think himself entitled to address me on any subject in the capacity of either judge, member of the legislative council, or amateur adviser. He was continually writing me letters or seeking interviews for the purpose of suggesting some desirable object of expenditure with little or no appreciation of our financial condition, or of criticising or opposing something I had done, was doing, or was reported as about to do.'

It is possible, though never stated, that Gorrie's plentiful physical energy grated on the nerves of des Voeux, whose health was a permanent problem as a result of yellow fever, sunstroke, two serious accidents which caused concussion of the brain and spine, and appalling seasickness, the latter a particularly unfortunate affliction in a colony such as Fiji, made up of a group of islands visitable only by boat.

They clashed on quite specific and well-documented issues, such as Gorrie's announcement that he intended to release from gaol all prisoners who had been, in his opinion, illegally convicted, and his insistence on moving to Suva and holding Supreme Court Sessions there for some months before the seat of Government was moved from Levuka to Suva, to the inconvenience of everyone but himself. Of des Voeux, Gorrie wrote:

> I have now before the Council a Criminal Procedure Code (which des Voeux in one of his tantrums delayed for a year) which will put the coolies on a par with the natives. It is not true that I gave a man penal servitude for accidentally shooting at a Fijian, but I gave a small settler in the back country six years penal servitude for rushing off to get his gun after a squabble with a Fijian and then deliberately waiting behind a bush until he saw the man's head above the stream when swimming away from him across the river, and then letting blaze at his head. He would have got ten years for it at home. I gave him six. But I regret to say he has got out by des Voeux yielding to public pressure. Of course the Colonial Settlers think firing at a native rather a good thing.

————◆————

In 1881 John Gorrie was knighted and in 1882, after his daughter Isabella Jane's marriage on Fiji to Hamilton Hunter, he took six months' home leave, his first since leaving Britain in 1869, though it is worth noting that when

Gorrie left, des Voeux had even more trouble with the next Chief Justice. In 1883, Gorrie was appointed Chief Justice to the Leeward Islands and was based in Antigua where he continued to make powerful enemies among the colonists. In 1884 his wife Marion became ill. A temporary return to Britain, away from the tropical heat, was recommended and the whole family made the trip, but Marion died on the boat and was buried at sea.

In 1885 Gorrie was appointed Chief Justice of Trinidad and took up the post early in 1886. The Legislative Council in Trinidad was made up of officials and of private citizens. The latter were known as the Unofficials, and it was they who were Sir John's chief enemies. In *A History of Modern Trinidad* Bridget Brereton writes: 'The Unofficials were able to exercise some control over the senior officials in the island. For instance, the episode of the Judicial Enquiry Commission illustrates the ability of the Unofficials to make life uncomfortable for officials who did not show proper deference to the local oligarchs, in this case Chief Justice Sir John Gorrie. From 1886, when Gorrie arrived, to 1891, when the Commission was appointed to investigate the administration of justice, the Unofficials conducted a persistent campaign against Gorrie. It was a group of Unofficials whose complaints led the Secretary of State to appoint the Commission, and they formed an 'Unofficial Committee' which acted like a prosecuting counsel during the inquiry, retaining legal help to cross examine Gorrie and his witnesses. Gorrie's unforgiveable sin was to administer justice impartially, and to reform judicial procedures so as to make the courts more accessible to lower-class suitors. Gorrie was correct when he said of the Unofficial Committee 'they are subject to every local bias and prejudice, men who have no sympathy with an impartial administration of justice, men who would not and do not hesitate to use their public position to make charges and demand inquiries with a view to getting control of the judiciary.'

The storm clouds were certainly gathering. In a September 1887 letter Gorrie writes:

> You may have noticed a question put by Baden Powell in regard to my mode of administering justice and the reply, by no means satisfactory, of the Secretary of State for the Colonies. It is rather hard that the spiteful action of a few disappointed litigants (you will find names and dates written) should as easily get expression in the House of Commons and through a man so respectable as Mr Baden Powell, and that before my reply is learned the House is up and there is no chance of getting the slur upon me removed.

In 1888 Gorrie's youngest, Jeanie, died in Trinidad of an unnamed infection, just four years after her mother had passed away. After each of these deaths there was a great outpouring of sympathy and affection from the local people.

In 1889, when the legislation that joined Trinidad and Tobago came into force, Gorrie automatically became Chief Justice of both islands. It was troubles in Tobago that helped to bring things to a head – there were near riots when he suggested that workers on Tobago should be paid the same rates as those in Trinidad. It was at about this time that a particularly vindictive and litigious Tobago doctor and planter, Dr Anderson, took against him, claiming miscarriage of justice in various cases in which Gorrie had found in favour of one of Anderson's employees.

To give an idea of the attitude of those who supported Gorrie, here are extracts from a one-page poem produced by a jobbing printer – who bravely printed his own name and address: A. de Peaza, No. 33A St Vincent Street – in answer to attacks building up in the press: 'All you who have the ears to hear and brain to understand,/ Come listen to Judge Gorrie's praises, the wisest in the land./ He likes the poor to get their right, the rich he does not fear./ He is the greatest blessing of this great jubilee year./ Before time, law was very bad, and justice very sad./ But he has changed that sort of thing out here in Trinidad./ The poor man now can get his rights, as well as can the rich./ And dollars do not dazzle their sight, power does not bewitch.'

Gorrie was also involved in commercial ventures in Trinidad. He tried to set up a People's Bank which would extend cheap credit to smallholders, which never got off the ground, and a Crop Advance and Discount Company, which did. At one point the Secretary of State 'instructed Gorrie to disassociate himself from any commercial undertaking', but Gorrie openly defied him, pointing out that his predecessor as Chief Justice had been 'the leading cocoa lord of the place', and that the Governor himself held shares in several commercial enterprises.

In the spring of 1892 a Commission of Enquiry was sent out from Britain to enquire into the administration of justice in Trinidad and Tobago and into specific charges of drunkenness made against Mr Justice Cook, Senior Puisne Judge under Gorrie. They found against Cook (in a trial containing some bizarre evidence) and he was suspended and left the island. When it came to the charges against Gorrie, the Chief Justice at first conducted his own defence, but retired on May 19th saying that the case had been prejudged against him during his temporary absence holding a court at Tobago.

There were three specific charges: that he had disregarded the facts in one of the cases involving Dr Anderson; that he had disregarded established principles of law and procedure; and that he had frequently used intemperate and offensive language in court. The *Times* of July 27 1892 reports the Commissioners as saying: 'with deep regret we have come to the conclusion, upon the evidence laid before us, that the complaints are to a considerable extent well founded... with regard to the first two heads of charge we do not attribute to the Chief Justice any unworthy motives. We see no reason to doubt that Sir John Gorrie was actuated by a desire to do justice. With regard to the last head of charge we must leave the language used, and the character of the imputations made, to speak for themselves.'

The *Times* continues: 'The Commissioners left the colony on the same day that their report was sent in, and returned to England after an absence of just three months. On June 20 the Legislative Council met, and the Governor submitted to the members a minute stating that the report had just been received by him and that its accusations against the Chief Justice were of such a grave nature that it was inadvisable that his Honour should preside in the Supreme Court of the colony until they had been disposed of by the highest authority. His Excellency further informed the Council that charges would be preferred against Sir John Gorrie without delay under the Colonial Regulations, with a view to suspension, but that he had also felt it his duty in the meanwhile to interdict the Chief Justice from any further performance of his duties. Subsequently, as we are informed, owing to severe indisposition, his Honour asked for, and obtained, some months' sick leave, and at once left Colony for England.'

Gorrie's departure from Trinidad, undoubtedly in genuinely bad health, was an emotional and dramatic affair. The *Port of Spain Gazette*, which was firmly on the side of his enemies, reported events with some scorn. About Gorrie's arrival at the dock by buggy a reporter wrote: 'Attached to the vehicle were two long ropes which were in the hands of some three dozen running persons. These latter, as I heard one enthusiastic gentleman say, were "hauling Judge, horse and buggy." It was a ludicrous sight to say the least of it. The crowd in the street had assumed great proportions, supplemented as it had been by cabs and drays. On the latter were some of the worst characters of the town who with foul oaths threatened to "lick down anyone who said anything against Sir John Gorrie". Haggard-looking, with a death-like pallor overspreading his face, Sir John Gorrie presented a woeful and sympathy-attracting appearance; yet his carriage was erect, his bearing defiant-looking, and there was to be seen from the Chief Justice's flashing eyes that the old temper was still un-extinguished. But if Sir John Gorrie's physical condition was so sad a one as to excite sympathy, surely the circumstances attending his drive from the office of the Crop Advance and Discount Company to the jetty were still sadder. That a man occupying his high position should have found himself the idol for the scum of the town was a sad commentary. Escorted by a howling, half-frenzied mob, composed of the chronic law-breaking element known as *diamantes*; lewd and lawless women vulgarly gesticulating and dancing; insolent and besotted draymen, Sir John Gorrie drove to St Vincent jetty. Thoughtful people looked on, wondered, and felt grieved and saddened that the highest judicial officer of the Colony should have had such a following to bid him adieu with never even one face among it representing the respectable section of the community.'

But the recorded comments of people on the jetty included: 'See Mrs Joseph. He get back she land for her when dey want tief it'; and 'Even the sun has come out to show its appreciation of Sir John Gorrie, the upright judge. His enemies ought to take notice of it.' One man, who was looking particularly depressed, was told that even if the Chief Justice was down now he would soon be on his feet again, as he was a very successful fighter, to which he replied 'No, no, him not get up again. Dis time him too meger.' His words were prescient.

Gorrie's ship docked at Plymouth and he had travelled only as far as Exeter when he was taken off the train, in a very bad way. Within a very short time, he was dead. Minnie, Isabella and Malcolm, who came to him during his final illness, always believed he died of a broken heart.

Gorrie's brother Daniel wrote to the Marquis of Ripon, Secretary of State for the Colonies, to ask if the shadow overhanging Sir John could in some way be lifted. He received a reply from Downing Street, dated September 7, 1892, which read: 'Sir, I am directed by the Marquis of Ripon to acknowledge the receipt of your letter of the 24 ultimo, and to inform you that the death of Sir John Gorrie has prevented further enquiry into the charges against him, founded on the report of the Commission appointed to enquire into the administration of justice in Trinidad and Tobago. I am to add that Lord Ripon would have been very glad if the further inquiry, which, but for Sir John Gorrie's lamented death, would have taken place, should have had the result of sustaining the high reputation which he had justly acquired in the earlier stages of his Colonial service. I am, Sir, your obedient servant. Edward Wingfield.'

For his part, Dr Anderson continued to bring cases of personal grievance against Gorrie even after his death, and also against two of his colleagues, who were at least alive and able to defend themselves.

When Gorrie died his family found that his personal affairs were in disarray and no provision had been made for them. His second daughter Isabella was married and secure. However his son, Malcolm, who had worked unofficially for his father for some years, now had no income, no savings and no job, and his eldest daughter Minnie had to support herself by travelling as a companion to wealthy women visiting the spas of Europe. Friends of Sir John tried to persuade the Government to pay to Minnie the widow's pension that would have gone to her mother had she lived, but to no avail.

———◆———

John Gorrie's life was a mixture of politics—colonial, inter-departmental and personal; courtroom drama; comedy both black and white (in every sense); and tragedy. Whatever people said to or of him, and however difficult they succeeded in making things for him, he was never intimidated or deflected from his beliefs. Some called him 'rough and vulgar in manner… and not a man to inspire confidence,' another 'one of the most ardent, capable and disinterested advocates of reform.' He was energetic, short-tempered, humorous, sometimes brusque, and intransigent. But throughout his career as a Colonial Judge he used all his energies against those white colonialists who abused their positions of power and trust.

Judy Allen

Illustration Credits

Cover

Numa Desjardins, 'Champ de Mars, Port Louis 1880'. Wikimedia Commons.

Jacques Gérard Milbert, *Atlas* (1812), p. 21 – Carte de l'Île-de-France. British Library HMNTS 10096.i.24. Courtesy of Flickr Commons and the British Library.

Text

Page viii, Page from John Gorrie's manuscript of 'Maid of Maurice.' National Records of Scotland (http://catalogue.nrscotland.gov.uk/nrsonlinecatalogue/welcome.aspx), GD1/1441/3/2, originally in the private collection of Judy Allen. Courtesy of Judy Allen.

Page 22, 'Chaussée in Port Louis before the fire of 1893', from From Allister Macmillan, *Mauritius Illustrated* (London: W. H. & L. Collingridge, 1914).

Page 33, 'The transport of sugar cane', from Macmillan, *Mauritius Illustrated*.

Page 56, 'La Flore Mauricienne in Port Louis', from Macmillan, *Mauritius Illustrated*.

Page 68, 'Cutting sugar cane', from Macmillan, *Mauritius Illustrated*.

Page 152, 'View of the harbour of Port Louis', from Macmillan, *Mauritius Illustrated*.

Page 161, 'Indian workers on Antoinette Estate', from Macmillan, *Mauritius Illustrated*.

Page 250 and back cover, portraits of Marion Graham Gorrie and Sir John Gorrie. National Records of Scotland, GD1/1441/2/1/1R and GD1/1441/2/2/1R, originally in the private collection of Judy Allen. Courtesy of Judy Allen.